The Apostle Paul
Guides the Early Church

The Apostle Paul Guides the Early Church

Nils Alstrup Dahl

TRANSLATED AND EDITED BY
Paul Donahue

CASCADE *Books* · Eugene, Oregon

THE APOSTLE PAUL GUIDES THE EARLY CHURCH

Copyright © 2021 Wipf and Stock Publishers. All rights reserved. Except for brief quotations in critical publications or reviews, no part of this book may be reproduced in any manner without prior written permission from the publisher. Write: Permissions, Wipf and Stock Publishers, 199 W. 8th Ave., Suite 3, Eugene, OR 97401. Earlier material Copyright © 1977 Augsburg Publishing House and © 2000 by J.C.B. Mohr (Paul Siebeck) and used with permission.

Cascade Books
An Imprint of Wipf and Stock Publishers
199 W. 8th Ave., Suite 3
Eugene, OR 97401

www.wipfandstock.com

PAPERBACK ISBN: 978-1-5326-8407-4
HARDCOVER ISBN: 978-1-5326-8408-1
EBOOK ISBN: 978-1-5326-8409-8

Cataloging-in-Publication data:

Names: Dahl, Nils Alstrup, author. | Donahue, Paul, editor and translator.

Title: The apostle Paul guides the early church / Nils Alstrup Dahl ; edited and translated by Paul Donahue.

Description: Eugene, OR: Cascade Books, 2021. | Includes bibliographical references and index.

Identifiers: ISBN: 978-1-5326-8407-4 (paperback). | ISBN: 978-1-5326-8408-1 (hardcover). | ISBN: 978-1-5326-8409-8 (ebook).

Subjects: LCSH: Bible—Epistles of Paul—Criticism, interpretation, etc. | Bible.—Epistles of Paul—Theology. | Paul,—the Apostle, Saint. | Mission of the church—Biblical teaching.

Classification: BS2655.M57 D34 2021 (print). | BS2655 (epub).

Manufactured in the U.S.A.   January 28, 2021

Contents

Editors Foreword | ix

PART I: STUDIES IN PAUL: SECOND EDITION

Preface | xv
Acknowledgments | xvii
Abbreviations | xix

1. Paul: A Sketch | 1

2. Paul and Possessions | 21

   Appendix I: Words and Phrases Referring to the Collection | 36

   Appendix II: On the Literary Integrity of 2 Corinthians 1–9 | 38

3. Paul and the Church at Corinth | 40

4. A Fragment and Its Context: 2 Corinthians 6:14—7:1 | 62

5. The Missionary Theology in the Epistle to the Romans | 70

   Appendix I: A Synopsis of Romans 5:1–11 and 8:1–39 | 88

   Appendix II: The Argument in Romans 5:12–21 | 91

   Appendix III: Confession and Comments in Romans 7:14–25 | 93

6. The Doctrine of Justification: Its Social Function
    and Implications | 96

7. Promise and Fulfillment | 122

8. The Future of Israel | 138

9. Contradictions in Scripture | 160

10. The One God of Jews and Gentiles (Romans 3:29–30) | 178

PART II: INTRODUCTION TO EPHESIANS

Translator's Preface | 195

11. Introduction to the Letter to the Ephesians | 197

General Bibliography | 311
Index | 313

Editor's Dedication

I dedicate my work in this volume to the memories of
Nils Alstrup Dahl and Donald R. Juel,
and of my parents, Frank and Ethel Donahue.
May they rest in peace and rise in glory!

Editor's Foreword

THE STUDIES OF NILS Alstrup Dahl in this volume will have the power to illuminate the texts they discuss as long as anyone chooses to read them. Dahl's essays do justice to the timelessness of the texts themselves. The essays have that illuminating power for those of any faith, or none, for they are the work of a great historian, steeped in the literature of the age he studied, gifted with an intellect of extraordinary power, both in its analytic skills and in its creative imagination.

I am grateful to all who made it possible, including Cascade Books of Wipf and Stock Publishing, Mohr/Siebeck, Augsburg Fortress Publishing, and especially Sister Eva Dahl, to put before English language readers a new edition of Dahl's studies on Paul and the Pauline school.

New Testament scholars have long regretted that their work has itself become a matter for controversy, quite apart from the results. It is my hope that Nils Dahl's works of exceptional scholarship will show that scholarship is entirely consistent with vibrant Christian faith and will provide all readers, whatever their stance toward biblical scholarship, some insight into the potential for scholarship to undergird and deepen faith in the gospel message. Christians would do better to concentrate on the central Christian truth, that God was in Christ, reconciling all persons to himself, and that the church continues God's saving ministry. These essays should help!

The challenge of interpreting the New Testament as historical texts is grossly underestimated by almost all. Two thousand years of interpretation, with many shared themes, often means that traditional interpretations replace the texts in the minds both of the faithful and of those hostile to faith. The texts date from a time almost completely alien to residents of the industrial West, who have never lived where getting water meant bringing a bucket to the well, not turning on a tap. What a changed context that is for the story of Jesus and the Samaritan woman! I used to begin my classes in Introduction to the New Testament with the question, "Is it easy to understand the New Testament, or hard?" The almost universal consensus was that it was easy. I repeated the question at the end of the term, and by then most of the students said that it was hard; they at least knew what I thought.

Reflecting on Nils Dahl, his life and work, has helped me define what I think the requirements are for scriptural interpretation of lasting value and power. First of all is empathy. A gifted interpreter must be able to empathize with the situation of the person whose writing he or she is seeking to interpret. Empathy is a personal characteristic shaped by many factors, but important among them in my view is variety of life experience.

Nils Dahl heard a radio broadcast for the first time on a crystal radio set assembled by a friend in a Norway in many ways closer to the ancient world than to the modern. He was a student in Hitler's Germany and had the vision to see where Nazism could lead, and the conscience to despise it. That led him to leave Germany for Strasburg to pursue his studies, which deepened, but more importantly broadened, his exceptional grasp and understanding of the whole gamut of biblical scholarship. Interpretations of lasting value must build on a mastery of what has already been done. In that, Nils Dahl had few peers.

I remember a story he told me of Christmas with a German family as the Nazi war machine was ramping up. A boy in the family had received a friction motor tank as a gift. Dahl asked the boy who had given him the tank, and received the answer: "the Christ child!" In telling the story, Dahl communicated that the story held an awful truth: Christians gave the world mechanized warfare.

Nils Dahl and his wife experienced the hardships of war in occupied Norway. He fled Norway, a refugee, but sure of a welcome in Sweden, where his wife had been able to travel legally.

This diversity of life experience, combined with the empathy which was already his, his profound learning, his analytic skills, his creative imagination, all these things made Nils Dahl the truly exceptional historian he was, an enduring resource for all who wish to understand an era that proved so significant in shaping all that followed.

But for the Christian reader who turns to his essays to understand better the faith that Paul and the other apostles shared, with their own age and ours, Dahl offers more. He was a man of deep faith, who, though he did not enter the ministry as first he planned, preached the gospel in word and work, and the illuminating power of his studies can help the Christian reader appropriate the liberating power of the gospel message Paul preached, and adopt the habits of life that live it out.

Paul's writing and Dahl's work show that Christians have disagreed on points of doctrine from the very beginning. For Paul, and for Dahl, "believers must visibly express their unity in the fellowship of the Lord's table," despite those differences. Perhaps these essays will give some modest impetus to an ecumenism based on love, hope and respect. Need we agree on every aspect of sacramental theology and on the nature of ministry to join at the Lord's table? Can we not trust in God's graciousness to fill up what may be lacking, or at a minimum want to express our respect for other Christians, and for the power of unity, by joining with them at table?

PART I: STUDIES IN PAUL

THEOLOGY FOR THE EARLY CHRISTIAN MISSION
SECOND EDITION

Preface

THE STUDIES COLLECTED IN this volume were originally prepared for various occasions, but they are all byproducts of regular courses on Pauline exegesis and theology which I have taught at Oslo and at Yale. The earliest study is a semester-opening lecture from 1947 (Chapter II). The latest was intended for the festschrift presented to Ernst Käsemann on occasion of his 70th birthday in 1976 (Chapter X). Some studies deal with favorite topics of my own (Chapters V and VI). In other cases, I was asked to write or to speak on a given theme (Chapters I and VII–VIII). The volume includes more or less experimental contributions to scholarly debate (Chapters III and IV) and the preliminary results of a research project that may never be brought to full completion (Chapter IX).

Due to the prehistory of the volume, the choice of topics is somewhat arbitrary. The attentive reader will detect that over the years I have gained new insights and even changed my opinion on some points. As the subtitle, "Theology for the Early Christian Mission," indicates, the volume represents a fairly unified perspective on Paul. In preparing the studies for publication, I found that diversity caused fewer problems than repetition. Both the diversity and the repetition are representative of my study of Paul. Never fully satisfied with the standard works, or with what I have myself said on some earlier occasion, I have again and again had to read and reread the text of his letters, approaching them from various angles, with new and old questions in mind. I assume that I will continue to do so, and hope that my studies will induce the readers to do the same.

By and large, I have left the original substance and form of the studies unaltered. I have, however, rewritten Chapter V, "The Missionary Theology in the Epistle to the Romans." I have also added appendixes to Chapters II and V and footnotes to Chapters I, II and IV. In the other chapters, I have only occasionally made some deletions or additions, mostly in the footnotes. The English translation is, at some points, an improvement, clarifying or modifying the original.

Only Chapter III has earlier been available in English. Chapters IV and X are here published for the first time. All the other chapters have been published in Norwegian; Chapter IX also in a German translation. Professor Terry Callan has translated that chapter from the German version, but his translation has been checked against the Norwegian original. For the chapters which have been translated directly from Norwegian, my wife prepared a first draft which has been thoroughly revised by Professor Paul Donahue. Only their devoted work has made the appearance of this volume possible. Paul Donahue has also volunteered to work as my assistant at every stage of the preparation of the whole manuscript. He has, in fact, acted as a co-editor of the whole volume. Jouette Bassler and Ben Fiore, both graduate students at Yale, have also rendered valuable help. I am very grateful to all these fellow workers.

My gratitude extends to a much wider circle of persons, who have invited me to give lectures or to write an article on Paul, or who have stimulated my thoughts by their own studies and by their reactions to mine. I would like to mention the members of the Commission on Theology of the Lutheran World Federation, who discussed the doctrine of justification in the period 1958-63, and the members of the Society of Biblical Literature Seminar on Paul who in 1970-75 dealt with the form and function of Paul's letters. Earlier versions of Chapters VII and IX were parts of the Nils W. Lund Memorial Lectures which I had the honor to give in 1968, at North Park Theological Seminary. I am indebted to scholars who have differed sharply among themselves, such as Rudolf Bultmann, Anton Fridrichsen, Johannes Munck and Paul Schubert in the past and Ernst Käsemann and Krister Stendahl in the present generation.

The scholarly dialog continues. I have profited greatly from communication with my own students, to whose contributions I have often drawn attention in the footnotes, which otherwise only refer to a somewhat arbitrary selection of current literature. Finally, I recall with gratitude the response of audiences who have listened to my lectures on Paul—colleagues, students, pastors, and others. It is my hope that this book might be of interest to an equally wide audience.

Nils A. Dahl
The Divinity School
Yale University

Acknowledgments

THESE ESSAYS APPEARED PREVIOUSLY in the following publications:

1. "Paul: A Sketch" first appeared in *Vestens Tenkere*, edited by E. Skard and A. H. Winsnes, Oslo: Aschehoug, 1962), vol. 1. In translation, it appeared in Dahl, *Studies in Paul: Theology for the Early Christian Mission* (Minneapolis: Augsburg, 1977) 1–21.

2. "Paul and Possessions" first appeared in *Kirke og Kultur* 52 (1947). In translation, it appeared in Dahl, *Studies in Paul: Theology for the Early Christian Mission* (Minneapolis: Augsburg, 1977) 22–39.

3. "Paul and the Church at Corinth according to 1 Corinthians 1:10—4:21" was first published in *Christian History and Interpretation: Studies Presented to John Knox*, edited by W. R. Farmer, C. F. D. Moule, and R. R. Niebuhr (Cambridge: Cambridge University Press, 1967) 313–36. It was then included in Dahl, *Studies in Paul: Theology for the Early Christian Mission* (Minneapolis: Augsburg, 1977) 40–61. It was subsequently reprinted in *Christianity at Corinth: The Quest for the Pauline Church*, edited by Edward Adams and David G. Horrell (Louisville: Westminster John Knox, 2004) 85–95.

4. "A Fragment and Its Context: 2 Corinthians 6:14—7:1" began as a paper read at the Annual Meeting of the Society of Biblical Literature in Toronto, 1969. It was first published in Dahl, *Studies in Paul: Theology for the Early Christian Mission* (Minneapolis: Augsburg, 1977) 62–69.

5. "The Missionary Theology in the Epistle to the Romans" was first published as "Misjonsteologien i Romerbrevet," in *Norsk Tidsskrift for Misjon* 10 (1956) 44–60. In translation, it appeared in Dahl,

Studies in Paul: Theology for the Early Christian Mission (Minneapolis: Augsburg, 1977) 70–94.

6. "The Doctrine of Justification: Its Social Function and Implications" was first published as "Rettferdiggjørelseslaerens sosiologiske funksjon og konsekvensene," in *Norsk teologisk tidsskrift* 65 (1964) 284–310. In translation, it appeared in Dahl, *Studies in Paul: Theology for the Early Christian Mission* (Minneapolis: Augsburg, 1977) 95–120.

7. "Promise and Fulfillment" was first published as "Paulus' syn på løftenes oppfyllelse," in *Israel, Kirken og verden*, edited by Magne Saebo, Gammeltestamentlig Bibliotek 2 (Oslo: Land og Kirke [Gyldendal], 1972) 99–114. In translation it appeared in Dahl, *Studies in Paul: Theology for the Early Christian Mission* (Minneapolis: Augsburg, 1977) 121–36.

8. "The Future of Israel" first appeared in Dahl, *Studies in Paul: Theology for the Early Christian Mission* (Minneapolis: Augsburg, 1977) 137–58.

9. "Contradictions in Scripture," was first published as "Motsigelser I Skriften—et gammelt hermeneutiskt problem," in *Svensk teologisk kvartalskrift* 45 (1969) 22–36. In translation it appeared in Dahl, *Studies in Paul: Theology for the Early Christian Mission* (Minneapolis: Augsburg, 1977) 159–77.

10. "The One God of Jews and Gentiles" first appeared in Dahl, *Studies in Paul: Theology for the Early Christian Mission* (Minneapolis: Augsburg, 1977) 178–90.

11. "Introduction to the Letter to the Ephesians" was first published as "Einleitungsfragen zum Epheserbrief," in Dahl, *Studies in Ephesians: Introductory Questions, Text- & Edition-Critical Issues, Interpretation of Texts and Themes*, edited by David Hellholm, Vemund Blomkvist, and Tord Fornberg, 3–106. WUNT 131. Tübingen: Mohr/Siebeck, 2000.

Abbreviations

BFCT	Beiträge zur Förderung christlicher Theologie
BHT	Beiträge zur historischen Theologie
CBQ	Catholic Biblical Quarterly
CTM	Concordia Theological Monthly
DTT	Dansk teologisk tidsskrift
FRLANT	Forschungen zur Religion und Literatur des Alten und Neuen Testaments
HNT	Handbuch zum Neuen Testament
HTR	Harvard Theological Review
IDBSup	Interpreter's Dictionary of the Bible, Supplementary Volume
JAC	Jahrbuch für Antike und Christentum
JBL	Journal of Biblical Literature
Judaica	Judaica: Beiträge zum Verständnis . . .
KD	Kerygma und Dogma
KJV	King James Version
MGWJ	Monatsschrift für Geschichte und Wissenschaft des Judentums
MNTC	Moffatt NT Commentary
NEB	New English Bible
NorTT	Norsk Teologisk Tidsskrift
NovT	Novum Testamentum

NTS	*New Testament Studies*
RB	*Revue biblique*
RevQ	*Revue de Qumran*
RSV	*Revised Standard Version*
SBLDS	SBL Dissertation Series
SBLSBS	SBL Sources for Biblical Study
SBT	Studies in Biblical Theology
SD	Studies and Documents
SNTSMS	Society for New Testament Studies Monograph Series
SO	Symbolae osloenses
SPB	Studia postbiblica
ST	*Studia theologica*
STK	*Svensk teologisk kvartalskrift*
TDNT	Gerhard Kittel and Gerhard Friedrich, eds., *Theological Dictionary of the New Testament*
TLZ	*Theologische Literaturzeitung*
TSK	*Theologische Studien und Kritiken*
UUÅ	Uppsala universitetsårsskrift
WMANT	Wissenschaftliche Monographien zum Alten und Neuen Testament
WUNT	Wissenschaftliche Untersuchungen zum Neuen Testament
ZNW	*Zeitschrift für die neutestamentliche Wissenschaft*
ZTK	*Zeitschrift für Theologie und Kirche*

1

Paul: A Sketch

DURING HIS TRAVELS AS an apostle of Jesus Christ, Paul arrived in Athens, a city which remained a center for Greek culture and philosophy despite its decline in political significance. Luke describes Paul's debate with Epicurean and Stoic philosophers living in Athens in Acts 17. These Athenian philosophers appear to have thought at first that Paul was simply one of the many sophists and rhetors who wandered from city to city preaching popular moral philosophy, or perhaps the cult of some Eastern deity. But Paul resisted easy classification; the novelty of his message appealed to the philosophers' curiosity. Despite their interest, these Athenian philosophers did not accept Paul as a colleague or consider him their equal.

Though he might occasionally allude to popular Greek philosophy or quote a Greek poet, Paul was not a philosopher, not even in the sense in which Philo, the famous Alexandrian Jew who lived at the beginning of the first century, was a philosopher. Philo tried to prove that the Law of Moses embodied true philosophy. Paul deliberately rejected philosophical argumentation and rhetorical polish as vehicles of his message. His sole intention was to proclaim "the word of the cross," the folly of God which put the wisdom of men to shame.[1] Paul did not attempt to solve

---

1 The Norwegian version of this survey article appeared in a collection of essays on "Thinkers of the West," from Socrates and Plato to Wittgenstein, Heidegger, Sartre, and others. I have added chapter and verse references and some footnotes to the English translation, without changing the non-technical form of presentation. For some important works on Paul, see the General Bibliography.

See 1 Cor. 2:1–5. Paul's own words and my paraphrase need some qualification. Paul's message does set him apart from the tradition of ancient philosophy and

the problems of existence by careful reflection on the meaning of data gathered by prior observation and investigation. Paul is an apostle; he is the representative of the one who sent him. He proclaims the message entrusted to him. For this reason, Paul does not recognize the validity of a judgment based on his personal performance as a speaker or as a thinker. He demands that those who hear him acknowledge the legitimacy of his commission and his faithfulness in carrying it out.

Does Paul warrant a place in the history of Western thought? Does he belong among the philosophers? Historians have to answer these legitimate questions with a resounding yes. They must recognize the significant impact of Paul's thought on the development of Western culture. Paul was the first to use formal logic to attempt to make clear the implications of faith in Jesus Christ. He is not only a religious hero, not only a missionary and church leader, but also a "thinker," the first Christian thinker whose writings have survived. Paul was not like some modern missionaries who both preach the word and carry on some quite separate scholarly pursuit like linguistics or anthropology. Paul's life as an apostle and his thought were integrally related to each other. His thought determined his daily activity, and the problems he encountered in his daily activity as a missionary provided the material for his reflection.

THE LIFE

Paul came to Greece in 50 or 51. We can date his arrival as closely as that because we know that Paul lived in Corinth when Gallio was Roman proconsul of Achaia (Acts 18). With this date as a point of departure, we can use other information (e.g., Gal. 1) to construct a Pauline chronology. Paul's conversion must have occurred early in the thirties, only a couple of years after Christ's death. At this time Paul was still a young man; we have nothing which would enable us to determine his age more exactly. Paul was a native of Tarsus in Cilicia, one of the many free Hellenistic cities which, in the centuries after Alexander, disseminated Greek culture in Asia. Since he was both a Jew and a Roman citizen, the cities of Jerusalem

---

rhetoric. Yet, if rhetoric is properly understood as the art of persuasion, Paul was himself a skillful rhetorician, at least when he wrote his letters (cf. 2 Cor. 10:10). In fact, depreciation of empty rhetoric and sophistry was itself part of philosophical and rhetorical tradition. See, e.g., H. D. Betz, *Der Apostel Paulus und die Sokratische Tradition* (Tübingen: Mohr, 1972). On the level of Paul's literary and rhetorical culture, see also Malherbe, 29–59.

and Rome jointly enjoyed a special significance for him. Paul came from a family of Pharisees, of the tribe of Benjamin. He was named for the tribe's most illustrious member, Saul, King of Israel. As was the case with many Hellenistic Jews, the boy also had a Graeco-Roman name, the Latin Paulus. We can speculate that one of Paul's ancestors was taken prisoner of war when Pompey conquered Palestine in 63 B.C., that he was sold as a slave, and was eventually emancipated by a Roman citizen belonging to the Roman *gens* Paulus. Such a history would explain both Paul's Latin name and his Roman citizenship.[2]

We do not know how much Paul learned of Greek culture during his childhood in Tarsus. His letters show a certain familiarity with the terminology and rhetorical style current in contemporary popular philosophy. Paul was completely comfortable with the Greek language without feeling the constraint of the formal rules of literary style. Acts 22 says that as a young man Paul went to Jerusalem to study and there he became a disciple of the most famous rabbi of the period, Gamaliel.[3] As was customary, he also learned a trade, tentmaking. Later in life, the apostle boasts that he supports himself by working with his hands. His educational career suggests that Paul's family was economically secure.[4]

Although Jerusalem was unique among the cities of the Graeco-Roman world, it was very much a part of that world. A Roman military administration governed Palestine, which by then had felt for centuries the impact of Hellenistic culture. Many Palestinian cities adopted Greek constitutions and the Greek language. Even in Jerusalem, the architecture of public buildings differed from that of the rest of the Graeco-Roman world only in the absence of sculpture. The Jews who lived throughout the Roman world were frequent pilgrims to Jerusalem, and were themselves a source of continuing Greek influence. Some Greek-speaking

2. Jerome reports that Paul's forebears were from the town of Gischala in northern Galilee but either migrated, or were deported, to Tarsus when a Roman army invaded and plundered the province, and that Paul went with them (*On Illustrious Men*, 5; *Commentary on Philemon*, v. 23). That is probably no more than a conjecture.

3. W. C. van Unnik has convincingly argued that the word *anatethrammenos* ("brought up") in Acts 22:3 implies that Paul came to Jerusalem as a boy. See his article "Tarsus and Jerusalem" (1962, reprinted in *Sparsa Collecta*, I, Leiden: Brill, 1973, 259–320). But the reliability of the biographical data in Acts remains disputed. In any case, Paul usually uses the Greek Bible (Septuagint), but his letters demonstrate that he had some training in rabbinical methods of studying the Scriptures. See Chapter 9, "Contradictions in Scripture."

4. See Chapter 2, "Paul and Possessions."

Jews settled in Jerusalem and organized their own synagogues in which to worship.

In the rabbinic schools, there was no time for the study of Greek literature. The Law, rabbinic traditions and their interpretation required all the student's time. Secular scholarship was the domain of others not called to the higher state of study of the Law, among them distinguished women. But even the scribal education which Paul received had itself taken shape both under the influence of and in reaction against the dominant Hellenistic culture, just as in our own time the national, cultural and religious renewal in the third world presupposes the profound impact of Western civilization.

Although many efforts have been made to distinguish the Greek from the Jewish component of Paul's thought, the task is hopeless: no real separation is possible. Even in the world of the young disciple of Gamaliel, the rabbinic academy at Jerusalem, Jewish and Greek elements were inextricably commingled. The dominating factor, however, which supplied the young Paul with a sense of direction, was Jewish in origin: his zeal for the Law. His service to the Law exceeded, at least in his own estimation, that of his pious contemporaries: even years later he could describe his conduct while a Jew as "blameless."[5]

Paul's zeal for the Law led him to take an active role in persecuting those who confessed their faith in the crucified Messiah, Jesus of Nazareth. Paul is likely to have believed that if Israel repented and obeyed the Law, then God would intervene on her behalf; he did not subscribe to the view that armed revolt would bring Israel's vindication. As a Pharisee, Paul found that the followers of the Nazarene weakened observance of the Law and diminished Israel's hope of entering the age to come. For the disciple of Gamaliel as for the apostle of Jesus Christ, there was an irreconcilable tension between the Mosaic Law and the crucified Messiah as ways to salvation.

When Paul set out for Damascus, he was not tortured by a troubled conscience, as the young monk Luther was. Rather, his enthusiasm remained undimmed. When Christ appeared to him, Paul had not wearied of the attempt to fulfill the Law perfectly. His view of the relation of the Mosaic Law to the crucified Messiah did not change when Christ called him to become his ambassador to the Gentiles; Paul simply abandoned one side of the fray to enter the lists on the other. He never doubted that

---

5. Phil 3:6. See, e.g., Stendahl, 80.

God himself had intervened in his life to reveal his Son to him: that fundamental presupposition underlies all of his subsequent life and thought. That event completely transformed Paul's values; the observance of the Law which he had once esteemed so highly he reckoned a complete loss, nothing more than refuse in comparison to his life's new direction: "To know Christ Jesus, my lord" (Phil 3:4–11). Paul began to preach the faith he had formerly sought to exterminate.

We know little about Paul's first years as a Christian. After his baptism, he spent several years in Arabia, by which we should probably understand the Nabataean kingdom south of Damascus. Later he paid a short visit to Jerusalem, where he met Peter. After a trip to his native Tarsus, he came to Antioch in Syria, a city which had become an important center for Greek-speaking Christians, non-Jews as well as Jews. From what we know about Paul, we may speculate that he worked as a missionary even during this first period. But his wide-ranging missionary journeys, carried out systematically, according to plan, began only after his stay in Antioch. At first Barnabas, who must have played an important role as a mediator between Antioch's Greek-speaking Christians and those in Jerusalem, and between Paul and the Jerusalem apostles, accompanied Paul on his missionary journeys.

Several years later, Paul went to Jerusalem once again with Barnabas. There the Jerusalem church and its leaders recognized the right of non-Jews to enjoy Christian fellowship without circumcision and without keeping the Law of Moses. Further, the agreement gave Paul the freedom to carry out his special mission to the Gentiles. The years which followed the Jerusalem Council (ca. 48–57) constitute the climactic period of Paul's apostolate. Long and difficult journeys took Paul around the Eastern littoral of the Mediterranean, into the inner recesses of Asia Minor, to Macedonia and to Achaia. At Corinth, the capital of Achaia, and at Ephesus, the capital of Roman Asia, he stayed for long periods of time. During this period Paul wrote letters to the Christian congregations in Thessalonica, Galatia, Corinth and Rome, possibly also to Philippi.

At the end of this period the apostle wrote: "But now, since I no longer have any room for work in these regions, . . ." (Rom. 15:23). This sounds strange to us, knowing as we do how incomplete the Christianization of the Eastern Mediterranean was. Paul wanted to preach Christ where no one had heard of him. When Paul—and others—had founded congregations in the central cities of the Eastern Mediterranean, Paul thought his work was complete: these central cities would represent the provinces, receiving Christ when, as Paul hoped, he would soon come again. Paul looked beyond the Greek to the Latin world: toward Rome, and then onward to Spain. For a time, problems in several congregations and the collection for the Jerusalem church delayed him. The collection was of great importance to Paul because he had agreed with the Jerusalem apostles to complete it, and because it symbolized for him the unity of Jew and Gentile within the church. If the Gentiles gave willingly, and if the Jerusalem church received their gift with gratitude, it would be a meaningful expression of mutual solidarity. Paul was vitally concerned that the Jerusalem church acknowledge his congregations by accepting the gift; therefore he himself went to Jerusalem to deliver it, aware as he was of the potential dangers (Rom. 15:26–32).

During his work as a missionary, Paul's life had several times been in danger; he had been arrested and punished more than once. In Jerusalem, Paul was arrested and imprisoned; for two years, he was a prisoner in Caesarea, the coastal capital of Roman Palestine; then he went on to Rome, where his imprisonment continued for two years more. At this point, Acts concludes its story of Paul. That Paul finally had his opportunity to preach the Gospel in the capital of the Empire is more important to the author of Acts than Paul's personal fate. Paul was executed in Rome during the reign of the Emperor Nero. According to Roman tradition, he was buried outside the city walls, where a famous basilica which bears his name stands today. But just as we are unsure of the date of his birth, so too the exact date of his death remains unknown.

LETTERS

Acts relates many episodes in Paul's life, although its account is both incomplete and at some points inexact. In his letters, Paul himself comes to life. His letters enable us to know more about Paul than about all but a very few other figures from antiquity. The form of Paul's letters is distinctly personal, differing both from common, casual correspondence and from polished, literary work. The style is richly varied, sometimes more like ordinary letters, with greetings, compliments, information and requests, and sometimes more like a sermon. The letters were in fact written to be read aloud in the congregation. Paul writes sometimes in the vivid, persuasive style used by popular Greek philosophers, appealing to an imaginary conversation partner; in other places, like a true rabbi, he uses quotations from Scripture to prove his point. On occasion Paul's thoughts tumble out with such intensity that they destroy the sentence structure, but the prose can also rise to nearly poetic, hymnic heights. Although we can detect certain fixed patterns which underlie his letters, Paul varies the structure according to the situation. We find sustained development of thematic sentences juxtaposed with digressions; sometimes an idea is mentioned and then abandoned, only to be taken up again at a later point.[6]

For Paul, the letter form was not simply a literary or didactic device. His letters always address particular situations. He feels a pastoral responsibility toward the congregations which he has left behind when he has moved to a new mission territory, as 1 Thessalonians shows. In Galatians, Paul sternly exhorts the inexperienced Gentile Christians not to adopt the Jewish rite of circumcision or other Jewish ceremonies. In 1 Corinthians, Paul rebukes the congregation for failings which have been reported to him orally, and answers questions which the congregation put to him in writing. Paul thanks the Philippians for a financial contribution to his work. Sections of Romans resemble a theological treatise presenting Paul's version of true Christian faith, but even this letter has a specific purpose: to prepare for his visit to Rome. It is important to Paul that the Roman church support his work in the West, and also that it pray that the Jerusalem church accept the collection which Paul is about to deliver.

In some respects, the Pauline letters have an official character. They represent a speech rather than a private conversation. The sender is not a private person, but an earthly ambassador of the heavenly Lord, the Risen Christ. However, Paul avoids when possible the use of his apostolic authority to enforce a solution. He does not write to his congregation like an oriental despot to his subjects; rather, the style recalls the manner Hellenistic kings adopted when writing to a free city, whose autonomy they acknowledged.[7] The congregations themselves enjoy a direct relationship with Christ; Paul therefore respects their freedom and independence, which they have in Christ. As a result, Paul's letters begin by acknowledging the bond of faith and love which ties him to his congregations. He reminds them of his own role, how he worked for their good, how he continues to pray for them and to suffer on their behalf. Paul works

---

6. See also Chapter V, "The Missionary Theology in the Letter to the Romans."
7. See Bjerkelund, 59–74.

to establish a foundation for his request that his congregations live in a manner appropriate to the privileges which they have received and that they amend their shortcomings. Only voluntary, comprehending obedience is the obedience of genuine faith. Consequently, Paul constantly appeals to the personal judgment of his readers; for him, reflection is a constituent element of the life in faith.

In his letters, Paul discusses a wide range of issues. He solves particular problems by relating them to the broad scope of what is essential in Christianity. If he exhorts his readers to think more about others and less about themselves, he may adduce as an example a hymn about Christ, who renounced his divine glory for the sake of men (Phil. 2). While discussing prophecy, speaking in tongues and other spiritual gifts, he stops suddenly to eulogize love in one of the New Testament's most eloquent passages, 1 Cor. 13. We observe frequently the transition from the recipient's concrete situation to God's act in Christ and to the universal scope of the gospel, with a subsequent return to the original problem, now viewed in a transformed light.

Because Paul seeks to convince his readers, to deepen their understanding rather than simply to compel their obedience, he accepts the premises of those to whom he writes. When Paul writes to the Christians at Rome, he makes clear his respect for their standing in the faith and for their autonomy; he introduces himself as a preacher of the common gospel, in order to continue with his attempt to prove that this common gospel implies the doctrine of justification by faith. When he writes to the Corinthians, he accepts their slogan, "All things are lawful to me," but he modifies and corrects this slogan by introducing the need to consider the position of the weak brother, by emphasizing that love requires that a Christian do nothing that might make his brother stumble. In 1 Corinthians Paul also appears to endorse the view that "it is well for a man not to touch a woman." Yet Paul's motivation for this endorsement is very different from that which prompted Corinthian ascetics to make that statement. Paul makes clear that the advantage of celibacy is that it makes possible an individual's complete devotion to Christ; he does not share the Corinthian ascetics' contempt for the body and for sexual love (1. Cor. 7–8).

On some occasions, Paul feels obliged to speak a plain, emphatic "No!", as when he forbids the Galatians to undergo circumcision (Gal. esp. 5:2ff.). But when possible, he attempts to accommodate his readers' presuppositions and experience. The same attitude characterized his missionary work as a whole; Paul made himself the servant of all, a Jew to the Jews, a Gentile to the Gentiles, a weak man to the weak: "I have become all things to all men, that I might by all means save some" (1 Cor. 9:22). He will not let unessential forms become an obstacle to his work; he refuses to compromise his loyalty to Christ. We can understand how Paul's opponents could interpret his flexibility as vacillation and inconsistency. To respond to such accusations, Paul points to God's unfailing word and to his covenant in Christ; Paul, in all that he does, simply acts as the servant of his Risen Lord (see, e.g., 2 Cor. 1:15-22).

Paul varies expression and argumentation to suit both his recipients and the particular situation which he confronts. He never confines himself to purely theological speculation, but always includes pastoral guidance and exhortation. It was by design and not by accident that Paul wrote letters and not theological or philosophical treatises. To recognize the variety of his pastoral concerns should not obscure his thought's inner unity, a unity which flows not from a thoroughgoing doctrinal system, but from the centrality in Paul's thought of faith in Jesus Christ.

CHRIST AND THE LAW

Some regard Paul as the second founder of Christianity, as the one who transformed the simple faith of Jesus into the dogmatic religion of the institutional church. Among other errors, this view wildly exaggerates Paul's historical significance. Between Jesus and Paul lies not only the preaching of the first apostles, both prior to and independent of Paul, but also the beginnings of Hellenistic Christianity and its establishment, e.g., in the cities of Damascus, Antioch and Rome. It was at Damascus that Paul became convinced of the truth of the faith that he had formerly tried to eradicate; he spent the rest of his life among Greek-speaking congregations. Paul's Christological statements in kerygmatic summaries, confessions and hymns are not innovative. That also applies to the sacraments: Paul depends on previously existing traditions and uses language which has already become standard. Some passages in the Pauline letters clearly reflect currently existing hymnic, liturgical and catechetical texts; in some cases, we may have more or less verbatim quotations.[8]

---

8. See, e.g., Bultmann, I, 133-52; A. M. Hunter, *Paul and His Predecessors* (London: SCM, 1961), 24-44, 65-78); E. Krentz, "The Early Dark Ages of the Church," *CTM* 41 (1970) 68-85.

Paul did not give belief in Christ any new content, but he did think through its meaning and consequences in a more radical way than others. Paul used material of widely different origin to construct and to elaborate his thought. One scholar has said that in order to gather the comparative material to illustrate one of Paul's sentences one must make a round trip through the thought world of antiquity.[9] Still, most important for the former Pharisee was to relate the new which had come with Christ to the old which was revealed in Israel's Holy Scriptures: the belief in the one God who had created the world, who had spoken through the prophets, who had acted in history, who had promised to send the Messiah to redeem Israel, and who is going to raise the dead and mete out to each person the just consequence of his deeds. Paul's thought not only has a single center, Jesus Christ, but a definite framework, the saving history depicted in the Old Testament and in later Jewish eschatological literature.

The "new" which had come with Jesus was not a new religion but rather a new creation. Christ is the new Adam, who came in the fullness of time, and who died for our sins, "to deliver us from this present evil age" (Gal. 1:4). This was God's great deed of love, the fulfillment of his promises. When he raised Jesus from the dead, God acted as Creator; similarly, God's creative power is constantly at work among believers. For Paul, Jesus' resurrection was not an isolated event, but the inauguration of the general resurrection which will take place at the end of the world. Those who have been baptized into Christ have, Paul says, already died with Christ and been buried with him, in order that they might share his resurrection life. He maintains that in the gospel the righteousness of God reveals itself as the power of salvation to all who believe. By "righteousness of God" Paul does not mean some passive attribute of deity, but the character of God's acting toward men, when, as Judge, he intervenes to vindicate himself and to bring salvation. Those who believe are already justified, they have been acquitted by the divine court, though they were once guilty. God's Holy Spirit, whose power the congregation experiences in its religious life, guarantees the coming glory which Christians will receive.

---

9. The scholar is Vilhelm Grönbech, the Danish historian of religion, whose early works made a great impact on Johannes Pedersen, Sigmund Mowinckel, and Scandinavian biblical scholarship in general. His book, *Paulus, Jesu Christi Apostel* (Copenhagen, 1940) is, in some respects, a splendid caricature but, unfortunately, not available to me at the moment.

A pervading feature of Paul's letters is the tension between "now" and "not yet." Believers are already acquitted, but they must still submit to the final judgment. They have received a share in Jesus' resurrection life, but they still live in the mortal body. They are in Christ, but also in the world, exposed to its anxieties and temptations. Christians must struggle constantly, and always face the possibility of failure. The present is for Paul nothing more than an interlude between the saving work of Jesus' life, death and resurrection, and the cosmic drama which unfolds when he comes again in glory. The Christian lives at the same time in two ages; he lives both in the old aeon of sin and death, and in the new aeon, which has arrived with Christ, of righteousness and life. Paul shares the Old Testament view of time as consisting of epochs with special content rather than as being an undifferentiated linear progression.[10]

The new order which had come with Christ was quite different from the Messianic age to which Paul had looked forward. The Messianic congregation, the saints, the chosen ones, by no means enjoyed a preeminent position in the world. On the contrary, in addition to the problems common to all people, they had also to confront persecution and suffering for the sake of their faith. To some extent, Paul can deal with this problem by using traditional Jewish reflection on the sufferings of the just: they are the means God uses to discipline the faithful in this life so that their reward in the next will be all the more glorious. But for Paul, another factor is decisive: the situation of the Christian corresponds to that of Christ himself, who lacked every aspect of worldly glory, who was in the end condemned as a criminal and executed. The believers' sufferings unite them with Christ; when they share his sufferings they also participate in his hidden glory. For Paul, the sufferings which he has himself endured are a proof of the legitimacy of his apostolate.

Paul's greatest theological problem was the relationship between Christ and the Law. When Paul accepted the gospel about Christ as true, when he came to believe that through this gospel God forgave sinners and judged the ungodly righteous, then he had to reject the Law as providing the proper rules for the relation of man to God. At the same time,

---

10. It is too simplistic to contrast a biblical concept of linear time with a Greek concept of cyclic time. One should, however, not forget that Paul does not himself speak of the "two aeons" in the way which has become customary among his interpreters after Albert Schweitzer's epoch-making works on Paul. The terminology of the two ages is simply an auxiliary construction which can help the modern reader to become aware of the apocalyptic context of Paul's theology.

Paul did not question the identity of the God who saved men through Christ with the God who had given the Law through Moses. Paul found the solution to his problem in the figure of Abraham, who had received a promise from God and who had trusted that God would keep his promise (Gal. 3, Rom. 4). Somewhat simplified, the juridical-theological reasoning runs as follows: the Law cannot be a permanent condition added after the fact to the original promise, for then it would make the promise void. The Law was therefore a temporary measure of limited validity. The Law was binding only until the coming of Christ, which fulfilled God's promise to Abraham. While he lived, Jesus himself obeyed the Law; his death marks its limits. The Risen Lord is no longer bound by the constraints of the Law, nor are those who are "in him" through baptism into his death. This new situation legitimizes Christian freedom from the Law.[11]

Paul also provides an explanation for God's purpose in establishing the Law as a temporary measure: without law, there can be neither crime nor punishment. The Law served to inhibit the proliferation of human sinfulness, but at the same time it transformed sin into transgression: when men sinned, they now violated the specific commands of a written code, and deserved punishment. That was exactly God's intention when he gave the Law. Not until man stood before God as a justly condemned transgressor could God display the full extent of his grace by granting completely unmerited pardon. Paul concludes that the Law's specific requirements were intended for the old aeon, and thus had only a limited validity for those who lived in the new aeon as well as in the old. The Law's eternally valid content is God's good and holy will. Paul does not denigrate the Law when he points out that its imperatives "You shall . . . You shall not" were unable to effect the results which they commanded (Rom. 7). The fault lies within man: God's righteous commands and prohibitions produce transgression. Man cannot convert his good intentions, formed by the Law, into action. All apparent lawfulness is only an illusion, for fulfillment of the specific commands becomes the ground for self-assertion, both before men and God. Such pride is the very essence of lawlessness, for the central thrust of the Law is complete self-surrender to God, grateful acknowledgment of his benefits, and love of neighbor as self.

Paul is convinced that the Law itself was his ally in his struggle for Christian freedom from the Law. To apply the Law's regulations to those

---

11. See Chapter IX, "Contradictions in Scripture."

who belong to Christ is to misread it. The Law's essential requirement—a right relationship to God and to other people—Christians meet when they live the new life in Christ, guided by the Spirit of God. Christian freedom from the Law does not mean that Christians are exempt from doing God's will. Paul repeatedly stresses that Christians must manifest their new life in their personal conduct. God's forgiving love is liberating and transforming: the one who is loved can love, and love fulfills the Law.

Paul's doctrine of the Law enabled him to interpret his own life experience. His zeal for the Law had led him to persecute the church of Christ. In Christ, God had granted him forgiveness for this grave sin. But more, Paul's doctrine of the Law provided a theological foundation for the ongoing Gentile mission and added to its impetus. Paul had not forgotten his pride in being a Jew and not a sinful Gentile. But when he had accepted Christ, he had, as had Peter and the others, acknowledged that before God the Jew had no advantage. Jews as well as Gentiles depended absolutely on God's grace. Thus, it was entirely inappropriate to introduce Jew-Gentile distinctions into Christian congregations, and to treat Gentiles as second-class Christians (Gal. 2:15ff.).

That many Gentiles accepted the gospel of Christ while most Jews rejected it posed another problem. Had God's promise to Israel come to nothing? Paul answers with an emphatic no. In the first place, God's promise did not extend to all of Abraham's descendents, but only to those whom God had chosen. God is sovereign, free to choose and to reject whom he will. Secondly, some Jews do believe; Paul himself is an example. They are at present the faithful remnant, the recipients of what God has promised Israel. Thirdly, Israel's present rejection of Christ does not bring God's saving purpose to an end. Ultimately, all of Israel will be saved. Gentile acceptance of the Gospel simply makes clear that both Jews and Gentiles are saved only by God's mercy and grace; it is the indirect path God has chosen which nevertheless leads to the salvation of Israel (Rom. 9–11). The salvation of Israel remains one of Paul's personal goals as well; he hoped that his work and success among the Gentiles would move Israel to healthy jealousy, a jealousy which would move Israel to accept the gospel.

Paul's hopes for Israel were not realized. Paul's view of God's plan for Israel illustrates, however, a fundamental conviction which pervades his thought: God does not act as people expect, nor as they imagine they merit. God rejects the strong and puts the wise to shame; he exalts the humble and turns the persecutor into his apostle. He has made those who were not his people, the Gentiles, his people, in order to bestow his grace on those whom he had first chosen, Israel. Paul's faith that the Crucified One is Lord determines this interpretation of history. Paul's interpretation also corresponds to Jesus' attitude toward outsiders, to his love for tax-collectors and sinners.

Most important for Paul is that men recognize that they cannot attain the right relationship to God, to their fellow men, or to themselves by their own efforts, by their privileged position, or by their own wisdom. When a man seizes the opportunity which God gives him in Jesus Christ, the consequences of that decision will transform his life. Paul does not need to develop his doctrine of justification, the Law and Israel in order to make this point to his Gentile readers. He can also use language more familiar to Greeks.

RENEWED HUMANITY

Paul draws his anthropological vocabulary both from the Old Testament and from general Greek usage; from the Old Testament terms like "heart" and "flesh," and from Greek terms like "body," "mind" and "conscience." He has no interest in specifying man's essence or his constituent parts. Paul's different anthropological terms refer to aspects of a human being rather than to discrete parts. Man as subject knows, wills, acts and suffers; as object he experiences the results of the knowing, willing and acting both of himself and of others.

Paul does not develop any doctrine of the immortality of the soul; his hope for life after death rests on his conviction that God has the power to raise the dead, and that Christ is Lord even over death itself. Paul is not concerned with dividing a man into a lower, animal nature and a higher, rational nature; rather he is concerned with the position of the whole man before God, his relation to the world and its powers, to other men and to himself. Paul's use of the word "flesh" provides a good example. Flesh is not merely something which a man has. Man is flesh; here Paul follows common Old Testament usage. But Paul also speaks of the flesh as a sphere of influence, a cosmic principle or power: man is in the flesh and can live "after the flesh." By "flesh" Paul does not simply mean the material and the sensuous; he means the whole realm of purely human desire and achievement, the world which takes into account lineage, position, worldly accomplishments, learning, circumcision and works of the Law, the world in which a man has grounds for boasting, but in which he encounters unhappiness, hatred and strife.

Paul considers men representatives of the social groups to which they belong. He speaks of Greeks and barbarians, but far more commonly of Jews and Gentiles or Jews and Greeks. The Jews demand signs and Greeks seek wisdom. Both groups display the same attitude toward Christ: the Crucified One is a stumbling block to the Jews and folly to the Greeks, "but to those who are called, both Jews and Greeks, Christ is the power of God and the wisdom of God" (1 Cor. 1:24). But these distinctions are fundamentally unimportant, for with reference to both groups Paul states: "There is no distinction; since all have sinned and fall short of the glory of God" (Rom. 3:22–23). To reach this conclusion, Paul argues, using Greek natural theology, that the world itself makes possible knowledge of God and of fundamental moral principles. He does not use natural theology to provide a rational foundation for morality, but simply to show that there is no decisive distinction between the religious situations of Jews and of Gentiles. Even those without the Law had an avenue to approach God, and therefore have no excuse for their failure to do so; they have merited the punishment they will receive. The Jews' possession of the Law has given them no real advantage, for there are also Gentiles who have done what the Law requires.

Responsibility and guilt are common to all men and the gospel is valid for all—God is certainly not God only of the Jews.[12] Paul never abandoned the exclusiveness of Jewish monotheism. God is the one God, who alone possesses Divine Majesty, who does not share divine dignity with any of the so-called gods, in contrast to Greek philosophical monotheism, where the divine source manifests itself in a multiplicity of divine powers, whose worship thereby becomes a worship of the divine source. For Paul, there is only one path which leads to a right relationship with God: faith in Jesus Christ. All, without distinction, are free to follow this path. From his Jewish and Christian presuppositions Paul can draw conclusions which approach the universalistic conceptions of his contemporaries without coinciding with them.

"There is neither Jew nor Greek, there is neither slave nor free, there is neither male nor female; for you are all one in Christ Jesus" (Gal. 3:28). This sentence does not imply that all national, social and physiological distinctions have disappeared. The Greek who becomes a Christian

---

12. See Chapter X "The One God of Jews and Gentiles."

remains a Greek, unlike the Greek proselyte to Judaism, who abandons his own community to become part of another. Paul thinks that Christian Jews ought to continue to live as Jews, as long as their adherence to tradition does not disrupt the unity of the Christian community.

Paul unreflectively accepted the social standards of his environment, with the roles they assigned both to slaves and to women, and he did not anticipate that his views would figure, on both sides, in the struggles over slavery and over women's liberation. But that does not mean that he did not anticipate substantial social change. The life in Christ had to make its mark on life in the world, on the relationship between Jew and Greek, husband and wife, master and slave. The life in Christ unites those who are different, and alters the relations between them, without destroying the differences.

The relationship between unity and multiplicity had for a long time occupied Greek thinkers; Paul sometimes appropriates the Greek stylistic traditions associated with this speculation. But it is characteristic that he prefers to use masculine terms rather than neuter: *heis* (the One, i.e., God) and *hoi pantes* (all the people), not *hen* (one) and *ta panta* (all things) or even *hen ta panta* (all things are one). Paul often applies cosmological language to the human situation and especially to the relation of Christ to the church. The church displays her multiplicity not only in the varieties of peoples whom she congregates, but also in the variety of gifts and ministries which the Spirit bestows on members of the church. We can look at such spiritual gifts from either of two perspectives. The Christian receives a spiritual gift to serve others; the service he renders testifies to the presence of the gift. Paul uses the image of the body and its members to illustrate this relationship, an image used in antiquity for civil societies and for the universe as a whole. Paul's fundamental conviction is that the church is the body of Christ, and that those who believe in his name become, through baptism, part of that body. Associated with this conviction is the view that every member of the church has a specific function and that in their very dissimilarity the members of the church are dependent on each other.

In the epistles to the Ephesians and to the Colossians, the image of the church as the body of Christ clearly has cosmic, universal components. Christ is the head of the church, which is his body, but he is also the sovereign head over all the universe's superhuman powers and principalities.[13] In Christ, God has bridged the gulf which separated Jews from Gentiles; the church by her very existence testifies to God's intention to reconcile what has been at odds. The church is the initial realization of God's plan to restore and unify the universe.

Paul has no interest, scientific or theosophic, in the structure of the universe or in the celestial hierarchy of powers and angelic beings, even though he takes their existence for granted. Paul stood at the boundary of a religious revolution which transformed fascination with the universe's divine order, and with the regular movement of the sun, the moon, the planets and the stars, into cosmic anxiety. The individual strove to win release from inexorable fate, from the power of the stars and from imprisonment in the material world by undergoing initiations into secret cults, by participating in religious rites, and by seeking to learn the knowledge which gave the knower the ability to escape (*gnōsis*). Astrology and other forms of mythological pseudo-science erased the boundaries between matter and energy and personal beings. In Paul we read both of powers and principalities and of the elements of the world (*RSV*—"the elemental spirits of the universe," Gal. 4:3). This second expression does not designate the four material elements of early natural philosophy (earth, water, air and fire), but rather the fundamental forces which govern existence, especially, perhaps, the power of the stars. Behind such conceptions lies the human experience that man is not master of his own fate, but subject to powers beyond his control, the hidden forces that govern nature, society and even the life of the individual.

Against this background, the Christian confession that Jesus is Lord includes the proclamation that all powers and principalities are subject to him. Those who believe are free from the cosmic powers, whatever they are. Christians have no need of rites and ceremonies which honor these beings in order to attain salvation, nor do they need to engage in ascetic practices in order to escape their realm of influence. Christians are free to use everything which God has created, giving thanks.[14] They have no reason to fear the cosmic powers: "For I am sure that neither death nor

13. The epistles to the Ephesians and Colossians represent a Pauline school of thought even if they were not written by Paul himself or at his request. My own position on the authorship of these letters has shifted somewhat over the years. Today I am most inclined to think that they were written after the death of the Apostle. See my article "Ephesians," in *IDBSup*, 268–69.

14. See Rom. 14:6, 14; 1 Cor. 10:23–30. Cf. also Col. 1–2 and the comments upon Colossians in F. O. Francis and W. A. Meeks, *Conflict at Colossae*, SBLSBS 4 (Missoula, MT: Scholars, 1973), esp. 197–200.

life, nor angels, nor principalities, nor things present, nor things to come, nor powers, nor height, nor depth, nor anything else in all creation will be able to separate us from the love of God in Christ Jesus, our Lord" (Rom. 8:38–39). Christian faith means freedom from the world and its powers as well as freedom from the Mosaic Law and its commandments.

On occasion, Paul speaks about freedom from the world using ordinary language rather than cosmic terms. The Christian cannot commit himself completely to earthly cares, to human ties, sorrows and joys: "(Let) those who deal with the world (live) as though they had no dealings with it" (1 Cor. 7:31). In antiquity, liberty implied the contrast to slavery, or to bondage, far more than it does today. But the liberty of which Paul speaks even the slave who is in Christ can share. Christian liberty does not confer moral license: the man who commits sin soon becomes the slave of Sin.

The concept of liberty is part of Western culture's Greek heritage. Paul too owes some debt to Greek philosophical ideas about the liberty of the wise man who knows that some things lie beyond his power. But Paul goes further; the freedom of which he speaks is not stoic apathy, the undisturbed peace of mind of a man who maintains an inner distance from worldly affairs. Paul integrates freedom with an engaged concern: that man is free who is Christ's slave, and who, moved by love, becomes the slave of other men. The free member of a Christian community respects the freedom of his brothers. Paul exhorts the Corinthians not to become the slaves of men, while at the same time reminding them: "For though I am free from all men, I have made myself a slave to all, that I might win the more" (1 Cor. 7:23; 9:19).

IMPACT ON WESTERN THOUGHT

Paul's formulation of the relationship between faith in Christ and the Law of Moses, his central theological concern, had a decisive impact on the church in its formative years. Paul was neither the first nor the only early Christian to carry the Christian message beyond the borders of Judaism. But without Paul, Christianity might very easily have split into two camps, one a sect within Judaism, and the other, entirely separate from Judaism, a mystery cult association which would soon have lost its identity in the welter of contemporary syncretism. Our knowledge of primitive Christianity before and contemporary with Paul is too limited for us to assess the probability of this danger with any accuracy. There is no doubt, however, that Paul made an important contribution which helped enable the church to retain the Old Testament while refusing to adopt specifically Jewish traditions. Only by combining both these elements could the church have developed as it did, into a universal institution, accessible to all, with a historic consciousness of its vocation as the People of God. Paul's penetrating theological analysis of these problems had a decisive impact on the whole subsequent history of the church, and thereby on subsequent world history.

Paradoxically, we can continue by saying that the Pauline problematic of the relation of the church to the Law and to Israel soon became irrelevant. The fall of Jerusalem to the Romans in 70 marked the end of the powerful influence of the Jerusalem church. Few Christians any longer perceived that the unity of Jews and Gentiles in the church was a problem. In a dramatic reversal of the situation which Paul had confronted, Jews who wished to become Christians had to abandon Judaism. The church retained the Old Testament, but read it as a Christian book; the use of the anachronism "Old Testament" itself helps convey the early Christian outlook.

As time went on, the hope faded that Christ would soon vindicate Christian faith by his coming again; Christians no longer felt in their own lives, as Paul and his contemporaries had, that a new Creation had dawned with Christ and with his resurrection. First generation problems gave way to those of the second and third. For those who had always been Christians, the Pauline contrast between "once" and "now," so vivid for mission congregations, lost its force. Christians continued to honor Paul, they collected his letters and read them, but more because they valued their general religious content than because they understood and approved Paul's solutions to his specific problems.

Paul's attempt to express his basically non-Greek thought structure using Greek language and concepts colored by Greek philosophy, made it easier for later Christian generations to combine Greek philosophy with Christian faith. In the second century, Gnostics and other heretics displayed an interest in Paul which the orthodox did not share, at least not to the same degree. The most important of these second century heretics, Marcion, even prepared his own critical edition of the Pauline letters, a process which may have prompted the church to fix more firmly the apostle's place in the canon. At the end of the second century, Irenaeus and other church fathers wrested Paul away from the Gnostics and used his writings to confute them. From that time on, Pauline elements have been an integral part of Christian theology.

Through the centuries Paul has exerted influence not as an original thinker but as the author of inspired writings. But a thread of Paul's thought runs through the whole fabric of Western intellectual history, in philosophical speculation about man and history, liberty and unity, as well as in theology. We cannot, however, distinguish the specifically Pauline from other Christian elements, from the impact made by the Gospels and other books of the New Testament, by the Old Testament, by church tradition and by theological interpretation.

At two points in the history of the West specifically Pauline ideas emerged with striking impact: at the time of Augustine and at the time of the Reformation. In these periods the Pauline doctrines of salvation by grace and justification by faith, without works, gained such weight that subsequent Western Christianity has continued to read Paul through the eyes of Augustine, and for Protestants, of Luther. In the Eastern church, the problem of the relation of faith to works has never had such a central position. In the East, Christians regard Paul as a saint, a mystic and a martyr. As to his theology, his image of the church as the body of Christ was more important than his doctrine of justification.

Augustine found Paul useful when, in his struggle against Pelagius, he emphasized the necessity of grace. Paul's belief that throughout history God chooses some and rejects others became the foundation for a doctrine of each individual's predestination to salvation or to condemnation. Luther found in Paul the solution to his personal problems of conscience, and took up Paul's insistence on Christian freedom in his struggle against monastic piety, ceremonial ritual and the church's hierarchical organization. Augustine and the reformers did recognize fundamental elements of Paul's thought, but they placed these elements in a non-Pauline context, a context shaped by the history of the church, by its practices of penance, and by a consciousness of sin far more introspective than that of Paul and of his congregations. Modern biblical study has attempted to take Paul's own situation seriously, to understand him as a man of his own time, to view his special contribution against the background of what his contemporaries and predecessors thought and said. The picture of Paul which has gradually emerged contains much that appears strange to us, but it has also shown that Paul was a thinker of wider scope and greater penetration than we would have guessed from the traditional stereotype.

2

Paul and Possessions

No reader of the New Testament can avoid confronting the sayings of Jesus about money: "Do not lay up for yourselves treasures on earth," "No man can serve two masters, . . . You cannot serve God and mammon," "Go, sell what you have, and give to the poor," "Woe to you that are rich." Nor need one read too far in the prophets or in James to find harsh pronouncements about wealth and its dangers. We find no such judgments in Paul's letters. At a first reading, Paul does not appear to have much to say about the problems of wealth. This apparent silence is very striking. Paul, who traveled through large cities in the Roman Empire making his living as a tentmaker, must have had far more experience dealing with money than Jesus, who was a carpenter in a rural town, Nazareth, before beginning his public ministry.

Of course, Paul does know something about the dangers of wealth; the word he most commonly uses to describe them is *pleonexia*. *Pleonexia* means the desire to have more. English translations use words like "covetousness," "ruthless greed," "rapacity," and "avarice." "Greed" occurs frequently in lists of pagan vices. Greed is idolatry. Just as adulterers, thieves and robbers cannot inherit the kingdom of God, neither can the greedy. Christians should not even mention greed; their lives should provide no opportunity to speak of its existence.[1] Here Paul speaks plainly. But it is difficult to avoid the impression that such warnings are reminiscences of elementary Christian instruction, almost truisms. Paul is much

---

1. Rom. 1:29; 1 Cor. 5:10f.; 6:10; Col. 3:5; Eph. 4:19; 5:3, 5. Ephesians and Colossians represent Pauline catechetical traditions even if not written by Paul. So do the Pastoral Epistles.

more zealous and eloquent when he discusses sins against moral purity and love. Only 1 Timothy speaks about greed as the root of all evil.[2]

Paul does not simply warn against economic abuses; he advocates a positive economic ideal for the individual to work quietly and eat one's own bread: "If anyone will not work, let him not eat." Everyone must manage his own affairs and work with his own hands. Nobody should have an opportunity to criticize the way Christians live. Christians must meet their economic obligations, including the payment of taxes to the Roman authorities.[3] To use a word current in Paul's time which in ours describes a certain socio-economic ideal, Paul advocates autarchy.[4] In Paul's letters, this word means that the individual must be content with what he has. But there is more to the word than that; in order to maintain his economic independence, the individual must at least have enough to get by, and he must avoid the entrapment of wealth.

The man who manages his own affairs prudently will also be able to provide for those in need. The Christian worker should strive to earn more than is necessary to provide for his own needs, in order to be able to relieve the suffering of those who cannot provide for themselves. The exhortation to do good, to provide for those who have nothing, is a constantly recurring element in Paul's moral teaching.[5] For Paul, next to the sacrifice of life itself, giving away all one's possessions is the greatest act of love. But he does not urge the members of his congregations to such extremes of charity; he writes: "But have (I) not love, I gain nothing" (1 Cor. 13:3).

There is no doubt that Paul advocates a high moral standard concerning the use of money. However, his exhortations are down-to-earth, little more than commonplaces. Paul neither condemns wealth nor glorifies its renunciation. He does not urge the Christian to leave everything and to imitate Jesus' life of poverty. What Paul demands of the Christian is honesty, industriousness, contentment and generosity. We get the impression that he demands solid middle-class respectability. It is obvious that Paul has appropriated the best of the ethical traditions of Judaism

---

2. 1 Tim. 6:10; cf. 6:6-9, 17-19.

3. See 2 Thess. 3:10-12; 1 Thess. 4:11f.; Eph. 4:28; and Rom. 13:1-7.

4. *autarkeia*: 2 Cor. 9:8 ("have enough"); 1 Tim. 6:6 ("contentment"); *autarkēs*: Phil. 4:11 ("content"). The idea can also be present where the word is not used, e.g., 1 Thess. 4:12: "So that you may ... be dependent on nobody," or: be in need of nothing.

5. See Rom. 12:13; 2 Cor. 9:8; Gal. 6:6-10; Eph. 4:28; 2 Thess. 3:13.

about possessions, traditions which largely coincided with the views of the Greek moralists. There is less of anything specifically Christian.

However, we have not yet presented the whole picture. There are elements which Paul adds to his treatment of money which make it unique. First, it is strange that Paul never speaks about money directly even though he writes several times about financial matters. This may reflect his environment, in which he had little reason to distinguish between money and other forms of property and income. He only uses the term "possessions" (or "property") once, in passing.[6] In every other case, he paraphrases. It appears that, consciously or unconsciously, he is striving to avoid using the appropriate nouns. His circumlocutions would not seem natural if they were not expressions of a unified outlook. Paul never looks at an individual's relationship to money in isolation.

References to money are always part of a total context, which includes the attitude to its use. Three factors in particular are decisive for Paul's attitude toward money: eschatology, the church, and his own situation as an apostle.

Second, Paul was aware that he was living in the last days. He expected to see Jesus' return and the end of the world. He knew that the Messiah had already come and that the process which would bring the world to an end had already started. The events which guaranteed the world's end, Jesus' death and resurrection, had already occurred. Christians, who were baptized into Christ Jesus, were already delivered from "this present evil age," they had already received the Holy Spirit as a first fruit and as a guarantee of their redemption.[7] In this situation property and money had little significance; they belonged to the age which was perishing. Paul uses phrases like "material benefits" ("carnal things": *KJV*) and "matters pertaining to this life."[8] The contrast is to the spiritual good, i.e., to matters that relate to God and to his kingdom. Economic affairs are trivial.[9] For those who already have a share in the new age, money can no longer

---

6. 1 Cor. 13:3: *panta ta hyparchonta mou* ("all I have"). Cf., e.g., Matt. 24:47 ("all his possessions"); Luke 11:21 ("his goods"), 12:33 ("your possessions").

7. See, e.g., 1 Cor. 10:11; 2 Cor. 1:21f.; 5:5, 17; Gal. 1:4; 4:4-6; 6:15; Rom. 6:1ff.; 8:9ff.; 13:11-13. On the social and economic conditions of the members of the Pauline congregations, see Malherbe, 29-31, 71-87; M. Hengel, *Property and Riches in the Early Church: Aspects of a Social History of Early Christianity* (London: SCM, 1974) esp. 35-41. Cf. also E. A. Judge, "St. Paul and Classical Society," *JAC* 15 (1972) 19ff.

8. *ta sarkika*, Rom. 15:27 ("material blessings"); 1 Cor. 9:11, ("material benefits"); *ta biōtika*, 1 Cor. 6:3 ("matters pertaining to this life").

9. *ta elachista*, i.e. the smallest things, 1 Cor. 6:2 ("trivial cases").

have any real importance. Paul is far from "dropping out" of society, however. He sharply rebukes those members of the Thessalonian congregation who had stopped working because they believed that the Day of the Lord was at hand.[10] Paul demands that those living in the last days manage their economic affairs with an inner integrity: "The appointed time has grown very short; from now on, let those who have wives live as though they had none, and those who mourn as though they were not mourning, and those who rejoice as though they were not rejoicing, and those who buy as though they had no goods and those who deal with the world as though they had no dealing with it for the form of this world is passing away."[11] A Christian shall obviously continue to work and earn money, but he shall at the same time maintain his independence.

This view echoes the teachings of the Cynic and Stoic philosophers contemporary to Paul; they too spoke about autarchy and about the wise man's independence of the external conditions of his life.[12] But although the exhortations are similar, Paul's advice had very different roots. Paul is not concerned with the self-sufficiency and personal integrity of the wise man, with his inner freedom and his mastery of the external conditions of his existence. Paul states the consequences of the objective situation in which Christians live at the end of the ages. What matters is their relation to their Lord in heaven. Christians must not attach themselves to money or to other earthly concerns, attachments which would weaken their commitment to the Lord. They ought not to be anxious about anything but to please him.

Paul did not insist that those whose livelihoods involved dealing with money change their occupation. On the contrary, Christians had an obligation to continue working in the profession they practiced before becoming Christians: "Only, let everyone lead the life which the Lord has assigned to him, and in which God has called him," "Every one should

---

10. Thus 2 Thess. 3:6ff., cf. 2:1ff. The exhortation to work in 1 Thess. 4:11–12 is part of traditional paraenesis, see R. F. Hock, "The Working Apostle: An Examination of Paul's Means of Livelihood" (PhD diss., Yale, 1974) 96–108. Nevertheless, eschatological expectations and the presence of "idlers" (*ataktoi*) seem to enhance its relevance for the Thessalonians, see 1 Thess. 4:13ff.; 5:14.

11. 1 Cor. 7:29–31.

12. The Diatribes of Epictetus provide the best known illustration of this attitude. For the necessity to distinguish between Stoics and Cynics and between differing trends within both schools, see A. J. Malherbe, "Cynics" and "Epictetus," in *IDBSup*, 201–3 and 271.

remain in the state in which he was called."[13] The end is near at hand, earthly affairs have lost their significance, and therefore Christians have no reason to alter their position in life. Paul applies this logic to the married and to the unmarried, to the circumcised and to the uncircumcised, to slaves and to the free.[14] There can be little doubt that his attitude toward the rich and the poor was much the same. The poor and the rich have the same Lord, who gives both groups a share in his bounty and who joins them in the same church: this is the strikingly new element in Paul's thought. The congregation becomes the decisive social reality for the Christian way of life, and communal life by necessity involves the use of possessions. Herein lies an important difference from the ideals of the Stoic sages and Cynic preachers. Here too we find part of the explanation for the difference between what Jesus and what Paul say about money.

The customary ethical rules have even greater weight within the community: the Christian should "do good to all men, and especially to those who are of the household of faith" (Gal. 6:10). Greed is especially shameful when it victimizes a Christian brother. Paul harshly rebukes Christians at Corinth who have filed lawsuits against one another as a result of their commercial dealings.[15] Worst of all for Paul is that they appeal to pagan courts to settle their financial differences. But the

---

13. 1 Cor. 7:20. Here *RSV* translates: "Every one should remain in the state in which he was called." In the Greek text (*en tē klēsei hē eklēthē*) the word *klēsis* refers, in accordance with normal Pauline usage, to God's effective call through the gospel. Paul's idea is that a person should remain in the state the person was in when the call reached him (whether he was or was not circumcised, was slave or free, married or single). Cf. 1 Cor. 7:17ff., esp. 7:24, *en hō eklēthē* ("in whatever state each was called"). Paul fails to take into account that his rule could not possibly apply to children as they grew up and to adults who had to find work in order to support themselves. He assumes that only a short period of time remains but, after all, he had been a Christian for some twenty years when he wrote 1 Corinthians. He may, in fact, presuppose that children continued to live in the house and to practice the trade of their parents. If so, this would provide some information about social conditions in the Pauline congregations. At least since Luther, the word *klēsis* in 1 Cor. 7:20 was taken to refer to the civil state or occupation as being a religious vocation. As a consequence, Paul's eschatologically motivated theory of status quo was turned into a biblical rationale for social conservatism.

14. The advice to slaves who have an opportunity to gain freedom (1 Cor. 7:21b) remains enigmatic. For information on an attempt to reach beyond the alternative renderings in the text and footnote in the *RSV*, see S. Scott Bartchy, *First Century Slavery and 1 Corinthians 7:21* (SBLDS 11, Missoula: Scholars Press, 1973).

15. 1 Cor. 6:1-11. See E. Dinkler, "Zum Problem der Ethik bei Paulus," *ZTK* 49 (1952), now in *Signum Crucis* (Tübingen: Mohr, 1967) 204-40.

congregation has already suffered a defeat when its members sue one another: "Why not rather suffer wrong? Why not rather be defrauded?" The issue of lawsuits gives Paul the opportunity to stress the basic idea that Christians must be willing to suffer injustice.[16] He views the whole problem in the light of the position that Christians will occupy when they participate in the judgment of the world, and in the light of the reality in which they already participate as a result of their baptism.

We know little about the social composition of the Pauline congregations. We can guess that the majority consisted of craftsmen and shopkeepers. We know that there were some slaves. As a whole, however, the congregation did not belong to the proletariat narrowly construed, though it did not come from the upper class: "For consider your call, brethren; not many of you were wise according to worldly standards, not many were powerful, not many were of noble birth."[17] Paul could no doubt have added: "Not many were rich." But he did not. For Paul, the gospel is more a judgment on those who think they are wise, who think they are noble, than a judgment on the rich. It is quite likely that the congregation at Corinth did have some rich members, even if they did not belong to the intellectual or social elites. In any case, the congregation includes not only slaves but also slaveowners. Paul provides moral instruction for both groups. When Paul speaks of a man and his household, he includes not only his immediate family but his slaves as well.[18] We know little about the individuals whose names we find in Paul's letters or in Acts; what we do know indicates that they were financially independent. Perhaps some of them were very wealthy. The poor have probably remained anonymous. By and large, that too indicates that we cannot assume that most of the congregation's members came from the proletariat.

What is the relationship of rich to poor in the Pauline congregation? Again, the texts provide little information. Paul never says: "There is neither rich nor poor." This is not a pressing question for Paul. But the

---

16. Paul shares the idea with Greek moralists in the Socratic tradition that it is better to suffer injustice. See also Matt. 5:39f.; 1 Peter 2:20; 3:9, 13f.

17. See 1 Cor. 1:26. In Rome and other cities in the Empire freedman and other people outside the families could be rich without being fully accepted in the higher circles. The Christian church, like other cults and associations, is likely to have found recruits among people who were moving upwards in society, as Wayne Meeks has pointed out in an unpublished paper.

18. 1 Cor. 1:16; cf. Acts 16:15; 18:8.

Corinthian correspondence makes it clear that economic differences did create problems. Even at the liturgical center of the congregation's life, in the Lord's Supper, groups formed along social lines. Here Paul clearly rebukes the well-to-do for their behavior. The rich have gorged themselves on the food they brought with them with the result that those who could only arrive later, slaves and workingmen, do not have enough to eat. Those who act in this way "despise the church of God and humiliate those who have nothing." Paul condemns the indifference to the significance of the sacrament implicit in such behavior.[19]

This is not the only image of congregational life at Corinth which Paul provides, however. He also mentions Christians who provide hospitality for the congregation gathered in their homes. When Paul writes from Corinth to the Christians in Rome, he refers to Gaius as: "host to me and to the whole church" (Rom. 16:23). It is probable that Gaius not only allowed the congregation to gather in his home, but also entertained it. This reference hints that the Pauline congregations soon begin to take wealth into the service of the church. It is not that the rich man sells all that he has and contributes to the poor or to the congregation's common fund; rather, he opens his home to the congregation and, perhaps, provides for it at his own expense.[20]

Philemon used his wealth in this way. The letter Paul wrote him gives us an example of Paul's attitude toward an individual's management of his personal financial affairs. The escaped slave Onesimus was Philemon's property. Paul begins by assuring Philemon that he thanks God for the love and faith which Philemon has displayed "toward the Lord Jesus and all the saints." He mentions the joy and comfort Philemon's love have afforded him, "because the hearts of the saints have been refreshed through you" (Philem. 4–7). Paul alludes to the generosity which Philemon's wealth has enabled him to show his Christian brothers, hoping that he will once more demonstrate this generosity. Paul does not mention the financial aspect directly, which is typical. What is important is that Philemon has manifested Christian love and that he has given his Christian brothers an opportunity to experience the reality of that love. Here the

---

19. See 1 Cor. 11:17–24.

20. See the references to the churches in the house of Prisca and Aquila (Rom. 16:3–5; 1 Cor. 16:19), of Philemon, Apphia and Archippus (Philem. 2), and of Nympha (Col. 4:15), and also the recommendation of Phoebe as the helper (*prostatis*) of many in Rom. 16:1–2.

material does not stand in opposition to the spiritual; rather, the material becomes a carrier, a medium, of the spiritual.

Paul writes to Philemon in order to intercede for an escaped slave, Onesimus, who had come to Paul and whom Paul had converted. Onesimus' escape from Philemon appears to have been compounded by some financial wrongdoing. Though Paul may not know exactly what happened, he presupposes that Philemon has a valid claim to make against Onesimus. He writes to Philemon with great solemnity that Philemon should charge Onesimus' debt to Paul's account: "I, Paul write this with my own hand, I will repay it" (Philem. 19). Indeed, the tone is so solemn that we detect an element of irony in it. The irony becomes more evident when Paul adds that he could have said that Philemon owed Paul his very self, because it was through Paul that he had become a Christian. Despite the irony, Paul is making a serious point. There ought to be proper order in financial affairs, even (and especially) among Christians. Paul is actually suggesting that Philemon renounce his claim against Onesimus, but he leaves it to Philemon to make his own decision. There is another suggestion which Paul makes only implicitly. There can be little doubt that Paul hopes not only that Philemon will welcome back his runaway slave, but also that he will then send Onesimus back to Paul to continue to serve him while he is in prison.[21] Paul refuses to ask this favor of Philemon directly; he simply suggests it (though indeed he suggests it very strongly!). He leaves it to Philemon to do more than what Paul has asked him to do, "in order that your goodness might not be by compulsion but of your own free will" (Philem. 14). Paul expects much of his fellow Christians, even in financial matters. But he expects them to act freely and lovingly, not under compulsion.

We find no trace of a communistic ideal in Paul's letters, not even of a voluntary consumers' communism as an expression of love. He does however mention the ideal of economic equality; he quotes from Scripture: "He who gathered much had nothing left over, and he who gathered little had no lack."[22] It is when speaking of the relationship between different Christian congregations that Paul speaks of equality (*isotēs*), viewing them as economic units. But certainly the ideal of mutual help and of equalizing abundance and scarcity applies to individuals as well. The

---

21. See John Knox, *Philemon among the Letters of Paul*, (2nd ed., Nashville: Abingdon, 1959), 24–32. The evidence does not prove that the legal question of Onesimus' status as slave or freedman was important to Paul.

22. See 2 Cor. 8:8–15, where Paul quotes Exod. 16:18.

method that Paul endorses is that those who have more than they need share what they have with those in want, not that everyone surrenders his possessions to a communal fund.

There may well have been a common congregational fund, but we have no real picture how that fund was managed. Paul lists acts of helping among spiritual gifts, he talks about serving, and about him who contributes.[23] It remains uncertain whether he refers to those whose resources enable them to help others or to those who administer a common congregational fund. In the earliest period perhaps both functions belonged to a single group of individuals. It is obvious that in his letter to the Philippians Paul presupposes a church office whose responsibilities include financial administration. When he mentions bishops and deacons, he does so because they are the ones who manage the congregation's common fund.[24] At the same time, these officials preside over the congregation's worship. Responsibility for the management of the congregation's financial affairs, for carrying on its charitable work and for presiding over its liturgies was inseparably joined together in these early congregations. The community's celebration of the Eucharist was also a common meal, the time when the congregation offered its gifts, gifts which were later distributed to the poor.[25]

When Paul mentions these matters, he never stresses the purely financial aspect which can be measured in dollars and cents. Paul stresses instead the giver's attitude: "Each one must do as he has made up his mind, not reluctantly or under compulsion, for God loves a cheerful giver" (2 Cor. 9:7). Paul concentrates on the joy and love which the gifts express, on the relationship to one another and on the community in Christ which the distribution of material goods realizes. Money becomes more than just money within the Christian church; it attains an almost sacramental significance: "A visible sign of an invisible grace."

23. *antilēmpseis* (1 Cor. 12:28) ("helpers"), *diakonia*, Rom. 12:7; *ho metadidous*, Rom. 12:8 ("he who contributes"; the reference to economic contributions is not beyond dispute). In Rom. 12:8 *ho proistamenos* is probably "a leader" (*NEB*, cf. 1 Thess. 5:12), not "he who gives aid"; *ho eleōn* ("he who does acts of mercy") probably refers to visiting the sick and similar charitable acts, rather than to almsgiving.

24. Phil. 1:1; cf. 4:10ff. and see below, note 37.

25. The picture drawn in the text depends more on inferences from what we know about early Christian practice in general than upon exact information provided by the letters of Paul. From 1 Cor. 16:2 we may possibly draw the inference that gifts for immediate use within the congregation were collected on the first day of the week, when Christians gathered for worship. See also Acts 2:44-47; 6:1-6.

The collection on behalf of the Jerusalem church makes this point most clearly. This collection was extremely important to Paul.[26] It became one of the principal foci of the last years of his work in Asia Minor and Greece; it was a project which Paul worked hard and long to complete. The economic need of the Jerusalem church was a fundamental presupposition underlying the project. But this is not the element which weighed most heavily on Paul. More important for Paul was that the collection was an obligation which he had assumed. At the Apostolic Council, which acknowledged that Gentile Christians were free from the requirements of the Mosaic Law, Paul and Barnabas had promised to "remember the poor" (Gal. 2:10). The fulfillment of this promise symbolized for Paul a ratification of the unity between Jewish and Gentile Christians. Paul's way of speaking about this gift is very characteristic. He uses words like "service," "fellowship," "blessing," and "grace." He regards the money itself as the embodiment of everything which giving the gift symbolizes, and he expresses himself in a way which is impossible to translate.[27] For Paul, the gift proves the reality of the love which binds all Christians together. The congregation in Macedonia has manifested exactly the right spirit: "Their abundance of joy and their extreme poverty have overflowed in a wealth of liberality on their part. For they gave according to their means, as I can testify, and beyond their means—not as we expected, but first they gave themselves to the Lord and to us by the will of God" (2 Cor. 8:2, 5). Indeed, Paul can appeal to Christ as a model: "Our Lord Jesus Christ, that though he was rich, yet for your sake he became poor" (2 Cor. 8:9).[28]

Paul wants the members of his congregations to give freely, willingly. Yet he regards the gift as a duty, as a repayment, because the Gentiles have come to share in the spiritual blessings which originally belonged to the Jews. The spirit with which the Jewish Christians receive the gift is as important to Paul as the spirit with which the Gentile Christians give it. By accepting the gift the mother congregation in Jerusalem ratifies its fellowship with Gentile Christians and confirms its recognition that Gentile

---

26. On the collection, see D. Georgi, *Die Geschichte der Kollekte des Paulus für Jerusalem* (Hamburg: H. Reich, 1965); K. F. Nickle, *The Collection* (SBT 48, London: SCM Press, 1966).

27. On the terms and metonyms for the collection to Jerusalem, see Appendix I below.

28. For the purposes of the present study, it does not make much difference whether 2 Corinthians 8 and 9 are fragments of two separate letters or originally belong in the present context. See Appendix II below.

Christians are brothers in Christ. If the gift is given and received with joy, it unites Jewish and Gentile Christians so that as a single community they can give thanks to God. In this way, the gift of money expresses what is for Paul most important: the unity of Jews and Gentiles in the church of Christ.[29] This is the reason that it was so important to Paul to deliver the gift in person, even though he fully understood the risk of a journey to Jerusalem.

Paul knew that his zeal to complete the collection exposed him to criticism; some have clearly impugned his motives. Paul took care to shield himself from such criticism as much as possible by conducting himself very scrupulously. The congregations themselves chose representatives who supervised the local collection and who accompanied Paul when he delivered it: "We intend that no one should blame us about this liberal gift which we are administering, for we aim at what is honorable not only in the Lord's sight, but also in the sight of men." (2 Cor. 8:20–21).[30]

Even apart from the collection, Paul's actions exposed him to criticism. The modern saying, "The pastor's purse is never full," reflects an attitude toward wandering preachers, sophists or philosophers widespread in antiquity. In his first letter to the Thessalonians, Paul tries to make it clear that he is not a preacher of that type: "For we never used either words or flattery, as you know, or a cloak for greed, as God is witness" (1 Thess. 2:5). Paul reminds them: "We worked night and day, that we might not burden any of you." Paul can recommend his own conduct as an example for them to follow.[31]

Even while stressing that he has worked with his own hands, that he has renounced their financial support, Paul emphasizes that he is entitled to that support. He uses arguments to support his claim: the analogy to soldiers, the image of gardeners who share in the harvest and shepherds who have a right to part of the flock, the commandments of the Mosaic

---

29. See Rom. 15:27–31; 2 Cor. 9:10–14. I have dealt with this aspect of the collection in other studies, see pp. 77, 111, and 142.

30. 2 Cor. 12:14–16 shows that Paul's handling of the collection was criticized. 2 Cor. 8:16–23 lists his precautionary methods.

31. See 1 Thess. 1:6 and cf. 1 Cor. 9 and 11:1. On 1 Thess. 2:3–12 see A. J. Malherbe, "Gentle as a Nurse," *NovT* 12 (1970) 203–17. On Paul's work with his hands, see Hock (note 10). Both Malherbe and Hock draw attention to the similarities between Paul and the Cynics.

Law and Jesus' own words.³² The saying of Jesus that the laborer deserves his food appears in Paul in the form: "Those who proclaim the gospel should get their living by the gospel." Paul adduces only this positive statement. He does not refer to the prohibitions against carrying a money belt or traveling bags, or against efforts to obtain more than simple hospitality. Paul's selection and interpretation of Jesus' instructions illustrate the difference between preaching the gospel in rural Galilee and preaching the gospel in the principal cities of the Empire.³³

Why does Paul stress so heavily a right to support which he has renounced? It is extremely important to him that his churches acknowledge this right because that acknowledgment means they recognize his legitimacy as an apostle. For this reason, Paul's congregations must understand that his renunciation of support represents a purely personal decision, a free will undertaking which exceeds his obligations. The financial sacrifices others make, Paul wants them to make voluntarily, with joy, not because of compulsion. He makes it clear that the same rule applies to him. He has earned the right to the congregation's support, but he has renounced it of his own free will. Thus, his renunciation is praiseworthy, something in which he can take justifiable pride.³⁴ To

32. See 1 Cor. 9:6-14. On Paul's use of sayings of Jesus, see D. Dungan, *The Sayings of Jesus in the Churches of Paul* (Philadelphia: Fortress), 3-80. Dungan's analysis of Matthew's redaction is unsatisfactory, but that does not impair the value of his study of Paul's handling of the saying in 1 Cor. 9:14 (Matt. 10:9; Luke 10:7).

33. As reported in Mark 6:8-11 (Luke 9:3-5) and Matt. 10:9-14/Luke 10:4-11, Jesus' instructions call the disciples to devote all their energy to their preaching and healing mission. The prohibition against carrying money presupposes that they should not earn money either, but trust that God would provide. According to Paul's interpretation, Jesus had stated the principle that the preacher of the gospel had a right (*exousia*) to receive support (1 Cor. 9:4, 6, 18; cf. Gal. 6:6). Missionaries like Paul and Barnabas, who founded new churches in Hellenistic cities, had either to carry money or to work in order to support themselves when they first came to a new place. Paul's practice was opposed by the itinerant charismatics who visited Corinth, but these "apostles" could rely on receiving their livelihood without work or money only because they visited cities where there was already a Christian community (cf. 2 Cor. 10:12-16; 11:12-15; 12:11-15). That the ancient practice of itinerant apostles and prophets could lead to abuse is also attested by Didache 11, cf. Hermas 43 (Mand. XI). G. Theissen has devoted several studies to the radicalism of itinerant charismatics and the contrast between them and Paul's church-founding missionary practice. See esp. "Wanderradikalismus," *ZTK* 70 (1973) 245-71, and "Legitimation und Lebensunterhalt," *NTS* 21 (1974/75) 192-221.

34. See esp. 1 Cor. 9:15-18; 2 Cor. 11:10, and. cf. Käsemann, "A Pauline Version of the 'Amor Fati,'" in *New Testament Questions of Today* (Philadelphia: Fortress, 1969), 217-235.

preach the gospel was the charge he had received from God, about which he had no choice; but to preach without asking for his deserved compensation was in itself his reward (1 Cor. 9:18). His sacrifice removed a possible stumbling block from the path of prospective converts; they had no cause to believe that he was motivated by greed.

Indeed, Paul was criticized because he refused to accept payment. When Paul speaks about the injustice he had done the church at Corinth by refusing compensation, about the lack of love he displayed by his sacrifice, the irony is obvious: "For in what were you less favored than the rest of the churches, except that I myself did not burden you? Forgive me this wrong!" (2 Cor. 12:13).[35] Paul assures them that he will not in the future ask for any help from the congregation at Corinth or from neighboring congregations. The reason for Paul's attitude may well be the criticism he has received at Corinth for the way he dealt with money. Paul did receive help from the congregations in Macedonia, even when he was living in Corinth. Paul says that he "robbed" other congregations in order to spare the Corinthians.[36] Perhaps some at Corinth accuse him of robbery because of his efforts to promote the collection for the Jerusalem church.

The congregation at Philippi in particular distinguished itself by helping Paul financially. They sent a gift to Paul when he was a prisoner in Ephesus (or Rome). The letter which Paul wrote to express his thanks for their gift is perhaps our best evidence for his attitude toward money.[37] One must be cautious about describing anything in world history as unique; but there is no letter of acknowledgement and thanks which compares to Philippians. I need not say too much about the letter; let me simply note that Paul gives thanks explicitly for the gift only at the end of the letter. What he mentions at greater length is fellowship in working

---

35. Cf. 1 Cor. 9:3ff.; 2 Cor. 11:7-12; 12:14-18.

36. 2 Cor. 11:8. See also 2 Cor. 11:9; 12:13 and Phil. 4:10ff.

37. The opening of Philippians adumbrates the thanks for the gift at the conclusion of the letter (4:10-20). The bishops and deacons (1:1) are likely to have administered the gift. The phrase *epi pasē tē mneia hymōn* (1:3) most likely refers to the support with which the Philippians had several times "remembered" Paul. See Schubert, *Form and Function of the Pauline Thanksgiving*, 61. Their "partnership (*koinōnia*) in the gospel" was manifested in financial support of Paul (Phil. 1:5; cf. 1:7). A note of joy pervades the whole letter (Phil. 1:18, 25f.; 2:2, 17f.; 3:1f.; 4:1, 4). The gift from Philippi was, certainly, one factor that made Paul rejoice. See also Webber, "The Concept of Rejoicing in Paul" (PhD diss., Yale 1970), 164-67, 178-83, 216-17, 245-50, 268-76, 286-88, 315-19, 353ff.).

for the gospel, joy and community in Christ. Paul, who was proud that he supported himself, that he did not burden anyone, was filled with radiant Christian joy because of the gift which he had received.

Paul is not expressing thanks merely for a gift of money. He gives thanks for the fellowship in Christ which the gift expresses. Here again we see that a gift of money within the Christian congregation can be an act of worship, nearly sacramental. Paul describes their gift as "a fragrant offering, a sacrifice acceptable and pleasing to God" (Phil. 4:18). Paul had not asked for the gift and he would have managed without it. As he told the Philippians: "For I have learned, in whatever state I am, to be content. I know how to be abased, and how to abound; in any and all circumstances I have learned the secret of facing plenty and hunger, abundance and want. I can do all things in him who strengthens me" (Phil. 4:11-13).

With this quotation we could have concluded. But we inquisitive modern men and women want the answer to one more question: what was Paul's own financial situation? His financial condition during the time he spent as a missionary seems fairly clear: working with his own hands enabled him to survive, with a minimum of outside help. Probably, he knew want more often than plenty. But what was the financial situation in the home in which he grew up? There can be little doubt that Paul came from a rather well-to-do family. Though he worked as a tentmaker,[38] the self-conscious pride he takes in earning his living by working with his own hands makes it unlikely that he came from a working-class family. Paul had learned to make tents because every Jew had to learn a trade, not because it was necessary in order for him to support himself.[39]

What little information we have about Paul's family and adolescence confirms the impression his letters create. The rabbinic training Acts attributes to Paul, if true, would not provide conclusive evidence about his economic status. Several of the rabbis were rather poor. If Paul did study in Jerusalem, however, that would suggest that he came from a family of

---

38. Only Acts 18:3 makes a reference to Paul's trade. The meaning of *skēnopoios* ("tentmaker") is not quite certain.

39. In his dissertation (see note 10), Hock points out that the evidence to which scholars usually refer is later than Paul. Hock therefore prefers to think that Paul followed the practice of some Cynics, e.g., Simon the Shoemaker. See pp. 6-21, etc., esp. "Conclusions," 163-65.

The Cynic analogies, however, in no way exclude the possibility that Pharisees also combined study with the practice of a craft. On Cynic influence on rabbinic Judaism, see H. Fischel, *Rabbinic Literature and Greco-Roman Philosophy* (SPB 21, Leiden: Brill, 1973).

independent means; not many working-class Diaspora Jews could have afforded to send their sons to Jerusalem for an education. That Paul's father was a Roman citizen also makes it more likely that he was well-to-do.[40] Perhaps it is not too rash to suggest that the close cooperation and friendship between Paul and Barnabas had its roots in similar social backgrounds. We know from Acts that Barnabas had a farm which he sold. He gave the money he received to the congregation's common fund, which the apostles in Jerusalem managed. He obviously belonged to the group which contributed most.[41]

If what I have suggested is true, what happened to the money which Paul inherited from his father? It is difficult to imagine that he did not receive an inheritance, though he might have been disinherited because of his conversion to Christianity. More likely Paul, like Barnabas, gave his property to the congregation's common fund, or perhaps he used the money to support himself during his early years of service as a missionary for Christ. We do not know, because the extant letters describe only his later, more successful work. If my conjecture is correct, then the silence of the sources is eloquent indeed. Paul's financial sacrifice is likely to have been greater than we can determine from his letters, but he chooses not to talk about it.

There is a pervading but quiet heroism which characterizes Paul's attitude toward money; to use Paul's words: "The love of Christ controls us." (2 Cor. 5:14).

---

40. See Acts 22:28 on Paul's Roman citizenship and 23:16–22 on the son of his sister.

41. See Acts 4:36–37. On the theme of possessions in Luke-Acts, see L. Johnson, "The Literary Function of Possessions in Luke-Acts" (PhD diss., Yale, 1976, to be published in the SBL Dissertation Series).

APPENDIX I

Words and Phrases Referring to the Collection

The following list illustrates the variety of terms and circumlocutions which Paul uses to speak about the collection for Jerusalem. The translation of the *RSV* is given in quotation marks, with the addition of parentheses where I have first given elementary lexical information. The list begins with more or less technical terms and proceeds to metonyms, metaphors, and other words and phrases which refer only within a specific context to the collection.

- *logeia*, collection, 1 Cor. 16:1, 2 ("contribution").
- *koinōnia*, partnership, sharing, etc., Rom. 15:26; 2 Cor. 9:13 ("contribution"); 2 Cor. 8:4 ("taking part").
- *diakonia*, service, Rom. 15:31; 2 Cor. 8:4 ("relief"); 2 Cor. 9:12 ("offering"); 2 Cor. 9:13 and, possibly, 1 Cor. 16:15 ("service"). The verb *diakonein*, serve, refers to the collection in Rom. 15:25 and 2 Cor. 8:19, 20.
- *leitourgia*, voluntary public service, or (priestly) ministry, 2 Cor. 9:12 (*hē diakonia tes leitourgias tautēs*, "the rendering of this service"); *leitourgein*, "to be of service," Rom. 15:27.
- *charis*, (gift of) grace, favor, 1 Cor. 16:3 ("gift"); 2 Cor. 8:6, 7, 19 ("gracious work"). Cf. 2 Cor. 8:1 ("grace," as in 2 Cor. 8:9; 9:14).
- *haplotēs*, simplicity, sincerity (in giving), 2 Cor. 8:2 ("liberality"), 9:11, 13 ("generosity").
- *eulogia*, blessing, 2 Cor. 9:5 ("gift," "willing gift"). Cf. 9:6, *ep' eulogiais* ("bountifully").
- *hadrotēs*, plenitude, 2 Cor. 8:20 ("liberal gift").
- *perisseuma*, "abundance," 2 Cor. 8:14.
- *endeixis tēs agapēs hymōn*, "proof of your love," 2 Cor. 8:24.
- *karpos*, fruit, Rom. 15:28 ("have delivered to them what has been raised," with the footnote: "Greek *sealed to them this fruit*").

- *sporos*, seed, sowing, 2 Cor. 9:10 ("resources"); cf. the quotation from Ps. 112:9 in 2 Cor. 9:9 and the allusion to Isa. 55:10 in 9:10. *ho speirōn*, "he who sows," 2 Cor. 9:6.
- *ta genēmata tēs dikaiosynēs hymōn*, "the harvest of your righteousness," 2 Cor. 9:10, with allusion to Hosea 10:12.
- *meros*, part, etc.; *en tō merei toutō*, "in this case," 2 Cor. 9:3.
- *hypostasis*, substance, reality, matter, etc., but hardly ever confidence; see Bauer-Arndt-Gingrich and H. Koester in *TDNT*, VIII, 572–589. *en tō hypostasei tautē*, 2 Cor. 9:4 ("for being so confident") probably means either "in this state of mind" (referring to Paul's boasting, 2 Cor. 9:3, cf. 11:17) or simply "in this matter." Only on the last interpretation does the word belong to this list.

Translation becomes especially difficult where Paul combines several of these words to speak about the collection; for example,

2 Cor. 8:4: *tēn charin kai tēn koinōnian tēs diakonias tēs eis tous hagious*, the grace of and the participation in the service for the saints ("the favor of taking part in the relief of the saints").

Some other words are associated with the collection without ever denoting it: *prothymia*, "readiness" or "good will," 2 Cor. 8:11, 12, 19; 9:2; *spoudē*, "earnestness," 2 Cor. 8:7, 8; cf. 8:16, 17; *agapē*, "love," 2 Cor. 8:7, 8, 24; *ergon agathon*, "good work," 2 Cor. 9:8.

APPENDIX II

On the Literary Integrity of 2 Corinthians 1–9

According to fairly widespread opinion, 2 Corinthians 8 and 9 are two fragments of separate letters which a redactor incorporated into the composite document which we know as 2 Corinthians. See, e.g., D. Georgi, "Corinthians, Second Letter to the," in *IDBSup*, 183–86. For the purposes of my study, it does not make much difference whether or not this is really so. Nevertheless, I would like to set forth some counter-arguments for which I am indebted to former and present students at Yale.

1. 2 Cor. 7:4 contains a thematic statement which is spelled out in 7:15–16; the argument here prepares for, and is continued in, chapter 8. See R. D. Webber, "The Concept of Rejoicing in Paul" (PhD diss., Yale, 1970), 225–45.

2. Throughout 2 Cor. 1–7 Paul expresses his confidence in the Corinthians and seeks to reestablish his own credibility. Only when mutual confidence is restored can Paul hope that the Corinthians will heed his advice concerning the collection for Jerusalem. See S. N. Olson, "Confidence Expressions in Paul: Epistolary Conventions and the Purpose of 2 Corinthians" (PhD diss., Yale, 1976), 99–215.

3. In terminology, in the use of examples, and in other features, the argument in 2 Cor. 8 (and 9) conforms to the style of deliberative or symbouleutic rhetoric. The most obvious examples occur in 2 Cor. 8:10; *gnomēn ... didōmi*, "I give my advice," and *touto ... sympherei* "it is best." In symbouleutic rhetoric, the credibility (or "ethos") was a matter of great importance, and so it is in 2 Corinthians. (S. N. Olson, D. Wilcox, D. Worley).

4. By handling the affair with the wrongdoer to Paul's full satisfaction, the Corinthian Christians had already passed a first test, see 2 Cor. 2:5–11; 7:7–13. The completion of the collection will be a second, decisive test of their faith, love, earnestness, and loyalty to Paul, see 2 Cor. 8:8, 24, 9:4ff., 13. Cf. also 13:5–10. (J. Espy).

5. The formula *peri men gar*, "now . . . about," in 2 Cor. 9:1 could, but does not need to, introduce a new topic. It could mark the transition from the recommendation of Titus and two brothers in 2 Cor. 8:16–24 to the resumed treatment of the collection itself in chapter 9. Even in 2 Cor. 9:3–5 Paul refers to the anonymous brothers, who apparently were representatives of the churches and members of the delegation that was to bring the collection to Jerusalem.

It is possible and even likely that Paul in his letter referred to the two brothers by name. If so, their names would for some reason have been deleted at an early stage of the textual history. Thus, there is indeed a possibility that the document which we read as 2 Corinthians underwent some editorial redaction at an early stage. But even if the document were composite, the seams should be located between chapters 8 and 9 and/or between chapters 9 and 10 but not between chapters 7 and 8 or between 7:4 and 7:5. On the special problem of 2 Cor. 6:14—7:1, see Chapter IV below.

3

Paul and the Church at Corinth according to 1 Corinthians 1:10—4:21

WHEN FERDINAND CHRISTIAN BAUR in 1831 published his famous article on "The Christ-party in the Corinthian Church,"[1] he was not raising a new question but making a fresh contribution to a discussion which had already begun. Yet his article is generally considered to have inaugurated a new epoch in the history of New Testament scholarship. Dealing with one specific question, Baur in his article gave a first sketch of his understanding of the historical dialectic in primitive Christianity. The main ideas were later developed in voluminous works by Baur and his pupils in the "Tübingen School," and have exerted a considerable influence upon students of the New Testament up to the present day.

In his essay Baur argued that in spite of the four slogans reported in 1 Cor. 1:12 there were, in fact, only two parties involved in the strife at Corinth: over against the adherents of Paul and Apollos stood those of Cephas, who claimed to be those who belonged to Christ. As the weaknesses of this theory have often been pointed out, there may be some reason for calling attention to its strengths. Baur observed that in 1 Cor. 1–4 Paul does not deal with a variety of parties, but in "this first apologetic section" gives a justification for his apostolic authority and ministry. Further, he was able to trace a continuity between 1 Cor. 1–4 and the later controversy of which 2 Corinthians, especially chapters 10–13, is

---

1. "Die Christuspartei in der korinthischen Gemeinde, der Gegensatz des paulinischen und petrinischen Christentums in der ältesten Kirche, der Apostel Petrus in Rom," *Tübinger Zeitschrift für Theologie* 4 (1831) 61–206. Cf. Baur, *Paulus* (Stuttgart, 1945), 259–332.

evidence. Baur could also relate the enigmatic slogan "I belong to Christ" to Paul's remark in 2 Cor. 10:7: "If any one is confident that he is Christ's, let him remind himself that as he is Christ's, so are we." Finally, Baur was able to integrate the Corinthian controversy into a comprehensive view of the earliest history of Christianity which he found to be determined by the tension between Paulinists and Petrine Judaizers. Yet, the arbitrary reduction of the four slogans to two parties caused numerous modifications of Baur's theory even within his own school.

More than one hundred years of research since Baur's essay has made it clear that there is no real trace of Judaizers at Corinth, at least not at the time of 1 Corinthians. According to Wilhelm Lütgert, Paul's chief opponents at Corinth, identified with the Christ party, were spiritualistic enthusiasts, an early type of libertinistic Gnostics.[2] This theory has been very influential in Germany. Adolf Schlatter modified it by tracing a Palestinian background for the "Corinthian theology."[3] The philologist Richard Reitzenstein explained both Paul's terminology and the Corinthian piety on the background of contemporary Hellenistic religiosity, mystery religions and syncretistic Gnosis.[4] More recently W. Schmithals[5] and, in a different way, U. Wilckens[6] have tried to reconstruct the doctrines of the Gnostics in Corinth.

Outside Germany scholars have been more reluctant to assume that Paul's polemic had to be directed either against Judaizers or against Gnostics. Johannes Munck published an essay on 1 Cor. 1-4, later incorporated in his book *Paul and the Salvation of Mankind*, with the provocative title "The Church without Factions."[7] He held that there were neither parties nor Judaizers, and, we may add, no Gnostics at Corinth. What caused the trouble was that the Corinthians, owing to their Greek background, misunderstood Christianity as wisdom: they took the Christian leaders to be teachers of wisdom, like rhetors and sophists who

---

2. *Freiheitspredigt und Schwarmgeister in Korinth* (BFCT 12, 3; Gütersloh, 1908).

3. *Die korinthische Theologie* (BFCT 18, 2; Gütersloh, 1914). Cf. also Schlatter's commentary, *Paulus, der Bote Jesu* (Stuttgart: Calwer, 1934).

4. *Die hellenistischen Mysterienreligionen* (3rd ed., 1910; Leipzig: Teubner, 1927), esp. 333-93, "Paulus als Pneumatiker."

5. *Gnosticism in Corinth* (1st ed., 1956; ET; Nashville: Abingdon, 1971).

6. *Weisheit und Torheit* (BHT 26; Tübingen: Mohr, 1959). See the critical review by H. Koester in *Gnomon* 33 (1961) 593ff.

7. "Menigheden uden Partier," *DTT* 15 (1952) 251-53. Incorporated as chapter 5 of *Paul and the Salvation of Mankind*.

took themselves to be wise and made all this a cause for boasting. More recently, John C. Hurd, Jr., has written a very stimulating book on *The Origin of 1 Corinthians*.[8] Following solid traditions of American scholarship, he avoids the generalizations of theology and comparative religion and tries to reconstruct the stages of the relations between Paul and the church at Corinth prior to 1 Corinthians. The result is that the controversies behind 1 Corinthians were not due to any extraneous influence upon the congregation, but to Paul's own change of mind in the time between Paul's Corinthian ministry and the previous letter referred to in 1 Cor. 5:9–11. This change is explained as due to the apostolic decree to which Paul in his previous letter felt obliged to be loyal; in accordance with John Knox and others, Hurd argues that the Corinthian ministry preceded the Apostolic Council, according to a chronology based on Paul's letters and not on the secondary evidence of Acts.[9]

This brief and eclectic, but fairly representative summary shows that while there is a wide negative agreement that in 1 Corinthians Paul is not opposing Judaizers, there is no consensus with regard to the background and nature of the controversies. As to the questions of exegesis, it is quite generally agreed that in 1 Cor. 1–4 Paul is addressing the church at Corinth as a whole, and that it is not possible to take any one section to refer to any one of the parties, if there were such parties. Likewise, while 1 Cor. 5–16 may attest the presence of various trends within the congregation, it has not proved possible with any degree of certainty to relate these trends to the slogans reported at the beginning (1:12). But this exegetical consensus is only a negative one.

No clear interpretation has been given to the slogans of 1:12. If there were no factions, but merely quarrelling, jealousy and strife, the difficulties are increased. Why, then, does Paul give the slogans such a prominent place? The major difficulty lies in the words "I belong to Christ" which quite a few scholars regard as a gloss.[10] The combination with 2 Cor. 10:7 favored by Baur and, on different presuppositions, by Lütgert and Schmithals, seems to provide the relatively best possibilities of interpretation, but the theories of these scholars are open to other objections.

8. *The Origin of 1 Corinthians* (New York: Seabury, 1965).

9. Cf. John Knox, *Chapters in a Life of Paul* (New York: Abingdon, 1950), 13–88 (in *Apex Books* edition).

10. J. Weiss and others, including Wilckens. For references cf. Hurd, 96–107, and (Feine-Behm) W. G. Kümmel, *Introduction to the New Testament* (Rev. ed.; Nashville: Abingdon, 1975), 273.

No clarity has been reached with regard to the relation between chapters 1–4 and the rest of the epistle. An increasing number of scholars doubt the integrity of 1 Corinthians; the present epistle is assumed to be a composition of fragments from two or more letters.[11] Hurd offers a valuable survey and critique of these theories, but fails to provide a reasonable explanation of the function of the first major section (1:10–4:21) within the letter as a whole. On the fairly dubious principle that "clearly the greater objectivity attaches to the written portion of the information,"[12] he bases his understanding of the background of 1 Corinthians entirely upon the hypothetical reconstruction of the letter from the Corinthians to Paul and Paul's previous letter. This may represent a sound reaction against other scholars who have based their theories mainly upon 1 Cor. 1–4. Munck deals only with these chapters, and Wilckens concentrates on 1 Cor. 1–2 alone! But personally I cannot share the optimism with regard to the objectivity of written documents such as statements issued by ecclesiastical bodies, and often find oral information more revealing with regard to what has been going on. In fact, Hurd is hardly able to make anything out of 1 Cor. 1–4, and the "tentative suggestion" which he finally makes is a bad relapse into a method which he has in principle overcome.[13]

Finally, no clarity has been reached with regard to the relation between the situations reflected in 1 Corinthians and in 2 Corinthians. Is Paul in 2 Corinthians, or in the fragments of which the epistle is often assumed to be composed, dealing with later developments of the same controversy as in 1 Cor. 1–4, or is he facing entirely new problems? Both views are held, and there are arguments which seem to favor both of them.[14] In the following pages it will be argued that while Baur was wrong in taking Paul's opponents in 1 Cor. 1–4 to be Judaizers, he was fully right in speaking of these chapters as an "apologetic section" in which Paul justifies his apostolic ministry. It is a main failure of theories like those of Munck and Hurd that they do not really take this into account.[15]

11. Cf. Hurd, 43–47, 69–71, 86–89, 131–42. Kümmel, *Introduction*, 202–5.

12. Hurd, 62. But cf. also 113: "Paul knew from his oral information that the Corinthians had not been altogether candid with him in the letter they addressed to him."

13. Ibid., 269–70. Cf. the summary on 295: "I Cor. 1–4 and II Cor. 11:17–33 concern the 'parties' which we suggested were the result of disagreement over the effect of the Previous Letter on the table fellowship between Jewish and Gentile Christians."

14. Examples are given by Kümmel, *Introduction*, 284–86.

15. Without making any impression upon Munck, I tried to draw attention to the

An attempt to reach beyond the present impasse in the interpretation of 1 Cor. 1–4 must be performed according to a strict method if the result is not going to add to a chaos which is already bad enough. I would suggest the following principles:

(1) The controversy must be studied as such. Due account must be taken of the perspective under which Paul envisages the situation at Corinth. But as far as possible, we must also try to understand the Corinthian reaction to Paul.

(2) While 1 Cor. 1–4 must be understood against the historical background, any reconstruction of that background must mainly be based on information contained within the section itself. Relatively clear and objective statements concerning the situation at Corinth must serve as a basis. Evaluations, polemical and ironic allusions, warnings and exhortations may next be used to fill out the picture. Only when these possibilities have been exhausted, and with great caution, should Paul's own teaching be used as a source of information concerning views held by the Corinthians; Paul may have adapted his language to theirs, but this assumption remains highly conjectural.

(3) The integrity of 1 Corinthians may be assumed as a working hypothesis which is confirmed if it proves possible to understand 1 Cor. 1:10—4:21 as an introductory section with a definite purpose within the letter as a whole. Materials from 1 Cor. 5–16 should therefore be used for the sake of comparison. Special attention should be paid to chapters 5 and 6 which in the present context stand at the transition from 1–4 to those sections of the epistle in which Paul handles questions raised by the letter from Corinth.

(4) In so far as they do not directly serve the purpose of philological exegesis, but provide materials for a more general historical and theological understanding, information from other Pauline epistles, Acts, and other early Christian, Jewish, Greek, or Gnostic documents should not be brought in until the epistolary situation has

---

apologetic aspect in an article, "Paulus apostel og menigheten i Korinth (I. Kor. 1–4)," *NorTT* 54 (1953) 1–23. The present essay is an attempt to restate and elaborate my case, with less attention paid to exegetical details, and with the addition of some new, more conjectural hypotheses. My interest in the topic has been renewed by the work of Hurd, but it is not a main purpose to discuss his theories.

been clarified as far as possible on the basis of internal evidence. Points of similarity, especially with 2 Corinthians, should be noted, but not used in such a way that the results of contextual exegesis are pre-judged.

(5) Any reconstruction of the historical background will at best be a reasonable hypothesis. A hypothesis will recommend itself to the degree to which it is able to account for the total argument and all details within 1 Cor. 1–4 with a minimal dependence upon hypothetical inferences derived from extraneous sources. The results achieved will gain in probability if they can without difficulty be integrated into a comprehensive picture of the history of primitive Christianity in its contemporary setting.[16]

The basic information contained in 1 Cor. 1:10—4:21 is what was reported by Chloe's people: there was quarrelling (*erides*) among the Christians at Corinth, each one of them saying, "I belong to Paul," or "I to Apollos," or "I to Christ." In 3:3–4, where only the names of Paul and Apollos are mentioned, Paul speaks about "jealousy and strife" (*zēlos kai eris*). As the implication of the slogans is controversial, only the fact of the quarrels is unambiguous. Another piece of evidence is, however, added at the end of the section: "Some are arrogant (*ephysiōthēsan*, lit. have been puffed up) as though I were not coming to you" (4:18). That the persons in question were "arrogant" (*RSV*), or "filled with self-importance" (*NEB*), is Paul's evaluation. But we do get the information that some assumed that Paul would not come back to Corinth. It seems likely that they expressed their view openly.[17] In view of this statement, the idea that Paul always deals with the congregation as a whole needs some modification; there are certain persons whom he regards as "arrogant." As often, he uses the indefinite pronoun *tines* to refer to definite persons whose names he does not want to mention.[18] This indicates that Paul is aware of the existence of some center of opposition to him within the church at Corinth.

---

16. The statement of methodological principles will make it clear why I discuss the theories of Munck and Hurd rather than those of Schmithals and Wilckens. This does not reduce the value of the immense amount of material gathered, especially by Wilckens.

17. This is made fairly clear by the emphatic *eleusomai de* at the beginning of verse 19, cf. verse 21 and 16:5–7.

18. Cf. Rom. 3:8; 1 Cor. 15:12, 34; 2 Cor. 3:1; 10:2, 12; Gal. 1:7; Phil. 1:15; 2 Thess. 3:11 (1 Tim. 1:6, 19; 4:1; 6:10, 21). Sometimes even *tis* or *ei tis* is used in a similar way.

The results of this search for objective information may seem to be very meager. But if combined the pieces of information disclose that the quarrels and the slogans at Corinth were related to the assumption that the apostle would not return. The general context supports this combination.

The whole section begins with Paul's appeal to his brethren in Corinth that they should agree and avoid divisions (1:10). It ends with an equally urgent appeal that they should be imitators of Paul: to that purpose he sends Timothy who will remind them of his instructions (4:16-17). Both in 1:10 and 4:16 we find periods headed by the verb *parakalō* ("I appeal," "beseech," or "urge"), a formal pattern which Paul uses when he sets forth what is a main purpose of his letters, expressing what he wants the addressees to do.[19] The *parakalō*-periods are distinguished from strict imperatives in that they call for a voluntary response. But Paul makes it quite clear that as the Corinthians' only father in Christ he does have authority to command, even if he does not do so, He hopes that he will not have to use his rod when he comes to Corinth which he plans to do if that is the will of the Lord (4:14-15, 19-21). At the beginning Paul asks for the mutual concord of the brethren; at the end of the section if not before, the reader understands that Paul at the same time asks his children to concur in harmony with their father in Christ. This is well brought out by John Knox, who has written, with reference to 1 Cor. 1-4: "He wants his converts to stand firm, not only in the Lord, but also in their loyalty to him."[20]

The general content of the section adds further confirmation to this. It deals with four main themes:

(1) Unity in Christ and the quarrels at Corinth, 1:10-13. This initial theme is taken up again in 3:3-4 and 21-23.

(2) Wisdom and foolishness, the power and wisdom of God over against the wisdom of men. Various aspects of this main theme are handled in 1:17-3:2, and taken up again in 3:18-21 and 4:7-10.

(3) The function of the apostles and Christian leaders, and the esteem in which they should be held, 3:5-4:6, cf. 4:9-13.

19. The clearest example of this epistolary use of *parakalō* is found in Philem. 8ff. Cf. John Knox, *Philemon among the Letters of Paul* (1935; 2nd ed., New York: Abingdon, 1959), 22f.; Bjerkelund, 118ff., 162ff.

20. *Chapters in a Life of Paul*, 95.

(4) Paul's relations to the church at Corinth. This theme is implicit throughout the whole section from 1:13 onwards and comes into the foreground at the end, 4:14–21.

It is clear how the first and the third themes are related to one another. The Corinthians are quarrelling because they "boast of men," i.e. of one of the teachers, and are "puffed up in favor of one (of them) against the other" (3:21; 4:6). It is somewhat less evident why the wisdom theme is given such a prominent place. However, Paul takes the Corinthians' boasting of the teachers to imply boasting of their own wisdom (cf. 3:18–21; 4:7–10). At the same time, he sees the quarrelling as clear evidence that the Corinthians are not as wise and spiritual as they imagine themselves to be (3:3–4). But in order to understand the structure of the total argument we have to realize that the fourth theme, the apostle and his relations to the church at Corinth, comes in at all important points of transition.

The initial appeal for unity immediately leads to Paul's activity at Corinth and to his commission as a messenger of the gospel (1:13–17). In 2:1–5 and 3:1–2 Paul returns to his own first preaching at Corinth, so that this provides the framework within which he deals with the word of the cross and with the way in which the Corinthian brethren were called (1:18–25, 26–31), as well as with the wisdom which is reserved for the mature (2:6–16).

From his first preaching at Corinth Paul returns to the present situation (3:2c–4; cf. 1:11–12). Even when he deals with the questions, "What then is Apollos? What is Paul?" he not only makes statements of principle, but points to the special ministry assigned to him (3:10–11), and asserts that no human court, but only the Lord, is to pass judgment upon him (4:3–4). Even when he contrasts the predicaments of the apostles with the riches of the wise Corinthians, Paul has first of all his own ministry and sufferings in mind (4:8–13). Thus the whole argument quite naturally leads to the conclusion, "For though you have countless guides in Christ, you do not have many fathers. For I became your father (*hymas egennēsa*) in Christ Jesus through the Gospel." It would be unfair to say that preparation for this statement is the main function of everything that has been said; yet, one aim of what Paul has to say about the strife at Corinth about wisdom and foolishness, and about the function of

Christian leaders, is to re-establish his authority as apostle and spiritual father of the church at Corinth.[21]

From the statement, "With me it is a very small thing that I should be judged by you or by any human court" (4:3), we may safely infer that some kind of criticism of Paul has been voiced at Corinth. And it is not difficult to find out what the main content of this criticism must have been. That becomes evident in phrases like, "Not with eloquent wisdom" (*ouk en sophia logou*, 1:17), "Not in lofty words of wisdom" (*ou kath' hyperochēn logou ē sophias*, 2:1), "Not in persuasiveness of wisdom" (*ouk en peithoi sophias*, 2:4),[22] "Milk, not solid food" (*gala . . . ou brōma*, 3:2). To what extent the phrases, and not merely their content, allude to what was reported to have been said, is immaterial. Since the Corinthians evidently understood themselves as wise because they thought themselves inspired, pneumatic persons (cf. 3:1), we must conclude that Paul was not merely held to lack the oratorical ability of a Greek rhetor, but also the gift of pneumatic wisdom. In 4:8 the apostles are not only said to be "fools for Christ's sake," but also "weak," and "in disrepute."[23]

In addition to Paul's alleged lack of wisdom, Paul's critics may have mentioned other failings. He had not baptized many (cf. 1:14). The catalog of sufferings in 4:11-13 deserves close attention. Hunger, thirst, and nakedness are common features in descriptions of persons in need (cf., e.g., Matt. 25:35-36). That he is "roughly handled" (*NEB, kolaphizometha*) refers in a more specific way to afflictions suffered during the apostolic ministry (cf. 2 Cor. 11:23-25). The lack of stability (*astatoumen*) is characteristic of the apostle who is "homeless" (*RSV*) and has

---

21. On several occasions the point that is most directly relevant to the actual situation comes towards the end of a section or an epistle, cf. 1 Cor. 10:23—11:1; 11:33-34; Rom. 15:30-33; Gal. 6:11-17; Phil. 4:10-18; 2 Thess. 3:6-15. Thus there are good analogies for the assumption that the issue involved in 1 Cor. 1-4 is most clearly to be seen in 4:14-21.

22. I am inclined to take this as the original text which by an early error was misspelled as *ouk en peithois sophias*. The other variant readings can all be understood as attempts to improve this. The problem has no material importance.

23. Adducing very interesting evidence, Munck demonstrates that Greek rhetors and sophists could be regarded as wise, powerful, and honored: *Paul and the Salvation of Mankind*, 158f. and 162f., with notes. But he does himself see that the Corinthians thought of their power as participation in the kingdom of God (p. 165). The Greek analogies therefore do not suffice. At this date there were hardly any sharp distinctions between philosophers, sophists, rhetors, hierophants and mystagogues. For Jewish analogies cf. D. Georgi, *Die Gegner des Paulus im 2. Korintherbrief* (WMANT 11; Neukirchen-Vluyn: Neukirchener, 1964).

to "wander from place to place" (*NEB*); but the choice of the term may very well allude to what was said at Corinth about the unstable apostle who was not likely ever to come back (4:18; cf. 2 Cor. 1:15ff.). An unambiguous reference to a practice of Paul's which is known to have caused objections at Corinth is contained in the clause "We labor, working with our own hands" (cf. 1 Cor. 9:3–18; 2 Cor. 11:7–11; 12:13). Paul goes on: "When reviled, we bless; when persecuted, we endure." This is what a follower of Christ should do (cf. Luke 6:27–9; Rom 12:14). But adding, "When slandered, we make our appeal" (*parakaloumen*, in *RSV*: "we try to conciliate"), he once more alludes to the actual situation; at Corinth he is slandered and responds, not with harsh words, but by making his friendly—though not exactly "humble" (*NEB*)—appeal.

Since the entire section contains an apology for Paul, and since the strife at Corinth was linked up with opposition against him, it becomes possible to interpret the slogans reported in 1:12. Those who said "I belong to Paul" were proud of him and held that his excellence surpassed that of Apollos or Cephas. The other slogans are all to be understood as declarations of independence from Paul. Apollos is mentioned as the most outstanding Christian teacher who had visited Corinth after Paul. Cephas is the famous pillar, the first witness to the resurrection, an apostle before Paul. The slogan "I belong to Christ" is not the motto of a specific Christ-party but simply means "I myself belong to Christ—and am independent of Paul." Understood in this way, all the slogans have a clear meaning in the context and in the situation. Paul had no reason to deal in detail with the various groups, and it becomes quite natural that he should concentrate his presentation on the relationship between himself and Apollos.

It may be added that on the interpretation proposed, the analogy between 1 Cor. 1:12f. and 2 Cor. 10:7 becomes clear. In 2 Cor. 10:7 there is no trace of a specific Christ-party: the wandering apostles simply attacked Paul and claimed to belong to Christ as his servants (cf. 11:23). Paul's answer is that he too belongs to Christ, and, more than they, he is distinguished as a servant of Christ by his sufferings. Here and there Paul finds it an anomaly that someone at the same time can claim to belong to Christ and yet oppose his apostle and faithful servant.

There is no reason to think that either Apollos or Cephas was in any way responsible for the use that was made of his name by people at

Corinth who claimed to be independent of Paul.[24] Paul himself stresses their solidarity and dependence upon God's work (3:5–9, 22; 4:6; 15:11; 16:12). But what then was the occasion for the strife and the opposition to Paul? One fact, especially, needs explanation. The church at Corinth had sent Stephanas, Fortunatus and Achaicus as a kind of official delegation to Paul. In all probability, the Corinthians had commissioned these delegates to bring a letter from the congregation to Paul, asking for his opinion on a number of questions. In this letter it was stated that the Corinthians remembered Paul in everything and maintained the traditions he had delivered to them.[25] Thus, the official attitude of the congregation seems to have been one of loyalty to the apostle. Yet, Chloe's people could orally report that there was strife in Corinth and that there was some opposition to Paul. This tension between the written document and the oral report requires some explanation.

We do not know anything either about Chloe or about her people. From what Paul writes we do, however, learn one thing, namely that it was not Stephanas and the other members of the delegation who reported the quarrels at Corinth. It may mean that the quarrels had started after the departure of the delegation, or it may mean that the delegates had not gossiped. In any case, Paul had his information about the quarrels and the opposition from some other source, and this may have been important both to him and to the recipients of his letter. The name of Stephanas is mentioned at the beginning of our section, in a very curious fashion. Paul first states that he baptized none of the Corinthians except Crispus and Gaius. But he has to correct himself and add that he also baptized the household of Stephanas. This lapse of memory may simply reflect that at the moment Stephanas was with Paul and not at Corinth. But even without much depth psychology one might suspect that Paul first forgot to mention the household of Stephanas because he did not wish to involve Stephanas in his discussion of the divisions at Corinth.

Much more important is the way Paul mentions Stephanas at the end of the letter. First Paul recommends Stephanas and his household;

---

24. The Corinthians may well have derived their knowledge of Cephas from what Paul had told them; at least Peter may have been a great authority far away, in spite of the renewal by C. K. Barrett of the theory that he had visited Corinth, "Cephas and Corinth," in *Abraham unser Vater: Festschrift O. Michel* (Arbeiten zur Geschichte des Spätjudentums und des Urchristentums, 5; Leiden: Brill, 1963), 1–12.

25. 1 Cor. 11:2. It is fairly generally agreed that Paul here alludes to what was said in the letter from Corinth. Cf. Hurd, 52 and 90f.

they were the first-fruits, i.e. the first converts of Achaia, and have devoted themselves to the service of the saints, which may mean that they have taken an active part in the collection for Jerusalem.[26] With remarkable emphasis Paul urges the congregation to be subject to such men and to every fellow worker (16:15–16). After 1:10 and 4:16 this is the third *parakalō*-period of the letter! Next Paul speaks about his joy at the presence of the delegation, adding a new injunction: "Give your recognition to such men" (16:17–18). It is risky to draw conclusions from such injunctions as to the state of affairs which they presuppose. But the double emphasis gives some reason to suspect that not everybody in Corinth was inclined to give due recognition to Stephanas, his household, and his fellow delegates. The evidence is so far inconclusive, but a hypothesis may be ventured: the quarrelling Corinthians were opposing Stephanas as much as they were opposing Paul. As Stephanas was the head of the delegation, he was quite likely also its initiator, and a chief advocate of writing a letter to Paul to ask for his opinion on controversial questions.[27]

The advantage of my conjecture is that it makes it possible to explain in a simple, perhaps somewhat trivial way, the data contained in 1 Cor. 1:10—4:21. The delegation and the letter it carried were themselves the cause of the quarrels. I can imagine myself hearing the objections, and I put them in my own language:

> Why write to Paul? He has left us and is not likely to come back. He lacks eloquence and wisdom. He supported himself by his own work; either he does not have the full rights of an apostle, or he did not esteem us to be worthy of supporting him. Why not rather write to Apollos, who is a wise teacher? I am his man! Or, if we do turn to anybody, why not write to Cephas, who is the foremost of the twelve. I am for Cephas! But, why ask anyone for counsel? Should we not rather say: I myself belong to Christ? As spiritual men we ought to be wise enough to decide for ourselves.

---

26. R. Asting mentions this possibility, but is more inclined to think that Paul refers to service rendered to Christian preachers, including himself. *Die Heiligkeit im Urchristentum* (FRLANT 46, nF 29; Göttingen: Vandenhoeck & Ruprecht, 1930), 151 and 182–83.

27. Hurd argues that the Corinthians' questions were veiled objections (113 and chapter 5, 114–209). In that case, the role of Stephanas may have been that of a mediator who succeeded in persuading the brethren that the objections should be presented to Paul in the form of a polite letter. But cf. notes 39 and 40 below.

The details of this picture are of course pure imagination. But they may help us visualize the delicate situation Paul was facing when he set out to write his answer to the Corinthians. He had to answer a polite, official letter that asked for his advice. But he had also received an oral report stating that some brethren at Corinth had objected to the idea of asking Paul for instructions. Quite likely, latent objections had become more open and had caused a good deal of quarrelling after the departure of the delegation. As a consequence, Paul had to envisage the possibility that his letter containing his reply might easily make a bad situation worse. Quarrel and strife might develop into real divisions of the church, if his recommendations were enthusiastically received by one group and rejected by others.[28]

If the situation was anything like what I imagine, Paul could not possibly go right ahead and answer the questions raised in the letter from the Corinthians. He had first of all to make it clear that he did not speak as the champion of one group but as the apostle of Christ, as the founder and spiritual father of the whole congregation. The first section, chapters 1–4, is therefore a necessary part of the total structure of the letter and has a preparatory function. This also explains the somewhat unusual pattern that a short thanksgiving (1:4ff.) is immediately followed by the first *parakalō*-period.[29] Paul had first of all to urge the Corinthians to agree, to be of one mind. Only on the presupposition that they did so, and that no divisions arose, would whatever else the apostle had to write be of any help.

Answering his critics, Paul is very careful to avoid giving the impression that he favors any one group in Corinth. There is no competition between himself and Apollos or Cephas, and still less between Christ and himself. Therefore even the slogan "I belong to Christ" is fittingly countered by the questions, "Is Christ divided? Was Paul crucified for you? Or were you baptized in the name of Paul?" There is only one Christ, and

---

28. While Munck rightly argues that the term *schismata* used in 1 Cor. 1:10 (cf. 11:18 and 12:25) does not prove that there were "parties" or "factions," he has a tendency to play down the serious danger of divisions within the church, *Paul and the Salvation of Mankind*, 136–39. I am still inclined to think that *schismata* corresponds to the term *maḥalāḳōt* used in rabbinic literature. Jonathan ben Uzziel, for instance, is said to have translated the prophets "in order that divisions should not multiply in Israel," b. Megilla 3a. Cf. my book, *Das Volk Gottes* (1941; repr. Darmstadt: Wisenschaftliche Buchgesellschaft, 1963), 224.

29. The closest analogy is the period introduced by the equivalent *erōtōmen* in 2 Thess. 2:1. See Bjerkelund, esp. 189ff.

therefore no distinction between the Christ to whom the Corinthians belong and the Christ preached by Paul. Paul is Christ's delegate and in no sense his rival. At Corinth he laid the foundation, and it is impossible to belong to Christ without building upon this foundation, which is Jesus Christ himself (cf. 3:10–11, 21–23).[30]

That Paul did not baptize many is for him a reason for thanksgiving. There is no risk that anyone will say that he was baptized in Paul's name and has been made his man. The task of the apostle was not to baptize but to proclaim the gospel (1:14–17). That he did not preach with eloquent wisdom was to the benefit of the Corinthians, and in accordance both with his own commission and with the nature of the gospel, which is the word of the cross. What may appear as sheer folly is God's saving power and wisdom (1:18–25). The Corinthians ought to know this from their own experience (1:26–31). When Paul in Corinth concentrated on preaching Jesus Christ as the crucified one, this was due to a conscious decision. He renounced all the effects of rhetoric and human wisdom, in order that the faith of the converts might rest in the power of God alone (2:1–5). But when he did not in Corinth elaborate the secret wisdom of God's way of acting, it was not because Paul lacked the pneumatic gift of wise speech, but because the Corinthians were immature (2:6—3:2).

My one-sided and incomplete summary of 1:14—3:2 may be sufficient for the purpose to show that everything Paul here says was relevant to the situation he faced. From 3:3 onwards he turns more directly to the present state of affairs. Using himself and Apollos as examples, he stresses their solidarity as servants and fellow workers for God. Those who make comparisons and are proud of the excellencies of their favorite fail to realize their own dignity as God's field, building, and temple (3:5–17). All things, including Paul, Apollos, and Cephas, belong to those

30. Even in 2 Cor. 11:4 the point is the identity of Jesus and not a variety of Christologies. Paul preached the true Jesus and made him the foundation of the church at Corinth. A Jesus who does not fit this teaching must be a false Jesus. The same holds true for a Spirit and a gospel which is received as if Paul had not already preached the gospel and as if those who then believed had not already received the Holy Spirit. Hurd (104-5) has well summarized the arguments against the existence of a separate Christ party. Paul's replies would "simply further the claims" of the party. But Hurd has failed to take into account the possibility that "I belong to Christ" could be an anti-Pauline slogan even if it is not the device of a special party. On that presupposition the replies become highly relevant just because "It is axiomatic that Christ is a unity," as Hurd says himself; Paul is not a rival, but the apostle, servant, and steward of Christ. The argument in 1 Cor. 1:13-15 is analogous with 3:5-11 and 3:21-23; 2 Cor. 10:7; 11:1-4; and 11:23.

who themselves belong to Christ (3:21-23). Yet it is also stressed that Paul had a special task of his own. He was the one who planted and laid the foundation, and this he did as a skilled master builder (*hōs sophos architektōn*). Certainly he did not lack wisdom (3:6, 10). While Paul has no authority of his own, all others have to build on the foundation laid by him. They have to take care, lest they build with materials that will perish, or even destroy the temple of God (3:10-17). The context suggests that those who vaunt their wisdom might easily be guilty of these offences.[31] When speaking about faithfulness as the one duty required of stewards, Paul once more immediately turns to the relations between the Corinthians and himself (4:2-5).

Even the riddle of the enigmatic statement in 1 Cor. 4:6 may possibly find a solution. The phrase *mē hyper ha gegraptai* ("not beyond what is written") is widely assumed to be the quotation of a slogan used in Corinth.[32] I would suggest that even this slogan was part of the discussions and quarrels connected with the delegation and the letter to Paul. The point would then be: "We need no instructions beyond what is written. As spiritual men we can interpret the Scriptures for ourselves. Why ask Paul?" Paul picks the slogan up and returns it. There is no contrast between the apostle and "What is written," but there might be one between the scriptures, Paul and Apollos on the one side and the assertive and quarrelling Corinthians on the other. By the example of Paul and Apollos they should learn not to go beyond what is written, viz., not to be puffed up, but faithfully to perform the appointed service, knowing that everything is a gift of God. In the context the slogan gets its content from the preceding citations from and allusions to what is written concerning the wisdom of God in contrast to the wisdom of men (cf. 1:19f.; 1:31; 2:9; 3:19f.).

---

31. I see no reason for making 3:18 the beginning of a new section.

32. In addition to the commentaries, cf. O. Linton, "'Nicht über das hinaus was geschrieben steht' (1 Kor. 4. 6)," *TSK* 102 (1930) 425-37; L. Brun, "Noch einmal die Schriftnorm 1. Kor. 4, 6," *TSK* 103 (1931) 453-56; M. D. Hooker, "'Beyond the things which are written,'" *NTS* 10 (1964) 127-32. Miss Hooker deals very well with the terminology and context, but I have not been convinced by her renewal of Lütgert's and Schlatter's suggestion that the Corinthians ventured to go beyond what was written. It seems much more likely to me that they exercised their wisdom as interpreters of scripture as suggested by the terms *Sophos, grammateus,* and *suzētētēs* in 1 Cor. 1:20. Only in 1 Corinthians does Paul use quotation formulas like, "It is written in the law," and "The law says" (9:8, 9; 14:21, 34); the reason might be that he agrees to play the game according to the rules set by the Corinthians themselves.

Paul does not, as his adherents are likely to have done, deny the facts which his opponents alleged against him. But what they meant as objections Paul interprets as indications of the faithfulness with which he has carried out his commission. Lack of wisdom, power, and honor is part of the lot that God has assigned to the suffering apostles of the crucified Christ (4:9–13). In order to forestall the possibility that quarrels could lead to divisions, Paul the whole time deals with the church at Corinth as a unity. Only at the end does he single out some persons and flatly deny what they have asserted (4:18f.), that he will not return to Corinth, and, therefore, that he no longer cares for the brethren there; it is simply not true. They are his dear children, and certainly he will come very soon, if the Lord wills. This assertion is repeated at the end of the epistle (16:5–7, cf. also 16:24).

We can now draw some conclusions:

(1) The section 1 Cor. 1:10—4:21 is correctly, even if not exhaustively, to be characterized as an apology for Paul's apostolic ministry.

(2) The quarrels at Corinth were mainly due to the opposition against Paul.

(3) Probably, the quarrels were occasioned or at least brought into the open by the letter and the delegation which were sent to Paul.

(4) The section has a clear and important function within the total structure of 1 Corinthians; before Paul could answer the questions raised, he had to overcome both false appraisals and false objections, and to re-establish his apostolic authority as the founder and spiritual father of the whole church at Corinth.[33]

A number of problems remain. I have to deal briefly with some of them. The first is the function of 1 Cor. 5–6. Why doesn't Paul after the introductory section immediately proceed to give his answer to the questions raised by the Corinthians? It is hardly more than a partial answer that in chapters 5–6, and in 1–4, he deals with matters about which he has only oral information.[34] In spite of theories that fragments from several letters are combined, chapters 5–6 seem to be closely related to their context. There are several points of contact between the preceding

---

33. As to Paul's authority, cf. 1 Cor. 5:3–4; 7:40b; 9; 11:16, 34b; 14:37–38; 15:1–2, 10; and 2 Corinthians, *passim*.

34. The section 11:17–34 is an example of material based on oral information and dealt with at a later place in the letter. Cf. Hurd, 79–82.

section and the beginning of chapter 5.³⁵ 6:12-20 anticipates several items in the latter part of the epistle.³⁶ 6:1-11 is related to chapter 5 by the idea of judgment, by the question of the relations to those outside the church, and especially by the catalogs of sinners in 5:10 and 11 and 6:9-10. Finally, 6:9-11 serves not only as a conclusion to 6:1-8 but also as an introduction to 6:12-20. There is no reason to doubt the literary integrity. The problem is that of the epistolary function of these short sections.

The most important point in this connection may be the allusion to the previous letter, 5:9-11. I have elsewhere argued that the content of what Paul wrote may best be reconstructed by a combination of 5:9-10 with 6:9-10.³⁷ He must have written something like: "Neither immoral men, nor the greedy, nor robbers, nor idolaters, etc., will inherit the kingdom of God. Do not associate with them, nor even eat with them." If this reconstruction is approximately correct, the fragment 2 Cor. 6:14-7:1 is hardly likely to have been part of the previous letter.³⁸ Closer parallels are found in the catechetical instructions in Eph. 5:3-7 and Gal. 5:19-21, cf. also Col. 3:5-6; 1 Thess. 4:3-6, and the free, epistolary variation in Rom. 1:18-2:11. Thus, the previous letter is likely to have contained a restatement of Paul's oral instructions, just like 1 Thess. 4:2ff.³⁹

It is fairly generally assumed that in Corinth what Paul had written was taken to imply that all social relations with unbelievers had to be broken off, and that, in 1 Cor. 5:9-13, Paul is correcting this idea, whether (as is sometimes assumed) it was his own original intention, which he subsequently altered, or whether it was the Corinthians' misunderstanding of what he wrote. Certainly the scope of his instruction may have been open to several interpretations, as can be seen by the analogous passage in Eph. 5:3ff. But neither theory—self-correction or misunderstanding—is

35. *pephysiōmenoi*, 5:1; cf. 4:19. Paul's absence and presence, 5:3; cf. 4:19f.; *kauchēma*, 4:6; cf. 3:21; 4:7. Cf. Hurd, 89, n. 1.

36. Cf. Hurd, 87-89.

37. See my article, "Der Epheserbrief und der verlorene, erste Brief des Paulus an die Korinther," in *Festschrift O. Michel* (see note 24), 65-77.

38. See Chapter IV below.

39. Hurd has seen that there are some signs of similarities between 1 Thessalonians and the previous letter. (231-233). In addition to the analogies between 1 Thess. 4:2-6 and 1 Cor. 5-6, statements like 4:4-5, 4:13-18, and 4:19-20 might in fact have occasioned questions like those which are treated in 1 Cor. 7, 12-14, and 15. But, instead of following this track, Hurd has elaborated the much less attractive hypothesis that the previous letter was occasioned by the Apostolic Decree.

necessary.⁴⁰ The point in 1 Cor. 5:9ff. may simply be a matter of clarification, with the purpose of stressing that what Paul wrote was highly relevant to the church at Corinth. I am therefore inclined to think that chapters 5–6 are still closely related to the controversies which the first main section of the epistle sought to clear up.

At Corinth someone may have felt that even in his previous letter Paul had only given them milk and not solid food; why ask for a new letter from him? Dealing with two concrete cases, and adding some general warnings against sexual license, Paul is able to illustrate his point, viz., that the brethren at Corinth are still badly in need of the milk of elementary instruction concerning a Christian way of life. Understood in this fashion, chapters 5 and 6 can be seen to have an important function as the transition from the introductory section to the answers given to the questions raised by the letter from Corinth. To put it more bluntly: Paul did not want to shame his children at Corinth by what he wrote concerning their quarrels and the opposition to him (4:14), but before he proceeded to answer their questions he did point out that there were cases of which they ought to feel ashamed (5:1–6; 6:5). If the incestuous man is to be identified as one of those who were puffed up, assuming that Paul would not return (4:18), the reasons for this would be quite obvious; but I see no possibility for deciding whether he was or not.⁴¹

In my essay I have explained the controversies reflected in 1 Cor. 1–4 in terms of the church policy and personal matters involved. This does not mean that I think the theological aspects of minor importance. But in practice theological debates usually involve questions of church policy and personal relations. I see no reason to assume that this was different at the time of Paul. Though we regard theology, church policy, and personal relations as separate and yet allow them, illegitimately, to influence one another, Paul makes no such distinctions. He does not distinguish person and office, but identifies himself and wants to be identified by his apostolic

---

40. I owe this observation to C. Douglas Gunn. To state "that we have in 1 Cor. 5:9-11 Paul's own word for the fact that his earlier statement on the subject had been misunderstood by the Corinthians," as Hurd does on p. 215, is not correct. But even if one accepts the probability of the inference, as I have earlier done myself, there is not sufficient evidence to justify the shift from Hurd's first conclusion that it is not possible to know whether or not the section 5:9–13a was occasioned by the Corinthians' letter, to his later assumption that this was indeed the case (Hurd, 83, 149–54, 215, 219f.).

41. In case he was, the further identification with Paul's opponent in 2 Cor. 2:5ff. and 7:12 would not be as improbable as most contemporary commentators think.

ministry.[42] Even his theology and his policy cannot be kept separate from one another. His theology is flexible, responsive to different situations. Yet it has a firm core. In shorthand fashion it may be called a theology of the cross, a term that is especially appropriate with regard to 1 Cor. 1–4. From this basis, he evaluates the trends within the church at Corinth. He finds that the Corinthians do not recognize the wisdom of God, manifested in the cross of Christ. Claiming to have a wisdom of their own, they fail to appreciate that wisdom which, to paraphrase a Lutheran term, is an alien wisdom, *sapientia aliena*. They think that they already possess the coming power and glory, not realizing that in this world the glory of the church and its leaders is, like the glory of Christ himself, veiled under weakness and sufferings (cf. 4:8ff.). Likewise, by passing judgments themselves, they fail to take account of the judgment that is to come, which both the apostle and his critics have to face (3:11–15; 4:5). Boasting that they are pneumatic, they prove by their behavior that they are psychic, sarkic, that they are just ordinary men (2:14–3:4). Still using the language of Lutheran theology, we may say that in the eyes of Paul the Corinthians uphold a false theology of glory.

To an adherent of *theologia crucis* any doctrine which he dislikes may appear to be *theologia gloriae*. The term is not very useful for characterizing any specific type of theology. We have to raise the question whether or not this does in an analogous way hold true to Paul's picture of the Corinthian theology. And certainly, Christians at Corinth may have quarrelled and passed critical judgments, both against Paul and against one another, they may have appreciated wisdom and rhetoric, and they may have been proud and even arrogant, without having any profound theological reasons for all this. Much of what Paul writes does not give us any information whatsoever about what was involved in the theological aspects of the controversies. And yet, there are some clear indications that Paul really did hit the nail on the head when he found that the main tendency in Corinth was to anticipate the eschatological glory to such a high degree that almost nothing was left for the future. To use modern slogans: the Corinthians upheld an "over-realized eschatology", overstressing the "already" and neglecting the "not yet".

The clearest evidence is to be found in 1 Cor. 15. Whatever may have been the exact views of those who said, "There is no resurrection of the dead," they evidently saw no reason for a future resurrection, since those

---

42. On Paul as an "eschatological person" cf. Fridrichsen, 3 and *passim*.

who were baptized already participate in heavenly glory.[43] That this was their attitude both the sacramentalism and the pneumatic enthusiasm at Corinth confirm (1 Cor. 10:1–13; 12–14).[44] The encratitic tendencies with regard to marriage and sexual intercourse, as well as the custom of allowing women to prophesy and speak in the assembled congregation, without restrictions, are likely to reflect the idea that there was no longer a distinction of male and female, since those who belonged to the new mankind were like the angels (1 Cor. 7; 11:2–15; 14:34–35). Even the knowledge and liberty claimed in relation to meat sacrificed to idols point in the direction of eschatological enthusiasm (chapters 12–14).

To Paul this type of enthusiasm is a perversion of the message he had preached at Corinth. Yet it is conceivable that it may have emerged spontaneously as a result of Paul's own activity.[45] To some degree the tendencies may also have been stimulated by the preaching of Apollos. I see no necessity for assuming any other extraneous influence at work. If the term "Gnosis" is to be applied, one would probably have to assume that in the spiritual climate of those days various types of Gnosis could emerge, mutually independent of one another.[46] But these are complicated questions. This short survey of theological trends at Corinth has only one purpose in this context: to show that the section 1 Cor. 1:10—4:21 not only has the function of re-establishing the authority of Paul as the founder and father of the entire church at Corinth, but also prepares for the content of the answers given to the questions raised and indicates the theological basis on which these answers are given.

43. Cf., long ago, Schlatter, *Die Korinthische Theologie* (see note 3), 28, 62–66, etc. Many details are still under discussion, as, for instance, how far 2 Tim. 2:18 is an adequate summary of the Corinthians' position; but a fairly wide consensus seems to be emerging, cf. Hurd, 195–200 with references, and further Munck, *Paul and the Salvation of Mankind*, 165–67, and E. Käsemann, "On the Subject of Primitive Christian Apocalyptic," in *New Testament Questions of Today*, 131–37.

44. In their letter the Corinthians must have written about their zeal for spiritual gifts, 1 Cor. 14:12 and 39. This explains the somewhat forced transitions in 12:31 and 14:1. This allusion is more obvious than others which have been widely recognized, but is not taken account of in the literature surveyed by Hurd, 67–68.

45. Hurd's reconstruction of Paul's first preaching in Corinth is reasonably independent of the dubious theory concerning the impact made upon the previous letter by the Apostolic Decree. Several points deserve serious attention. Cf. 273–88.

46. If Wilckens is right that there was a fully developed Gnostic Christology at Corinth, the balance of probability would weigh in the other direction. The data discussed in my paper is not favorable to this hypothesis, but it is not excluded by my own reconstruction.

The way in which Paul identifies his cause and his person, his policy and his theology, may be astonishing and strange to us. We know that even at Corinth the reactions were mixed. The letter apparently made its impact. In 2 Corinthians we hear no more about the concrete questions discussed in 1 Corinthians; probably Paul's instructions were accepted. The proposals to appeal rather to Apollos or to Cephas may not have been very serious, and proved to be failures. What did not come to an end was the criticism directed toward the apostle. Many of the objections which Paul countered in 1 Cor. 1–4 were voiced again, partly in modified, partly in sharpened forms.[47] The relations between the apostle and the church at Corinth in the time between 1 and 2 Corinthians were both complex and troublesome. It is easy to understand that many were quite willing to listen when some new, wandering apostles arrived. And thus, the apostle had once more to write an apology for his apostolic ministry, this time in a sharper and more direct form (2 Corinthians, especially chapters 10–13). The picture here drawn of the situation in Corinth at the time of 1 Corinthians does therefore harmonize very well with our general knowledge of the Corinthian church and of primitive Christianity as a whole.

In later days, and even in scholarly literature, the Corinthians' mixed feelings with regard to Paul have found many echoes. Paul has been hated and loved more than most persons of the past. The book on Paul by Vilhelm Grønbech, the Danish historian of religion, might be mentioned as a highly sophisticated version of such reactions with many features in common with the Corinthians' portrait of Paul.[48] John Knox is one of the few who have tried to do justice both to the opponents and to the admirers of the apostle past and present.[49] While the debate will go on, we should not forget that Paul did not care about judgments passed by the Corinthians or by any human court. He would hardly have cared more about the tribunal of history if he had been familiar with that concept. His only ambition and passion was to be found a faithful servant in the judgment of his Lord. For the historian, the chief task must be not to express sympathy or antipathy or to evaluate virtues and

---

47. When Paul is said constantly to recommend and defend himself, this might well be a direct reaction to 1 Corinthians. Cf. 2 Cor. 3:1; 5:12; 12:19. It was admitted, however, that "His letters are weighty and strong," 10:10.

48. V. Grønbech, *Paulus: Jesu Kristi Apostel* (Copenhagen: Natur och Kultur, 1940). Cf. E. Hirsch, *ZNW* 40 (1941) 229–36.

49. "The Man and His Work," in *Chapters in a Life of Paul*, 89–107.

shortcomings, but to try to understand Paul as he wanted to be understood, as an apostle of Jesus Christ. He is an amazing person. In 1 Cor. 1–4 he proves able to handle delicate matters of church policy or trivial matters of church politics in such a way that his words are still worth reading. He has something to say which is potentially most important, and which remains reasonably clear in spite of the hypothetical nature of our historical reconstructions.[50]

---

50. Conversations with colleagues and students have convinced me that the characterization of 1 Cor. 1:10—4:21 as an apologetic section is one-sided and may be misleading, for two reasons:

A. In contrast to parts of Galatians (esp. chapters 1–2) and 2 Corinthians (esp. chapters 10–13), 1 Corinthians 1–4 is not written in the style of an apologetic letter.

B. To call the section "apologetic" is to downplay the degree to which Paul is critical of his own adherents as well as of his opponents.

Nevertheless, the section lays a foundation for the subsequent parts of the letter, it serves to reestablish Paul's true authority, and it does contain apologetic elements, see esp. 1 Cor. 4:2–5 and 18–21. I have therefore decided not to rewrite this study but to let it remain fresh, one-sided, and at some points conjectural. For other approaches to 1 Cor. 1–4, see, e.g., R. W. Funk, "Word and Word in I Corinthians 2:6–16," in *Language, Hermeneutic, and the Word of God* (New York: Harper & Row, 1966), 275–305; W. Wuellner, "Haggadic Homily Genre in I Corinthians 1–3," *JBL* 89 (1970) 199–204; J. H. Schütz, *Paul and the Anatomy of Apostolic Authority* (Cambridge University Press, 1975), 187–213.

4

A Fragment and Its Context: 2 Corinthians 6:14—7:1[1]

IT IS GENERALLY RECOGNIZED that the section 2 Cor. 6:14–7:1 is a self-contained unit, beginning with the exhortation, "Do not be mismated with unbelievers," and concluding with the injunction "Since we have these promises, let us cleanse ourselves from every defilement of body and spirit, and make holiness perfect in the fear of God." The injunctions are motivated by a series of rhetorical questions, "For what partnership have righteousness and iniquity?" etc. The central affirmation, "We are the temple of the living God," is supported by a chain of scriptural quotations freely adapted. Read in isolation from its context, the section makes perfectly good sense, whether one reads it as addressed to some particular issue, such as mixed marriages or participation in pagan religious ceremonies, or as a general warning against association with outsiders.

Taken at face value, the section is not related to its context. If it is left out, there is a smooth transition from 6:11–13 to 7:2. I quote the key sentences: "Our mouth is open to you Corinthians; our heart is wide . . . In return, widen your hearts also. Make room for us . . ." As a consequence of such observations a number of scholars have drawn the conclusion that 2 Cor. 6:14–7:1 is an interpolation.[2] There has been a good deal of discussion as to whether the fragment was taken from some other letter of Paul, presumably the lost "previous letter" to the Corinthians, mentioned in

---

1. A paper read at the Annual Meeting of the Society of Biblical Literature in Toronto, 1969, unaltered but with footnotes added.
2. See, e.g., D. Georgi, in *IDBSup*, 183–84.; Kümmel, 287ff.

1 Cor. 5:9-11, or whether it was derived from a non-Pauline source.[3] The vocabulary and phraseology are not typically Pauline. If the fragment had recently been discovered on a sheet of papyrus, the idea of Pauline authorship would hardly have occurred to anybody. Yet, Paul's style and language are so flexible that it is difficult to say with certainty that Paul could not possibly have written the text.[4] I would think that this problem has been solved by the discovery of the Qumran documents. Even persons like myself who are reluctant to assume much direct influence of the Qumran sectarians upon the New Testament will have to admit that 2 Cor. 6:14-7:1 is a slightly Christianized piece of Qumran theology. Christ has been substituted either for God or for the Prince of Light (resp. Michael) as the opponent of Belial (Beliar); the designation of the members of the holy community as *pistoi* (believers) and of the outsiders as *apistoi* (unbelievers) seems to be Christian. But most of the other terms and ideas, the dualism between light and darkness, the term Belial, the notion of the community as the temple of God, the chain of quotations, the call for separation and for purification, are all typical for the Qumran documents. This has been demonstrated conclusively by Joseph Fitzmyer and others, whose arguments need not be repeated.[5]

Assuming that the fragment is of non-Pauline origin, I see no reason to think that it was originally part of Paul's lost letter and only later incorporated into our 2 Corinthians. There is no exact agreement, but only a vague similarity, between the fragment and what must have stood

---

3. Theories about the composite nature of the Pauline Epistles started with the conjectures that 2 Cor. 6:14-7:1 was a fragment of Paul's lost "previous letter" to the Corinthians mentioned in 1 Cor. 5:9-11; that 2 Cor. 10-13 belonged to the letter which Paul wrote "with many tears" (2 Cor. 2:4), and that Romans 16 was (part of) a letter to Ephesus. In the course of time hypotheses have multiplied and become increasingly complicated—and less credible. See Harry Gamble, "The Redaction of the Pauline Letters and the Formation of the Pauline Corpus of Letters," *JBL* 94 (1975) 403-18.

4. Several words and phrases used in 2 Cor. 6:14-7:1 do not occur elsewhere in the Pauline Epistles, as pointed out in commentaries and special studies. Yet, other words and phrases indicate that the fragment has been reworked in a Pauline style, see note 13 below.

5. See esp. J. Gnilka, "2 Cor. 6:14-7:1 In the Light of The Qumran Texts and The Testaments of the Twelve Patriarchs" (1963); ET in J. Murphy O'Connor, ed., *Paul and Qumran* (Chicago: Priory Press, 1968) 46-68; J. A. Fitzmyer, "Qumran and the Interpolated Paragraph in 2 Cor. 6:14-7:1," *CBQ* 23 (1961) 271-80, repr. in *Essays on the Semitic Background of the New Testament* (SBLSBS 5, Missoula: Scholars, 1974) 205-17. In some respects, the Book of Jubilees contains even closer parallels to 2 Cor. 6:14ff. than any of the clearly sectarian writings; cf. Jub. 1:15-26; 2:19-22; 22:14-24; (30:11; 33:11-20).

in the previous letter. It is unnecessarily complicated to conjecture that a non-Pauline text was first quoted by Paul in one letter and later on interpolated into another. I therefore assume that 2 Cor. 6:14–7:1 is a fragment of non-Pauline origin, now to be read as part of our 2 Corinthians. The fragment may be either pre-Pauline or post-Pauline. Neither of these possibilities can be excluded a priori. On the one hand, David Flusser has shown that the most striking New Testament parallels to Qumran texts belong to the layer of tradition common to Paul, John, 1 Peter, Hebrews, etc., presented by Bultmann under the heading "The Kerygma of the Hellenistic Community."[6] On the other, a writing as late as the Shephard of Hermas contains parallels to Qumran as close as those of any New Testament document. Thus neither the content nor the affinities help us to decide whether the fragment was quoted by Paul or interpolated by a later redactor. Whoever incorporated the fragment can, possibly, also have altered its wording.

Scholars who have upheld the integrity of 2 Corinthians have tried to show that a warning against intermingling with the Gentiles fits the context. Most of these explanations have been somewhat strained and far-fetched.[7] Many of those who assume a secondary interpolation argue that our 2 Corinthians as a whole was contrived by a redactor who combined fragments from a number of Pauline letters into a new composition.[8] Some of them, especially Günther Bornkamm, have been able to trace some pattern for the redactional arrangement. But none of them seems to have offered a rational explanation for the interpolation of our fragment between 6:13 and 7:2. A cautious scholar like Kümmel takes this to be a major weakness of the whole interpolation theory.[9] Thus, the apparent lack of meaningful connection between the fragment and its context can be used as an argument in both directions.

6. See D. Flusser, "The Dead Sea Sect and Pre-Pauline Christianity," *Scripta Hierosolymitana*, 4 (1958) 215–66. On the general problem of Qumran and the New Testament, see the cautious comments of P. Benoit in *NTS* 7 (1960/61), esp. 288–95, the comprehensive study of H. Braun, *Qumran und das Neue Testament*, I-II (Tübingen: Mohr [Siebeck], 1966) esp. II, 165–80; on our passage, see I, 201–3, and the summary of J. A. Fitzmyer in *IDBSup*, 216–19.

7. One example may suffice: In his supplement to Lietzmann's commentary (HNT 9, 4 ed. 1949), Kümmel considered 2 Cor. 6:3–10 as an excursus on the apostolic ministry, whereas Paul in 6:14ff. continues the ethical paraenesis he had begun in 6:1–2.

8. See, e.g., Georgi, *IDBSup* 183ff., who thinks that 2 Corinthians is a composition of five different letters (accepting 6:14–7:1 as non-Pauline).

9. See Kümmel, 288.

Under these circumstances I propose that we temporarily bracket the whole question of the integrity or composite nature of 2 Corinthians and simply try to read the text as it stands. We should not only ask for the original meaning of the fragment but try to understand its function in the present context. Once the question is put this way, the answer follows. The transition from Paul's interrelations with the Corinthians to the contrast between light and darkness is created by two injunctions: "Widen your hearts also," and "Do not be mismated with unbelievers!" If the exhortation and the warning are read in conjunction, the meaning is clear: "Widen your hearts for us (i.e., Paul), and do not be mismated with unbelievers who refuse to do so." The rest of the fragment serves to support this exhortation and this warning. As there is no accord between light and darkness, and between Christ and Belial, the Corinthians should not make common cause with the unbelievers, who reject the apostle. They ought to welcome him; that is the only behavior appropriate for those who are the people of God. Obviously the fragment was not originally written to serve this function, but it is equally obvious that read this way it makes good sense in the context.

The possibility of this simple solution has not even occurred to the majority of commentators.[10] Yet if the total context of 2 Corinthians is taken into account, the section 6:11–7:4 can hardly be read in any other way. The term *apistoi* occurs only once in 2 Corinthians outside our fragment, in 4:3–4: "And even if our Gospel is veiled, it is veiled only to those who are perishing. In their case the God of this world has blinded the minds of the unbelievers, to keep them from seeing the light of the glory of Christ, who is the likeness (*eikōn*, image) of God." Within its context this passage contains an indirect warning to the Corinthians; they should take care not to side with the unbelievers to whom Paul's gospel is veiled. A similar idea is suggested by the passage in 2:15–16: "We are the aroma of Christ to God among those who are being saved and among those who

---

10. Ph. Bachmann (in *Kommentar zum N.T.*, ed. Zahn [Leipzig: Deichert, 1909], 294), considered the possibility that Paul suggested that the Corinthians would join forces with the unbelievers by locking the door to Paul, but rejected it in favor of the theory of a misplaced fragment from the "previous letter." In *A Commentary on the Second Epistle to the Corinthians* (New York: Harper & Row, 1973), C. K. Barrett finds the transition from 6:13 to 14 abrupt but by no means impossible. He paraphrases (on p. 194): "If you turn to God and to me as his messenger, it means a break with the world." This makes sense, but in the context it makes better sense to turn the logic of the argument around: "If you really break with the world, it means acceptance of God and of me as his messenger."

are perishing, to the latter a fragrance of death to death, to the former a fragrance of life to life." The contrast between life and death in this passage is as sharp as the contrast between righteousness and iniquity, light and darkness, in 6:14ff. Two groups of men, those who are saved and those who perish, are separated by their opposite reactions to the gospel and to the apostle. In chapter 3 the apostle is further identified as the minister of the new covenant, a covenant with glory and righteousness.

The fragment in 6:14ff. has to be read against this background. The apostle of Christ is the representative of righteousness and light. A refusal to welcome him would mean that the Corinthians sided with unbelievers, with iniquity, darkness, and Belial against righteousness, light, and Christ. We may paraphrase the injunctions in 6:13–14 by supplementing them from what has been said earlier: "Widen your hearts to me, and do not be mismated with the unbelievers whose minds the god of this world has blinded."

The immediately preceding section, from 5:11 onwards, reinforces this way of reading our fragment and its context. Here the nature of Paul's ministry, including his dealing with the Corinthians, is defined by means of references to the love of Christ and to the action of God, who in Christ reconciled the world to himself and entrusted Paul with the ministry of reconciliation. As an ambassador for Christ, through whom God makes his appeal, Paul makes a petition (*deometha*): "Be reconciled to God" (5:14–20).[11] Applied to the Corinthians, this appeal takes a special form, "We entreat you not to accept the grace of God in vain" (6:1). After a parenthetical citation of Isa. 49:9 with the comment "Behold now is the day of salvation" etc., Paul continues by stressing that he in no way poses any obstacle but in all his sufferings and doings commends himself as God's servant (6:3–10). The reason for this self-recommendation is, no doubt, the presence at Corinth of people who are said to pride themselves on external matters and to be in need of letters of recommendation (5:12; 3:1), letters which probably, as argued by Dieter Georgi, contained enumerations of their charismatic performances, their *res gestae*.[12] Paul engages in an emulation (a *emulatio, sygkrisis*) of them, but not without

---

11. Paul has begun to exhort the Corinthians in 2 Cor. 5:20: "We beseech" (*deometha*). 5:21 is a delayed conclusion to 5:17–19; cf. Rom. 3:22b–23; 7:25b; 10:17, and see "The Missionary Theology in the Letter to the Romans," Chapter V, 77, 85, n. 27.

12. See D. Georgi, *Die Gegner des Paulus im 2. Korintherbrief*, (WMANT 11; Neukirchen, Neukirchener, 1964), 241–46; A. Fridrichsen, "Peristasen-katalog und Res Gestae," *SO* 8 (1928) 78–82.

a sense of irony in stressing the paradox of strength in weakness. Thus he gives the Corinthians cause to take pride in him, in the hope that, knowing him, they may be able to answer his critics (5:11–12).

After inserting this self-recommendation, Paul formulates his appeal more specifically. The exhortations to be reconciled to God (5:20) and not to receive the grace of God in vain (6:1) are narrowed down to the request that the Corinthians should be open to Paul as his heart is open to them. The three appeals are not identical in content, yet the sequence suggests that it would be difficult to conform to the former injunctions without also accepting the last one. Thus the insertion of the fragment in 6:14–7:1 only reinforces the note of urgency which is already present in the context. For the Corinthians, to refuse to welcome Paul might mean to receive the grace of God in vain or, in other words, to be mismated with unbelievers.

Within the context, the final exhortation in the fragment, like the first one, takes on a very specific meaning. The first seven chapters of 2 Corinthians, from 1:12 onward, stress the integrity and purity of Paul's conduct towards the Corinthians (cf. 1:17; 1:23; 2:4, 17; 4:1–2). Listing his afflictions in 6:3–10 (a "peristasis catalog"), Paul again asserts his integrity and reliability (vv. 6–8). Immediately after the inserted fragment he writes: "Open your hearts to us; we have wronged no one, we have corrupted no one, we have taken advantage of no one" (7:2). In this context the injunction, "Let us cleanse ourselves from every defilement of body and spirit, and make holiness perfect in the fear of God," must be read as a call for reciprocity. The Corinthians' attitude toward Paul ought to be marked by the integrity and sincerity which characterized his conduct towards them.

The interpretation might be further elaborated. What I have said should be sufficient to prove that the fragment makes good sense within its present context. The contextual sense is different from the original meaning, but just as a more or less verbatim quotation, the fragment has a clearly definable function where we now read it. Its present location cannot be due to an accident; whoever inserted the fragment must have known what he was doing. Whether this person was Paul himself or a later redactor remains an open question, dependent upon the literary analysis of 2 Corinthians as a whole.[13] The text of the letter seems to have

13. While I remain convinced that 2 Cor. 6:14—7:1 is based on a fragment with remarkable similarities to the Dead Sea Scrolls and the Book of Jubilees, I am also convinced that the fragment has been reworked and adapted to its present context: The

been altered before it came into the Pauline collection of epistles. Personally, I find the deletion of the names of the brethren who accompanied Titus to be most unambiguous evidence for this (cf. 8:18, 22, 23; 12:18). Other problems are well known. I would, therefore, consider it unfair to assign the whole burden of proof to those who deny the integrity of our 2 Corinthians.[14] Although I am presently unwilling to commit myself to any definite solution of these complex issues, I am fairly convinced about one thing, namely, that the person who inserted the fragment in 6:14–7:1 is the same one who added chapters 10–13 at the end of the letter.

The quotation of the fragment serves as a serious warning to the Corinthians and makes the situation envisaged in chapters 1 through 7 resemble the difficult situation envisaged in chapters 10–13 much more than the text of 1–7 would do without the fragment. Moreover, the admonition to cleanse away every defilement in 7:1 is paralleled by the harsh statement about those "who have not repented of the impurity, immorality and licenciousness which they have done," in 12:21. The false apostles are branded as servants of Satan (11:14). Most important, what is implicit in 6:11–7:4 is made explicit in a slightly different form in 11:2–4: "I am afraid that as the serpent deceived Eve by his cunning, your thoughts will be led astray from a sincere and pure devotion to Christ." The reference here is to the false apostles who preach Christ as if he had not already been preached by Paul and who make the Corinthians receive the Spirit as if they had not already received it when they accepted the gospel preached by Paul. Disloyalty to the apostle is equated with infidelity to Christ who sent him, to the Spirit originally received, and to the gospel proclaimed by Paul. The willingness of the Corinthians to welcome the

---

phrase *eohontes oun* . . . (since we have . . .) in 2 Cor. 7:1 has analogies in 3:12 and 4:1, cf. 3:4; 4:7; 5:1. The clause, "For we are the temple of the living God," (6:16), has a closer analogy in 1 Cor. 3:16 than in any of the Dead Sea Scrolls. The address *agapētoi* (beloved) in 7:1 occurs also in 2 Cor. 12:19, and the verb *epitelein* (7:1) occurs also in 2 Cor. 8:6, 11. Concepts like "righteousness," "light," or "unbelievers" are even elsewhere in 2 Cor. used in a dualistic context, see, e.g., 3:9ff.; 4:3–6; cf. 2:15–16.

14. In his article, "2 Cor. 6:14–7:1: An Anti-Pauline Fragment?," *JBL* 92 (1973) 88–108, H. D. Betz has suggested that the fragment originated among the opponents Paul combats in his letter to the Galatians or in a similar group. It is not impossible that both Paul's opponents and Paul himself, or a later disciple of Paul's, made use of the same traditions and scriptural passages, reworking them in opposite ways and using them in different contexts. I refrain here from a fuller discussion of Betz's conjecture, and of other problems. In a seminar paper in the fall of 1976, David Rensberger presented a more comprehensive study of 2 Cor. 6:14—7:1. Hoping that it will some day be published, I have not here incorporated his observations.

"superlative apostles" to the neglect of their own apostle makes Paul fear that Satan will seduce them. What is merely suggested by the insertion of the fragment (in 6:14-7:1) is here stated in plain words: to join the false apostles in their opposition to Paul would mean to side with Satan/Belial in his opposition to Christ.

Read in isolation, the fragment 2 Cor. 6:14-7:1 is a very important piece of evidence for some kind of connection between the Qumran community and the early church. Read within the context of 2 Corinthians, the same fragment attests an understanding of Paul which tends to identify rejection of the apostle with rejection of Christ and siding with the devil. If the fragment is a secondary interpolation, its insertion would be a most interesting example of early "Paulinism", to be considered along with the deutero-Pauline epistles. The lack of links with the context and the absence of any full analogy to a quotation of this type and extent may still favor the theory of interpolation. But I have to confess that I find it somewhat difficult to imagine a later redactor who was capable of expressing his understanding of Paul's unique apostolic ministry in such an indirect and subtle way, leaving it to the readers to understand the function of the fragment within its context. The possibility that the apostle himself incorporated the fragment may after all have to be reconsidered.

5

The Missionary Theology in the Epistle to the Romans

PAUL HAS BEEN ACCLAIMED as the first Christian theologian and as the greatest Christian missionary of all time. Scholars have, however, often failed to realize how closely these two aspects are interrelated. In modern times there has often been a separation between theology and mission.[1] Foreign missions have frequently been conducted with more enthusiasm than theological reflection, and the study of Christian mission has only slowly obtained its proper place in the theological curriculum. This modern separation between theology and mission has had a great impact on the image of Paul. Many scholars have described his theology as a dogmatic system without much inner relationship to his missionary work. Other scholars have gone to the opposite extreme and argued that Paul's genius was that of a great missionary and religious personality. Only recently have an increasing number of scholars begun to recognize that there is something wrong in the very distinction between Paul's mission and his theology. His theology and his missionary activity were inseparable from one another.[2]

---

1. The classical example of this reaction is A. Deissmann, *Paul* (1911, 2.ed. 1925; ET, London: Hodder & Stoughton, 1911, trans. W. E. Wilson). See also G. Warneck, *Paulus im Lichte der heutigen Heidenmission* (Berlin: Warneck, 1914).

2. In contrast to the works of Bultmann and Ridderbos, those of J. Munck and K. Stendahl are characteristic, in some respects extreme, examples of the more recent trend, as is also, in another manner, the booklet of C. J. Roetzel. For references, see the general bibliography.

Paul's theology was no academic dogmatics thought out at the desk and presented in the classroom. A systematic outline of his theological doctrines becomes at best an accurate and useful map, a two dimensional projection without depth or movement. Paul does not develop a system like the scholastic philosophers, orthodox Protestants, or German idealists. This, however, does not mean that Paul's theology has no inner unity. The word "system" applies to structures as diverse as the array of the planets around the sun and as a language where an infinite number of statements, which may even contradict one another, are possible. This flexibility enables us to call Paul's theology a "system" which has one center of gravity, Jesus Christ, and in which variegated statements are interrelated with one another as parts of an encompassing totality. The perimeter is conditioned by the sacred Scriptures and traditions of Israel, including faith in God, biblical history, and eschatology, as well as by the social world and the changing circumstances that Paul had to face.

Paul does not stand outside the history of salvation and reflect on it. He is much more actively involved and has a special role to play in the period between the death and resurrection of Christ and his coming in glory. Thus he is not developing a Christian philosophy of history, even though portrayals of his theology from a "history of salvation" perspective run the risk of giving that impression.[3] He argues theologically in order to make the missionary congregations understand their own place within the divine economy, what God has granted and promised to them and therefore also what he can expect of them. To put it very briefly, we may characterize Paul's theology as a christocentric theology of mission with biblical history and eschatology as its framework.

Paul understands himself as an apostle of Jesus Christ, commissioned to preach the gospel to Gentiles who had not previously heard it. In Pauline usage, the words "gospel" and "apostle" are correlates,[4] and both are missionary terms. But Paul's concept of an apostle implies much more than our word missionary. The apostle has his commission from the risen Christ himself with authority to be his ambassador and representative, as long as he does not disregard his commission but remains

---

3. See Bultmann's critical review of O. Cullmann, *Christ and Time* in *TLZ* 73 (1948) 659-66 (= *Exegetica*, Tübingen: Mohr, 1967, 356-66).

4. Already in his early article, "To euaggelion hos Paulus," *NorTT* 13 (1912) 153-70, 209-56, A. Fridrichsen stated that gospel and apostle are correlated concepts (p. 250). See also his later study, *The Apostle and His Message*, 8ff., and my critical review in *Nuntius Sodalicii Neotestamentiei Upsaliensis* 2 (1949) 11-14.

faithful to the gospel. Paul maintains that he preached the same gospel as Peter and the others who were apostles before him (e.g. 1 Cor. 15:11). What made Paul's "gospel to the uncircumcised" different from Peter's "gospel to the circumcised" was Paul's special commission: to preach the good news about Christ to non-Jews. That meant that the time had already arrived when salvation was to be offered to the nations.

When Paul summarizes the content of the gospel, he often adds something about his own call and work.[5] Quite likely, he referred to his own conversion and commission even in his missionary preaching. That would explain that he could be accused of proclaiming himself (see 2 Cor. 4:5). In his letters, he not only calls the congregations to imitate his conduct, he also presents himself as an example of God's grace, which makes all Jewish privileges and zeal for the Law irrelevant (see Phil. 3:4-11; Gal. 1:11-16; 2:19-20). At least in retrospect, Paul claims that he received the call to preach among the Gentiles when the risen Christ appeared to him. But his experience was at the same time a conversion which changed the direction of his life and turned his convictions upside down.[6] Thus, an inner unity of mission and theology can be traced back to the beginnings of Paul's life as a Christian, even if the theology which we know from the letters was articulated under the impact of Paul's later missionary experience.

Paul's apostolic ministry was not limited to missionary proclamation of the gospel. He aimed further than that. In Rom. 15:16 he refers to his ministry as priestly service whose goal is "that the offering of the Gentiles may be acceptable, sanctified by the Holy Spirit." In 2 Cor. 11:2

---

5. See Rom. 1:1-6; 1 Cor. 15:3-11; 2 Cor. 4:4-6; 5:17-21; Gal. 1:6ff.; 2:7-9. Cf. also Phil. 2:5-3:17 and 1 Thess. 1:3-2:11. In Ephesians, Colossians, and the Pastoral Epistles the correlation between the gospel and the apostle is expressed in more stereotyped phraseology, see Eph. 3:1-12; 6:19f.; Col. 1:23-29; 1 Tim. 1:11ff.; 2:5-7; 2 Tim. 1:8-12; Titus 1:1-3. There is a more distant analogy to this correlation in the kerygmatic speeches in Acts, which not only summarize the story of Jesus, relating it to Old Testament testimonies, but also refer to those who are witnesses to this story, Acts 2:32; 3:15; 5:32; 10:39, 41; 13:31; cf. Luke 24:48. For the author of Acts, Paul does not belong to the primary witnesses, but his calling is reported three times, in Acts 9, 22 and 26. From Gal. 1:23-24 we learn that the story of Paul's conversion circulated at a very early date. See my article, "Evangelium og Apostel," *NorTT* 44 (1943) 193-217. Cf. also J. H. Schütz, *Paul and the Anatomy of Apostolic Authority* (SNTSMS 26; Cambridge University Press, 1975) esp. 35-158.

6. Stendahl, 7-23 ("Call rather than Conversion"), objects to the phrase "Paul's conversion"—for good reasons if the term "conversion" carries connotations of a change of religion. But certainly, the call of Paul resulted in a radical change of direction.

he uses nuptial imagery: "I betrothed you to Christ to present you as a pure bride to her one husband." In several letters Paul states the goal of his intercession and whole endeavor in terms like these: "so that you . . . may be pure and blameless for the day of Christ," or "guiltless in the day of our Lord Jesus Christ."[7] Paul was not just a herald who hurried to proclaim the gospel to all nations. His ministry also had a more pastoral aspect. He is the intercessor on behalf of his congregations who pleads their cause before God and he is the advisor who counsels them, in order to be able to present them to Christ at his coming, which Paul expected in the near future.

It is only when we are aware of the various aspects of Paul's ministry that we can fully understand how intimately his theology is bound up with his missionary activity. He is the herald of the gospel, Christ's ambassador to the Gentiles, an example for his churches and their intercessor and counselor, and all of this is part of his eschatological mission. It is therefore one-sided to see Paul's theology as an existential interpretation of the kerygma which he proclaimed as a missionary.[8] It would also be one-sided to see Paul's theology mainly as a rationale for his Gentile mission and as a defense of its results.[9] Paul develops his theology in ongoing dialog, reminding, warning, exhorting and counseling his churches,

---

7. See Phil. 1:10-11; 1 Cor. 1:8, and cf. 1 Thess. 3:13; 5:23; Phil. 1:6 (Col. 1:22f., 28). On Paul as an intercessor (or paraclete), see my article "Paulus som förespråkare," *STK* 18 (1942) 173-82 (a reaction to N. Johansson, *Parakletoi* [Lund: Gleerup, 1940]). Cf. also the recent study of G. P. Wiles, *Paul's Intercessory Prayers* (SNTSMS 24; Cambridge University Press, 1974).

Since L. Bieler, *Theios Anēr* (Vienna: Höfels, 1935) it has become customary to use the term "divine man" (*theios anēr*) in a wide sense and to apply it to Paul's opponents (esp. in 2 Cor.). But in this wide sense, one would have to consider Paul himself as a divine man, albeit as a very peculiar representative of the category—as H. Windisch did in his book *Paulus und Christus* (Leipzig: Hinrichs, 1934). Paul was a divine messenger, a missionary, preacher and teacher, tested in the agony of suffering, a charismatic person and miracle worker, and he was a paraclete, the intercessor of the Gentile churches and of his own people. One ought, however, to use the term in a more restricted sense, as the ancient sources do. See Carl Holladay, "Theios Anēr in Hellenistic Judaism: A Critique of the Use of the Term in Christology" (PhD diss., Cambridge, 1974, to be published in the SBLDS).

8. Bultmann tends, in his *Theology of the New Testament*, to substitute an existentialist systematization of Paul for the traditional dogmatic interpretation. See my review article in *The Crucified Messiah*, 90-128.

9. Stendahl, e.g., 27, 80f., 130f., views Paul's teaching about justification under this perspective. To me that seems to be a one-sided approach, even if a necessary corrective. See Chapter VI.

polemicizing against misunderstandings of the gospel and against anything that might distort the integrity of the communities which he hopes to present to Christ. For this reason each of his letters has its own distinctive features, depending on the audience and the circumstances to which Paul speaks. Writing letters and "doing theology" were part of his mission.

In most of his letters Paul deals with practical issues in young churches or, as in 2 Corinthians, with the relationship between them and himself. The letters move back and forth from specific problems to matters of principle which provide guidelines for their solution. Only the Letter to the Romans stands apart. Here the epistolary introduction and conclusion serve as a framework for discussion of theological themes that apparently have little or no close relationship to the immediate concerns of the recipients. For this reason, the Letter to the Romans has been the starting point for presenting a systematic outline of "Pauline Theology," or what German scholars in the 19th century called "Paulinism." The interpretation of Romans is therefore decisive for testing the interrelation of Paul's theology and his missionary work to see whether or not it is really as close as I have maintained. The following comments are intended to show that it is.

The prescript of Romans (1:1–7) is as unique in the history of epistolography as is the letter itself. Its pattern follows the Pauline variant of epistolary convention and includes three elements: 1. The name of the sender. 2. The recipients. 3. A greeting formula.[10] The first of these three parts, however, has been expanded in a very unusual way. Paul introduces himself as "a slave of Christ Jesus, called to be an apostle," adding that he has been set apart for the gospel of God. Then he inserts a reference to God's promise in the Old Testament and a summary of the gospel and concludes by returning to his own commission. It is from the promised Son of God, Jesus Christ our Lord, that Paul has received grace to be an apostle and to bring about obedience of faith among all the Gentile nations. Due to these expansions, the opening identification of the sender has almost become an exordium, a prologue to the whole letter. A closer analysis would show that the prescript of Romans anticipates a number of themes that are elaborated in the body of the letter. The primary function

---

10. See, e.g., W. G. Doty, *Letters in Primitive Christianity* (Philadelphia: Fortress, 1973) 29–31; Roetzel, 29–30. Cf. also J. A. Fitzmyer, "Some Notes on Aramaic Epistolography," *JBL* 93 (1974) 201–25: F. X. J. Exler, *The Form of the Ancient Greek Letter.*

of the opening paragraph is to set forth Paul's full credentials for addressing the Christians in Rome with an apostolic and didactic letter.

In a Greek letter prescript, the second part is the identification of the addressees. The normal form is a dative in the third person, as in Rom. 1:7a: "To all God's beloved in Rome, who are called to be saints." It is one of the peculiar stylistic features of the prescript to Romans that before he has formally identified the addressees, Paul has already turned directly to them, addressing them, using a second person plural pronoun to state that they too are included among the nations to whom the Lord has sent Paul, giving him grace to carry out his apostolic task. This irregularity is an example of the freedom with which Paul varies epistolary conventions, combining formality with intimacy.

Paul had made it a rule that he would not build on an "alien foundation," by preaching the gospel where others had preached the gospel before him and had already laid the foundation of a Christian community (see Rom. 15:20-21; 2 Cor. 10:13-16). In the case of Rome, however, he intended to make an exception, hoping to reap some harvest in the world capital by his missionary work as he had among the rest of the Gentiles (Rom. 1:13-14). In Greco-Roman antiquity, a written message was regarded as a substitute for personal presence and oral communication.[11] Thus, that Paul addressed an apostolic letter to the Christians in Rome, preaching the gospel in writing, was a departure from his rule, not to intrude upon churches which he had not founded himself. Using the prescript to give his full credentials, Paul makes it clear that his apostolic commission to preach the gospel and bring about obedience of faith extends to all nations, including Rome. At the same time, he also makes it clear that he respects the independence of the Christians in Rome: they are already "God's beloved, called to be saints," and "called to belong to Jesus Christ," just as Paul is himself "called to be an apostle."

As usual the prescript is followed by some opening sentences that express the sender's attitude toward the addressees of the letter.[12] Paul usually assures his audience of his thanksgiving and intercession. That is an expression of appreciation, appropriate for the apostle, as the spiritual father and counselor of a congregation. Writing to the Christians in Rome, Paul is not in this position. The reason for his thanksgiving is that their faith is reported far and wide, i.e., it has become generally

---

11. On the practice and theory of ancient letter writing, see my article, "Letter," in *IDBSup*, 538-40, with bibliography.

12. Schubert (See General Bibliography).

known that Christianity has spread to Rome. Giving a very polite twist to a conventional epistolary phrase, Paul does not write that he prays for the well-being of the addressees but that he prays for his own well-being, that he may at last succeed, by the will of God, in coming to visit the Christians in Rome.[13] Having written that he hopes to strengthen them with some spiritual gift he corrects himself. What he has in mind is mutual encouragement (Rom. 1:12). Paul is very careful to make it clear that he does not want to intrude upon the Roman Christians, but at the same time he excuses himself for his failure to come earlier (Rom. 1:13).

The epistolary conclusion confirms that the writing of the letter to the Romans was a delicate task that called for diplomatic tact and politeness. Paul assures the addressees that he is confident of their ability to take care of themselves and to instruct one another (Rom. 15:14). He considers his own letter a reminder; he concedes that he has written somewhat boldly, and he goes on to give a further explanation of his apostolic mission and his future plans (Rom. 15:15-33). Here we learn that the letter was written towards the end of Paul's missionary activity in the Eastern provinces, probably during his last visit to Corinth. At this moment Paul can write: "I no longer have any room for work in these regions" (Rom. 15:23). I take the meaning of this astounding statement to be that representative churches had finally been so well established that they would, with the help of God, be able to prepare themselves for the day of the Lord, without the supervision of the apostle. What had hindered Paul from going to Rome earlier was, obviously, trouble in some of the congregations and the delayed conclusion of the collection for "the saints" in Jerusalem.

Paul wrote his letter to the Romans at a turning point in his career, shortly before he left on his last journey to Jerusalem. Various circumstances at the time of writing are reflected in the letter. It is easy to find reminiscences of the conflicts in which he had recently been involved and of which we have evidence in his letters to the Corinthian and Galatian Christians. It is also possible to read the letter as a draft of the "collection speech" which Paul intended to deliver in Jerusalem. One obvious purpose of the letter was to prepare for Paul's arrival at Rome. One does not have to read much between the lines to see that Paul also wanted

---

13. Cf. Rom. 1:10, *ei pōs ēdē pote euodōthēsomai* ("that I may now at last succeed") with 3 John 2, *euchomai se euodousthai* ("I pray that all may go well with you," followed by: "I know that all is well with your soul"). A similar use of *euodousthai* is fairly common in papyrus letters.

to refute objections to, and forestall possible misunderstandings of, his teachings and whole attitude. But we should not belittle the stated purpose of the letter either; Paul wrote to the Christians in Rome in order to exhort and strengthen them without intruding upon them and without doubting the genuineness of their Christian faith. What Paul does in his letter is what he had for a long time hoped to do in person: he preached the gospel to those in Rome (see 1:15). He had all the more reason to do so in writing as troubles in Jerusalem might possibly hinder him from ever coming to Rome (see 15:31f.). To some extent, the letter anticipates the mutual encouragement that Paul hopes to enjoy in Rome (1:12). He not only suggests that the Christians in Rome will support his mission to Spain, but he also explicitly asks for their intercession for his journey to Jerusalem (see 15:24, 30-32). The appeal for intercession may, indeed, be a main reason why Paul wrote *this* letter to the Romans. The Christians in Rome needed to know what Paul taught and how he understood his own mission if they were going to ally themselves with other Pauline churches and intercede for a favorable reception of the collection.[14]

Like Paul's other letters, Romans has the characteristics of a genuine letter. It is a written communication between two parties who are spatially separated and is a substitute for personal presence. The letter form serves to provide information and to make requests, and also to promote friendly relations between sender and addressees. Even the didactic nature of the main body of the letter is conditioned by the specific epistolary situation. The relationship between theology and missionary activity is as intimate in Romans as in any of Paul's letters, but the perspective is different. The letter contains little, if anything, that gives us specific information about the origin and organization of Roman Christianity. Paul may himself have been fairly well informed.[15] But if he was, it is all the more

---

14. On recent studies on the composition and purpose of Romans, see G. Klein, "Romans, Letter to the," in *IDBSup*, 752-54, who concludes by stating an emergent consensus: "In any case, recent debate shows that Romans can be adequately interpreted only by seriously viewing it as an occasional letter in the form of an essay that goes beyond the occasion." Cf. also Käsemann's commentary on Rom. 15:29 (see General Bibliography).

15. This would certainly be the case if the list of greetings in Romans 16 is an original part of the letter to Rome, as I think it is. A strong case for the integrity of the letter has been made by Harry Gamble Jr., *The Textual History of the Letter to the Romans* (SD 42; Grand Rapids: Eerdmans, 1977). On p. 91ff., Gamble rightly stresses the commendatory character of the greetings. Cf. also W. Wuellner, "Paul's Rhetoric of Argumentation in Romans," *CBQ* 38 (1976) 330-51.

remarkable that he does not address more directly any internal problems. He was not the spiritual father of the Roman Christians, and he leaves it to them to make specific applications of his teaching. It would almost seem as if he was more in need of their understanding, intercession and loyal support than they were in need of his advice. It is not the problems of a local church but the universal gospel and Paul's own mission which in this letter provide the point of departure for theological discussion. This is made very clear by the way in which Paul introduces the theme of the letter.

Writing about his travel plans, Paul states: "I am indebted to Greeks and to barbarians, both to the wise and to the simple" (Rom. 1:14). What Paul owes to mankind is nothing but the gospel of Christ.[16] The thematic statement about the gospel as God's power of salvation is introduced as a motivation for Paul's disposition not to be ashamed of the gospel but to confess it boldly to all people everywhere, even in Rome. We should also observe the back reference to the letter opening: the gospel in which the righteousness of God is revealed is identical with the missionary kerygma that Paul summarized in Rom. 1:2-6.

In Rom. 1:16-18 Paul sets forth three thematic statements: 1. The gospel is God's power for salvation, for Greeks as well as for Jews. 2. In the gospel the righteousness of God is revealed, "from faith to faith." 3. The wrath of God is revealed from heaven against all ungodliness and wickedness of men. Editors and commentators usually make the third thesis, Rom. 1:18, begin a new paragraph and a new section of the letter. They are uncertain whether the thesis in 1:16-17 should be considered part of the letter opening (1:8-17) or a short thematic paragraph by itself. But in the Greek text, the four sentences in Rom. 1:15-18 are all logically connected with one another by means of a *gar* ("for"). The thematic statements all serve as a warrant for the preceding one. The question of whether a sentence belongs to the preceding or to the following paragraph is anachronistic since the text was to be read aloud and the original handwriting did not set the paragraphs off from one another. In many manuscripts not even the words are separated from one another. As the text was to be heard, rather than seen, the transition from one unit of thought to another had to be indicated by other means than by typographical or scribal arrangement. In Romans, as elsewhere, the conclusion of one section frequently introduces the theme of the following

---

16. Cf. my article, "Evangelium og plikt" (Gospel and Duty), in *Festskrift til Regin Prenter* (Copenhagen: Gyldendal, 1967), 142-54.

section. Greek prose style was in general closer to oral speech than are modern literary products.[17] In order to follow the flow of thought in the Pauline letters, one should pay more attention to thematic statements, gradual transitions, and "ring composition" than to the division into chapter and verse or to headings and systematized outlines supplied by modern translations and commentaries.

The last two of the three thematic statements in Rom. 1:16-18 are formulated in antithetical parallelism and spelled out in reverse order. Paul first deals with the revelation of the wrath of God (Rom. 1:18–3:20) and only after that with the revelation of his righteousness (3:21ff.). At the point of transition, Paul links the two units of thought. In 3:21 Paul has turned to the theme of God's saving righteousness, but in 3:22b-23 he inserts a delayed conclusion to the preceding section: "There is no distinction, for all have sinned and fall short of the glory of God." The opening statement in 1:17 had already referred to "all ungodliness and wickedness of men." In 1:19-32 Paul spells this out with respect to Gentiles, who are without excuse for their idolatry and punished by their vices. But then Paul gives his accusation an unexpected twist, indicting any person, even the Jew, who condemns Gentile vices but does similar things (2:1-5). The chapter division between 1:32 and 2:1 is misleading because it obliterates the central position of the description of God's impartial judgment in 2:6-11 which repeats the phrase "the Jew first and also the Greek" from 1:16, concludes the treatment of the revelation of God's wrath and introduces the theme of divine impartiality.

Theologians and exegetes have long struggled with the problem that Paul teaches justification by faith, without works of the Law, but at the same time asserts, without any qualification, that the outcome of the last judgment will depend upon what a person has done. There is indeed a problem here, but apparently Paul himself did not pay much attention to it. The most obvious reason for this is that Paul stressed the same point in both cases. There is no distinction between Jew and Greek, because God shows no partiality, neither when he justifies the ungodly nor when he renders to every man according to his works.

In Rom. 2:12-29 Paul applies the dogmatic axiom of God's impartiality to the Gentiles who have sinned "without the law" and to the Jews

---

17. At this point I owe important insights to A. Wifstrand, "Grekisk och modern prosastil" (Greek and Modern Prose Style), in *Tider och Stilar* (Lund: Gleerup, 1944), 5-38.

who sinned "under the law."[18] The Gentiles can get a fair trial because they know what the Law requires (2:14-16). The Jew will have no advantage in possessing the Law if he has broken it (2:17-24). It is not the external circumcision of the body but only the inner circumcision of the heart that counts before God (2:25-29, cf. 2:13). Having reached this point, Paul raises the question: "Then what advantage has the Jew?" (Rom. 3:1). The condensed series of questions and answers in 3:1-8 shows how important it was to Paul to refute false consequences drawn from his teaching and objections raised against it. He will return to a fuller refutation later in his letter (see esp. chapts. 6-7 and 9-11).

Undergirding his accusation against Jews and Greeks with a catena of scriptural quotations, Paul draws the conclusion that no human being will be justified by works of the Law (3:9-20). Against this negative background he turns to its positive counterpart, the theme that was first stated in Rom. 1:17, the revelation of the righteousness of God. The basic exposition of the theme in 3:21-26 deals with "the redemption in Christ Jesus," in whom God has set things right. The consequences are drawn in a new series of questions and answers (3:27-31) and supported by an interpretation of Abraham's faith in God attested in Gen. 15:6 (Rom. 4). Paul insists that there is no distinction, that God is the God of Gentile nations as well as of Jews, and that Abraham is the father of all believers, whether they are circumcized or not (3:21, 29-30; 4:11-12). To Paul, the existence of uncircumcized Gentile believers is fully legitimate because it is based on faith in the God in whom Abraham believed (see Rom 4:5, 17, 24-25).[19]

Through the end of chapter 4 the composition of Romans is fairly clear in so far as Paul has first treated the theme of God's wrath and righteous judgment (1:18—2:11 + 2:12-29 and 3:1-8 and 9-20) and after that has taken up the theme of God's righteousness (1:17; 3:21-26 + 3:27-31 and 4). The analysis of chapters 5-8 has created more difficulties. Older

---

18. I have found the most convincing analysis of the argument in Romans 1-2 to be that of M. Pohlenz, "Paulus und die Stoa," *ZNW* 42 (1949) 69-104 (repr. 1964). As I suggested in *STK* 18 (1942) (see note 7), Paul's argument would gain in force if it presupposes the idea that the Torah and/or the *mitzvoth* (commandments observed) will act as advocates for the Israelites in the judgment of God. Cf. Aboth 4:13 and other passages collected by N. Johansson, *Parakletoi*, 174-78. Paul's idea would then be that the Gentiles have similar defenders (or accusers). Jouette Bassler is preparing a dissertation on the idea of God's impartiality, esp. in Rom. 2:11 and context.

19. See Käsemann's commentary, with bibliography. H. Moxnes, Oslo, is working on a fresh investigation of Abraham's faith in God, centering on Rom. 4:17ff.

Protestants tended to think that Paul first dealt with justification (1:16–5:21) and then with sanctification (6–8). In the 19th century it became more common, especially in Germany, to distinguish between two lines of thought in Paul: Rom. 6–8 contained a "mystical-ethical doctrine of salvation" to be distinguished from the "forensic" doctrine in the earlier chapters.[20] In either case, the exegetes failed to pay sufficient attention to the formal composition of Romans and to the eschatological and missionary dimensions of Paul's theology. A number of more recent scholars, however, have preferred to connect Rom. 5 with 6–8 rather than with 1–4, since already in Rom. 5:1–11 Paul proceeds from justification to the final salvation and the life of those who are justified by faith.[21]

There is no doubt that Rom. 5:1–11, like 3:21–26, has a fundamental importance within the total composition and serves as a basis for subsequent comments and elaboration. The analogy between Adam and Christ in 5:12–19 illuminates and supports the main thesis in 5:1–11, that justification is a sure ground for the hope of final salvation and life. Moreover, Romans 8 restates more fully several ideas that are already present in 5:1–11: the sufferings that believers experience are not contrary to their standing in grace; the Holy Spirit, which they have received, and the love of God, evidenced by Christ's vicarious death, assure them that their hope is not in vain.[22]

---

20. The distinction between two separate lines of thought in Paul goes back to H. Lüdemann, *Die Anthropologie des Apostels Pautus* (Kiel: Universitätsbuchhandlung, 1872); cf. A. Schweitzer, *Paul and His Interpreters*, 28ff. Schweitzer's own eschatological approach contributed much, although largely in an indirect way, to the overcoming of the duality. In recent decades, the problem has receded into the background; cf., e.g., H. D. Wendland, *Die Mitte der paulinischen Botschaft* (Göttingen: Vandenhoeck & Ruprecht, 1935); P. Schubert, "Paul and the New Testament Ethic in the Thought of John Knox," in W. Farmer, ed., *Christian History and Interpretation*, 363–88. Most recently, the problem has been restated by E. P. Sanders, esp. 474–511. This important book appeared so late that a discussion is impossible. Sanders distinguishes between "juristic" and "participatory" (rather than "ethical" or "mystical") categories, and thinks that "the main theme of Paul's theology is found in his participationist language rather than in the theme of righteousness by faith" (p. 552). One question would be if Paul's theology is not, in its very center, more polemical than Sanders will allow for.

21. See, e.g., the commentaries on Romans by Dodd, Nygren, Barrett, and Käsemann.

22. See my synopsis of Rom. 5:1–11 and 8:1–39 in my article "Two Notes on Romans 5," *ST* 5(1951) 37–48. A revised version of the synopsis is included as Appendix I to this article. For a more detailed argument, see P. van der Osten-Sacken, *Römer 8 als Beispiel paulinischer Soteriologie* (FRLANT 112; Göttingen: Vandenhoeck & Ruprecht, 1975), esp. 57–60.

Yet, Rom. 5:1-11 can also be seen as a (preliminary) conclusion to the preceding argument. The transition from an argument in the third person to the use of an inclusive "we" begins already in 4:24-25 and continues through 5:1-11. It is clear that Rom. 5 is part of the exposition of the first theme introduced in Rom. 1:16ff.: "The gospel is a power of God for salvation," etc. But the exposition of that theme continues through Rom. 9-11 ("Jew first and Greek") and right up to the conclusion of the paranaesis in 15:7-13. We should therefore not take Rom. 1:16 as a specific theme for the section Rom. 5-8. It is, rather, the encompassing theme for the whole main body of the letter (1:16-15:13). The theses about the revelation of God's righteousness and of his wrath (1:17-18) are subthemes, and are treated in a reverse order. Whether the main line of division should be drawn before or after chapter 5 is a minor problem. More important, analysis of the composition confirms that the overarching theological theme of Romans coincides with the motivation for Paul's missionary zeal. "Justification by faith" is not in itself the theme of the letter but part of, and a criterion for, Paul's missionary theology.

Even within Romans 5-8 the chapter divisions and inserted headlines tend to obscure the flexible, yet orderly progression of Paul's argument. Here, too, discrete units of thought conclude with theses that are then elaborated or that give rise to questions. The main examples are: 5:9-11 + 5:12ff.; 5:20-21 + 6:1ff.; 6:14 + 6:15ff.; 7:5-6 + 7:7ff.; 7:12 + 7:13ff. (7:25a + 8:1ff; see below); 8:17b + 8:18ff. The problems raised and discussed in chapters 6 and 7 cause some difficulties for analysis since they are not directly related to the main positive argument set forth in chapters 5 and 8. One might consider the discussions of problems related to sin and the Law as digressions,[23] but would then have to add that they feed into the main argument and enrich it, as can easily be seen by a comparison between Rom. 5 and Rom. 8. It would be more appropriate, however, to consider the units introduced by the questions in 6:1, 6:15, 7:7 and 7:13 as refutations of objections against Paul's doctrine and thus as integral parts of his argumentation.[24] Earlier in the letter Paul has

---

23. In *ST* 5, 41 (see note 22), I spoke about Rom. 6:1-7:6 and 7:7-25 as "two digressions." Cf. also J. Jeremias, "Zur Gedankenführung in den paulinischen Briefen," in *Studia Paulina in honorem J. de Zwaan* (ed. van Unnik, Haarlem: Bohn, 1953), 146-54; J. Dupont, "Le problème de la structure litteraire de l'Epître aux Romains," *RB* 62 (1955) 365-97; B. Noack, "Current and Backwater in the Epistle to the Romans," *ST* 19 (1965) 155-66. On the function of Rom. 5:12-21 within this context, see Appendix II to this chapter.

24. A digression may, of course, carry as much weight as the main argument but, in

already envisaged the objection that his doctrine gave free rein to sin and abrogated the Law (see 3:4-8 and 31). It is obvious that this objection or false consequence posed a real threat to Paul's missionary work. If left unrefuted, it would be fatal to Paul's credibility in Rome.

But why, then, does Paul in Rom. 6 drop the terminology of faith and justification and shift to a baptismal imagery of death, burial and resurrection with Christ and later to an argument from moral philosophy (6:15ff.) and to a somewhat strained comparison with marriage law (7:1-4)? It is not satisfactory to answer that Paul shifts to another, more "Hellenistic" and mystical line of thought. Outside the letter to the Romans, the attempt to distinguish between "forensic" and "mystical-ethical" terminology becomes artificial.[25] Even in Romans, Paul ascribes a "forensic" importance to the sacramental death with Christ (see Rom. 6:7 and 7:1-4). It would seem to have been entirely possible for Paul to move directly from the reign of grace through righteousness (Rom. 5:21) to the moral consequences of being under grace (6:15ff.). The main reason for the introduction of a new set of terms and images in Rom. 6:1ff. may be very simple. Paul wanted to persuade his Roman audience. The juridical terminology of righteousness and judgment, transgression and pardon was most appropriate for the argument that, ultimately, it made no difference whether or not a person knew the revealed Law, since God is the impartial judge and had set things right by letting his Son die for all, without any distinction. Having argued that the Law was only an interim order that came in to make the crime greater, he is faced with a different task. Refuting the alleged consequence, that his doctrine favored sinning, he turns the point around and exhorts his readers that they should put themselves and their capacities for action at the disposition of God, in the service of righteousness. To further this purpose he appeals to their own experience: they have been baptised into the death of Christ, they have become obedient to the "standard of teaching" to which they have been handed over as to a master, and they have received the Spirit of Christ (see Rom. 6:3ff., 17ff. and 7:5-6 + 8:2-17).

---

ancient rhetoric, refutation of real or possible counterarguments is an integral part of the art of persuasion. For this insight I am indebted to Stan Stowers, who is preparing a study of "Paul and the Diatribe," centering upon the dialogical elements in the style of Romans.

25. Cf., e.g., 2 Cor. 5:14-21; Gal. 2:16-21; 3:23-4:6; Phil. 3:8-11 (Eph. 2:1-10; Col. 2:9-15). See, e.g., R. C. Tannehill, *Dying and Rising with Christ* (Berlin: Töpelmann, 1963).

Having refuted the notion that his teaching favored sinning, Paul has to face other objections that he equated the Law with sin and made the Law responsible for the death of the sinner (Rom. 7:7, 13). In the answers to these objections the wider, missionary perspective seems to drop out of sight. Paul speaks in the first person singular, and even if the "I" is rhetorical, used to express a typical experience, the distance from the description of social vices in Rom. 1:24ff. and 2:17ff. is obvious. Parts of Rom. 7:14-25 read like a confession of sin with inserted comments.[26] The point of these comments, and already of 7:7-12, however, is the exculpation of the Law. The blame is to be put on sin, the power that reigns over mankind since Adam. Just because it is holy and righteous and good, the Law made an end to the state of moral indifference and caused evil desire (7:7-12). Recognizing that the results of his actions do not correspond to his good intentions, the sinner bears testimony to the goodness of the Law—and to his own slavery under sin.

The confession in Rom. 7:14-15, 18-19, 22-23 concludes with a cry for deliverance and a thanksgiving (vv. 24-25a). As the thanksgiving marks the transition to the assertions of liberation and new life in Romans 8, many commentators have assumed that the final comment in v. 25b has been misplaced, or that it is a secondary gloss. I prefer to see it as a "delayed conclusion" that refers back to the statements in 7:5-6 and clarifies them.[27] There Paul spoke about "sinful passions, aroused by the law" and about slavery "under the old written code" (lit. "under the oldness of the letter" *palaiotēti grammatos*) which he contrasted with enslavement in the new order of the Spirit (*en kainotēti pneumatos*). In the conclusion Paul makes it clear that he does not blame the Law but sin for the enslavement and death of the carnal man, who lives in the flesh without the lifegiving power of God. His mind may be subservient to the Law of God and recognize it to be good, but with his flesh (and that means in practice) he is a slave to the law of sin. For Paul, the Law requires deeds and not good intentions. Just by bringing about evil in spite of his own good intentions, man proves that he is enslaved, incapable of liberating himself.

---

26. See Appendix III to this chapter. Stendahl, 83, has rightly stressed that Rom. 7:7-25 is part of an argument about the Law but overreacted in considering the "supporting argument" simply "a common sense observation."

27. For other examples of delayed conclusions, see Rom. 3:22b-23; 10:17; 2 Cor. 5:21. The correspondence between Rom. 7:6b and 7:25b is an example of rhetorical inclusion.

The treatment of Law and sin (Rom. 7:7-25) has a double function in the context, to refute objections and exculpate the Law, and to provide the dark background for the liberation in Christ and the new life in the Spirit. Under both aspects, the section gives a fuller elaboration of ideas that Paul had earlier stated in a condensed form (see Rom. 3:7-8, 19-20; 5:20-21, and also 3:31). In Rom. 1:18-3:20 Paul accused Gentiles and Jews because of the vices that were current among them. In Rom. 7:7-25 he analyzes more deeply the general human predicament in this world, which since the fall of Adam has been under the sway of sin. In Romans 8 Paul elaborates what was already said in 5:1-11 about the reasons for confident hope in the midst of sufferings, but he does so against the background of man's slavery under sin, as described in 7:7-25. The Holy Spirit, given to those who believe in Christ, is the lifegiving and guiding power which makes it possible to fulfill the just requirement of the Law, as well as the surety of future life and glory. In order to refute objections and to encourage and admonish the Christians in Rome, Paul has added depth to his missionary theology.

In Rom. 9-11 Paul returns to the role of Jews and Gentiles, resuming the question about the faithfulness of God to his people (see 3:1-4). We find similar compositional devices as in the rest of the letter. A brief introduction is followed by a thematic statement which covers the following discussion: "It is not as though the word of God failed" (9:6a). Two subthemes (9:6b and 7) are treated in a reversed order. Paul proves from Scripture that "not all are children of Abraham because they are his descendants" (9:7-13). Later on, he develops the other theme that was introduced first: "Not all who are descended from Israel belong to Israel" (9:6b, cf. 9:22-29, 30-33; 10:16-21; 11:1-10). At this point, the argument becomes somewhat complicated because Paul also refutes objections (9:14ff. and 19ff.), supports his argument with scriptural quotations and, at a remarkably late point, states the reason why he had to deal with the question of whether or not the word of God to Israel had failed (cf. 10:1-17).[28] There is no need to go into detail here. The inner unity of Paul's mission and theology is nowhere more obvious than in Rom. 9-11. Within the doctrinal body of the letter, it is only here that Paul explicitly refers to his own ministry as apostle to the Gentiles—and as

---

28. Rom. 10:4 is another example of a conclusion that introduces the theme of the following section. Rom. 10:17 is the conclusion to 10:4ff., but already in 10:16 Paul has introduced his next theme, the disobedience of (part of) Israel. Rather, he returns to this theme, cf. 9:30-33; 10:1-3.

intercessor for Israel.[29] Moreover, Paul's vision of future salvation for all Israel provides the right perspective for the collection with which Paul is, at the moment of writing, ready to go to Jerusalem, pleading that the Christians in Rome should intercede with their prayers that it might be well received.

There is no need to discuss the exhortations in Rom. 12:1-15:13 in any detail either. By and large they represent the same type of paraenesis that we find in 1 Thess. 4-5 and in other letters as well. Various subsections are introduced by thematic appeals. Most of the exhortations pertain either to the mutual relations between Christians or to their relations to those outside, including the governing authorities. Especially the discussion of the strong and the weak in Rom. 14:1-15:6 seems to presuppose that Paul had some knowledge of internal problems in Rome, but even here he deals with typical rather than with specific cases, thus avoiding intruding on a church that he had not himself founded. We can further note that the warning against haughty thoughts in Rom. 12:3 and 16 picks up a theme from the more specific warning that Paul addressed to the Gentiles in 11:20.

Not only in 11:18ff. but already in 6:11-13 Paul had shifted to a hortatory mood. This is one indication among others that the paraenesis is organically related to the theological argument in Romans. The initial, and thematic, request in Rom. 12:1: "to present (*parastēsai*) your bodies as a living sacrifice, holy and acceptable to God," especially, recalls 6:13: "yield (*paristanete*, present) yourself to God." The difference is that in 6:13 Paul used military rather than sacrificial metaphors. The sacrificial imagery reappears in Rom. 15:16, where Paul speaks of the goal of his own ministry: "that the offering (*thysia*, sacrifice) of the Gentiles may be acceptable, sanctified by the Holy Spirit." Here the Gentiles are seen as the sacrifice to be presented by Paul, whereas Paul in Rom. 12:1 calls his readers to sacrifice themselves. Neither the similarity nor the difference between the formulations in 12:1 and 15:16 can be accidental. As a minister of Christ Jesus to the Gentiles, Paul is to present them as a sacrifice to God. But he can only achieve this goal if his constituency responds with a voluntary obedience and learns to discern what is the will of God for themselves (see Rom. 12:2 and cf. Phil. 1:9-11 and Rom. 15:14). Both the opening sentences in 12:1-2 and the whole paraenetic section in

---

29. For a fuller treatment of Rom. 9-11, see Chapter IX. On Paul as intercessor for Israel, see Wiles, *Paul's Intercessory Prayers*, 253-58.

Romans confirm that Paul considers the Christians in Rome to be part of his constituency and yet he is careful to respect their independence.

Concluding his exhortations, Paul writes: "Welcome one another, therefore, as Christ has welcomed you." The formulation is a generalized resumption of 14:1: "As for the man who is weak in faith, welcome him." We are hardly to identify the weak and the strong in Rom. 14:1–15:6 with Christian Jews and Gentiles. Christ's ministry to the circumcised, that confirmed the promises to the patriarchs and made the Gentiles praise God for his mercy, is rather to be seen as a paradigm for Christian conduct in general (Rom. 15:7–13). The conclusion to the paraenesis and to the main body of the letter refers back to the thematic statement in Rom. 1:16: "a power for salvation . . . to the Jew first and also to the Greek," and even to the opening summary of the gospel which God had promised beforehand (1:2–6). The conclusion reaches beyond the opening, however, in making the praise of God's faithfulness to his people and his mercy toward the Gentiles the ultimate goal (see the Psalm quotations in Rom. 15:9–12).

The analysis of the composition of Romans could easily have been carried on at greater length and in more depth. I hope that my somewhat scattered remarks have been sufficient to illuminate the inner correspondance between the form, the content, and the setting of the letter. Paul's letter to the Romans gives us the most comprehensive representation of Paul's theology because it was written for a very particular purpose. The theology of Romans is closely tied to the Pauline mission with its historical and eschatological perspectives. If we are to take the letter seriously as a canonical, normative writing, it will neither suffice to use it to nurture personal piety nor to integrate Paul's teachings into a systematic theology. The task is rather to regain the unity of theology and evangelism, and of justification by faith and world mission.

APPENDIX I

A Synopsis of Romans 5:1–11 and 8:1–39

The parallelism between the two segments of the letter pertains to themes and argumentation rather than to vocabulary, phraseology, or order. I have therefore not written out the text of Rom. 8, assuming that the reader will have a Bible at hand. In order to draw attention to verbal similarities, I have inserted some transliterations of the Greek text. The equivalent English words and phrases can easily be identified in a translation.

Romans 5:1–11		Romans 8
1.	Therefore, since we are justified (*dikaiōthentes*) by faith, we have peace with God through our Lord Jesus Christ.	1–2 30 (*edikaiōsen*) 33 (*ho dikaiōn*)
2.	Through him we have obtained access to this grace in which we stand, and we rejoice in our hope (*ep' elpidi*) of sharing the glory of God (*tēs doxēs tou theou*).	20 (*eph' (h)elpidi*) 24–25 (*tē . . . elpidi . . . elpis . . .*) 17b (*hina kai syndoxathōmen*) 18 (*tēn mellousan doxan . . .*) 21 (*eis tēn eleutherian tēs doxēs tōn huiōn tou theou*) 29–30 (*toutous kai edoxasen*)
3.	More than that, we rejoice in our sufferings (*en tais thlipsesin*) knowing that suffering produces endurance (*hypomonē*)	17b (*eiper sympaschomen . . .*), 18 35–37 (*thlipsis ē stenochoria*) 25 (*di' hypomonēs . . .*)
4.	but endurance produces a tested mind and a tested mind produces hope (*elpis*),	24–25

5.	and hope does not disappoint us, because God's love (*hē agapē tou theou*) has been poured into our hearts (*en tais kardiais hēmōn*) through the Holy Spirit which has been given to us.	17, 28–30, 35–39 31–32 26–27 (*ho de ereunōn tas kardias*) 2, 4, 9–11, 13–17a, 26–27 23 (*... pneuma theou oikei en hymin*)
6.	While we were yet helpless, at the right time Christ died (*apethanen*) for the ungodly.	34 (*X. I. ho apothanōn*)
7.	—	
8.	But God shows his love for us in that while we were yet sinners Christ died for us.	35, 39 (*apo tēs agapēs tou theou tēs en Christō Iēsou*) 34 (*X. I. ho apothanōn*)
9.	Since, therefore we are now justified by his blood, much more shall we be saved by him from the wrath of God.	30, 33 34 31–34
10.	For if (*ei gar*) while we were enemies we were reconciled to God by the death of his Son (*... huiou ...*), much more (*pollō mallon*), now that we are reconciled, shall we be saved by his life (*en tē zoē autou*)	10, 11, 13b, 17a (*ei de ...*) 31–32 (*ei ho theos ... tou idiou huiou ... pōs ouchi kai ...*) 33–34 34 (*mallon de egertheis ...*)
11.	Not only so, but we also rejoice in God through our Lord Jesus Christ, through whom we have now received our reconciliation.	31–39, *passim*.

Comments: Apart from the climactic chain in Rom. 5:3–4 and the aside in Rom. 5:7, all major themes in Rom. 5:1–11 reappear in Romans 8: Justification and a restored relationship to God as the basis for the hope of future salvation and glory, in spite of present sufferings; the gift of the Holy Spirit, the death of Christ, and the love of God as warrants for this hope; a note of exultation. Yet, the difference between the two segments of the letter is not simply one of order, style, and phraseology. As the terminology shows, 5:1–11 is still closely linked to chapters 1–4 and brings the argument there to a preliminary conclusion: "By faith" and "grace" in 5:1–2; Christ's death for the ungodly, while we were still "helpless," "sinners," "enemies" in 5:6–10; "by his blood" and salvation "from the wrath" in 5:9. By contrast, the restatement of the argument in chapter

8 is set forth against the background of 5:12—7:25: Liberation from the sway of sin and death; the contrasts between the flesh and the Spirit, i.e. between our mortal bodies and the Spirit of God, and between slavery and freedom; participation and conformity with Christ; the Holy Spirit as guide and power for moral life and as helper and intercessor in weakness and sufferings, not only as a warrant of salvation.

APPENDIX II

The Argument in Romans 5:12-21

Since the main text did not deal with the Adam-Christ analogy in Rom. 5:12-21, I may add some comments here.[30] The main function of this segment of the letter is to support the argument in 5:1-11, in much the same way as the interpretation of the story of Abraham in chapter 4 supports the main thesis in 3:21-26. Paul argues that Christ's "act of righteousness" (*dikaiōma*), i.e. his obedience unto death, will bring life as well as justification to all who receive God's grace through him. The fall of Adam, which made sin come into the world and which became the cause of death for all mankind, provides an analogy and a warrant for this conclusion. In this respect, Rom. 5:12ff. restates the argument in 5:1-11, using the analogy between Christ and Adam to add a universal perspective. But in the course of his argumentation, Paul changes direction, going from an argument from analogy to an argument from a minor to a major cause (*a minori ad maius*, see esp. Rom. 5:15, 17). One reason for this is a conviction which Paul shared with the rabbis: the mercy (or grace) of God is greater, and will have more far-reaching effects, than the judgment with which he reacts to sin (cf. Exod. 20:5-6 and 34:6-7). But this is hardly the whole explanation.

The breakdown of the sentence structure in Rom. 5:12ff. indicates that there is a specific factor which makes the analogy between Christ and Adam less than complete. It was only in the period before Moses that everybody died as a consequence of Adam's fall which had brought sin and death into the world (cf. Rom. 5:13-14). Later on, sinners were also accountable for their own transgressions of the Law (cf. *ek pollōn paraptōmatōn* ["following many trespasses"], Rom. 5:16). By contrast, Christ's act resulted in a righteousness that remains a free, undeserved gift, a grace that outweighs the many transgressions of the Law as well as the sin of Adam. Thus, it was only in the time between Adam and Moses that the relation between the one and the many was the same in the order of sin and death as in the order of righteousness and life. Paul can draw

---

30. This is a summary and restatement of the second of my "Two Notes on Romans 5," *ST* 5 (1951) 37-48.

the conclusion that it is all the more certain that all who have received justification through Christ will also obtain life through him.

Thus, the Law is the factor which disturbs the analogy in contrast between Adam and Christ. That this is indeed so is confirmed by the conclusion of the chapter, Rom. 5:20-21. Here Paul raises the question of the function of the Law and of its relation to sin, a question that had remained unanswered, or had only received partial answers, in the preceding parts of the letter (see Rom. 3:20, 31; 4:13-15). The answer given in Rom. 5:20-21 introduces the theme of the argumentation that follows in Rom. 6-8. All of this means that Rom. 5:12-21 supports and extends the argument in 5:1-11, but at the same time serves as a transition to the renewed treatment of sin and the Law in chapters 6-7, which in turn provides the background for the restatement of themes from 5:1-11 in chapter 8. The whole of Romans 5 is connected with both the preceding and with the following sections of the letter, 5:1-2 serving as a transition from the exposition in 3:21-4:25, and 5:20-21 serving as a transition to the questions raised in 6:1ff. The problem of whether a main line of division should be drawn between chapters 4 and 5 or between 5 and 6 or, possibly, between 5:11 and 5:12 becomes acute only if we ask for some systematic outline and fail to follow Paul's vivid argumentation.

APPENDIX III

Confession and Comments in Romans 7:14–25

	Confessional Statements	Comments
14.	We know that the Law is spiritual, but I am carnal, sold under sin.	
15.	For I do not what I want, but I do the very thing I hate.	I do not understand my own actions.
16.		Now, if I do what I do not
17.		want, I agree that the Law is good. So then it is no longer I that do it, but sin
18.	nothing good dwells within me, I can will what is right, but I cannot do it.	which dwells within me. For I know that nothing good dwells within me, that is, in my flesh.
19.	For I do not do the good that I want, but the evil I do not want is what I do.	
20.		Now if I do what I do not want, it is no longer I that do it,
21.		but sin which dwells within me. So I find it to be a law that when I want to do right, evil lies close at hand.
22.	For I delight in the Law of God, in my inmost self,	
23.	but I see in my members another law, at war with the law of my mind and making me captive to the law of sin which dwells in my members.	
24.	Wretched man that I am! Who will deliver me from this body of death?	
25.	Thanks be to God through Jesus Christ our Lord!	
		So then, I of myself serve the Law of God with my mind, but with my flesh I serve the law of sin.

The text might have been arranged in other ways, but the distinction between confessional statements and comments is fairly clear. The comments in the right column undergird Paul's rejection of the idea that the Law is responsible for the death of the sinner. Sin is to be blamed. The left column, by contrast, reads like a confession of sin, a lamentation over slavery under the power of Sin, introduced by the phrase "but I . . ." which is used in a similar way in some of the Psalms and in Qumran hymns.[31] The concluding cry for deliverance and the thanksgiving in 7:24–25a are also in harmony with the confessional style.[32]

The comments are obviously made in retrospect, from Paul's Christian point of view. The confession of sinfulness contrasts sharply with Paul's self-evaluation as a Pharisee: "As to righteousness under the law blameless" (Phil. 3:8). It contrasts equally with his evaluation of himself as a Christian: "I am not aware of anything against myself" (1 Cor. 4:4). But the common opinion that Rom. 7:7-25 gives Paul's Christian evaluation of existence under the Law[33] is not quite satisfactory either, as it fails to give a satisfactory explanation for the confessional style. Especially the cry for deliverance at the end would seem artificial if the intention was simply to give a Christian interpretation of pre-Christian existence.

In spite of all that has been written about Romans 7, there is still room for a careful, comparative investigation of the style. Here I shall only make some common sense remarks:

1. The "I" form is no doubt used as a rhetorical device, but the use of this form would hardly be meaningful unless both the speaker and his audience can in some way identify with the experience of the typical "I".

---

31. See Pss 22:7; 69:29(30); 73:2; 1QS 11:9; 1QM 1:21; 3:23f.; 4:33, 35; 11:19; 12:24; 18:25, 31 and frag. 1:4; 3:11; 52:3. For the sequence in Rom. 7:14, "We know . . . but I am . . . ," see 1QH 1:21: "These things I have known . . . , yet I am but a creature of clay and a thing kneaded with water," etc., and 3:20-24: "And I knew there was hope . . . But I, a creature of clay, what am I?" For similarities and differences between Rom. 7 and analogous passages in the Dead Sea Scrolls, see esp. H. Braun, "Römer 7, 7-25 und das Selbstverständnis der Qumran-Fromme," in *Gesammelte Studien zum Neuen Testament und seiner Umwelt* (Tübingen: Mohr, 1962), 100–119 (repr. from *ZTK* 56, 1959).

32. Cf. E. W. Smith, "The Form and Religious Background of Romans 7:24–25a," *NovT* 13 (1971) 127–35.

33. See esp. the very influential study of W. G Kümmel, *Römer 7 und die Bekehrung des Paulus* (Leipzig: Hinrichs, 1929). In spite of many variations, Kümmel's main thesis has been accepted by a great number of scholars.

2. If genuine, a confession of sin is a very personal matter. Yet, the confession may be best expressed in stereotyped language, perhaps in the form of a ritual prayer.

3. When we confess our sins before God, our self-evaluation is very different from what it normally is when we communicate with other people. The Dead Sea Scrolls contain very clear examples of this, but I would think that the observation also holds true for Pharisees, for saints, and for ordinary people.

The confessional statements are so general that everybody can make them their own. They are not autobiographical in any narrow sense, but they do express Paul's personal experience. His intention was good, as he was motivated by zeal for the Law. Yet, the result of his action was evil: he persecuted the church of God. The "I" who makes the confession is the person who is now legally dead and, thanks to the liberation in Christ Jesus and the power of the Spirit, even effectively dead (see Rom. 7:1-6; 8:9-11; and cf. Gal. 2:19-20). Yet, even those who have received the Spirit still groan, as they wait for the redemption of the body (Rom. 8:23). We have no evidence to prove that confession of sin before God was practiced in the Pauline communities, as it was, more or less regularly, at Qumran, in the Synagogue liturgy and, apparently, in some early Christian circles (see 1 John 1:9). It is hard to say whether or not an argument from silence would be conclusive. In any case, Paul does not in Rom. 7 use the "I" form in order to give biographical information, to set forth anthropological doctrines, or to give an abstract interpretation of pre-Christian existence under the Law. He wants to engage his readers, so that they concur both in the conclusion that the Law is good and in the thanksgiving for the liberation in Christ and, thus, let the Spirit, not the flesh, direct their lives.

6

The Doctrine of Justification: Its Social Function and Implications

BY THE DOCTRINE OF justification I mean the Pauline doctrine outlined in Rom. 3:28: man is justified by faith apart from works of the Law. This doctrine Paul develops in the letters to the Romans and the Galatians. In the letter to the Galatians the form is polemical and pointed whereas the letter to the Romans gives a more comprehensive, positive account intended to ward off misinterpretations. Brief statements of the doctrine can also be found in other Pauline letters (2. Cor. 5:21; Phil. 3:7ff.; cf. Titus 3:5-7; Acts 13:38f.). Words such as righteous, righteousness and justify can also appear outside the context of the doctrine of justification, and the substance of the doctrine can be present even where the technical terminology of the doctrine is missing.[1]

I presuppose common knowledge of the content of the doctrine and shall neither try to penetrate its theological depths nor take a stand with regard to the contested parts of its interpretation. A close discussion of exegetical details in the central texts would exceed the limits of my essay. My question is simpler and pertains to Paul's use of the doctrine of justification. The phrase "social function and implications" indicates that I see the doctrine as something more than a dogmatic doctrine or an answer to the question of how the individual is to find a gracious God. In this study, I want to point out that this doctrine not only concerns the

---

1. The substance of this paper has, in various versions, been given as a lecture at several theological schools in the United States and at a pastors' institute sponsored by the Theological Faculty at the University of Oslo.

individual and his relation to God but is also of importance for the common life of Christians. This is no new insight but is an aspect which has only infrequently received due attention in treatments of Paul's doctrine.

Before we turn to Paul's specific doctrine, I shall make some remarks about the teaching about God's righteousness and his justification of man in Judaism and early Christianity. Here I use the common term "pre-Pauline" Christianity to refer to teachings which Paul is likely to have had in common with other early Christian teachers and preachers. We shall next turn to Paul's special doctrine of justification by faith, as we find it in Romans and Galatians, and conclude with some remarks about analogies in other New Testament writings and about the use of Paul's doctrine in the later history of the church.

1. RIGHTEOUSNESS AND JUSTIFICATION: EARLY CHRISTIANITY AND QUMRAN

The question of the background and origin of the terminology which Paul uses in his doctrine of justification has, usually, been answered in one of two ways. Many scholars have assumed that Paul made an antithetical use of rabbinic terminology. Whereas the Jewish theologians taught that man became righteous and guiltless before God by observing the commandments, Paul maintains that it is through faith and not through works of the Law that we become righteous in God's judgment.[2] Others have assumed that Paul drew upon the usage in the Old Testament, perhaps mediated by the Septuagint. Especially in the Psalms and in Second Isaiah, God's "righteousness" means his saving righteousness, his vindication of himself and of his convenant people. Being faithful, he sets things right for the poor and oppressed.[3]

The choice between these two possibilities has certain consequences for the understanding of the term *dikaiosynē theou* (righteousness of

---

2. Especially in older literature, the rabbinic doctrine was presented as a direct contrast to Paul's view and thus caricatured. For more recent and balanced accounts, see, e.g., A. Oepke, "Dikaiosynē Theou bei Paulus in neuer Beleuchtung," *TLZ* 78 (1953) 257-63; H. Ljungmann, *Pistis* (Lund: Gleerup, 1964), 24-28.

3. See esp. C. H. Dodd, *The Epistle to the Romans* (MNTC; London: Hodder & Stoughton, 1932), 9-12. More recently, E. Käsemann has tried to interpret "God's righteousness" against an apocalyptic background, see *New Testament Questions of Today*, 168-82. The same approach is followed by P. Stuhlmacher, *Gerechtigkeit Gottes bei Paulus* (Göttingen: Vandenhoeck & Ruprecht, 1966).

God). Interpreted as antithetical to rabbinic doctrine, Pauline *dikaiosynē theou* means the righteousness from God, the righteousness which God imputes and gives to believers. If Paul's use of the term is derived from the Septuagint's usage, it is more natural to understand the genitive as a subjective genitive: God demonstrates his saving righteousness when he, as an act of grace, acquits or pardons sinners. This understanding informs the translation of Rom. 1:17 in *The New English Bible*: "Here is revealed God's way of righting wrong."[4]

It is not necessary to make an exclusive choice between the two possible explanations. Combinations or compromise solutions are also possible. Some scholars suppose that in different contexts Paul assigns somewhat different meanings to the term.[5] But the alternative, polemical or biblical terminology, is out of date today. Like many other problems, the question of the terminology of justification must be reconsidered in the light of the Dead Sea Scrolls. Some of the Scrolls from Qumran speak of the sin of man and of God's righteousness in a manner that sounds strikingly Pauline, not to say Lutheran. Especially some of the hymns stress that all men are sinners, the members of the sect and the "I" who prays not excepted: "And when he is judged, who will be just before Thee?" (1QH 7:28; cf. 9:14f.; 12:19; 16:11). "It is by Thy goodness alone that a man is justified and by the immensity of Thy mercy" (13:16f.). The praying person—is it the Teacher of Righteousness himself?—elaborates at length his own misery. He is made of clay, kneaded with water, conceived in uncleanness and sin, "a spirit of straying, and perverse" (1QH 1:21f.) He leans on God's acts of grace and his rich mercy, because God in his righteousness wipes out sins and cleanses away guilt (1QH 11:30f.): "For I leaned on Thy favors and on the greatness of Thy mercy. For Thou pardonest iniquity and clean[sest m]an of sin by Thy righteousness" (1QH 4:37).

The confession of redemption through the righteousness of God alone is most clearly expressed in the hymnic conclusion of The Scroll of the Rule: "But to God I will say, My righteousness" (1QS 10:11).

---

4. On the most recent discussion, see G. Klein, "Righteousness in the NT," in *IDBSup*, 750–52; M. T. Bauch, "Perspectives on 'God's righteousness' in recent German discussion," in Sanders, 523–42, Appendix.

5. This opinion was held by several of the older commentators (e.g. Lietzmann) and has been restated by Sanders, 491–95.

For to God belongs my justification,
and the perfection of my way,
and the uprightness of my heart
are in His hand:
by His righteousness are my rebellions blotted out. (11:2f.)

―――

and from the fount of His Righteousness comes my justification.
From His wondrous Mysteries is the light in my heart . . . (11:5)

―――

As for me, I belong to wicked humanity,
to the assembly of perverse flesh. (11:9)

―――

No, men cannot establish their steps
for their justification belongs to God,
and from His hand comes perfection of way.
By His understanding all things are brought into being,
by His thought every being established,
and without Him nothing is made.
And I, if I stagger,
God's mercies are my salvation for ever;
and if I stumble because of the sin of the flesh,
my justification is in the righteousness of God
which exists for ever.

―――

He has caused me to approach by His Mercy
and by His favors He will bring my justification.
He has justified me by His true justice
and by His immense goodness He will pardon all my iniquities.
And by His justice He will cleanse me of the defilement of man
and of the sin of the sons of men,
that I may acknowledge His righteousness unto God
and His majesty unto the Most High. (11:10–12, 13–15)[6]

The translation of this part of the Rule is beset with several difficulties. It is sometimes hard to know how to render a word, e.g., the plural of

―――

6. The translation is taken from A. Dupont-Sommer, *The Essene Writings from Qumran*, trans. G. Vermes (Cleveland: World, 1962).

ḥeṣed (mercy or acts of grace?). Punctuation and tense cause other problems. For our topic it is the interpretation of the noun *mišpāṭ* which is the most difficult and most important problem. If one consistently translates it, as Dupont-Sommer does, with "justification," the text sounds considerably more Pauline than if one renders it with "right" or "righteousness." There are good arguments for abandoning the attempt to find a single translation; the word *mišpāṭ* shifts nuance: right, legal rule or decision, righteousness, etc. Even in these quotations we must take into account the interaction of several nuances. The concept must not be one-sidedly rendered as either "imputed righteousness" or ethical righteousness as a human quality; the meaning is more comprehensive. The right, justice and righteousness of the praying person depend through and through upon God. By his own strength he can neither do the right thing nor obtain righteousness. God alone, in his righteousness, can forgive sin and acquit him, and only God can make his life right.

Without any detailed exegesis of the texts we may state that the beliefs voiced by members of the Qumran community correspond to a number of the classical formulations of the doctrine of justification. The ungodly is righteous only through grace. A man is saved not by his own righteousness but by God's saving righteousness. Man is at the same time sinful and righteous. Thus: *justificatio impii—sola gratia—justitia salutifera—justitia aliena—simul justus et peccator!* Expressions like these would not have the meaning they acquire in Lutheran dogmatics if applied to what is taught in the Qumran community. Nevertheless, the parallels are striking and raise both historical and theological questions. Where is the difference between Essene and Pauline doctrine to be located? Does a direct or indirect connection exist?[7]

One must be careful not to draw conclusions which are too rash. Père Benoit and other sensible scholars have, with good reason, called for caution. What the Qumran texts really prove is that the Old Testament idea of God's righteousness was alive in Judaism at the time of the New Testament, at least in certain circles and in some connections: God's *ṣĕdaḳa* is not a revenging or distributive justice but the saving righteousness he shows in his treatment of his chosen ones. It is not necessary to

---

7. On this question, see, e.g., S. Schultz, "Zur Rechtfertigung aus Gnaden in Qumran und bei Paulus," *ZTK* 56 (1959) 155-85; W. Grundmann, "Der Lehrer der Gerechtigkeit von Qumran und die Frage nach der Glaubensgerechtigkeit in der Theologie des Apostels Paulus," *RevQ* 2 (1960) 231-54. For more recent literature, cf. note 3 above.

suppose that the Pauline terminology is directly taken over from circles in Qumran or related groups. At the same time, however, it is obvious that we no longer stand before the alternative that the terminology of justification is either shaped in opposition to the Pharisaic doctrine or taken over from the Septuagint: it has a positive connection to a religious language still existing in Judaism. It is also important to point out that what we find in the Qumran texts is not merely the use of Old Testament terms like "God's righteousness": these expressions appear in a new context marked by a deep sense of the sinfulness of man, a mood of penance and practice of piety, and, moreover, a personal hope for salvation, all of this within a special group of chosen ones. The similarity with Paul's doctrine of justification through the saving righteousness of God is truly remarkable.

At this point I would like to refer to an observation made by David Flusser, professor at the Hebrew University in Jerusalem. The closest parallels in the New Testament to the Dead Sea Scrolls are, by and large, not to be found in thoughts and formulations which are especially characteristic of any one of the authors of the New Testament. They appear in terminology or phraseology which is common to Paul, John, the letter to Hebrews, and, to a certain extent, 1 Peter and other works.[8] This means that they are found in the layer of tradition which Bultmann presents in his *Theology of the New Testament* under the title "The kerygma of the Hellenistic church aside from Paul." This observation should be linked with the conclusion which a number of scholars have drawn from completely different observations. Paul has in his doctrine of justification made use of a terminology already current among the Christian congregations. Not only the noun *dikaiosynē* (righteousness) but also the verb *dikaioun* (justify) occur in the New Testament outside the context of Paul's special doctrine of justification, sometimes in a way which is rather close to the technical use of the terms. It is sufficient to mention the tax collector who "went down to his house justified" (Luke 18:14; cf. also Rom. 6:7; 1 Cor. 4:4). Especially remarkable are a few Pauline texts which seem to reflect traditional early Christian language and doctrine and at the same time have close parallels in the Qumran Scrolls.

Concerning the unrepentant, the Scroll of the Rule says: "When he dissembles the stubbornness of his heart he shall not be justified (*lô yiṣdāḳ*), . . . he shall not be absolved (*lô yizzākeh*) by atonement nor

---

8. D. Flusser, "The Dead Sea Sect and Pre-Pauline Christianity," *Scripta Hierosolymitana*, 4 (1958) 215-66.

purified by lustral waters, not sanctified by seas and rivers, nor cleansed by all the waters of washing. Unclean, unclean shall he be for as long as he scorns the ordinance of God" (1QS 3:3-6). Whether the verbal forms are to be viewed as passive or reflexive is open to some question. In either case, the thought is probably that the unrepentant is not to be admitted to the purifying rites of the community and that these rites would have no effect without conversion of the heart and adherence to a way of life in accordance with the Law as it was interpreted in Qumran.

With this statement in the Scroll of the Rule one must contrast and compare what is said in 1 Cor. 6:11: "But you were washed, you were sanctified, you were justified in the name of the Lord Jesus Christ and in the Spirit of our God." In these two texts the words for washing, sanctifying and justifying are used in close, nearly synonymous, parallelism; in the Scroll, in connection with the cleansing rites of the sect, in 1 Cor., in connection with Christian baptism. The negative formulation of the words in the text from Qumran does not, by and large, make any significant difference: the presupposition is obviously that anyone who is really converted is justified and guiltless, purified and sanctified through the cultic means of expiation and purification.

In 1 Cor. 6:11 Paul stresses something he regards as well-known. Among scholars today there is widespread agreement that the formulation does not express a specific Pauline doctrine. Justification is here linked to the name of Jesus and to the Spirit in a way not typical of passages where Paul develops his doctrine of justification through faith. Paul has here formulated his words in conformity with common teaching about baptism in the pre-Pauline congregations.

In other cases, too, one suspects that Paul has used more or less fixed formulations. The words in Rom. 4:25, "who was put to death for our trespasses and raised for our justification," seem to reflect confessional language. The formal parallelism, the elevated style and the unusual connection of the resurrection of Jesus with our justification indicate that the words are a loose quotation. Furthermore, it seems that a kind of confessional formulation forms the background for the well-known text in Rom. 3:24-26. Here too the style is elevated and several words occur which are unusual for Paul (e.g., *hilastērion* and *paresis*). In this case it is hardly a direct quotation but rather a free paraphrastic use of the given confession. The inserted *dia pisteōs* (by faith) in v. 25 is likely to be a Pauline comment. One can assume, however, that the pre-Pauline fragment spoke about the righteousness of God. Among the traditional formulations we can perhaps also include Rom. 8:29f., which may reflect baptismal theology, and Rom. 8:33, the introduction to the closing hymn in Rom. 8. Finally, we may mention the relative clause in 1 Cor. 1:30: "He is the source of your life in Christ Jesus, whom God made our wisdom, our righteousness and sanctification and redemption."[9] Characteristic for all these passages, and probably for pre-Pauline doctrine as a whole, is that words like *dikaioun* and *dikaiosynē* are used together with other more or less synonymous terms and that the statements do not have any polemical intent. Justification is linked to the death and resurrection of Jesus and to the name of Jesus and the Spirit of God active at baptism. One should perhaps note that according to Titus 3:5-7 it is "by the washing of regeneration," baptism, that we are "justified by his grace."

It would be hard to prove that in such early Christian texts terms like justify and God's righteousness have a meaning different from that which they possess in the Qumran texts. At least, a very subtle analysis would be necessary to prove any significant difference in the nuance of the words. What is said in the texts from the New Testament and in the Dead Sea Scrolls is nevertheless not the same. The difference, however, is due to the context and to the purpose of the statements rather than to word usage per se.

The Qumran texts, mostly hymns and prayers, refer to God's justifying righteousness. The praying subject expresses his confidence that God in his grace, faithfulness and righteousness will forgive the sins which are due to the weakness of the flesh. The members of the sect, who in the last days of wickedness live according to the right interpretation of the Law, can trust in God's righteousness and goodness. Prayers and hymns are not to be interpreted merely as personal confessions: they also give prototypical expressions of the right attitude toward God and thus contain a didactic element. The person who becomes a member of the sect must learn to trust God's mercy alone, but at the same time he must convert with his heart and adhere to the Law. Nowhere, however, do we find in the Qumran texts anything like the statement, "you have been justified."

---

9. On Paul's use of current terminology in passages like Rom. 3:24-26; 4:25; 1 Cor. 6:11, see E. Lohse, "Die Gerechtigkeit Gottes in der paulinischen Theologie" and "Taufe und Rechtfertigung bei Paulus," in *Die Einheit des Neuen Testaments* (Göttingen: Vandenhoeck & Ruprecht, 1973) esp. 218-23, 240-44. On Rom. 3:24-26, see also Käsemann's commentary and my *The Crucified Messiah*, 155f. with note 43 on p. 187. On Rom. 8:29f., see J. Jervell, *Imago Dei* (FRLANT 76; Göttingen: Vandenhoeck & Ruprecht, 1960), 271ff.

The contrast between "once" and "now" is much more sharply expressed in early Christianity than in the Essene sect.[10] It is not difficult to understand why this is the case. For the Qumran sectaries the revelation of God's saving righteousness and his justification of sinners is never linked with any event in history comparable to the death and resurrection of Christ. Accordingly, the initiation and purification ceremonies did not make the same kind of difference in the life of the members as baptism in the name of Jesus did for Christians. Christian baptism is important because it makes the believer participate in the grace of God as it was manifested in a saving event which occurred once and for all.

So far we have dealt with passages which relate justification to the death and resurrection of Jesus and to baptism in his name. Such baptismal reminders are rather common in the New Testament epistles. Those baptized are called to remember what they once were and what they now are, to realize the greatness of God's mercy and promise, and to understand what consequences it all must have for their behavior in the church and in the world. Paul constantly calls the congregation back to its beginnings: the first preaching of the Gospel, the foundation of a local congregation and the admission of individuals into the church.[11]

The terminology used in such reminders varies. One form indicates that the Christians have been justified. To the Christians in Corinth the apostle writes that they were unrighteous and committed all kinds of sins, but now they are purified, sanctified and justified. How can they then continue to do wrong, to make demands and to insist on their rights against Christian brothers, and to go to worldly courts for help in making these claims valid (1 Cor. 6:1-11)?[12] The reminder of baptism sounds paradoxical here. In spite of their injustice and wrongdoing they are nevertheless justified in Christ. But this in no way means that they may complacently assume that the Christian is simultaneously righteous

---

10. I assume that the Qumran convenanters were among those whom Pliny, Philo, and Josephus describe as "Essenes." On the contrast between "once" and "now", see *Jesus in the Memory of the Early Church*, 33-34; P. Tachau, *'Einst' und 'Jetzt' im Neuen Testament* (FRLANT 105; Göttingen: Vandenhoeck & Ruprecht, 1972).

11. See Chapters III and V, and also "Form-Critical Observations on Early Christian Preaching," in *Jesus in the Memory of the Early Church*, 30-36. (By a mistake it was not indicated that this essay had originally appeared in German in W. Eltester, ed., *Neutestamentliche Studien für Rudolf Bultmann* (BZNW 21; Tübingen: Mohr, 1954), 3-9.

12. On this passage, see E. Dinkler, "Zum Problem der Ethik bei Paulus," *ZTK* 49 (1952) 167-200 (= *Signum Crucis*, [Tübingen: Mohr, 1967], 204-40).

in the sight of God and sinful in his moral conduct. On the contrary, Paul stresses with great emphasis that those who have been justified are not to go on with their wrongdoings. Rightly understood, justification has very practical consequences, even for conduct in legal and economic matters. In the Qumran sect the Mosaic Law and the many rules of conduct remain obligatory in spite of the believer's knowledge that it is solely through God's grace that he can become guiltless and learn to do right. To an even greater extent, for early Christianity as well as for Paul, justification by grace was the very foundation and motivation for a new way of life—whether or not the word justification is used.

These remarks have shed some light on historical conditions. There is no reason to assume that Paul took over the terminology of justification directly from Essene circles. It is not the specific Pauline formulation of the doctrine but rather pre-Pauline theology which coincides in many respects with what we find in the Qumran texts. The possibility of a direct link between certain early Christian circles and the Qumran sect remains open, but one cannot exclude the possibility that the similarity reflects a common tradition interpreted by groups with a certain structural resemblance and not direct influence. It was not only in Qumran that the Old Testament concept of God's saving righteousness was alive in Judaism.[13] Both in Qumran and in early Christianity, personal certainty of salvation was connected with membership in a religious sect, a new covenantal congregation. This assurance may have generated in both groups, independently, a renewal of the Old Testament concept that God's righteousness proves itself in his salvation and justification of those who belong to the covenant. The nature of the new covenant is the determining factor for the meaning of justification. Thus, justification meant something very different to the Qumran covenanters, who had vowed to observe strictly the Torah as their community interpreted it, from what it meant to the early Christians, who were members of the community of the covenant in the blood of Jesus.

It is now possible to give a preliminary answer to the question of the function of the doctrine of justification in early Christianity. It is not merely a word of consolation to troubled consciences. Neither is it simply a polemical doctrine developed in controversies with the Jews. In what appears to be the more traditional early Christian usage, the references to justification serve to remind all members of the congregation of what

13. cf. Stuhlmacher, *Gerechtigkeit Gottes*, 166–73. There is, however, no evidence that "God's righteousness" was an apocalyptic term.

God has done for them and with them in Jesus Christ. In this general, not specifically Pauline, form the doctrine of justification has its setting (*Sitz-im-Leben*) in Christian teaching, perhaps especially in teaching addressed to the newly baptized. It is possible that the terminology of justification was also used in missionary preaching or in formal liturgical language, but as far as I can see, the sources do not permit more definite conclusions.

2. THE DOCTRINE OF PAUL

When Paul simply reminds Christians that they are justified through Christ he is probably applying current terms and teachings of a commonly accepted doctrine. However, the Pauline doctrine of justification through faith, not through works of the Law, further develops the terminology. In its specifically Pauline form, the doctrine has a polemical purpose. The words "justify" and "justification," receive a stress that makes it difficult to substitute synonyms. Such substitution is all the more difficult because of the closeness of the doctrine of justification in this narrower sense to scriptural exegesis.

The more common use of the terminology of justification has its background in the language of the Old Testament, a background which it shares with the equivalent expressions in the Qumran documents. Paul's more theologically developed doctrine depends on quotation of, and comments upon, specific Old Testament passages. To interpret these texts, Paul uses exegetical methods common to the Judaism of his day. Nevertheless, he achieves results which directly contradict those which Jewish and Judaizing exegetes obtained. The reason for this is his presupposition that these passages agree with his understanding of God's act and revelation in Jesus Christ. That does not mean that Paul simply finds scriptural prooftexts to undergird his theological position. Paul's scriptural exegesis has a more constitutive significance; it makes it possible for him to articulate his theological convictions.

One of the texts on which Paul builds is Psalm 143:2 (LXX 142:2): "For no man living (*pas zōn*) is righteous before thee." For Paul this means: "For no human being (*pasa sarx*) will be justified in his sight by works of the Law" (i.e., before God's court; Rom. 3:20; Gal. 2:16). Paul knows that there is justification in God's sight, but its foundation is different from works of the Law.[14]

Paul found a positive counterpart to the Psalm's negative statement in Hab. 2:4: "The righteous shall live by his faith" (LXX, "by my faithfulness"), or as Paul quotes it: "He who through faith is righteous shall live" (Rom. 1:17; Gal. 3:11). For Paul, this verse means that only through faith in Jesus Christ shall the righteous man receive life—and that only by faith is he righteous. Paul's understanding of Hab. 2:4 is analogous to the interpretation we find in the Qumran commentary on Habakkuk: "God will deliver them from the House of Judgment because of their affliction and their faith in the Teacher of Righteousness" (lQpHab. 8:2f.). The difference between them is, however, more striking than the similarity. The Qumran document stresses trust in the Teacher of Righteousness and faithfulness to his interpretation of the Law. Faith in the Teacher is in no way opposed to adherence to the Law but is the presupposition for its right observation, and therefore also for obtaining life. The interpretation of Hab. 2:4 is not related to the praise of God's saving righteousness, even though this concept occurs in hymnic texts from Qumran. In Rom. 1:17, by contrast, Paul quotes Hab. 2:4 to support his statement that the gospel reveals God's righteousness and, for that reason, is the power of God for salvation. Identifying the faith of Hab. 2:4 with faith in the crucified and risen Christ, Paul even draws the conclusion that the quotation proves that nobody is justified by the Law, since righteousness and life are given to those who have faith (Gal. 3:11).

For Paul, the quotation that the righteous shall live by faith contradicts the statement of the Mosaic Law that the one who keeps the Law's commandments and ordinances shall live by them (Gal. 3:12; Rom. 10:5). Paul's entire exegesis depends on the presupposition that faith and works of the Law exclude each other, that the Mosaic Law and faith in Christ cannot simultaneously express the proper way for man to relate to God. At the same time, Paul takes for granted that the Mosaic Law was from God, that it was good and holy. To extricate himself from the dilemma that these two views taken together create, Paul asserts that God never intended the Law to last forever. It was a temporary measure, valid only until the coming of Christ made faith in him possible. Paul finds in the

---

14. For the hermeneutical principle that warrants the apparently arbitrary addition of "by works of the Law," see Chapter IX, "Contradictions in Scripture."

Law itself evidence that its function was only provisional, preparatory: the story of Abraham.[15]

The most important quotation is Gen. 15:6 (LXX): "And Abraham believed God, and it was reckoned to him as righteousness." Paul combines this quotation with Psalm 31(32):1f. (LXX): "Blessed are those whose iniquities are forgiven, whose sins are covered. Blessed is the man against whom the Lord will not reckon his sin" (Rom. 4:3–8; cf. Gal. 3:6). Thus, Paul equates reckoning faith as righteousness with not reckoning sin; this is justification. Abraham is a model of the sinner who receives justification by faith without having earned it. Paul associates Gen. 15:6 with the promises which Genesis records, that Abraham would be the father of a multitude of nations and that in him would all the nations of the earth be blessed. Abraham's faith is for Paul faith that God would do as he had promised and, with an allusion to the birth of Isaac, faith in the God who brings the dead to life, the same God who raised Jesus from the dead. Vital to Paul's argument is that God promised and Abraham believed before Abraham's circumcision; circumcision cannot therefore be a condition for the fulfillment of the promise. The Law was not proclaimed on Mt. Sinai until long afterward, so the fulfillment of God's promises cannot depend on adherence to the Law any more than it can on circumcision (Rom. 4:9–16; Gal. 3:15–18). If obeying the Law was a condition for the fulfillment of God's promises, those promises would in fact have become invalid (Rom. 4:13–15; Gal. 3:18–23). Accordingly, the Law is simply an interim measure, which serves to identify sin as sin and thereby increases it, so as to emphasize the essence of grace: it is completely undeserved (Rom. 5:20–21).

Paul deduces from all this that Jews and Gentiles are justified in the same way, by faith alone. Those who believe in Christ, men and women of every nation, are the true children of Abraham, heirs according to promise. Paul uses other scriptural quotations as well to advance his argument (e.g., Rom. 10:6–17; Gal. 4:21–31). To the scriptural argument he adds an argument from experience: it is by the proclamation of faith that God has given the Holy Spirit to Gentiles as well as to Jews, as a down payment on, and guarantee of, their inheritance. In this way the Gentiles have come to share in the promises God made to Abraham (Gal. 3:1–5, 14; 4:6f.; cf. Rom. 8:15–17; etc.).

---

15. For Paul's interpretation of the story of Abraham, see B. Schein, "Our Father Abraham" (PhD diss., Yale, 1973), and cf. note 19 to Chapter V.

THE DOCTRINE OF JUSTIFICATION 109

For our purposes it is neither possible nor necessary to follow Paul's argument in detail. It is enough to emphasize how Paul has refined the doctrine of justification which he held in common with others:

1. Paul bases his doctrine on specific quotations from the Old Testament and expresses it as a pointed theological thesis;

2. Paul stresses that justification occurs specifically *through faith*, not just, more generally, in Christ and through baptism. There is no contradiction here; for Paul, as for the early church generally, baptism and faith belong together. When, however, Paul uses Gen. 15:6, Hab. 2:4 and other scriptural quotations to emphasize faith, he understands that faith as faith in Christ; the preaching of the gospel produces justifying faith;

3. Paul asserts that faith excludes works of the Law as a condition for justification and salvation; he expresses this view in an extreme form when he refers to God as the God who justifies the ungodly (Rom. 4:5);

4. Paul emphasizes the universal dimension of justification. As all men have sinned, Jews and Gentiles alike, so are all men justified only through faith: there is no distinction between Jews and Gentiles.

The Pauline formulation of the doctrine of justification has a clear social relevance; it implies an understanding of what Christian community is, and it provides guidelines to show the members of that community how they ought to relate to one another. In Galatians, Paul presents the doctrine in the context of his polemic against the requirement that Gentile believers in Christ be circumcised and obey at least some of the ceremonial commandments and ordinances of the Mosaic Law. He completely rejects that demand; if Christ makes justification and salvation available at all, he makes them available to those who have faith; there is no other requirement. The doctrine of justification proves that Christian Gentiles need not and should not become Jews, not even in part, in order to become full members of the church, true children of Abraham and legitimate heirs to all that God has promised. As Christians, Gentiles should remain part of the ethnic group from which they came, Greek, Galatian or whatever. Without rejecting the validity of the Old Testament, Paul can, with the help of his theologically formulated doctrine, assert uncompromisingly the universality of the gospel and of the church. That assertion had historical and social consequences that we cannot overlook.

It is not by accident that we find the quotation: "There is neither Jew nor Greek, there is neither slave nor free, there is neither male nor female; for you are all one in Christ Jesus" (Gal. 3:28; cf. 5:6; 6:15; Rom. 3:29f.; 10:12f.) in the context of a discussion of the doctrine of justification. Of course, Paul does not claim that there are no differences among individuals in sex, nationality, or social position. The codes of household duties are not the only evidence that this is not what Paul means. But if it would be a mistake to attribute to the Apostle a modern humanistic ideal of equality, it would be just as wrong to suppose that he is making an abstract theological statement about unity and equity before God which does not have social implications. The doctrine of justification which Paul so emphatically asserts has practical social consequences.

The most obvious example is the episode at Antioch which Paul describes in Gal. 2:11ff. Paul does not criticize Peter's theology; he presupposes that Peter's theology is essentially the same as his. If Peter did hold certain views which would later on have been classified as—let us say—crypto-semipelagian, I suspect that Paul would have passed over them in silence. Paul himself is not always as careful in his choice of theological formulations as strict Augustinians and orthodox Lutherans might wish. But the issue in Antioch was not theological clarity and precision. Peter, considering the problems of Christian Jews, thought it wise and prudent to withdraw from table fellowship with Gentile Christians. For Paul, the behavior of Peter and Barnabas constitutes their rejection of the doctrine of justification by faith. To preserve Christian unity at the Lord's table, Gentile Christians would have to "judaize"; in practice, the commandments of the Mosaic Law would regain their validity. But if the Law remained valid, then Christ had died to no purpose. Then—and only then—those who had sought their justification in Christ and not in works of the Law would be shown to be lawbreakers. Paul could be tolerant about differences in formulating doctrine. But when the unity of the church, as it was realized in fellowship at the common table, is at stake, Paul becomes adamant, forceful, uncompromising. For him, justification by faith and the truth of the gospel message are in danger, and he springs to their defense.

As Paul formulates the doctrine of justification, it has a polemical application.[16] Nevertheless, it would be wrong to understand it as purely polemical. In his letter to the Christians at Rome, Paul introduces himself and the gospel which he preaches, in order to win the Romans' support for his projected work in the West. At the same time—and I consider this one of his most important reasons for writing—Paul asks the Roman Christians to support him and his congregations in Macedonia and Achaia with their prayers, that the gift which Paul's Gentile congregations offer might prove acceptable to the saints in Jerusalem (Rom. 15:15–22). With this request in sight, Paul develops his doctrine of justification, attempting as he goes along to guard against misunderstandings, to avoid providing a pretext for Christians continuing to sin and to safeguard the holiness of the Law. Paul insists that he has not turned his back on his own people; on the contrary, salvation for Israel is the ultimate goal toward which he is working as an apostle to the Gentiles. In other words, the doctrine of justification appears in Romans as an essential and decisive component of a comprehensive theology of mission.[17]

Justification does not simply involve the individual and his salvation. Paul's perspective includes history and eschatology: Adam, mankind and Christ, the promise to Abraham and the Law given to Moses on Sinai, the gospel preached to Jews and to Gentiles, God's work in the past and in the future, the Apostle's own work in the present, the first fruits among the Gentiles and the remnant of Israel, the unity of Jews and Gentiles in the local congregation and in the worldwide church, Christ's dominion over principalities and powers, and the all-encompassing ultimate goal of God's plan for his creation. Obviously, the doctrine of justification is not primarily social; it is theological and soteriological. But the framework which Paul uses to locate the doctrine is social and historical rather than psychological and individualistic.

This does not give us any reason to doubt that the doctrine of justification is closely connected to Paul's personal experience and convictions. A confession like the one in Phil. 3:3–11 is enough to prove this

16. The characterization of the doctrine as a *Kampfeslehre* (polemical doctrine) goes back to W. Wrede, *Paul* (1904, ET 1907, trans. E. Lummis; repr. Lexington: American Theological Library Association, 1962).

A. Schweitzer and, most recently, E. P. Sanders have also expressed the opinion that the doctrine is part of Paul's polemics and not at the center of his theology. E. Käsemann agrees that the doctrine is polemical but stresses that it is constitutive for the gospel, see *An die Römer*, 24, 94f.; cf. Chapter X below.

17. Cf. Chapter V.

connection (cf. also Gal. 2:15–21). But Paul's description in Philippians makes it clear that his road to the doctrine of justification was different from Luther's. Paul's life as a Pharisee was, by the Law's standards, "blameless"; his zeal for the Law made him a persecutor of the church. He rejected everything in which he had once hoped, he accepted a status equivalent to that of pagan sinners, in order to obtain a righteousness which was not his own but a gift from God.

Paul knows that as an apostle he is nothing more than a sinner who has received God's grace and who now works as its instrument. But the sin that comes to his mind is always that he once persecuted the church of God. Paul knows that he is not perfect and that God will judge him (Phil. 3:12; 1 Cor. 4:4), but it is extremely difficult to find in Paul's letters any allusion to sins committed during his life as a Christian or in his work as an apostle. The person and the office are inseparable: what Paul is, he is as an ambassador of Christ. Paul's remarks in Romans 7 about the differences between intention and action do not disprove this assertion. In context, Romans 7 proves that it is sin in the flesh and not the Law itself which causes the Law to bring men to death rather than to life. The end of the chapter stresses the sinner's terrible plight more than is necessary to establish the holiness of the Law, but only to emphasize that the Christian's new life is not his own achievement, that it is the work of God and of his Spirit (Rom. 8). Romans 7 is not introspective religious autobiography.[18]

Justification really is the merciful acquittal of sinful men; Paul emphasizes that both Jews and Gentiles are without excuse for their sinfulness. He discusses with stark realism the sin and injustice present in his own congregations. Yet, nothing indicates that interior feelings of sin and guilt afflicted the Galatians and the Romans to whom Paul wrote. If they were troubled, it was for more obvious reasons: their fear that their uncircumcision made them second-class Christians; the doubt about the status of their relationship to God which their difficulties and sufferings prompted; the anxiety which different beliefs and practices within the congregation caused, especially in a congregation where "the weak" were inclined to judge and "the strong" to despise their brethren. Confronting such attitudes, Paul emphasizes that we are justified by faith; he interprets the tension between suffering and glory, weakness and power, as a necessary element of Christian existence in this world; he warns against boasting of one's religious accomplishments and against unwarranted

---

18. see Stendahl, esp. 78–96; cf. Chapter V, Appendix III.

self-confidence, and he reminds his readers that it is God who will judge. Even though many aspects of the congregation's life are not as they should be, Paul retains a striking, steadfast conviction: "He who began a good work in you (those who believe), will bring it to completion at the day of Jesus Christ" (Phil. 1:6).

Even where Paul does not use the terminology of justification, he can still express the underlying idea. At the root of the divisions within the church at Corinth Paul finds a fundamental misunderstanding of the gospel: the Corinthians distort the wisdom of God, the foolishness of the cross, into mere worldly wisdom. From this distortion flows boasting about the superiority of one's favorite teacher, self-complacency, and dissension, at the expense of unity in Christ (1 Cor. 1–4).[19]

The Colossian heresy was obviously an example of an encratitic, mystical piety: as Christ had put aside the earthly and had been elevated above the principalities and powers, so the Christian too had to free himself from the material by pious ascetic practices, in order to enter the heavenly sanctuary and to join the angels in their worship of God.[20] The letter to the Colossians denounces these attitudes as "human tradition." In Christ, as the gospel proclaims him, the believers already have everything they need for salvation. In baptism they died, were buried and have been raised with Christ, and when Christ, their life, appears, they will also appear with him in glory. Most important is that they continue in the faith which was preached to them. It is by day-to-day compassion, love and thanksgiving that a Christian puts to death what is earthly and seeks the things that are above. God gives salvation and liberation completely, unreservedly, through Christ's work of reconciliation—*sola fide*. For this very reason, "household instructions" have a fundamental theological importance, contrary to encratitic observances and mystical experiences.

Throughout his letters, Paul emphasizes that the believers neither obtained nor continue to possess justification, holiness, wisdom, power and life through their own efforts. They received everything because as members of his church they belong to Christ. An individualistic interpretation of Paul's ethic will almost inevitably lead to perfectionism, an attitude alien to the Apostle.[21] When Paul mentions growth toward

---

19. Cf. Chapter III above.

20. See F. O. Francis, "Humility and Angelic Worship in Col. 2:18," in Francis and Meeks, *Conflict at Colossae* (SBLSBS 4, Missoula: Scholars, 1973), 163-95.

21. This point was stressed by A. Fridrichsen in an article on "Helgelse och fullkomlighet hos Paulus," (Sanctification and Perfection in Paul), *Den nya kyrkosynen*

Christian maturity and perfection, he means a growth within the congregation, serving one's brothers on the foundation which Christ laid once and for all. The Christian virtues (to use a word which some mistakenly avoid) are the fruit of the Spirit, but that does not mean that good works and righteous living automatically follow faith. Speaking in tongues is the only gift of the Holy Spirit which does not activate man's will and understanding. The Spirit provides the discernment that is necessary for knowing what is good and the power to do it. Christians must strive to realize what they have become, due to God's grace, in order to understand what God wills in situations which demand moral decisions and social action. Their judgments and their behavior will show whether or not they have understood what justifying faith means.

In his requests and exhortations, Paul puts heavy stress on Christians' relationships with one another. The commandment to love one's neighbor is interpreted to be a commandment to love one's brothers within the community (Rom. 13:8–10; Gal. 5:14–15). In the life according to the Spirit which Christians live and in their mutual love, they fulfill the real requirements of the Law, on the basis of justification (Rom. 8:4). That God is Judge and that the gospel is for all men determines the Christian's relationship to those outside the community, but Paul underlines that Christian brotherly love fulfills the Law as he clarifies the relationship between Christ and the Law, between faith and works, in the doctrine of justification.

3. ANALOGIES IN OTHER WRITINGS

In the non-Pauline writings of the New Testament we find different conceptions which correspond more or less exactly to Paul's doctrine of justification. The Johannine writings, especially 1 John, provide the most interesting basis for comparison. Thus, 1 John 1:8–2:2 describes how Christians repeatedly sin and receive forgiveness for Christ's sake.

Seemingly contradictory statements appear next to one another in 1 John. The author writes: "If we say we have no sin, we deceive ourselves, and the truth is not in us" (1:8) and also: "No one born of God commits sin; for God's nature (*sperma*, seed) abides in him, and he cannot sin because he is born of God" (3:9). We can resolve this tension if we assume that both statements polemicize against the teachings of docetic-gnostic

---

(Uppsala, 1946), 62–91.

heretics. They appear to have believed that the pneumatic's inner, "real" self was of divine origin and substance, and was for this reason without sin. The pneumatic's self-awareness made it possible for him to do things without guilt that would have been sinful for others. The freedom from sin that they imagine they possess leads to the illusion that there is no danger in committing sinful acts. Against this background, the meaning of the contradictory formulations in 1 John is clear: the sins of the baptized are real sins; sin is never a matter of indifference, so the Christian must always avoid it. But for those who confess their sins, there is forgiveness.

The Reformation view that the baptized constantly need forgiveness has a firmer foundation in 1 John than in Paul. 1 John is the New Testament book which most closely approximates the paradoxical formulation, *"simul peccator, simul justus."* Especially important from the perspective of this article is that 1 John emphasizes that Christian community and brotherly love are the identifying marks of God's children (1:6f.; 2:7-11; 3:16-18; 4:7-21; 5:1-3). The Gospel of John also stresses the believers' common life. It is not simple affection that we encounter in John; it is a "juridical mysticism" which includes the ideas both of community and of mission. Unfortunately, it would carry us too far afield to pursue further the Johannine correspondences to the Pauline doctrine of justification.[22]

In general, only if one includes the social aspect of the doctrine of justification can one assert that the doctrine is central, that it sums up the message of Scripture. The Old Testament testifies that God in his undeserved love has chosen and preserved a people, a people unworthy of his goodness. Revealing his saving righteousness, God gives his people victory, salvation and peace. He has pity on the wretched and guards the rights of the oppressed. Those whom he justifies receive the status and position reserved for the righteous. It is impossible to separate the religious from the social even when faith expects God's future intervention to show forth his righteousness and to bestow salvation on the faithful.

Jesus speaks rarely, if ever, of justification. But if we think of his beatitudes of the poor, his miraculous help to the disturbed and his solidarity with outcasts, we can be sure that his work was a "justification of the ungodly." He did not come to call the righteous, but sinners to repentance. The Pharisees could certainly be aware of their sins. Thanksgivings

---

22. See Théo Preiss, "Justification in Johannine Thought," in *Life in Christ* (trans. H. Knight; SBT 13; Naperville: Allenson, 1954) 9-31. Cf. also my *Jesus in the Memory of the Early Church*, 115-17.

and confessions of sin had their place both in the communal worship of the synagogue and in the prayers of the individual. Jesus associated with notorious sinners, people whom the Law condemned as unclean, who were excluded from the community of the righteous. In some of his parables, Jesus explained that it was just such people whom God loved. The joy which marked the meals Jesus shared with tax collectors and sinners corresponds to the joy in heaven over a sinner who repents.

To come to the point, what Paul stated systematically, Jesus had already lived, in his attitudes and in his activities. The correspondence between them becomes clearer when we realize that Paul does not present the doctrine of justification as a dogmatic abstraction. As Jesus' work destroyed the significance of the distinction between sinners and the righteous in Israel, so Paul's fidelity to the truth of the gospel had to forbid discriminating within the church between Jews and Gentiles.

4. PAUL AND HIS INTERPRETERS

Many have wondered why the Pauline doctrine of justification seems not to have played an important role for Christians in the period after Paul. This impression depends on a number of factors. Protestant scholars have often been unjust in their evaluation of the Apostolic Fathers, the Apologists, and other early Christian authors. Viewed with an Augustinian or Lutheran understanding of Paul, they may seem superficial, with a tendency to interpret the gospel as a new law. But for them as for Paul it is of fundamental importance that God in his grace has established a new covenant and created a new people, a people reborn and sanctified in the baptismal bath. The questions which the Pauline doctrine of justification answered directly were no longer of interest to a church composed principally of Gentile Christians, who took for granted that the ritual commandments of the Mosaic Law did not apply to them. As time went on, other questions became more pressing. The change from the darkness of paganism to the light of Christ was not a personal experience to the same extent for later generations as it had been for the Pauline mission congregations. Christian sinfulness became a problem which could not be easily solved simply by recalling the beginning of one's life as a Christian, what one was because of the change worked by the gospel, faith and baptism. The question of the possibility of a second repentance arose, especially for Christians guilty of apostasy or of other serious sins. A Christian penitential practice developed, and it does not seem that anyone saw Paul's doctrine of justification as a possible answer to the problems with which that practice dealt. Even where one finds phrases reminiscent of the Pauline doctrine, it is doubtful that the doctrine of justification had much social relevance in the ancient church before Augustine.

Augustine was the first Christian thinker after Paul to assign central significance to the doctrine of justification. According to Augustine, God's grace was at work not only in baptism and at the beginning of the Christian life, but also in the sanctification which continued throughout that life and in the final perfection which would be its culmination. It would be wrong to suggest any direct incompatibility between Augustine's view and Paul's. But the context and the emphasis have shifted. Paul develops an eschatological theology of mission, while Augustine reflects theologically on human and divine activity in those justified by baptism. The author of the *Confessions* was also far more religiously introspective than the Apostle to the Gentiles or than the men of antiquity in general. It is not without reason that Augustine is sometimes called the first modern man.

Augustine's ideas about the *Civitas Dei* were probably more important in molding medieval society than his doctrine of grace. From his time onward, however, the struggle between Augustinianism and Pelagianism, the problem of relating the divine and human roles in salvation, remains a central concern for Western theology. This controversy has profoundly shaped Christianity in the West, whereas the Eastern church has never shown much interest in it.

The Augustinian monk Martin Luther stands in this Augustinian tradition. The Reformation presupposes, both in a positive and a negative way, the late Middle Ages, with its practice of penance, its scholasticism and its mysticism. It was in this context that Luther rediscovered the Pauline doctrine of justification, which gave him the answer to the question of how to find a gracious God. From the severity of the commandments of the Law and from God's wrath, the troubled conscience could flee again and again to the God revealed in Christ, who justifies by grace for Christ's sake, through faith.

The relationship between Paul and Luther has been very much discussed.[23] Not only Catholic scholars or radical Protestants like W. Wrede

---

23. To my knowledge, the best works on Paul and Luther are those of W. Joest, esp. *Gesetz und Freiheit* (Göttingen: Vandenhoeck & Ruprecht, [1951] 3.ed. 1963); and "Paulus und das lutherische *Simul Justus et Peccator*," KD, I (1955) 269-320. Cf. also

and A. Schweitzer, but even conservative theologians like A. Schlatter and Paul Althaus have maintained that Luther's interpretation of Paul is one-sided or even misleading. Others have shown how much Paul and Luther have in common. The question is complicated. If my view is right, they differ because they asked different questions, not because they gave different answers to the same questions. For this reason, it is not enough to list differences to prove fundamental disagreement any more than it is enough to list similarities to prove fundamental agreement. To use a musical image, we might say that the melody is the same, but that the harmony and the key are different. Or rather, Luther here furnishes a classic example of the inadequacy of the mere restatement of biblical themes; in order for these themes to have their full effect, they must be completely refashioned to fit the conditions and presuppositions of a different age. Yet, no transformation avoids the danger of one-sidedness.

I am not going to address here all the questions at issue. Certainly, what Paul had to say about the Mosaic Law and circumcision, about feasts and sabbaths, gained new currency when Luther applied it to the Catholic practices of penances and indulgences, to the piety of monastic life and to church ceremonies. The doctrine of justification, as it emerged from the new Lutheran exegesis, had social consequences which are impossible to ignore. For Luther and for the Lutheran confessions, the doctrine of justification by faith is not simply one doctrine among many; it determines the whole understanding of Christianity in a way that revolutionized the structure of the church and of society. It accomplished this negatively by abolishing monastic life and church hierarchy, by breaking away from canon law and from the papacy, and positively by giving enhanced religious meaning to service in secular vocations, in the family and in society.

Taking his stand on the doctrine of justification, Luther aimed at a reformation of the whole catholic church. The historical result was the establishment of different Reformation churches with the doctrine of justification by faith alone as their confessional mark. Confessional controversies and struggle led to ever more precise dogmatic formulations.

O. Modalsli, *Das Gericht nach den Werken: Ein Beitrag zu Luthers Lehre vom Gesetz* (Göttingen: Vandenhoeck & Ruprecht, 1963). For the discussion within the Lutheran World Federation Commission, 1958-1963, cf. the report by J. Rothermundt and other items in *Justification Today: Studies and Reports* (Lutheran World, Supplement to No. 1, 1965).

Even during the orthodox period the doctrine of justification by grace through faith was more than a theological abstraction. The doctrine served as a foundation for life in Lutheran and Reformed countries. But a certain narrowing also occurred, not only in relation to Paul but even in relation to Luther. The focus of the doctrine became the individual's relationship to God; justification became a decisive step on the road to salvation, a part of the *ordo salutis*. The pattern could vary somewhat, but generally followed these lines: first, awakening through the Law, then rebirth through faith, and with it justification, the acquitting judgment in the heavenly court, after that sanctification, and so on. Justification lost its all-encompassing character.

This last statement applies especially to pietism, even to those branches of the movement that gave a central place to the doctrine of justification. For the last several centuries it has been mainly pietists (or evangelicals) who have meaningfully retained the doctrine of justification as the essential element of the religious life, rather than merely clinging to a confessional standard which preserved denominational identity.

We should not overlook that even in its pietistic form, the doctrine of justification appears socially relevant. I am thinking especially of the revivalist and missionary movements. Of course, these are immensely complicated historical phenomena. One essential impetus was no doubt the personal experience of sin and grace, and concern for the salvation of every individual scattered around the world. This made preaching the gospel of salvation by faith for Christ's sake to the whole world a necessity. As one factor which prompted the growth of the world mission, the doctrine of justification has in recent centuries been a power at work, with other factors, breaking down old societies and creating something new in their place, contributing to sweeping changes both in the churches and in the world at large.

The revivalist movement and the evangelical world mission provide obvious examples that the doctrine of justification can have far-reaching social consequences, even as the result of strictly religious movements which do not have those consequences in view. But it is hard to deny, precisely on the basis of the experience of the missionary churches, that a Christianity which limits the doctrine of justification to personal religious experience and salvation is insufficient. Young Asian, African and Indian Christians today ask for guidance to overcome the problems which their societies and their churches confront. Like many Westerners, they have trouble finding the answers in pietistic-evangelical religiosity.

Missionaries brought not only the justifying gospel, but also Western patterns of behavior and a "ceremonial law" enacted by the traditions of the different churches. The questions are complicated. One example is polygamy. "The missionaries preach salvation by grace alone," said one African pastor, "but in practice that turns out to mean salvation by only one wife." What can we answer?

Because of this feeling of inadequacy which a one-sided view of the doctrine of justification sometimes prompts, it often happens, even among Lutherans, that some, more or less consciously, move the doctrine of justification into the background in order to bring other aspects of Christianity into the foreground, e.g., sanctification, social responsibility, the idea of the church, etc. But it is a mistake to attempt to redress a distortion in the presentation of the doctrine of justification by emphasizing other doctrines. The urgent task is rather to rediscover the social relevance and implications of the doctrine of justification. That does not mean a project in systematic theology, to deduce a social ethic from the doctrine of justification. The task is paradoxically both more limited and more comprehensive. We can formulate the question in this way: to what extent does the current practice of the church deny *de facto* the doctrine of justification, because it excludes certain groups of people from free access to God's grace in his church?

Racial discrimination provides an obvious and painful example. This problem is not something outside the task of preaching the gospel, something the church might attack as an addition to her central responsibilities. It belongs to the heart of the gospel message that God shows no partiality, and that for this reason neither can the congregations which gather in his name, wherever they may be. If the Christian churches in the United States, or elsewhere, had been able to resolve this problem in their midst, it would have meant far more than countless pious appeals for tolerance, far more than demonstrations; it would also have made it easier to find political solutions to the problems of racial discrimination.

The social implications of the doctrine of justification mean that believers must visibly express their unity in the fellowship of the Lord's table, as Paul so forcefully insists. Even Lutheran churches have continued in practice to disavow their confession that true preaching of the gospel and right administration of the sacraments are sufficient grounds for the unity of the church. Has the message of the doctrine of justification: "There is no distinction," had any impact on the social structure of the churches? Today, does not full acceptance into a suburban congregation presuppose a certain social standard and certain patterns of behavior? Do I go too far to suggest that middle class social standards and stereotyped forms of conversion experience and of religious expression have become the ceremonial and ritual law of our time?

I must rest content with raising questions of this sort to suggest points at which the doctrine of justification could have practical, tangible social consequences today. It would go far beyond the limits of an article and of my ability to attempt to sketch what the results would be if we really rediscovered the doctrine of justification, what the consequences would be if it really shaped church practice and Christian life styles.

That could be the task of a whole generation of theologians, not that biblical and systematic theology could solve the problem. No: here everything depends on what Christ's ministers preach from their pulpits and on how the faithful respond.

7

Promise and Fulfillment

BOTH IN EDIFYING LANGUAGE and in theological usage, it is common to talk about the fulfillment of promises. Therefore, it may come as something of a surprise to learn that this is not common biblical language.

The Pauline letters, Luke-Acts and Hebrews use the Greek word "promise" to signify God's commitment or pledge, but only Acts 13:33 uses the expression that God has "fulfilled" his promise. In the biblical perspective, God confirms his promises or he does what he has promised (Rom. 15:8; 4:21). We find the word "fulfillment" in other contexts: the fulfillment of the Law and the fulfillment of the Scriptures. A prophet's oracle can be fulfilled, and so also time. The words for promise and for fulfillment occur in similar contexts, but normally not in direct association with one another.

This observation becomes less striking when we consider ordinary usage in everyday conversation. We say that a prediction is fulfilled, but that a man keeps his promise, or that he does what he has promised. A promise is not a prediction. A prediction that two persons will marry is fulfilled when they have married.

But an engagement, the promise to enter into a marriage, is only confirmed at the wedding. The promise made in an engagement is kept only by living the married life. Using the terminology of modern semantics, a promise is a "performative utterance," a self-involving statement, or to use another phrase, a "self-obligating pledge." I commit myself to do all in my power to accomplish what I have promised, to move what I have pledged from the realm of possibility to that of reality. The person who makes a prediction which is not fulfilled has made a mistake. The person who breaks a promise is either untrustworthy or powerless.

We can make promises without using any specialized vocabulary. We can say quite simply: "I shall do that," or "I give you my word." To say: "He kept his promise," is to say no more than: "He kept his word." The Old Testament generally refers to God's promises as "the word of the Lord." Not even prophecies are understood simply as descriptive statements about future events; they are words of the Lord, with God's trustworthiness and power as guarantees, whether they threaten punishment or promise salvation. What we call a promise is a personal pledge rather than an objective statement. But it ought to be obvious that the personal self-involving character of a promise does not exclude an objective content. A person may commit himself to another by promising to do something for him or to give him something. The story of Abraham serves as a good example: God not only commits himself to Abraham, but he promises to give him the land.

We can apply this preliminary analysis of the promise concept to Paul's use of *epaggelia*, as the summary at the end of Romans makes clear: "For I tell you that Christ became a servant to the circumcised to show God's truthfulness, in order to confirm (*bebaiōsai*) the promises given to the Patriarchs, and in order that the Gentiles might glorify God for his mercy. As it is written, . . ." (Rom. 15:8–9). This statement introduces a series of quotations about praise and rejoicing among the Gentiles who shall hope in the root of Jesse.[1] The promises to which Paul refers are those which God made to the Patriarchs, Abraham, Isaac and Jacob, and to their descendants, the sons of Israel; these promises are a prominent feature of the book of Genesis. The promises are part of Israel's patrimony, as Paul writes in Rom. 9:4. By sending Christ as a servant to Israel, God has reaffirmed his commitment to do what he had promised; his fidelity to his promises proved his truthfulness. In Paul, promise clearly means more than mere prophetic prediction. Prophecy and fulfillment may be understood to mean that there is an exact correspondence between what is predicted and what actually happens. Christians have for centuries sought in this way to prove that Jesus was the Messiah predicted in Scripture. Such a view permitted Christians to restrict the role of Israel after the period during which the Old Testament was composed to transmitting the Scriptures which contain the messianic promises. When

---

1. The passages quoted are Ps. 18(17):49; Deut. 32:43 LXX; Ps. 117(116):1; Isa. 11:10 LXX.

those promises had been fulfilled, Israel's unique role had run its course. This perspective has been common among Christians since the time of Justin Martyr.[2] Paul's view of promise is different: by making promises, God has involved himself, he has committed himself to those to whom he gave his word.

The Greek perfect which Paul uses in Rom. 15:8 implies that Christ remains a servant to the circumcised. His work as a servant demonstrates that God has confirmed his promises to the fathers. Consequently, Paul does not believe that Jesus' earthly ministry fulfilled God's promises. On the contrary, Jesus' work reaffirmed the commitment of the God who is faithful. This does not mean that Christ's work has significance only for Israel. But Paul does not say that God has proved his trustworthiness to the Gentiles by confirming a promise made earlier. Rather, God has shown them mercy, and for that the Gentiles will praise his name. True, Scripture did foretell that the Gentiles would praise God, but God had not given them his promises. Israel receives the confirmation of prior promises; God shows mercy to the Gentiles "according to the Scriptures," but in a broader sense.

One would go too far to claim that Paul always maintains the distinction between confirmation of promise and the more general idea that events happen according to the Scriptures. In another context he can stress that the promise to Abraham is valid for believing Gentiles: "That is why it depends on faith, in order that the promise may rest on grace and be guaranteed (*einai bebaian*) to all his descendants—not only to the adherents of the Law but also to those who share the faith of Abraham" (Rom. 4:16). We might paraphrase Paul by saying that God gave his promises to the Jewish Patriarchs and to their descendants, but that they do include blessings for the Gentiles. Indeed, Christians live in the age of fulfillment, and whatever has been written has been written for them (cf. Rom. 4:23; 15:4; 1 Cor. 10-11). For this reason, we ought not to attempt to define too precisely our title: "Promise and fulfillment" in Paul. Rather, we consider the title a catchphrase which draws together an extensive and complex group of issues. Explicit statements about God's promises must of course receive greatest attention, but Paul's varied use of Scripture makes it impossible to set definite limits for our study.

---

2. An earlier version of this model is already present in Luke–Acts, see W. Kurz, "The Christological Proof from Prophecy in the Writings of Luke and Justin Martyr" (PhD diss., Yale, 1976). For the lexical data, see *TDNT*, 2:576-86.(Schniewind-Friedrich).

Paul is a biblical theologian. Judged by the standards of modern scientific exegesis, his exegesis often seems arbitrary. Exegetes tend to regard Paul's quotations from and allusions to Scripture as embellishments which support his thought without being integral to it. But Paul is not a systematic theologian. He is more like a good preacher, who can vary his use of the texts depending on the situation and purpose of the sermon. If the preacher is well prepared, then he has an exegetical basis to support his use of the text, even though he would make that basis explicit only when he has special reasons to do so. Paul has done his homework well. If we study his use of Scripture against the background of the hermeneutics of his day, we shall soon see both method and meaning emerge.

This does not imply that Paul uses some special exegetical method. The concept of promise and confirmation is important and has its own special function. But it constitutes only one of several possible models; we find patterns like prophecy and fulfillment, thematic statement and scriptural proof, typology and allegory. It is neither possible nor necessary to go into detail here. But we must make clear that Paul does not know the modern distinction between the meaning of a text as an ancient document within its original context and the meaning of a text for contemporary conditions and questions. For Paul, the Holy Scriptures are the words of God, of a God who through them speaks directly to the present. Conversely, present experience and events of the recent past belong within the Scriptural sphere. For Paul, there is an ongoing interplay between interpretation of Scripture and Christian existence in the present. Scripture helps to interpret events and experiences, and events and experiences help to reinterpret Scripture.[3]

At this point we should remark that our emphasis on Paul as biblical theologian does not mean that we should view him only against his Old Testament and Jewish background, ignoring his Hellenistic environment. "Jewish" by no means excludes "Hellenistic." By Paul's times, Hellenistic culture had influenced Judaism for centuries, both by making positive impressions and by causing negative reactions. The Old Testament is not simply one element of the historical background like others, but has a special status: it functions as Holy Scripture. The histories both of Judaism and of Christianity demonstrate that scriptural interpretation, like other cultural phenomena, is open to the influence of environment,

---

3. In this respect, Paul's use of Scripture agrees with Jewish Midrash. See J. Goldin's introduction to Shalom Spiegel, *The Last Trial* (New York: Pantheon, 1967); and cf. *The Crucified Messiah*, 144, 159f.

including that of changing spiritual climate. Time and place, the world in which one lives, help determine the questions addressed to Scripture, the method and presuppositions used for interpretation and, finally, the results of the exegesis itself. Theologians who make conscious use of contemporary science and philosophy still seek to establish a scriptural basis for that use. We could name as classic examples both Philo in Alexandria and Bultmann in Marburg. Contemporary thought and current problems influence less philosophical exegetes more unconsciously.

Paul uses hermeneutical techniques both from contemporary Hellenism and from Jewish and early Christian tradition. This is true even when his exegesis itself is novel and revolutionary. Paul's exegesis is original because interpretation of Scripture has become an integral part of his ministry as the apostle of Jesus Christ among the Gentiles.

2 Corinthians 1:20 states succinctly Paul's view on how God had acted to keep the promises he had made: "For all the promises of God find their Yes in him (Christ). That is why we utter the Amen through him, to the glory of God." As in Rom. 15:8, the theme is the ratification of his promises which God accomplishes in Christ. There is, however, a change of context from one discussion to the other. In Rom. 15:8, the context is Jesus' earthly ministry among his countrymen; in 2 Cor. 1:20, the context is the apostolic proclamation that Jesus is Lord.

In 2 Corinthians, one accusation among others which Paul tries to refute is that he vacillates; his Corinthians opponents used Paul's changed travel plans as an example of his unreliability. Paul answers by assuring the Corinthians that he has been honest and open in his dealings with them, motivated only by his concern for their well-being.[4] Paul wastes little time discussing the particulars of the case against him; in a transition characteristic of Paul which must have exasperated his opponents, he changes topics. From justifying his travel decisions he moves to a solemn affirmation of the truth of the gospel which he preaches. He emphatically rejects the charge that he hesitates between saying yes or no and offers in evidence the following statement: "For the Son of God, Jesus Christ, whom we preached among you, Silvanus and Timothy and I, was not Yes or No; but in him it is always Yes" (2 Cor. 1:19). The statement quoted above, that Christ is God's Yes to all his promises, follows immediately.

---

4. See 2 Cor. 1:12, 15–18; 1:23–2:11; 2:17; 4:1–6; 5:11–13. For a fuller analysis of 2 Cor. 1:15–22 and the context in 2 Cor. 1–7, see S. Olson, (Chapter IV, Appendix II.2, p. 38 above), Chapter 3, esp. 121–36.

The section 2 Cor. 1:19–22 refers to what the Corinthians have themselves experienced. The apostle and his co-workers had preached Christ as the confirmation of God's promises: those who accepted the proclaimed Christ gained a share in those promises. Those who were being baptized responded with their confession of faith, their "Amen!" The concrete situation was perhaps their response to questions of faith put to them before they received the sacrament itself. With their "Amen!" they have said "Yes!" to Christ, and thereby confessed their belief that God remains faithful to his promises. Christ, whom they received when they accepted Paul's preaching, is himself the agent of God to whom the Corinthians make this confession. God has confirmed the apostolic preaching and the Corinthian confession by sealing the Corinthians with the Holy Spirit, a gift which guarantees that God will fulfill all his promises. Clearly, Paul is not an observer who asserts that God's promises have already been fulfilled. Rather, he views his own work as an apostle of Christ as part of the process by which Christ ratifies that his promises are valid for those who believe in him.

In 2 Cor. 3:1–4:6 Paul discusses another aspect of his role. As minister of the new covenant, Paul parallels Moses, though Paul's ministry is of a higher order. The preaching of the gospel is not simply a report about the new covenant; as performative speech it effectively mediates the covenant promises. The existence of the church at Corinth not only testifies to the success of Paul's work, like a letter of recommendation; it even certifies the validity of the new covenant, as the stone tablets of the Law confirmed the validity of the old. The Spirit of the living God is the inscription on the Corinthians' hearts.[5] In 2 Corinthians 3 Paul speaks about the glory of the new covenant, and not directly about God's promises. But it is evident that here as in 2 Cor. 1:19–22 Paul views the preaching of the gospel as a mediation of God's promises, not as a logical demonstration that they have already been fulfilled.

2 Cor. 7:1 mentions God's promises explicitly: "Since we have these promises, beloved, let us cleanse ourselves from every defilement of body and spirit, and make holiness perfect in the fear of God." The promises

---

5. 2 Cor. 3:3 with allusions to Exod. 34:1; Jer. 31:33; Ezek. 36:26, etc. In his treatment of the ministry of the new covenant (2 Cor. 3:4—4:16), Paul draws not only upon Exod. 34 but also upon other passages, esp. Num. 12:7–8; Jer. 31:31–34; Gen. 1:26–27 and 1:3. For the exegetical traditions used, see now esp. M. R. D'Angelo, "Moses in Hebrews" (PhD diss., Yale, 1976). On 2 Cor. 3:1–3, see W. G. Baird, "Letters of Recommendation: A Study of II Cor. 3:1–3," *JBL* 80 (1961) 166–72.

to which Paul refers, he enumerates in the immediately preceding section, which consists of loose quotations of Old Testament passages. Paul begins the catena with the covenant promise: "I will live in them and move among them, and I will be their God and they shall be my people,"[6] and he concludes with a "democratized" form of the promise to David contained in Nathan's oracle: "And I will be a father to you, and you shall be my sons and daughters."[7]

2 Cor. 6:14–7:1 is a self-contained unit, whose content and form strikingly resemble material found in Jewish sectarian literature. But the pericope also makes sense in its present context. Other passages in 2 Corinthians show that Paul regards rejection of his gospel, and of himself, its proclaimer, as Satan's work: the devil hardens the hearts of the unbelievers (2 Cor. 4:3f.; cf. 11:3). In 2 Cor. 6:13–7:2 Paul has transformed a warning against social intercourse with outsiders into a warning against making common cause with unbelievers by adopting their attitude toward Paul and his gospel.[8] The promises call for sincere purity and sanctity, to be demonstrated in the mutual relations between the Apostle and his beloved Corinthians.

In his letter to the Romans, Paul introduces himself as: "A servant of Jesus Christ, called to be an apostle, set apart for the gospel of God which he promised beforehand through his prophets in the holy scriptures" (Rom. 1:1-2). Paul's special task is to preach to the Gentiles the saving message which God had promised to Israel (cf. Rom. 1:1-6). Here too Paul includes a reference to his own work when he speaks about the gospel and about God's promises. In Rom. 1:1-3 Paul states explicitly that it is the gospel itself, "the gospel of God, . . . the gospel concerning his Son," which God has promised. Paul continues in vv. 3-4 with a christological formula which summarizes the content of the gospel. The summary itself is based on a specific promise, the promise to David in Nathan's oracle in 2 Sam. 7:12-14, interpreted as referring to Christ. Jesus, descended from David according to the flesh, is the Messiah whom God promised David. In accordance with the spirit of holiness, he was designated Son of God at his resurrection from the dead, just as it was promised: "I shall be his father, and he shall be my son." It is quite likely that the christological

---

6. The quotation in 2 Cor. 6:16 conflates Ezek. 37:27 with Lev. 26:11., cf. Jer. 21:34f. etc. 2 Cor. 6:17 is based upon Isa. 52:11.

7. 2 Cor. 6:18, cf. 2 Sam. 7:14. Generalized ("democratized") versions of the same promise occur also in Jub—. 1:24-25; 2:19-20; and in Rev. 21:7.

8. On 2 Cor. 6:14–7:1 see also Chapter IV above.

formula in Rom. 1:3-4 results from primitive Christian exegesis of 2 Sam. 7.[9] Paul wants to assure the Romans that the gospel he was called to preach is the gospel which God had promised beforehand, the same gospel in which the Romans themselves have believed.

Paul refers to the gospel about Christ, as briefly summarized in the letter's opening statements, when he writes: "For I am not ashamed of the gospel: it is the power of God to salvation to everyone who has faith, to the Jew first and also to the Greek. For in it the righteousness of God is revealed through faith for faith" (Rom. 1:16-17). Paul takes this thematic statement up again in Rom. 3:21: "But now the righteousness of God has been manifested apart from Law, although the Law and the prophets bear witness to it." The reference to the Law and the prophets[10] implies general scriptural attestation, but the specific concept of God's fidelity to his promises may be implicit in what follows. According to Rom. 3:26, God put Christ Jesus forward as an expiation by his blood in order "to prove at the present time that he himself is righteous and that he justifies him who has faith in Jesus."

The expression "God's righteousness" (*dikaiosynē theou*) includes both the righteousness by which God himself is righteous and the righteousness by which God makes the believer righteous. That God shows himself righteous means in this context that he has kept his promise and thereby confirmed his fidelity. Neh. 9:8 expresses the same idea: "Thou hast fulfilled thy promise (*debarēka: thy words*), for thou art righteous." The statement in Rom. 3:5: "Our wickedness serves to show the justice of God," paraphrases Psalm 51:4: "(Against thee, thee only, have I sinned, . . .) so that thou art justified in thy sentence and blameless in thy judgment." The verse means that God keeps his word, and that he is

---

9. See, e.g., D. C. Duling, "The Promises to David and their Entry into Christianity," *NTS* 20 (1973/74) 55-77, esp. 72f. Cf. also my article "The Messiahship of Jesus in Paul," in *The Crucified Messiah*, 37-47. In Rom. 1:3-4 the phrases *kata sarka* (according to the flesh) and *kata pneuma hagiosynēs* (according to the Spirit of holiness) have been taken to refer to two natures or aspects of the person of Jesus. Most recent interpreters prefer to think of two contrasting spheres of existence (cf. 1 Tim. 3:16; 1 Pet. 3:18). But it may be better to interpret the phrases in analogy with Gal. 4:21ff. There the contrast *kata sarka/kata pneuma* is equivalent to the other contrast *kata sarka* and *di'epaggelias* (Gal. 4:29 and 4:23). In Rom. 1:3-4 Jesus is a descendant of David by virtue of his biological ancestry; he is the Son of God in accordance with the promise (cf. 2 Sam. 7:14) or, as Paul writes, "according to the Spirit of holiness." The Spirit of God inspired the prophets; it is also the life-giving Spirit of God who raised Jesus from the dead (cf. Rom. 8:11; 15:8-10).

10. Cf. Rom. 1:2, 17; 4:1-25; 9:32-33; 10:6ff.; 15:8-12.

vindicated. Rom. 3:25-26 probably has the same meaning. The passage is difficult to interpret for several reasons, among them the uncertainty about the meaning of the unusual word *paresis*. Several translations presuppose that it means tolerance; e.g., the RSV translates: "Because he had passed over former sins." Some interpreters believe that *paresis* is synonymous with the more common *aphesis* and means forgiveness. There is another possibility. The word *paresis* may refer to the dismissal of a criminal charge.[11] This last meaning fits the context of Rom. 3:25 well. The passage would then mean that God let Christ die to expiate the sins of men, so that he could justly dismiss the case against men, and thereby dispense with the just condemnation that men's sins had warranted. In this way God preserves his own righteousness, for justice prevails; he remains faithful to his word by declaring the person righteous who has faith in Jesus Christ (*ton ek pisteōs Iēsou*).

Paul develops more fully his thesis that a man is justified by faith apart from works of the Law in his discussion of the faith of Abraham (Rom. 4). Arguing from Gen. 15:6: "And he (Abraham) believed the Lord; and he reckoned it to him as righteousness," Paul presents Abraham as the father of and model for all believers. We cannot pause here to consider this passage at length, but it is worthwhile for our purposes to make a few observations. Using Abraham as an example, Paul is able to portray justifying faith as belief in God's promises. Even though he did have good reason to doubt, Abraham was firmly convinced that God had both the power and the will to do what he had promised (Rom. 4:17-22). Abraham believed in the God who gives life to the dead; Christians believe in the God who has raised the Lord Jesus from the dead (4:17, 24). Though they live in the time of fulfillment, Christians too believe in God's promises; they share Abraham's conviction that God remains faithful to his word. Paul interpreted the promise of the land (Gen. 15:7, 18, etc.) to mean that Abraham and his descendants would inherit the entire world (Rom. 4:13). At this point, Paul endorses an exegetical tradition from Jewish eschatology. But unlike his Jewish predecessors, Paul does not hope for political power in an earthly kingdom. For Paul, the promise guarantees participation in Christ's universal sovereignty. If the believers suffer with Christ, they will also be glorified with him and become heirs together with him (cf. Rom. 8:17-30).

---

11. Dionysius of Halicarnassus (VII, 37) distinguishes between dismissing a case (*paresis*) and temporarily delaying it. On Rom. 3:24-26, cf. also *The Crucified Messiah*, 154-57.

Finally, Paul stresses that Abraham's faith was reckoned to him as righteousness before he was circumcised; therefore the promise is not dependent on the Law. Paul maintains that if fulfillment of the Law is the condition for participation in the promise, then faith is nullified and the promise void (cf. esp. Rom. 4:14–15). Paul further spells out the relationship between Law and promise in Galatians; his statements there will serve us as a basis for further discussion.

Paul's conviction that the crucified Jesus is the Messiah underlies his understanding of God's promises, faith and the Law. At Damascus, Paul came to believe that God had raised Jesus from the dead, thereby vindicating his status as Messiah. In Romans, the concept of the messiahship of Jesus appears in texts like 1:2–4 and 15:8–12. In Galatians, a series of scriptural testimonies about Jesus the Messiah forms a partially concealed substructure for the whole argument concerning the promise and the Law.

In Gal. 3:16, Paul emphasizes that the scriptural promise to Abraham uses the singular form "his offspring" (*tō spermati autou*) rather than the plural form "thine offsprings" (*tois spermasin*). From this observation, he concludes that "thine offspring" refers to Christ and not to the Jewish people as a whole. His argument completely ignores the collective significance that both the Greek and Hebrew terms for seed, descendants or offspring (*sperma, zerá*) have. Scholars have often adduced this text as an example of Paul's use of arbitrary rabbinic exegesis. It is true that Paul's exegesis conforms to rabbinic hermeneutics both in method and in terminology. But the exegesis is not arbitrary. It depends on an exegetical inference by analogy. Just as "thine offspring" in the promise to David refers to the Messiah, so does "thine offspring" in the promise to Abraham.[12] Paul's allusion in Gal. 3:19 to Gen. 49:10, the Shiloh oracle, another text which tradition interpreted messianically, reinforces this

---

12. The messianic interpretation of "your offspring" in 2 Sam. 7:12ff. goes back to pre-Christian Judaism, see "Florilegium" from Qumran (4QFlor 1.10–11). A paraphrase of Gen. 49:10 combines this text with 2 Sam. 7:10 (4QPatrBl). Probably by analogy with 2 Sam. 7:12, rabbinic exegesis could also interpret Gen. 4:25 (*zēra 'aher*, RSV "another child") and Gen. 19:32 (*zera'*, "Offspring") messianically. The Messiah descends from Seth and, through Moab (Gen. Rab. 51:8; Ruth Rab. 7:15). Already the Septuagint seems to have taken the words about the woman's offspring in Gen. 3:15 to refer to the Messiah, since it uses the masculine form of the personal pronoun (*autos*). On Jewish and early Christian use of the Nathan oracle, see Duling (note 9) and D. Juel, *The Messiah and the Temple* (SBLDS 31, Missoula, MT: Scholars, 1977), Chapter IX; M. R. D'Angelo (note 9), Chapter II (on Heb. 1:5 and 3:1–6).

assertion. The enigmatic *s l h* was vocalized *še lô*, which made it possible to take the clause to mean "until the Messiah comes." Paul's paraphrase is freer still: "Till the offspring should come to whom the promise had been made."¹³

Gal. 3:14a already presupposes the messianic interpretation of "the offspring of Abraham": "that in Christ Jesus the blessing of Abraham might come upon the Gentiles." The text which underlies this verse is Gen. 22:18 (LXX), part of the report about God's oath to Abraham after he had proved faithful to God by demonstrating his willingness to sacrifice Isaac: "and in your offspring shall all the nations of the earth be blessed, because you have obeyed my voice." In Paul's paraphrase, the expression "the blessing of Abraham," derives from Gen. 28:4, and "in Christ Jesus" replaces "in your offspring."

It is possible that the promise in Gen. 22:18 is more generally the background for the Pauline expression "in Christ Jesus," especially when we find it in contexts like "the redemption which is in Christ Jesus" (Rom. 3:24), or "who has blessed us in Christ" (Eph. 1:3). In any case, it is clear that Gal. 3:14 refers to Gen. 22:18; further, it is likely that all of Gen. 22 underlies Paul's statements in Gal. 3:13-14 about Christ's vicarious death. Paul writes: "Christ redeemed us from the curse of the law, having become a curse for us," and then adds a free quotation of Deut. 21:23: "Cursed be everyone who hangs on a tree." This text perhaps served in early Jewish polemics as an argument against Christianity. Since Jesus died by hanging on the cross, he was cursed under the Law and could not possibly be the Messiah. According to Acts, the Jewish leaders handed Jesus over to the Gentiles who hanged him on a tree. Thus Jesus was apparently under the curse of Deuteronomy, but God vindicated him, raising him from the dead (Acts 5:30f.; 10:39f.).

In Gal. 3:13f. we encounter a more profound answer to the objection: Jesus did fall under the curse, when he suffered, though innocent, in the place of the guilty. This interpretation may depend on a combination of Deut. 21:23: "For a hanged man is accursed by God," with Gen. 22:13: "And behold, behind him was a ram, caught in a thicket by his

---

13. Gal. 3:19. In the translation of Dupont-Sommer, Vermes, the comment on Gen. 49:10 in 4QPatrBl reads: "Until the Messiah of Righteousness comes, the branch of David; for to him and to his seed has been given the covenant of the kingship of his people for everlasting generations." The Fragment Targum paraphrases: "Until the king Messiah comes, for the kingdom belongs to him." Targum Neofit has: "Until the time king Messiah shall come, whose is the kingship; to him shall all the kingdoms be subject" (trans. M. McNamara and M. Maher).

horns." Both later texts and Christian art show the ram bound to a tree. As the ram was offered as a sacrificial victim in place of Isaac, so Christ was hanged on a tree, incurring the curse of Deut. 21, in place of Israel which had incurred the curse of Deut. 27:26 by failing to observe the Law. Christ thus redeemed Israel, saving them from the condemnation which the curse entailed. This interpretation overcomes the offense of the crucified Messiah by assigning a positive significance to his death on the cross. Jesus is the Messiah (the Redeemer), not despite his humiliating death on a cross, but because of it. The redemption granted Israel in Christ means that the blessing of Abraham will come to the Gentiles, according to God's promise in Gen. 22:16-18.

The division in Gal. 3:13-14 between "us" and "the Gentiles" shows that Paul uses an early tradition, which must have had its origin in internal Jewish debate about the messiahship of Jesus. In the observation which concludes verse 14, Paul lets fall the distinction between Jews and Gentiles; he identifies the promised blessing with the Spirit, which "we" (now all Christians) have received through faith. In good rabbinic fashion, Paul applies existing exegetical traditions to new situations. In Gal. 3, Paul uses the exegetical argument that Jesus is Abraham's messianic offspring against the Judaizers in Galatia, who argued that the Law retained its validity even for Gentiles who came to believe in Christ.

Affirmations about the Spirit which the Galatians received when they came to believe constitute the framework of Paul's discussion of the promise to Abraham (Gal. 3:1-5; 4:6-7). Structure and content form a single whole, not two independent arguments for the Pauline doctrine of justification, one from experience and one from scripture. The exegetical argument proves the validity of what the Galatians experienced when they heard the gospel preached and received the Spirit, a gospel which imposed neither circumcision nor any of the other observances prescribed in the Law of Moses. With an emphatic "thus" (*kathōs*, just as) Paul emphasizes the analogy between what the Galatians have experienced and what Scripture says of Abraham, that he believed God and it was reckoned to him as righteousness (Gal. 3:6; Gen. 15:6). Using this analogy, Paul concludes that believers are the sons of Abraham (Gal. 3:7). That this is true not only for Jews but also for Gentiles, Paul deduces from the promise to Abraham: "In you shall all the nations be blessed" (Gal. 3:8-9; cf. Gen. 12:3, etc.).

The argument in Gal. 3:6-9 relates closely to the image of Abraham as the father of and model for believers which we find in Rom.

4. According to the exegetical tradition which underlies Gal. 3:13–19, however, it is Jesus alone who is the promised messianic offspring of Abraham. In Gal. 3:26–29 Paul weaves together these two strands of thought. In this passage, Paul interprets baptism with reference to Gen. 1:27; Christ, as the image of God, is the prototype of redeemed mankind: "There is neither Jew nor Greek, there is neither slave nor free, there is no 'male and female'[14]; for you are all one in Christ Jesus" (Gal. 3:28). Since in baptism the Gentiles have put on Christ, the offspring promised to Abraham, they too have become "Abraham's offspring, heirs according to promise." Returning to the beginning of his argument in 3:1–5, Paul is able to add an additional proof. God has accepted those to whom he has given the Spirit of his Son as sons and heirs (Gal. 4:6–7).

Thus, the Galatians' reception of the Spirit, and their experience of its work among them, proves that God has justified them, given them a share in the blessing of Abraham and made them his sons and heirs. Justification and the gift of the Spirit are inseparable from one another. Paul makes no distinction between the forensic and the pneumatic. The gift of the Spirit is evidentiary proof of God's acceptance. Paul views the Spirit which the believers have received as the first fruits of the glory which is coming, as a pledge, a down payment on the inheritance which God has promised.[15] He can therefore in Gal. 3:14b, 22 identify the content of the promise with the Holy Spirit.

In Galatians, the interpretation of the promises to Abraham as referring to Christ and to the Spirit serves to prove that Gentile believers are no longer under the Law. At this point, Paul goes beyond the early Christian tradition of which he has made use. If we read Gal. 3:13–14a in isolation, we learn that Christ, by his vicarious death, has redeemed Israel from the curse which had come upon them because they had transgressed the Law.[16] In its present context, however, the passage states that freedom from the curse is actually freedom from the Law itself. Paul asserts emphatically that because the righteous man obtains life through faith (Hab. 2:4), he cannot do so on the basis of works of the Law. As a consequence, no one is accepted as righteous "in the Law." Indeed, all those who rely on works of the Law stand under the curse on those who transgress the Law (Gal. 3:10–12). Furthermore, Paul affirms

---

14. I have translated "no 'male and female'" rather than "neither male nor female" in order to make the allusion to Gen. 1:27 clearer.

15. Cf. Rom. 8:23; 2 Cor. 1:22; 5:5; Eph. 1:13–14; 4:30.

16. Cf. Dan. 9:11; Deut. 27:15–26; 28:15–68. See also Chapter IX, esp. note 19.

that the promises which were solemnly ratified at the "covenant between the pieces" (Gen. 15) have a validity which is wholly independent of the Law which, according to rabbinic chronology, was given 430 years later. The Law is not a codicil which states conditions for the validity of the covenant. If it were, the promise would have been rendered void. But the covenant with Abraham was unconditional, given in the form of a gracious promise (Gal. 3:15–18).

Paul's insistence that the promise is independent of the Law does not lead him to compromise the integrity of the Law as a part of Scripture. As an interpreter of Scripture he must therefore uphold the Law; he must make its purpose clear. Paul's answer is that the Law was never intended to be more than a temporary expedient, valid only for the period from Moses to the Messiah (Gal. 3:19–20).[17] God did not give the Law to enable men to live justly and thereby to attain salvation, but rather to multiply sins and to make sin into transgression liable to punishment. Understood as serving this negative, merely preparatory function the Law does not stand in opposition to the promise but aims at its fulfillment in Christ (Gal. 3:21–29; cf. Rom. 5:20–21; 7:7–8:4). Any attempt to prolong the validity of Law, to extend into the period after Christ its use as a moral code which governs the fellowship of Jews and Gentiles within the church implies for Paul both a denial of faith and a misunderstanding of the Law (cf. Gal. 2:11–21).

Paul's doctrine of the Law deviates radically from the common Jewish view. Jewish scholars have properly emphasized that using Paul's statements about the Law to describe Pharisaic Judaism produces a completely misleading caricature. Many of them have often also asserted that Paul cannot have been familiar with the classical Jewish doctrine that the Torah is God's life-giving revelation.[18] This simply does not follow. Paul knows very well that Jews rejoice at their possession of the Law (Rom. 2:17–20). But he explicitly denies that the Law was able to make alive (Gal. 3:21). He does not give a historical, objective description of the Jewish view of the Law; that was clearly not his intention. On the contrary, in Gal. 3 and elsewhere he constructs a specifically Christian view of the Law and of its function as a part of Scripture. Methodologically,

---

17. On Gal. 3:20, see Chapter IX note 21.

18. See, e.g., H. J. Schoeps, 213–18 etc. At this point I am in basic agreement with E. P. Sanders: "It is the Gentile question and the exclusivism of Paul's soteriology which dethrone the law, not a misunderstanding of it or a view predetermined by his background" (497).

the argument agrees well with Jewish hermeneutic, but it persuades only when approached with specific Christian assumptions.

Paul's discussion of the relation between promise and Law centers on the presupposition that the crucified Jesus is the promised Messiah. It ought to be obvious that belief in a crucified Messiah was not a detail which could be inserted into the structure of Pharisaic Judaism without profoundly changing the structure itself. Zeal for the Law had made Paul a persecutor of the church. Belief in the crucified Messiah, hanged on a tree under the curse of the Law, must have appeared to Paul to be a shocking and offensive denial of the Law's validity. The appearance of the Risen Christ to him totally reversed his religious perspective and attitudes (cf. Phil. 3:4-11). Paul's Christian understanding of the Law's function differs from the Jewish view no more radically than his faith in the crucified and risen Jesus Christ differed from traditional Jewish messianic expectations. Both for the apostle and the persecutor, the Law and faith in Christ mutually exclude one another as ways to attain life.

As a Christian, Paul identifies the faith about which Scripture speaks with faith in Christ. While for the pious Jew faith and works of the Law were two sides of the same coin, for Paul the statement in Hab. 2:4: "The righteous shall live by his faith," excluded the statement in Lev. 18:5: "You shall therefore keep my statutes and my ordinances, by doing which a man shall live; I am the Lord." If the Law really had been able to make alive, then this contradiction would have been insoluble. Then Scripture would contain two incompatible doctrines of justification. By maintaining that the Law was not meant to give life, but to increase sin and the awareness of sin and by so doing to make grace pure grace, Paul manages to resolve the contradiction. In this way he can uncompromisingly maintain his Christian view of promise and yet retain the Law as a part of Scripture which had a legitimate, but limited, validity. Those who possess the Spirit are free of the Law, but at the same time it is precisely they who are able to fulfill the Law, in love and in freedom (Gal. 5:13-23; cf. Rom. 8:4-13; 13:8-10).

According to Paul, God has shown, by sending Jesus Christ and by his death and resurrection, that he remains faithful to his promises even though men have broken his Law. God has not yet fulfilled his promises, but he has confirmed that he will fulfill them. The believers have received a guarantee that they are God's children and coheirs with Christ, but they have not yet taken possession of their inheritance. The whole created order still groans in travail, Christians still suffer. The tension between

God's promises and empirical reality, a serious theological problem for Jews, remains. The belief in God's promises is still a belief that God has the power to do what he has promised. But the Christian view of present suffering and future hope has a very different character from that of Judaism. In the midst of suffering Christians experience not only the Spirit's helping presence but also union with the crucified Christ (cf. esp. Rom. 8:18–39). The future hope is first of all a hope to participate in the glory of the Risen Christ; little remains of the Jewish eschatological expectation that God will gather the dispersed sons of Israel, that he will reestablish them in the land, free from foreign domination. Although Paul has, by the standards of Jewish expectations, dissipated the promise's objective content, he nevertheless remains committed to the view that by his promises to the fathers God obligated himself to Israel. By his act in Christ Jesus, the servant to the circumcised, God confirmed his promises rather than voided them. This conviction leads naturally to the question of Paul's view of the future of Israel.

8

The Future of Israel

IN ONLY ONE OF the Pauline letters which have come down to us does Paul discuss thematically the future of Israel—in Romans 9-11, especially at the end of chapter 11. Two other texts, both difficult to interpret, may also deal with the topic, 1 Thess. 2:14-16 and 2 Cor. 3:16. 1 Thess. 2:14-16 contains one of the strongest anti-Jewish statements in the New Testament. After describing the Jews as persecutors, Paul continues: "But God's wrath has come upon them at last." Some have tried to reconcile this statement with the different view which Paul expresses in Romans 11 by assuming that the wrath of which Paul speaks in 1 Thessalonians is only provisional, that at the end God will show the Jews mercy. This interpretation is, however, syntactically implausible. Still, Paul can hardly mean that God's wrath has come upon the Jews forever; such a statement would completely contradict the carefully developed argument in Romans 11. Most likely is that in 1 Thess. 2:16 Paul is not discussing the future of Israel at all, but only a punishment which God has already meted out to the Jews.[1]

Some translations and some commentators make 2 Cor. 3:16 a general statement which refers to Israel: "But when a man turns to the Lord, the veil is removed."[2] It is more likely that here Paul is referring to Moses:

---

1. The relationship between 1 Thess. 2:14-16 and Rom. 11:24-26 has often been discussed. It was treated at length by N. Månsson, *Paulus och Judarna* (Stockholm: Diakonistyrelsen, 1947). B. A. Pearson has argued that the passage in 1 Thessalonians is an interpolation, dating from the time after the destruction of Jerusalem, in "1 Thessalonians 2:13-16: A Deutero-Pauline Interpolation," *HTR* 64 (1971) 79-94.

2. Recent Norwegian translations use the plural: "When they turn..." The French *Traduction oecumenique* is even more paraphrastic: "C'est seulement par la conversion

"But when he turns to the Lord the veil is removed." In 2 Cor. 3:16 Paul freely quotes Exod. 34:34, then in 2 Cor. 3:17-18 he both comments on the verse and applies it.[3] The whole section attempts to relate the ministries of the Old and New Covenants. Only in the light of Romans 11 can one find expressed in 2 Corinthians 3 hope for the conversion of Israel. Thus, we are free to concentrate on Romans 11 to develop Paul's view of the future of Israel.

Paul's statements about the future of Israel in Romans are well known. The literal sense is fairly clear. There ought to be no doubt that the statement in Romans 11:25, that all Israel will be saved, applies to the people of Israel, not to the church as a new Israel. The details of Paul's view about the future of Israel remain unclear; scholarly exegesis has made only limited progress in bringing them to light. For this reason I have chosen to concentrate on the question: what place does Paul's view of the future of Israel have in the composition of Romans and in the theology of Paul?

Many commentaries, monographs and articles discuss the interpretation of Romans 9-11.[4] In spite of the vastness of the literature, two aspects of these chapters have not received enough attention. Scholars rarely consider Paul seriously as an interpreter of Scripture. We still have no detailed investigation of Paul's use of the Old Testament in Romans 9-11, comparing it to other Christian and Jewish interpretations of the passages quoted, and examining their wording in textual tradition and in translations. The other aspect which scholars have neglected is a formal analysis of the composition and style of Romans 9-11. Here I hope to make a few useful suggestions.

---

au Seigneur que le voile tombe."

3. The *NEB* makes this explicit: "However, as Scripture says of Moses, 'whenever he turns to the Lord the veil is removed.'" The formal analogy with 2 Cor. 3:13-15 favors this interpretation:
  A. Text: "Moses put a cover over his face" (2 Cor. 3:13a, cf. Exod. 34:33 (35));
  B. Comments (2 Cor. 3:13b-15).
  A'. Text: "Whenever he turned to the Lord" etc. (2 Cor. 3:16, cf. Exod. 34:34);
  B'. Comments (2 Cor. 3:17-18).
Thus, in 2 Cor. 3:16-18 Moses is seen as a type for all who behold (or reflect?) the glory of the Lord with an uncovered face.

4. Two examples may suffice: J. Munck, *Christ and Israel*, and Chr. Müller, *Gottes Gerechtigkeit und Gottes Volk* (FRLANT 86; Göttingen: Vandenhoeck & Ruprucht, 1964). See also Käsemann, *An die Römer*.

The discussion of the place which chapters 9–11 occupy in the composition of the letter as a whole has oscillated between two poles. Some scholars regard Romans 9–11 as nothing more than a postscript to Paul's doctrinal presentation in chapters 1–8. Others completely reverse this view; they regard chapters 1–8 as a prelude to chapters 9–11. Only in these chapters does Paul state what he wanted most of all to make clear to the Christians of Rome. Strong arguments support both positions.

Although Romans 9–11 constitutes an internal unity, with its own beginning and conclusion, without any direct connection to the immediately preceding (6–8) or succeeding (12–13) sections, it nevertheless belongs to the development of the theme of the letter stated in 1:16: "I am not ashamed of the gospel: it is the power of God for salvation to every one who has faith, to the Jew first and also to the Greek." Paul discusses the relation between Jews and Gentiles in Romans 1–4, but only in chapters 9–11 does he make clear what he means by "to the Jew first." It is also true that the concluding sections of the letter presuppose what Paul has said in chapters 9–11 (cf. Rom. 15:7-13, 25-33). Thus, there is no need to choose between the two extreme points of view.

It is important to note that the argument in Romans does not move steadily forward in a straight line.[5] The best way to grasp the outline of the letter is to observe that a number of thematic formulations introduce various segments of the letter. Several times Paul introduces a theme and appears to leave it undeveloped only to take it up again later in the letter.[6] He raises objections to his own arguments and discusses them in sections which seem to interrupt the main line of argumentation but which enrich and deepen it. Thus, in the midst of Paul's description of the revelation of God's righteousness and of the salvation which results from it, we find discussions of the Christians' relation to sin, to the Law, and to the trials which beset them.[7] In chapters 9–11 Paul answers the questions he asked but did not answer in 3:1-5: What advantage has the Jew?

Will God be faithful to his promises to Israel? The peculiar construction explains why the letter has no fewer than three climactic conclusions, praising God for the completion of the work of salvation (Rom. 5:1-11; 8:31-39; 11:28-36; cf. also 15:7-13).

---

5. See Chapter V.

6. See, e.g., Rom. 3:1-8; 4:15-16; 5:20a.

7. Sin and the flesh: 6:1—7:6; 8:1-17; cf. 3:7-8; the Law: 7:5-8:4; cf. 3:20,31; 4:13-15; 5:20-21; tribulations, 8:17-39; cf. 5:3-4. See also Chapter V, Appendix I.

The doctrinal exposition of Romans is inserted into an epistolary framework. Most scholars, however, have failed to notice that epistolary style is somewhat more evident in chapters 9–11 than in 1:17–8:39. In Rom. 9:1 Paul addresses the recipients in very personal terms, asserting that he speaks the truth in Christ, that he does not lie.[8] The reference to the testimony of his conscience in the Holy Spirit corresponds to oath-like assurances in other sections where the epistolary character is clearer.[9] In 9:1–3 Paul tells the Romans what he feels, his sorrow for Israel, and in 10:1 he speaks of his intercession on behalf of the Israelites. In general, Paul confines his assurances to his recipients of his thanksgiving, his intercession and his joy to the opening sections of a letter.[10] In Romans 9:1ff. and 10:1ff. Paul's assertions concern a third party, his kinsmen by race, Israel.[11] The phrase in 10:2, "I bear them witness," is a common recommendation of a third party.[12] The same is true of the style in 9:4–5, where the characterization, "who are Israelites," is followed by three other relative clauses. Paul uses parallel, attributival relative clauses with the same antecedent much more frequently in recommendations than in other contexts.[13]

In large parts of Romans 9–11 we find the same argumentative style as in some earlier sections of the letter, with thematic formulations, rhetorical questions and dialog with an imaginary discussion partner, scriptural quotations, etc.[14] But Paul also addresses his audience as "brethren".[15] When he discloses the mystery of Israel's salvation, he uses

8. Cf. 2 Cor. 11:10; Gal. 1:20.

9. Cf. Rom. 1:8; 2 Cor. 1:12, 23; Phil. 1:8.

10. See, e.g., 1 Cor. 1:4–9; Phil. 1:3–11; Philemon 4–7. Even within the main body or at the conclusion of letters, such assertions occur in epistolary contexts, cultivating good relations between sender and recipients of the letter, e.g., 2 Cor. 1:23–24; 7:4, 16; Phil. 4:10, 14, 19; 1 Thess. 3:9–13.

11. The nearest analogy to this would be Col. 2:1–2. Except for Rom. 9:3, the expression "my kinsmen" (*syggeneis*) appears only in greetings; Rom. 16:7, 11, 21.

12. Cf. 2 Cor. 8:3; Col. 4:13.

13. See Rom. 16:3–4; 1 Cor. 4:17; Phil. 4:3; Philemon 9–13. I owe this observation to the complete survey of Pauline relative clauses by H. H. Lester, "Relative Clauses in the Pauline Homologoumena and Antilegomena" (PhD diss., Yale, 1973), Appendix I, 331–337. Passages like Rom. 4:16–18; 1 Cor. 15:1; 2 Cor. 1:10 are not fully analogous.

14. See Rom. 9:6–33; 10:4–21; 11:1–7, 11–12, 19–24; cf. 2:1–3:9; 3:27–31, etc.

15. Thus in the opening and closing sections of the letter, 1:13, 15; 15:14, 30; 16:17; also in the request in 12:1 and in 7:1, 4 and 8:12 but not in the more essay-like parts of the letter.

a conventional epistolary introduction to important information: *ou gar thelō hymas agnoein, adelphoi* (I want you to understand, brethren).[16] In 11:13 he addresses one part, probably the majority of his audience: "Now I am speaking to you, Gentiles." He continues by writing about his own vocation, as he otherwise does only in the epistolary opening and conclusion of the letter.[17] His praise of his own ministry recalls the thematic statement in 1:16 that he is not ashamed of the gospel.[18]

Attention to such details shows that in Romans 9–11 Paul not only unfolds the theological theme of the letter as a whole, but also addresses the epistolary situation more directly than in most parts of Romans 1–8. The content confirms that this is the case. Paul's statements in Romans 9–11 are closely related to what he says in Romans 15 about his approaching journey to Jerusalem. In chapter 11 Paul describes the Christians in Israel as the chosen remnant, and the Gentiles as wild branches grafted on to the cultivated olive tree; in chapter 15 Paul tells the Gentile Christians that they are indebted to the saints in Jerusalem because they have come to share in their spiritual blessings.[19] It is only in the light of Romans 9–11 that we are able to understand why Paul had worked so hard for the collection, and why it is so important to him that the Christians in Rome should support him with their intercessory prayers.[20]

The epistolary situation also explains the differences between Romans and Galatians, differences which are very obvious in Romans 9–11.[21] The tendency of the two letters at some points runs in opposite

---

16. Cf. Rom. 1:13; 1 Cor. 10:1; 12:1; 2 Cor. 1:8; 1 Thess. 4:13. On this and similar disclosure formulas, see J. L. White, "Body-opening Formulae in the Pauline Letter," *JBL* 89 (1970) esp. 91–92, and T. Y. Mullins, "Disclosure: A Literary Form in the New Testament," *NovT* 7 (1964) 44–50; and idem, "Formulas in the New Testament Epistles," *JBL* 91 (1972) 380–90.

17. See Rom. 1:1-6, 9–15; 15:15-21. In Rom. 10:15, 17 and 15:21 Paul applies passages from Isa. 52:7; 53:1 and 52:15 to the preachers of the gospel, including himself.

18. See Rom. 11:13f., and cf. also the concluding praise of Paul's ministry in 15:15-21. The concluding doxology in Rom. 11:33-36 corresponds to the opening thanksgiving in 1:8ff., and is followed by a request, introduced by *parakalō* (I appeal). For analogies, see 1 Cor. 1:9; 2 Cor. 9:15; Eph. 3:20-21; 1 Thess. 3:11-13.

19. See Rom. 11:5-6, 15-24 and 15:27. For a somewhat similar view, cf. Eph. 2:11-22.

20. See Rom. 15:22-31.

21. The differences are especially clear in the treatment of Abraham and his offspring in Rom. 4 and 9:5, 6-16 on the one hand and Gal. 3 and 4:21-31 on the other. There is also a striking difference between the whole tenor of the two letters and between the conclusion in Gal. 6:11-17 and Rom. 11:25-36 and 15:25-33. See my article

directions, contrary to one another. In Galatians Paul reacts passionately to opponents who claimed that his good reputation among the apostles and churches in Judea proved that in special circumstances Paul himself "preached circumcision," and that it was due to a missionary tactic of adaptation that he had refrained from telling the Galatians to observe the Law. Paul answers by maintaining that through a revelation of his Son, God himself had commissioned Paul to preach to the Gentiles and that Paul had everywhere and under all circumstances defended the gospel which he preached in Galatia, without any compromise.[22]

In Romans, by contrast, one of the purposes is to refute false rumors that Paul had rejected the Law and his own people. In this letter it is important for him to prove that he is neither an antinomian nor an apostate from Judaism. Paul may have had a special reason to stress this. In A.D. 49 a decree of the Emperor Claudius expelled Jews from Rome, Christian Jews among them. Many of them returned when Claudius was succeeded by Nero in 54, and shortly afterwards Paul wrote his letter to Rome.[23]

For many centuries, Romans 9–11 has been read as a Pauline theodicy. Since Augustine, the problem of predestination and free will has been at the center of discussion in the Western part of Christendom. The preoccupation with these problems has often obscured the realization that in Romans 9–11 Paul is dealing with God's faithfulness to his people Israel. The section does indeed contain statements that raise the issue of predestination and its relation to human responsibility; still, that issue is not Paul's principal concern. Only neglect of the formal composition and of the historical setting has allowed that issue to dominate the discussion of Romans 9–11.

Even interpreters who have recognized that the theme of Romans 9–11 is God's dealings with Israel in the past, the present, and the future have often failed to liberate themselves from the common dogmatic approach. As a result, the analysis of the composition is dominated by questions about God's election and Israel's responsibility. The following

---

"Der Name Israel: I. Zur Auslegung von Gal. 6, 16," *Judaica* 6 (1950) 161–70.

22. I presented an interpretation of Galatians along these lines in a paper, "Paul's letter to the Galatians: Epistolary Genre, Content, and Structure," delivered at the SBL Seminar on Paul, 1973. I hope some day to be able to return to the topic and to revise the paper for publication.

23. Several scholars have made this suggestion, see, e.g., G. Harder, "Der konkrete Anlass des Römerbriefes," *Theologia Viatorum* 6 (1954–58) 13–24.

summary sketches the most common outline of Paul's argument, which a number of commentaries reproduce with minor variations:

I. The failure of Israel is not incompatible with God's promises because in his absolute sovereignty God is free to elect and to reject whomever he wills. (Romans 9)

II. The 'hardening of the hearts' is due to the Jews' own guilt; their lack of faith is at fault. (Romans 10, or 9:30–10:21).[24]

III. The current situation, the Jewish rejection of Christ, will not last forever; at the end, God will show mercy and save all Israel (Romans 11).

According to an analysis of this type, Paul in Romans 9–11 gives three relatively independent answers to the problem raised by the Jews' negative reaction to Christ. The further question then is how the three answers relate to one another; are they really independent, or are they complementary to one another? Is Paul's argumentation an early example of theological dialectics, or has he committed the logical error of proving too much? Such questions have been discussed for a long time and many answers have been proposed. But, at least on the surface, Paul's argumentation is more straightforward than most of his commentators have assumed.[25] The argument appears to be more complicated than it really is, because Paul at various points in Romans 9–11, as in 1–8, refutes objections, clarifies presuppositions, or takes up special problems.

In Rom. 9:1–5 Paul affirms his own sorrow and the privileges of the Israelites. But at this point he does not explicitly state what the reason for his sorrow and anguish was. He immediately proceeds to formulate his thesis: "But it is not as though the word of God has failed" (Rom. 9:6). Paul has in mind God's promise to Israel; it is still valid. This is the sum and substance of what Paul wants to say in Romans 9–11. He begins his

---

24. Many commentators, including Käsemann, connect 9:30–33 with chapter 10 rather than with chapter 9. It is true that the passage introduces the 'theme' of chapter 10, but it is in itself a conclusion and transition. In 10:1 Paul makes a new start.

25. J. Munck, *Christ and Israel*, is one of the few exegetes who have succeeded in liberating themselves from the common way of treating the composition and the problems of Romans 9–11. His own interpretation could not carry conviction because of the strained effort to prove that Rom. 9:30–10:4 dealt with "The unbelief of the Jews toward Christ during his life on earth" (79–84), whereas chapter 10 shows "that God has not ceased to call Israel" (85) but "has done everything in order that the Jews may believe" (89ff.), as the preaching of the apostles has reached them everywhere (95–96).

exposition of the theme with two subordinate theses: "For not all who are descended from Israel belong to Israel," and "Not all are children of Abraham because they are his descendants" (Rom. 9:6b, 7a). Paul proves the second thesis by citing scriptural statements contrasting Isaac with Ishmael and Jacob with Esau. From these examples Paul deduces that God's promise and election matter, and not ancestry or merit. The specific application which Paul intends in the context is clear: even in the present God's word and promise stand firm; the relation between the chosen remnant and the rest of Israel is analogous to the relation between Isaac and Ishmael, Jacob and Esau (cf. Rom. 9:27–29; 11:1–6).

In the course of his argument, Paul develops the first of his sub-theses, that not all who are descended from Israel are "Israel" in the strict sense of the word. In Rom. 9:14, however, he inserts an objection: "Is there injustice on God's part?" The objection is caused by Paul's comment that the difference between Jacob and Esau was not due to anything they had done but merely to the call of God who chose one and rejected the other. A quotation from Mal. 1:2–3 supports this notion of God's selective choice: "Jacob I loved, but Esau I hated." For Paul, Scripture not only poses the problem but provides the solution, for God said to Moses: "I will have mercy on whom I will have mercy and will have compassion on whom I have compassion," and to Pharaoh: "For this purpose have I raised you up, for the very purpose of showing my power in you, so that my name may be proclaimed in all the earth" (Exod. 33:19; 9:16). Paul deduces from these verses that salvation does not depend on human will or effort but on the mercy of God, who has mercy upon whom he will and who hardens the heart of whom he will. We should not, however, overlook the context of the Exodus narrative. The hardening of Pharaoh's heart and his destruction served God's purpose, the liberation of Israel, a liberation which resulted in the proclamation of God's name to all the earth.

Paul's observations raise still other problems: "Why does he still find fault? Who can resist his will?" Paul answers with counter-questions based upon the biblical image of the potter and the clay.[26] Paul's reply does not even attempt a rational explanation. It simply recalls that God is God and man is a sinner who has no right to make complaints against his Creator.

---

26. See esp. Isa. 29:16; 45:9; Jer. 18:1–6.

In Rom. 9:21ff. Paul returns to his main theme. He applies the image of the potter and his products to the situation of his own time.[27] The syntax of verses 22-23 poses some problems. There is a conditional clause without any independent clause. The point becomes clear when we observe that Paul has modeled these verses after God's statement to Pharaoh quoted in verse 17. The schematic diagram below makes the correspondences clear.

Romans 9:17	Romans 9:22-24
For the very purpose of showing my power in you,	What if God, desiring to show his wrath and to make known his power,
I have raised you up	has endured with much patience the vessels[28] of wrath made for destruction,
so that my name may be proclaimed	in order to make known the riches of his glory for the vessels of mercy, which he has prepared beforehand for glory,
in all the earth	even us whom he has called not from the Jews only but also from the Gentiles?

Paul puts the non-believing Jews of his time on the same level not only with Ishmael and Esau, but also with Pharaoh and with Babylon (Jer. 50:25), the last-named a symbol for a world power hostile to God. The expression "the vessels of wrath" probably implies both that they are targets of God's wrath and that they are instruments of it. According to Paul, even though vessels of wrath are destined for destruction, they have a teleological function. Pharaoh's destruction not only demonstrated God's power, but also freed Israel, an act which made God's name known all over the earth. In the same way, Paul thinks, the hardening of the heart of a part of Israel will both show God's power and wrath and also demonstrate God's abundant goodness toward the vessels or tools of his mercy.

27. The Greek word *skeuos* is used for all kinds of utensils or tools, not only for hollow vessels. In Jer. 27:25 LXX (= 50:25 TM), *ta skeuē orgēs autou* refers to the tools or weapons (RSV) of God's wrath. Cf. also Isa. 10:5: "Ah, Assyria, the rod of my anger," and Isa. 13:5 (Hebrew and Symmachus).

28. Here the "vessels of wrath" seem to be instruments used by God, even if they are themselves under his wrath. The verb *ēnegken*, translated "has endured," can also mean "has carried forth." It probably alludes to Jer. 27(50):25 LXX: "The Lord has brought forth the tools of his anger." It corresponds to the phrase "I have raised you up" (*exēgeira se*) which Paul has himself introduced in the quotation from Exod. 9:16 in Rom. 9:17.

In an appended relative clause, Paul identifies the vessels of mercy with us, those whom God has called, "not from the Jews only, but also from the Gentiles." He adds passages from Hosea: "Those who were not my people I will call 'my people,' and her who was not beloved I will call 'my beloved.' And in the very place where it was said to them, 'You are not my people,' they will be called 'sons of the living God.'"[29] Paul understands these quotations as scriptural proof that the Gentiles also are to be called and to become God's people; yet it is not likely that he has overlooked that in Hosea the symbolic names refer to God's mercy toward the rejected Israel. As a rule, Paul reserves the designation "people of God" for Israel.[30] The relative clause inserted in Rom. 9:24 is probably to be understood as a parenthesis. The quotations from Hosea do not refer to the Gentiles alone, but to all the vessels of mercy. The phrases "in the place" and "there" (*ekei*) in 9:26 make better sense when we include the Israelites among those to whom it was said: "You are not my people," but who are to be called "sons of the living God." Possibly, Paul has Jerusalem in mind.[31] Throughout the letter, Paul represents God as the one who justifies the ungodly, who makes the dead to live, who loves his enemies and who in his mercy accepts those who are not his people as his people, indeed as his own children; this applies to Jews and to Gentiles without distinction (cf. Rom. 4:5, 17; 5:6-8; 11:15; 28-32).

The traditional interpretation of Romans 9:24-26 results from reading the verses in the light of later thought of the Gentile Christian church as God's new people. The context might at first seem to support that view; the promises to those who are to be called God's people precede quotations from Isaiah to the effect that only a remnant of Israel will find salvation (Isa. 10:22-23; 1:9). But the thought in 9:25-29 conforms to the introductory section 9:6-11. The promises for the future in Hosea correspond to the promises made at the births of Isaac and Jacob; they

---

29. Rom. 9:25-26, cf. Hos. 2:23; 2:1 and 1:10 (= 2:25; 2:1 and 1:10 TM).

30. See Rom. 11:1-2; 15:10. In the New Testament the term "God's people" is much less frequently transferred to the Christian church than one might assume from the reading of later Christian writings and modern scholarly literature, including my own book *Das Volk Gottes*. The transfer usually occurs in the form of quotations of biblical passages, see 2 Cor. 6:16; Heb. 4:9; 8:10; 1 Peter 2:9-10; Rev. 18:4; 21:3; cf. Titus 2:14.

31. Munck, *Christ and Israel*, 72-73, thinks that "there" (*ekei*) refers to Jerusalem as the place where the Gentile nations will be gathered and proclaimed the sons of the living God. On the basis of this interpretation, Munck (12-13) assumes that Paul expected his collection journey to open the way for Israel to the salvation determined by God.

confirm that God's promises remain valid. The prophecies from Isaiah about the remnant agree with the thesis that not everyone who descends from Israel is Israel. Not all Israel will be saved, but only a remnant, those among Israel who are vessels of mercy. Paul adds almost as an aside that there are Gentiles among these vessels of mercy, a point he develops later on (cf. 9:30–33; 10:18–20). Both the analogy to the Exodus story and the quotations from Hosea point ahead to the statements about the future of Israel in chapter 11. The hardening of hearts and God's wrath are the negative factors in a design whose principal purpose is the demonstration of God's mercy.

The question: "What are we then to say?" introduces a provisional summary of Paul's view of the contemporary situation (9:30). The Gentiles have embraced the righteousness that stems from faith whereas Israel (here the majority of Israel which does not belong to the remnant) has not reached the goal it pursued, namely righteousness based on Law (9:31). Israel tripped over the stumbling block, Christ. As in Galatians 3, traditional scriptural testimonies to Jesus as Messiah, here Isa. 8:14 and 28:16, are interpreted in the context of the Pauline contrast between faith and works. The crucified Messiah is a stumbling block, an offense to those who want to gain righteousness by their own efforts, while at the same time he is the cornerstone about whom the prophet spoke: "He who believes in him will not be put to shame."[32]

The summary in Rom. 9:30–33 functions as a transition to the following section of the letter. Yet, Paul makes a new start in 10:1–3, reaffirming his concern for his compatriots. Only at this point does Paul explain what prompts the sorrow and anguish about which he spoke in 9:1–3.[33] The Jews have a genuine zeal for God, but they lack understanding. Their attempt to establish their own righteousness has prevented them from subordinating themselves to the righteousness of God revealed in Christ. Here Paul inserts a new, final explanation of the relation between the Mosaic Law and Christ: "For Christ is the end (*telos*) of the Law, that every one who has faith may be justified." Paul supports this thesis by contrasting

---

32. Rom. 8:33 is a conflation of Isa. 8:14 and 28:16. The same combination recurs in 1 Peter 2:6–8, where also Ps. 118:22 is alluded to. Paul is likely to draw on traditional testimonies to the crucified Jesus as the Messiah. In Rom. 10:11–13 he uses Isa. 28:16, in combination with Joel 2:32 (3:5 TM), to interpret Deut. 30:14 and to prove that the promise pertains to all who believe, without distinction between Jew and Greek.

33. On epistolary expressions of joy, grief, and similar moods (or dispositions), see R. D. Webber, "The Concept of Rejoicing in Paul" (PhD diss., Yale, 1970), 96–156.

Lev. 18:5 with a quotation of Deut. 30:12-14 adapted and amplified by additions from other passages (Deut. 9:4; Psalm 106 (107):26 LXX). In the context of Deuteronomy, the word that is near is the commandment of the (deuteronomic) Law (Deut. 30:11). Paul, however, attributes the quotation to the personified righteousness by faith and takes it to refer to Christ and to the "word of faith" which the apostles proclaim.

The reinterpretation is not quite as amazing as it appears to be. In Judaism, the Torah was identified with Wisdom, and in early Christianity statements about Wisdom were often applied to Christ.[34] Paul is possibly drawing upon some traditional Christian interpretation. But there is also another possibility. In order to come to terms with what appeared to him as two contradictory scriptural passages, Lev. 18:5 and Deut. 30:11ff., Paul introduces a distinction between two concepts of the Law. Lev. 18:5, which states that the man who performs the commandments shall live by them, represents the Law (*nomos*) in the narrow sense, the commandments and prohibitions revealed at Sinai, in isolation from the encompassing divine economy. The statement in Deuteronomy about the commandment that is not too hard, not far off but near by, Paul, by contrast, takes to refer to the entire Law, the Law that together with the prophets bears witness to the righteousness of God (cf. Rom. 3:21).

In any case, Rom. 10:4-17 provides an excellent example of the process by which scriptural passages and present events reciprocally influence one another's interpretation. Combining Deut. 30:14 with quotations from Isa. 28:16 (already quoted in Rom. 9:33b), Joel 3:5 (2:32) and Isa. 52:7 and 53:1, Paul draws a picture of Christian preaching, faith, and confession; he also finds a reference to the failure of some hearers to obey the gospel they have heard. The whole section demonstrates how closely Paul's view of Israel is interrelated with his doctrines of justification and of the Law, with his Christology, with his conviction that "there is no distinction between Jews and Greek," and with his own mission and preaching of the gospel. But it is neither possible nor necessary to elaborate on those themes here.

For our purpose it is important to recognize that Romans 10 is not a part of Paul's answer to the question of whether or not God had repudiated his promises to Israel. The chapter is a delayed explanation of the factors which caused him to raise that question. From 10:4 onward Paul

---

34. See esp. Prov. 8; Sir. 24; Baruch 3:24-4:4; and John 1:1ff.; Col. 1:15ff.; Heb. 1:2-3. Baruch 3:29-30, like Rom. 10:6ff. makes use of Deut. 30:12f. See, e.g., J. Suggs, "The Word is near to you," in Farmer, 289-312.

digresses from his main line of argumentation, though at the conclusion of the section he returns to it. At the end of chapter 10 Paul repeats the same point he made at the end of chapter 9: the Gentiles have found the God they did not seek, while Israel has proven to be a disobedient and recalcitrant people. Paul proves this point with quotations from Deut. 32:21 and Isa. 65:1-2. Later on we shall see that the first of these quotations has a special significance for Paul: "I will make you jealous of those who are not a nation; with a foolish nation I will make you angry."[35]

After this analysis of the existing state of affairs, Paul returns in 11:1 to his main theme. The question implicit from the beginning of chapter 9 emerges in a pointed form: "Has God rejected his people?" Paul answers immediately with an emphatic denial. He first mentions that he himself, the Apostle to the Gentiles, is an Israelite, a descendant of Abraham, of the tribe of Benjamin. Once more it becomes clear that Paul does not interpret Scripture and history with scholarly detachment; he is vitally involved in what he is writing about. In 11:2 Paul presents a new formulation of his main thesis that God's word has not failed: "God has not rejected his people whom he foreknew."[36] Referring to an analogous situation at the time of Elijah, Paul points out that due to God's merciful choice and not on the basis of works, a remnant of Israel remains faithful (11:2-6).

Whereas in 9:27-29 Paul emphasized that only a remnant remained, in 11:5-7 he stresses that a remnant does in fact remain. Thus he has reached the conclusion of the line of argumentation introduced in 9:6. As Isaac, not Ishmael, as Jacob, not Esau, as the seven thousand at the time of Elijah, not the many who bowed the knee to Baal, so the Jews who believe in Christ, not the rest, are the children of the promise, chosen by grace. The remnant that remains proves to Paul that God has not rejected his people and that his word stands firm. At the same time it becomes clear that the hardening of the hearts of the large part of the people and their disobedience is not incompatible with God's promises; on the contrary,

---

35. See Rom. 10:19 and 11:11. Deut. 32:21 alludes to a hostile nation; Paul takes the saying to refer to Christian Gentiles. But both in Deut. 32 and in Romans 9–11 God's wrath and mercy toward his disobedient people are at issue. Already Munck, *Christ and Israel*, 90, stressed that "chapter 11 clearly resumes the thread of 9:29," and that the intervening passage (9:30—10:21), "is not some incidental parenthesis, but a necessary and basic explanation." That is also my conclusion in spite of disagreements with Munck's exegesis (see notes 25 and 31).

36. Even here Paul alludes to scriptural passages, esp. Ps. 94:14 and 1 Sam. 12:22; cf. also Deut. 31:6; Josh. 1:5; Jer. 31:37.

the Scriptures themselves show that the number of the faithful is small. Paul reinforces this point in 11:8–10 by citing a series of quotations about the hardening of hearts.[37]

The question which remains concerns "the others," those who do not belong to the remnant: "Have they stumbled so as to fall?" (11:21). Again Paul responds with an emphatic denial: "By no means! But through their trespass salvation has come to the Gentiles, so as to make Israel jealous." Just as the hardening of Pharaoh's heart led to salvation for the Israelites, so the hardening of the hearts of the Israelites who rejected the gospel has led to salvation for the Gentiles. We should not overstress the correlation of cause and effect. We do not need to consider Jewish rejection of the gospel a necessary condition for its acceptance by the Gentiles. Paul interprets what has actually happened. The crucified Messiah became an offense to Jews but brought salvation to the Gentiles.[38] The Gentiles had become participants in the messianic salvation at a time and in a way contrary to all expectations, not as a consequence of the liberation of Israel, but before Israel had herself accepted her salvation. For Paul, however, this does not mean that God's promise of salvation is taken from Israel and given to the Gentiles, but only that the order of events has been reversed.

Using the quotation from Deut. 32:21 cited in 10:19, Paul argues that the purpose of what has happened is to make the Israelites jealous. He believes that when the Jews realize that through the gospel God has reconciled the Gentiles to himself they too will want to share in its richness. Paul goes so far as to interpret his own ministry to the Gentiles in the light of his hope for the Jews: "I magnify my ministry in order to make my fellow Jews (lit. "my flesh") jealous, and thus save some of them" (11:13–14). Paul's hope for the future of Israel (which he goes on to state with greater clarity) coincides with the aim of his own work.

The reference to Paul's ministry occurs between two analogous syllogisms (11:12, 15). The trespass of the Israelites was an evil which had positive consequences for the Gentiles; how much more must their complete obedience, their "full inclusion" (*plērōma*) have positive consequences! (v. 12). The conclusion from the minor is restated in verse 15: "For if their rejection meant reconciliation of the world, what will

---

37. The quotations in Rom. 11:8–10 are taken from Deut. 29:4 (29:3 TM) combined with Isa. 29:10 (cf. 6:9–10) and from Ps. 69:23–24. Both Psalm 69 and Isaiah 29 appear often in the New Testament, e.g., Matt. 15:8f.; 27:40; Rom. 9:20; 15:3.

38. Rom. 9:30–33; 10:8–21; cf. 1 Cor. 1:23–25.

their acceptance mean but life from the dead?" One can question the logical cogency of these syllogisms, but one should recognize that Paul draws upon well-established Jewish tradition when he asserts that Israel's restoration will have worldwide consequences. Paul retains this idea in a christianized form, and argues for it by appealing to the positive consequences of the Jews' rejection of Christ. He may also presuppose the idea that God's mercy has in general a greater and more widespread effect than his judgment.[39]

Paul sees an alteration in Israel's relation to Christ as more than a hypothetical possibility. He thinks that it will occur eventually and says so, using figurative language: "If the dough offered as first fruits is holy, so is the whole lump; and if the root is holy, so are the branches" (11:16). The "lump" and the "branches" must refer to Israel, including "the others" as well as the chosen remnant. The argument presupposes that what is holy, consecrated to God, cannot permanently remain opposed to Christ or separated from him. It is less clear to what the metaphors "first fruits" and "root" refer, to Israel's forefathers or to the remnant. In the first case, the statement would say much the same thing as Rom. 11:28f.: "They are beloved for the sake of their forefathers. For the gifts and the call of God are irrevocable." In the second case the statement would recall the beginning of chapter 11: the presence of a remnant proves that God has not rejected his people but remains committed to the promise granted to the whole nation. This would correspond to the view found both in the Old Testament and in Jewish tradition that the remnant represents the whole people of Israel. It does not make much difference which interpretation we choose. In either case, God's election and promise is constitutive for the holiness of Israel. Possibly Paul had both ideas in mind. The metaphor of first fruits is more appropriate to the remnant, those Jews who are already consecrated to Christ in faith. The whole nation is consecrated through them, as the new harvest is consecrated through the offering of the first loaves made from the newly gathered wheat.[40] The metaphor of the root seems rather to suggest the patriarchs, from whom all Israelites descend.

---

39. Cf. Exod. 20:5-6; 34:6-7, etc., and also Rom. 5:15, as well as the rabbinic doctrine that the measure of mercy is greater than the measure of judgment.

40. Cf. the idea that the first converts are the first fruits of their provinces, Rom. 16:5; 1 Cor. 16:5. The Law commanding the offering of the first loaf appears in Num. 15:17-21.

In the following section Paul elaborates the image of the root and the branches (11:17-24). He portrays the remnant as branches which the gardener left in place when he pruned the olive tree and cut off other branches. The Gentiles are branches from wild olive trees which God has grafted onto the domesticated olive tree. Paul here uses the rhetorical technique of addressing directly the individual Gentile Christian, whom he warns against self-sufficiency and against boasting at the expense of the unbelieving Jews. He turns God's impartiality and sovereign freedom against Christians of Gentile origin. Though the language is figurative, Paul obviously is speaking about Israel, Gentile Christians, and Jews who have rejected Christ.[41] Paul portrays unbelieving Jews as branches broken off, but he stresses that their exclusion was a result of their lack of faith, that it was not definitive: "God has the power to graft them in again" (11:23). That means, in non-figurative terms, that God has given the Israelites his promises and that he is able to do what he has said. Paul even turns the warning addressed to Gentile Christians into a supporting argument by drawing a conclusion from the greater to the lesser: if God in Christ has accepted Gentiles, to whom he had not committed himself, how much more will he welcome the Jews, who received his promises (11:24).[42]

The question concerning "the others" raised in 11:11 receives its final answer in 11:25-26: "A hardening has come upon part of Israel, until the full number of the Gentiles come in, and so (*houtōs*, in this manner) all Israel will be saved." Paul introduces this statement as the disclosure of a revealed mystery. Yet the solution draws the conclusion of the preceding arguments.[43] We should probably not think of a sudden, unmediated revelation granted to Paul but rather of a mystery hidden in Scripture until its explanation was unveiled.[44] It is easy to find biblical passages which announce salvation for Israel.[45] The mystery which Paul reveals

---

41. Therefore, it does not matter whether or not grafting of wild branches into the domesticated olive tree was ever practiced. On Israel as an olive tree, see Isa. 11:16.

42. Paul still uses metaphors, although branches that have been pruned away are not grafted back onto the tree at a later stage.

43. See esp. 11:11-12, 15-16, 23-24.

44. Thus, the term "mystery" seems to refer to a mystery that is present in Scripture but only known by inspired interpreters. The term is used in a similar way in Eph. 5:32 and in the Dead Sea Scrolls. See, e.g., R. E. Brown, *The Semitic Background of the Term 'Mystery' in the New Testament* (Philadelphia: Fortress, 1968).

45. Cf. the rabbinic view that all Israel has a part in the world to come, m. Sanh. 10.

is not Israel's ultimate salvation, but rather the way in which Israel will achieve that ultimate salvation. Salvation will come to Israel indirectly, after a period during which the hearts of many Israelites will be hardened. The Gentiles will participate in this salvation first. Paul's view that Gentile Christians will make the Israelites eager to participate in Christ reemerges,[46] as his comment on the mystery he has just revealed makes clear: "Just as you were once disobedient to God but now have received mercy because of their disobedience, so they have now been disobedient in order that by the mercy shown to you they may also receive mercy" (Rom. 11:30-31).

The context makes clear that "all Israel" refers both to the remnant and to "the others." Paul does not affirm that every individual Israelite will attain salvation, but that God will grant salvation to both parts of his people, to those who have rejected Christ as well as to those who have believed in him. To support his view Paul quotes the Septuagintal form of Isa. 59:20-21, adding a line, "When I shall have taken away their sins," from Isa. 27:9.[47] In this way, Paul ties together God's covenant with Israel in the last days with the remission of sin, probably alluding to Jeremiah 31. Paul identifies the people's disobedience with their rejection of Christ, and looks forward to the disappearance of this disbelief, and to the forgiveness which God will grant.

Even though the order in Paul's argument as a whole is clear, it is hard to organize its component parts into a coherent picture of the future. From the quotation in Rom. 11:26-27, one could assume that Christ himself is going to save Israel when he appears at the end of days, but no other passage suggests such a view. Paul hopes that his own work among the Gentiles will lead to the conversion of some Jews, and he connects salvation for Israel with what he calls the coming in of "the full number of the Gentiles." Unfortunately, what Paul means by this phrase is far from clear. The word *plērōma* (fullness, "full number") has a positive value but it can have various nuances of meaning. One possible paraphrase of Rom. 11:25b would be: "Until the Gentiles enter the kingdom of God in the

46. See the quotation from, and allusion to, Deut. 32:21 in Rom. 10:19 and 11:11-14.

47. In Rom. 11:26-27, Paul connects the first clause in Isa. 59:21 with the preceding verse. For Paul, Isa. 59:21 states that the Deliverer will come from Zion, while the Septuagint has "for the sake of Zion" and the Hebrew text "to Zion." Does Paul expect that at his parousia Jesus will appear "from Zion"? Or does he make use of a form of the text that had been adapted in order to prove that Jesus, who was crucified in Jerusalem, is the Deliverer?

full number that God has decreed from the beginning." Another possibility is: "Until the salvation of the Gentiles occurs to its full extent."[48] However we translate the clause, it seems clear that Paul believed that his mission and that of others had succeeded in fulfilling its condition in the Eastern provinces of the Roman Empire, from Jerusalem to the shores of the Adriatic.[49] Paul's vision extended only to the lands around the Mediterranean. What he actually had in mind in speaking about the *plērōma* (fullness) of the Gentiles may therefore have been the successful completion of his mission to Spain.[50]

It is even harder to specify what specific consequences Paul expects to result from the "full inclusion" (*plērōma*) or the "acceptance" (*proslēmpsis*) of the Israelites. In Rom. 11:12 he speaks in general terms of "riches;" in 11:15 he states that the result will be life from the dead. Does Paul expect that the resurrection of the dead will follow upon God's acceptance of Israel, or does he speak figuratively about new life for the whole world? Since the entry of the "full number" of Gentiles is to precede salvation for all Israel, it is unlikely that Paul looked forward to a great missionary epoch in which the gospel message would spread to new, unknown areas. It is somewhat more likely that he expected the small congregations, which he and others had founded, to expand to include the entire regions they represented, just as the division between the faithful remnant and the rest of Israel would be overcome. Probably, the contrast between the "reconciliation of the world," that followed upon the (temporary) rejection of those Jews who failed to believe in Christ and the "life from the dead," which will follow upon their acceptance by God, is qualitative rather than quantitative. Whatever else Paul has in mind, he stresses that the enrichment of the whole world, which is to follow upon the restoration of Israel, is going to be an act of the God who makes the dead alive.

---

48. The latter translation, mainly based upon the analogy with Rom. 11:12, means the "full inclusion" of the Israelites rather than their "full number." Munck, *Christ and Israel*, 132, argues for the translation: "until the fullness of the Gentiles begins." His argument that Paul does not think in terms of predestination of a specific number to be obtained is more convincing than the proposed translation.

49. See Rom. 15:19-23.

50. This is argued in a forthcoming paper by Roger D. Aus, on the basis of numerous passages in the Old Testament and rabbinic writings which refer to Spain as the most distant land from which Gentiles will make pilgrimage to Jerusalem. For the more general idea, cf. Mark 13:10; Matt. 24:14.

Paul does not draw an exact map of future events, neither in Romans 9–11 nor elsewhere. Attempts to coordinate what Paul writes in Romans 11 with other eschatological statements in the Pauline letters do not succeed in constructing a unified Pauline doctrine about the last things.[51] It is harder still to reconcile Paul's view with that of other New Testament writings, e.g., Revelation. Paul has no interest in giving a detailed description of what is going to happen at the end of time. He does not speak abstractly about the distant future but concretely about a course of events already in progress, of which his own work as apostle to the Gentiles is an important part. Certain aspects of Paul's eschatology emerge clearly, but Paul does not integrate them into any eschatological dogmatic. Like Paul's theology in general, his statements about the eschatological future vary with the circumstances and the purpose of each letter. He writes to his congregations about the future in order to guide, to warn or to comfort them. Nevertheless, Paul's fundamental theological outlook underlies these varying formulations.

The initial thesis in Rom. 9:6 formulates Paul's fundamental conviction that God's word has not failed; that God has not rejected his people. This conviction provides the basis for what Paul says in Romans 9–11 about the future of Israel, about Christ, and about the Gentiles. But to a higher degree than the text reveals directly, what Paul says flows from his faith in Jesus Christ. Paul says more clearly in other places that God's promises to Israel concern Christ, but that presupposition underlies the discussion in Romans 9–11 as well.[52] Paul applies scriptural quotations about Israel's disobedience, the hardening of the Israelites' hearts and their temporary rejection to their refusal to accept Christ. He identifies the faithful remnant with those Jews who do believe in Christ. That God in the last days will again show mercy and restore his disobedient people to favor means that he has promised that all Israel will share in the salvation Christ alone makes available. Paul does not discuss what else the future holds for Israel, because for him Israel's relation to Christ is the decisive problem.

---

51. Cf. J. G. Gager, Jr., "Functional Diversity in Paul's Use of End-Time Language," *JBL* 89 (1970) 325–37. The 'functional diversity' extends to passages like 1 Cor. 15:22–28 and 1 Thess. 4:13—5:11.

52. Therefore, I cannot give as much weight as Stendahl (4) does to the observation that Paul does not use the name of Jesus Christ in Rom. 10:17—11:36. Cf. also his article "In No Other Name," in *Christian Witness and the Jewish People* (Geneva: Lutheran World Federation, 1976).

Paul does not spiritualize the Old Testament as radically as some of his hellenistic Jewish contemporaries did. Although Paul's Christology completely determines his scriptural interpretation and his view of Israel's future, he continues to insist that the Scriptures *do* speak about Israel and about their future. Paul knows from his own experience that the Gentiles have proved more willing to accept the gospel than the Jews. This phenomenon leads naturally to the question, has God rejected his people? An affirmative answer is impossible for Paul, not only because he is himself a Jew, but also because the Scriptures contain God's pledge to Israel. Christ's work as a servant to Israel confirmed God's promises, and God could not be God if he did not remain faithful to his word.

Paul's scheme, which provides the framework for his exegesis, follows the workings of God's mercy from Israel to the Gentiles, and from the Gentiles back to Israel, for the ultimate good of all. Paul, in a sense anticipating Hegel and Marx, sketches a dialectic of history, with thesis, antithesis and synthesis. But Paul is not interested in the orderly progression of history; he seeks to come to grips with God's sovereign freedom, a freedom which extends even to his treatment of those whom he has chosen. For all, Jews and Gentiles alike, the salvation made available in Christ comes as undeserved mercy, as clemency toward the disobedient, as justification of the ungodly. We could say that Romans 9–11 illustrates Paul's doctrine of justification by faith. However, we express ourselves more correctly when we say that from the beginning Paul's view of the relation of Israel to the Gentiles profoundly shaped his doctrine of justification. Only later, especially in the thought of Augustine and of Luther, did the doctrine of justification become fundamentally important apart from the problem of Israel and the Gentiles.[53]

Paul completes his description of Israel's future with a doxology which praises God's inscrutable wisdom (Rom. 11:33–36). Paul largely models the style and the wording after Old Testament prototypes.[54] But the closing declaration of God's omnipotence, "For from him and through him and to him are all things," follows Greek patterns. In philosophical contexts similar formulations refer to the one "ground of being" or to nature. Paul strips the formula of its pantheistic overtones. He applies it to God's sovereign action in history, from the creation to the consummation, to the omnipotence of God's love. The combination of Jewish

---

53. See Chapter VI, the last section, pp. 116–21.
54. See Isa. 41:3; Job 15:8; 41:3 (TM 41:3), etc.

and Greek stylistic elements both here and elsewhere in Romans is not accidental. Paul's faith in Christ has provided him with a new answer to a question which inescapably confronted Judaism amidst the universalism of the Hellenistic world: how could the one God be at the same time the God of the whole world and the God of Israel? Paul's answer is that God is not God for the Jews only but for the Gentiles as well.[55] There is no difference; all have sinned, all have fallen short of the glory of God, and all are justified in the same way, by accepting the unmerited offer of salvation which God gives through faith in Jesus Christ. But Christ, though Lord of all, became incarnate as an Israelite; God, though God of all, chose Israel to be his people, and by his word committed himself to Israel. In the future, God will keep the promises he has made. God's ways are unsearchable, but he is absolutely trustworthy.

The doxology in Rom. 11:33–36 serves to conclude not only the discussion in Romans 9–11, but the exposition in chapters 1–11 as a whole, both in form and in content. It is not only God's way of dealing with Israel which is miraculous, which surpasses man's understanding. That no man holds God in his debt, so that what he receives from God is never merited, is a fundamental idea which underlies all of Romans. Hardest for men to understand is that God uses man's disobedience and sinfulness to further his ultimate purpose, to show mercy to those who do not deserve it.[56]

When Paul calls God's judgments unsearchable and his ways inscrutable, he does not mean to imply that man can know nothing about God's way of acting. Paul has himself sought to understand exactly how God has acted with Israel and with the Gentiles, and how he will act in the future. The thought is more simply that God's ways are not man's ways, nor his thoughts man's thoughts. The doxology further explains why Paul does not presume to give an exact description of the future; he must leave room for surprises and for riddles.

Today, nineteen hundred years later, we know that the future did not unfold as Paul hoped and expected. His journey to Jerusalem with the collection he had gathered did not excite the envy of his compatriots in the way he had hoped. Israel has not accepted Christ, the parousia has not yet occurred. What has happened was precisely what Paul warned against. Christian Gentiles made themselves great at the expense of

---

55. Rom. 3:29–30. See Chapter X.
56. Rom. 11:30–32, cf. 1:18–3:26; 5:20–21.

Israel. Already Ephesians had to remind the Gentile Christians about the greatness of the mystery that has given them access to Christ and to God's promises together with Israel.[57] Gentile Christians soon came to believe that God had rejected Israel, that, much to the advantage of the Gentiles, he had gathered for himself a new people from among them; Jewish Christians they treat as a special case.

The controversy over the messiahship of Jesus and over exegesis of the scriptures began as a debate within Israel, between Jews who believed in the crucified Messiah and those who did not. When Paul writes, Gentile Christian churches have become a significant new element, but the Apostle is himself a Jew, and he knows that in Christ God has confirmed his promises to Israel. Later on, the ancient church read the Old Testament as a part of its sacred Scriptures, often using them to support its anti-Jewish polemic. When Christianity became the state religion of the Roman Empire, the polemic between two minority groups developed into active Christian discrimination against Jews. We know all too well the sad history of persecutions and pogroms which followed.

Paul does not envision any mission among the Jews by Christians of Gentile origins. This does not necessarily mean that such a mission is wrong, even though it has more often been pursued with zeal than with understanding. Paul thought that when Jews saw the richness of the spiritual benefits which the gospel had conferred on Gentiles, that they too would wish to share the blessings God had made available in Christ. What Paul hoped for has not happened, and no one can reproach the Jews for that.

In America it is sometimes said about the race issue: "It is not the black man's problem, but the white man's." In the same way, we could say of the relation of Christianity to Judaism: "There is no Jewish problem, but there is a Christian problem."

---

57. See esp. Eph. 2:11-22 and 3:4-10. The author of Ephesians was a disciple of Paul who belonged to a younger generation but was, possibly, himself a Jew. Cf. "Introduction to the Letter to the Ephesians, Part II" in this volume.

9

Contradictions in Scripture

THE BIBLE IS FULL of contradictions. This fact is often used to discredit both the orthodox doctrine of inspiration and more recent fundamentalism. For scholarship, however, recognition of disagreement within and among the individual writings of the Bible has another, more positive meaning: it is an aid in establishing chronology and in discerning the use of sources or the development of traditions, and through this an aid to historical reconstruction in general.

It also occupies an important place in the debate over biblical hermeneutics. Rudolf Bultmann, for example, defends his program of demythologization by observing that statements in the New Testament would contradict themselves if they were objectified and interpreted as literal truths about God and the world beyond; therefore, they must be interpreted existentially. At the other extreme, a book published in the United States a number of years ago, suggestively titled *The Varieties of New Testament Religion*, understood the contradictions in the New Testament as a basis for confessional relativism and denominational pluralism.[1] Others have asserted that contradictions are to be overcome by seeing the canonical scriptures as part of the emergence of catholic tradition, allowing for variation and organic development. In opposition to this Ernst Käsemann has emphatically insisted that the gospel is the center of the canon and has used it in relentless critique of all which is opposed to it, however firm its place in the canon.

---

1. E. F. Scott, *The Varieties of New Testament Religion* (New York: Scribners, 1944).

In view of the importance of the problem of contradictions in the Bible, one might expect that its history would already have been investigated. However, there is little literature on this topic, although the question of contradictions in Scripture has been discussed almost as long as the canon itself has existed. At the time of the definitive fixing of the Jewish canon, rabbis discussed, among other things, the possibility that Ezekiel contradicted the Pentateuch and that contradictions existed in Proverbs and Ecclesiastes. Marcion and others rejected the Old Testament writings on the grounds that they were self-contradictory and opposed to the gospel. Church fathers such as Irenaeus and Tertullian energetically opposed him and sought to prove the inner unity of the two testaments. A unique compromise is known from the pseudo-Clementine homilies. They assert that Moses and Christ are in complete agreement, but at the same time concede that the Pentateuch contains contradictions and falsehoods. This they explain by the theory that false pericopes came into the Law in the course of its oral transmission.

The question of contradictions also plays a role in the discussion about which New Testament writings were canonical. Shortly after 200, the otherwise orthodox Roman, Gaius, rejected the Gospel of John and the Book of Revelation on the grounds that these writings stood in opposition to the other Gospels and to the letters of Paul. To refute Gaius, Hippolytus wrote at least one reply explaining the disagreements. Like many other theological polemicists, Hippolytus seems to have misrepresented the position of his opponent.[2]

The discussions about the extent of the canon show that both Jews and Christians thought that the Holy Scriptures could contain no irreconcilable contradictions. But the discussions also reveal that there was an awareness of contradictions and that attempts were made to deal with them. The assumption that an apparent contradiction requires

2. According to Hippolytus, Gaius believed that it was the heretic Cerinthus who wrote the Fourth Gospel and the Apocalypse. This assertion of Hippolytus is constantly repeated. But from a fragment preserved by Eusebius (*Hist. Eccl.* III, 28.2) it seems probable that Gaius said only that Cerinthus lied when he introduced the revelation in the Apocalypse as written by a great apostle, and as given to him (the apostle) by angels. This is confirmed by excerpts from Dionysius of Alexandria who was probably also dependent on Gaius (*Hist. Eccl.* VII, 25.2). The fragments of Gaius' writing which were preserved by Dionysius bar Salibi and, without naming him, by Epiphanius, show that Gaius attacked the apostolic and canonical character of John and Revelation. Cerinthus was probably mentioned only incidentally; like the Montanists, Cerinthus had cited the Apocalypse as support for his chiliastic fantasies. A more detailed investigation is being prepared by J. D. Smith.

explanation opened the way to creative exegetical endeavor. A classic example of this is the question, familiar from the Gospels, of how the Messiah could be David's son if David himself calls him Lord (Mark 12:35-37 par.). The answer is not made explicit but is clearly to be found in the identification of the Lord at the right hand of God with Jesus of Nazareth, who is of David's family. In several places Paul deals with contradictory passages in Scripture which refer to Israel and to Gentiles or to the promise and to the Law. My own interest in this problem and its history was awakened particularly by his argument in the third chapter of the epistle to the Galatians. Here Paul cites Hab. 2:4, "But the righteous shall live by his faith" (or as Paul understands, "He who through faith is righteous shall live"). To this he opposes Lev. 18:5 which says about the commandments of the Mosaic Law, "For the man who does these things will live through them . . . ," i.e., he shall have life in them.

The Jewish scholar Hans Joachim Schoeps has recognized that Paul's discussion of these two passages must be understood against the background of the treatment of contradictory scriptural passages in contemporary Jewish hermeneutics.[3] But Schoeps neglects to investigate the latter closely enough, and consequently what he says about rabbinic hermeneutics in this connection is as unreliable as his exegesis of Paul. The pertinent hermeneutical rule is the last of R. Ishmael's 13 *middoth*, or hermeneutical principles. Schoeps renders it, paraphrasing freely, "If two verses contradict one another, one seeks a third to set aside the contradiction." This rendering relies upon a widespread traditional understanding of the rule which is untenable for two reasons.

First, as was already noted by Prof. Adolf Schwarz at the beginning of this century,[4] the rule thus interpreted is not in accord with the usual rabbinic practice. Normally an apparent contradiction is resolved by means of an exegetical distinction. It is assumed that the two contradictory statements refer to different things, or that they apply under different circumstances. Only in exceptional cases is a third statement introduced to resolve the conflict. Second, the traditional interpretation

---

3. *Paul: The Theology of the Apostle in the Light of Jewish Religious History*, trans. by H. Knight (Philadelphia: Westminster, 1961), 177f.

4. A. Schwarz, *Die hermeneutische Antinomie*, Wien/Leipzig: A. Möller, 1913. Like other works of this scholar, this investigation has played only a small role in later discussion. This is understandable in view of Schwarz's inclination to uncertain, partly fantastic hypotheses. The correct conclusions were drawn from his data by V. Aptowitzer in a review in *MGWJ*, n.f. 24 (1916) 174-181.

is also unsupported by the text of the rule. Literally translated the rule says, "Two scriptural passages which contradict one another until a third passage comes and decides between them." The formulation merely declares in what case the rule holds, without describing how to resolve the conflict. An older, more complete formulation known from the tannaitic midrashim, where it is ascribed to R. Akiba, but which also occurs in the traditions of the school of Ishmael makes clear how to deal with the two biblical passages: "Two scriptural passages which correspond to one another yet conflict with one another, should be upheld in their place until a third passage comes and decides between them."[5]

Thus the basic rule is that the two scriptural passages should be upheld, each in its place; i.e., they should be so interpreted that they do not negate one another, but rather both remain valid, each with a specific meaning within its own context. The third passage is mentioned only in a subordinate clause which adds a condition: the resolution of a conflict between two scriptural passages on the basis of contextual exegesis must be abandoned if it turns out that a third passage requires another resolution of the conflict.

One of Hillel's famous antinomies best illustrates the application of the basic rule and this condition.[6] Concerning the Passover sacrifice, Exod. 12:5 states: "From the sheep and the goats shall you take it." But Deut. 16:2 says, "And you shall slaughter the Passover for the Lord your God, sheep and cattle, in the place where the Lord will choose that his name dwell." The narrative in 2 Chron. 35 seems to take both regulations into consideration since King Josiah gives 3000 lambs and kids for the Passover sacrifice—in addition to cattle for holy sacrifice, which were cooked and distributed to the people. But the parallel account in the apocryphal Greek book of Ezra differs from this, making no explicit distinction between small cattle and large (1 Esdras 1:6–13). A certain Ezekiel reworked the Exodus narrative as a tragedy in Greek style and

---

5. Mekilta, Pisha 4 (ed. Lauterbach, I, 32) on Exod. 12:5; Sifre Num. 58 on Num. 7:89.

6. Palestinian Talmud, Pesahim 6:1 (33a). The tradition refers to three exegetical problems which caused Hillel to come from Babylonia to Palestine. Another of the three problems was an antinomy between Exod. 12:15 and Deut. 16:8, which Hillel resolved by giving proof for the Pharisaic dating of the day when the first sheaf of grain was offered and thus for Pentecost (Lev. 23:10–16). The third question concerned the interpretation of Lev. 13:37: "He is clean and the priest shall pronounce him clean." Such double statements in a single text were often discussed in the same way as antinomies between two texts.

had God explicitly give Moses the command that the Passover sacrifice should be both sheep and cattle.[7] Thus here the two prescriptions are harmonized in that the rule in Exodus is combined with the more encompassing rule in Deuteronomy. This solution is rejected by Hillel. To our knowledge he was the first to formulate with full consciousness the exegetical problem of how one can uphold two texts which differ from one another. He resolved the antinomy through a distinction: Exod. 12 refers to the Passover lamb while Deut. 16, which also permits large cattle, does not refer to the Passover lamb, but rather to the festal sacrifice for Passover (the Hagigah).

Hillel's solution was generally accepted. However, the tannaim continued to discuss the problem on an academic level. An obvious objection could be made to Hillel's solution. Exod. 12 contains a series of regulations which applied only to the first Passover in Egypt, e.g., the command to paint blood on the doorposts. If the two contradictory scriptural passages were supposed to be interpreted in their own contexts, it could be argued that the command to take a lamb or a kid applied only to the first Passover in Egypt, while Deut. 16 contained the regulations for the Passover celebration in the following generations.

I assume that this line of argument was purely scholastic in character, but it had to be refuted. A series of counter-arguments was adduced, based either on the exact wording of Exod. 12:5 or on supporting texts. It is in this connection that R. Akiba quotes in its full form the rule about two scriptural passages which contradict one another.[8] He finds the decisive third passage in Exod. 12:21: "Choose and take sheep for yourselves according to your families and slaughter for the Passover." Thus the clause, "Until a third passage comes and decides between them," is used when an antinomy admits to more than one solution. It serves as legitimation for departing from a solution which contextual arguments could support.[9] The stipulation is probably a later addition which pre-

---

7. Eusebius, *Praep. Ev.* IX, 29.13.

8. Mekilta Pisha 4. Other arguments were attributed to R. Ishmael and his pupils R. Josia and R. Jonathan, while two different proofs were ascribed to R. Eliezer b. Hyrcanus (Lauterbach I, 30-32). In the interpretation of Deut. 16:12 two variants occur. It is either assumed that the text as a whole concerns the festal sacrifice, or that it speaks both about the Passover lamb taken from the small cattle and about the festal sacrifice taken from the large cattle. See J. Z. Lauterbach, *Mekilta de-Rabbi Ishmael*, (Philadelphia: Jewish Publication Society, 1949), I, 30-33.

9. See also Sifre Num. 58; Mekilta Bahodesh 9 on Exod. 20:22; and Sifre Lev. 16:1 (Weiss 79b). No other references to a third, deciding scriptural passage seem to occur

supposes learned discussions in the rabbinic academies. The basic rule is that two scriptural passages contradicting one another should be upheld with the help of a distinction in the interpretation of the two contexts. In this form—without the additional stipulation—the rule corresponds to Hillel's practice, and certain indications suggest that Schwarz was right in his assumption that the formulation of the basic rule also goes back to Hillel.[10]

In any case it is only the basic rule which can be presumed to have been known and used at the time of Paul. Thus the task which confronted an exegete when he encountered an apparent contradiction in Scripture was not to find a third passage which could resolve this conflict. It was necessary first to establish which text contained the valid halakah, the correct statement, or the fundamental teaching. Then it was requisite to find a satisfactory explanation of the conflicting text to maintain its validity. This is clear from the typical rabbinic formulation of the problem: "One scriptural passage says . . . , but another passage says, . . . How are both of these passages to be upheld?" It is also evident in controversies, e.g., between Pharisees and Sadducees, where the participants take opposing positions and both can adduce scriptural passages as the basis for their argument. The one who could show the probative force of his own text and at the same time explain the text of his opponent prevailed in the discussion. A good example of this is found in the controversy between the Pharisees and Jesus about divorce—especially as it is presented in Matt. 19:3-9. Jesus answers the question about divorce by referring to the story of creation (Gen. 1:27 and 2:24), but can also explain why Moses commanded the writ of divorce (Deut. 24:1): it was on account of their hardness of heart.

In rabbinic literature there is a whole series of examples of the discussion of scriptural passages which contradict one another. Gradually, it became a kind of game to detect contradictions and to find explanations for them. This led to the discovery in Scripture of a series of legal rules,

---

in tannaitic traditions. The use of references to Scripture to support the interpretation of one of the contradictory passages is something different.

10. According to Jewish scholars of the twelfth century (Abraham b. David, Hillel b. Elyakim, and the Karaite Judah Hadassi) the fourth of Hillel's seven hermeneutical rules was simply "two scriptural passages." This is probably right—and other textual variants are corrupt. It makes far more sense that Hillel's fourth rule be a rule for two contradictory texts, than that it be a second rule for *Binyan ab*; according to the standard texts, Hillel's third and fourth rules deal with the derivation of an interpretation from one and from two scriptural passages respectively.

historical explanations and theological teachings which were not directly expressed; they had to be presupposed if seeming contradictions were to find a satisfactory explanation. In this way the study of contradictory statements in Scripture became an important factor in the steady growth of halakah and haggadah. Most of the rabbinic material dates from the second century after Christ or even later. However, it can be shown indirectly that the question of contradictions in Scripture must already have been discussed to a considerable extent at the time of Paul, as is evident even from the sparse traditions about Hillel and his immediate followers.

Harmonization of dissimilar religious traditions certainly took place at all times in the history of Israel. Only when the canon was defined and the text substantially fixed did the problem arise of how to maintain two scriptural passages which contradict one another. Even when the Pentateuch and eventually also other writings had achieved canonical status, the problem still did not arise immediately and everywhere. The exegetes of the Qumran sect, for example, seem not to have been interested in questions of this kind. Methodical discussion of contradictions in Scripture presupposes not only the existence of Holy Scriptures, but also contact with Greek philosophy and scientific method. The encounter with Hellenistic culture sharpened the problems and furnished the means of mastering them through logical distinctions and dialectic.

Biblical monotheism made a strong impression on many outsiders. Hellenistically educated Jews found support for their faith when they saw that the philosophers agreed with Moses, although they had not perceived the truth about the *one* God as clearly as he had. However, at the same time Moses could speak of God with anthropomorphic expressions and make use of mythopoetic language which agreed neither with reason nor with his own teaching. How could it be said, for example, that God descended on Mount Sinai when he is present everywhere? Or how can it be said that God rested on the seventh day since both nature and the Scriptures show that he is constantly active?

The first author known to have concerned himself with questions of this sort was the Jewish philosopher Aristobulus, who dedicated an apologetic work to Ptolemy VI Philometor (181–146 BC).[11] Later, questions of this kind appear again and again both in Philo and in the rabbis. According to the Letter of Aristeas, the Alexandrian delegation in

---

11. Cf. N. Walter, *Der Thoraausleger Aristobulos* (TU, 86; Berlin: Akademie, 1964). The most important fragments are preserved in Eusebius, *Praep. Ev.* VIII, 10 and XIII, 12.

Jerusalem raised the question of how, if creation is one, some animals could be considered unclean and therefore not to be eaten or even touched. The High Priest answered by explaining that the laws of ritual purity served a pedagogical purpose. They served to keep Israel separate and contained moral instruction in allegorical form.[12]

More than the rabbis, the Jewish exegetes in Alexandria tended to explain contradictions in Scripture by means of allegorical interpretation. In this respect the allegorical interpretation of internal contradictions in Homer, as it was practiced by Alexandrian scholars, served as a model. But the contrast between Alexandrian allegorism and Palestinian literalism should not be overstressed. It may be more important that both Philo and his predecessors and Hillel and his successors deal with the problem of conflicting scriptural passages, while this problem is unknown to the Teacher of Righteousness and to other exegetes in the Qumran community. Allegorical interpretation was neither unknown in Palestine nor the sole order of the day in Alexandria. Several times Philo mentions interpreters who tried to explain all the disagreements in the laws without seeking any deeper meaning in the text. These interpreters evidently discussed problems like those which the Palestinian rabbis tried to solve. Philo himself has little use for their sagacity. In his systematic exposition of the laws he usually passes over legal antinomies or tacitly harmonizes them.

There are two scriptural passages which Philo repeatedly contrasts with one another in a formal antithesis: Num. 23:19 and Deut. 8:5. These are almost always cited in abbreviated form so that the contrast emerges sharply. The first passage says "God is not like a man;" the second, on the contrary, says "like a man (God educates his son)." Philo designates these two statements as the chief summaries (*kephalaia*) of Scripture.

He uses them as a hermeneutical key to the explanation of other contradictions in the laws.[13] The truth is that God is not like a man, and neither is he like the world or anything else. But it is only "friends of the soul" who are able to grasp this truth in its purity. Therefore God is portrayed in Scripture like a man: with hands and eyes, ascending and descending, and with human emotions like anger, envy and remorse. This portrayal is a pedagogical device, intended for those who cannot

---

12. Letter of Aristeas 129f.

13. The chief text is *Deus imm.* 51–73; cf. among others *QG* I 55; II 54; *Sacr.* 89–101; *Conf.* 96–101; *Somn.* I 233–237.

free themselves from the corporeal. They need elementary instruction about God in simple terms.

Philo is full of praise for the wisdom of Moses. As the best of lawgivers he cared for all for whom he legislated—both for those who could perceive the truth about God and for those who had need of elementary instruction and firm discipline. It was precisely with the latter in view that Moses portrayed God as a man who educates and disciplines his son. The verb *paideuein* can, as is well known, express both. Once Philo even uses the image of a doctor who must tell a lie in order to prevent his patients' being discouraged and thereby worsening their condition. The lie makes the patients willing to submit to a painful treatment.[14] This is a surprising image, implying as it does that there are lies in Scripture. I can understand it only as an apologetic argument directed against those Jews who asserted that the Law of Moses contained falsehoods and therefore rejected it, wholly or partly. Philo answers by agreeing that there are falsehoods in the laws, but he emphasizes that they are useful lies, fully justified in pedagogical and therapeutic terms.

A careful analysis shows that the idea of "white lies" is a secondary development of the image of the doctor who must cause his patients pain in order to heal them, just as a master must educate a bad slave with threats and punishment. This indicates that the resolution of the conflict between "God is not like a man" and "like a man" was not originally related to true and mythopoetic language about God; Philo has adapted the discussion of the summaries to bear on this problem, which was his particular concern. This is also indicated by his statement that the distinction between "like a man" and "not like a man" corresponds to the distinction between "fear of God" and "love for him." Further, it should be kept in mind that ordinarily the Ten Commandments are called "summaries" of the Law. The texts designated as the chief summaries must therefore stand in some relation to the Ten Commandments; if so, however, they can hardly refer primarily to the use or absence of anthropomorphisms.

The original idea underlying these chief summaries is evident from the full text and context of the scriptural passages in which they are found, more clearly in Hebrew than in Greek. Num. 23:19 deals with God's gracious and unalterable purpose: "God is not a man that he should lie, nor a son of man that he should repent of anything." Deut. 8:5 speaks of his educative discipline: "that the Lord your God educates you, as a man educates his son." It is no accident that the fullest discussion of the

---

14. *Deus imm.* 64–66.

two summaries occurs in Philo's commentary on Gen. 6:6–8. The judgment on the generation of the flood illustrates God's educative discipline; the salvation of Noah and his family illustrates his unalterable salvific purpose.

The Septuagint, which translates both Num. 23:19 and Gen. 6:6–7 in free paraphrase, avoids the statement that the Lord regretted the creation of man. In spite of this, Philo explicitly deals with the question: does God regret or change his mind? This indicates that he is making use of a tradition which ultimately goes back to a Hebrew midrash which dealt with the opposition between Gen. 6:6–7 "The Lord regretted" and Num. 23:19 "God is not a man that he should lie, nor a son of man that he should regret anything."

In any case, there are indications which suggest that the distinction between the two summaries, "God is not like a man" and "like a man", was originally related to the distinction between what Philo calls the two powers of God and the rabbis call his two measures, namely kindness and punishment or mercy and judgment.[15] Philo adapted the discussion of the two summaries, bringing them to bear on the problems facing the Jews in Alexandria. But the material which he has adapted forms an early stage of the discussion among the rabbis about the relationship between judgment and mercy, or fear and love.

With reference to Paul, the texts of Philo are especially interesting because they discuss problems in a literary fashion preserving the complexity of the arguments. The rabbinic traditions point out antithetical scriptural passages and give the exegetical solution to the conflict. And there is a pertinent similarity between Philo's exposition in "On the unchangeability of God" and Paul's in Galatians 3. The similarity is all the more interesting because there is no question of any historical connection between the two. In both cases, it is not merely isolated scriptural passages which stand in opposition to one another, but rather opposing principles, both of which have their place in Scripture, although only one of them contains the real teaching of Scripture. For Philo Num. 23:19 contains the truth, while Deut. 8:5 summarizes the pedagogical aspect of

---

15. While the rabbis connected mercy with the Tetragrammaton and judgment with the divine name *Elohim*, Philo presupposes a tradition which said the opposite. In neither case could they be separated absolutely, and in one sense that was the main point: the gracious God is just, and the God who judges is merciful. This was evident from the inconsistent use of the names for God in Scripture. Greater use of the materials in Philo might have confirmed the principal thesis of H. Ljungmann, *Guds barmhärtighet och dom* (Lund: Gleerup, 1950).

the Law. For Paul the truth lies in the Habakkuk passage "to live by faith," while Lev. 18:5 refers to the function of the Law as a guardian of children.

A formal similarity is especially notable; the important scriptural passages are summarized in short catch phrases, for Philo "not like a man" and "like a man," for Paul "by faith" (*ek pisteōs*) and "by works of the law" (*ex ergon nomou*). The Pauline formulas are best understood as abbreviations for "The righteous shall live by faith" and "He who does them shall live by them." This kind of abbreviation has a still closer analogy in the rabbis who applied the formulas "out of fear" and "out of love" to human acts depending on whether they conformed to the commandments to fear God or to love him.[16]

With respect to hermeneutical terminology and method, Paul is much closer to the rabbis than to Philo. This could be illustrated from many details of Gal. 3.[17] But what is most important is that the argument becomes clear and comprehensible when it is interpreted in the light of the treatment of conflicting scriptural passages in contemporary Jewish hermeneutics. The interpretation of Scripture is interspersed with expressions of dismay at the new direction taken by the Christians in Galatia, combined with reminders of what they experienced when they first came to faith (Gal. 3:1–5; 4:6–11). Paul's thesis is that those who have heard the preaching of faith and received the Holy Spirit no longer stand under the Law. What happened to them corresponds exactly to what happened to Abraham: "Abraham believed in God, and it was reckoned to him as righteousness" (Gal. 3:6; cf. Gen. 15:6). From this Paul draws the conclusion that those who are "of faith" are sons of Abraham. For Paul, the promise that in Abraham all the nations shall be blessed proves that this also holds true for Gentiles (Gal. 3:8–9; cf. Gen. 12:3 etc., as understood at the time of Paul).

Paul concludes *e contrario* that since only those who are of faith (*ek pisteōs*) are blessed, those who rely on the works of the Law stand under

---

16. Relevant material, e.g., in R. Sander, *Furcht und Liebe im palästinischen Judentum* (Beiträge zur Wissenschaft vom Alten und Neuen Testament 68; Stuttgart: Kohlhammer, 1935).

17. Cf. for example the personification of Scripture in v. 8 and v. 22, the formulation "it does not say . . . , but . . . ," and the epexegetical "This is (the) Christ" in v. 16. In v. 17 Paul presupposes the usual rabbinic explanation for the contrast between Gen. 15:13 (400 years) and Exod. 12:41 (430 years). The first number, which applied to Abraham's offspring, is reckoned from the birth of Isaac; the other number is reckoned from the "covenant between the pieces" in Gen. 15. Paul has the latter in mind when he speaks of a legally valid covenant in Gal. 3:15–18.

the condemnation of those who do not keep all of it (Gal. 3:10; cf. Deut. 27:26). Thus, Paul presupposes that those under the Law can only incur its curse; they cannot receive its blessings (Deut. 28:1–14). For this view, he provides another scriptural proof. According to Hab. 2:4, the righteous shall live by faith; therefore, the opposite principle cannot also be valid at the same time—and righteousness, life and blessing cannot be dependent on doing all the things which the Law prescribes (Lev. 18:5). The whole train of thought in Gal. 3:1–12 rests on the presupposition that Hab. 2:4 and Lev. 18:5 contradict one another, and that the two corresponding principles "by faith" and "by (works of) the law" mutually exclude one another as qualifications for justification and life.[18]

A pious Jew would see no contradiction here: for him, keeping the commandments is part of genuine faith. This was certainly also Paul's view in his Pharisaic past. But as a Christian, he identified the faith spoken about in Scripture with faith in the crucified Messiah, Jesus, who hung on the tree under the curse of the Law. Because of this, the contradiction is complete. The conviction that faith in the crucified Messiah is incompatible with the enduring validity of the Law made Paul a persecutor of Christians in his early life; and he held fast to this conviction as an apostle.

Paul is confronted by the problem that Hab. 2:4 and Lev. 18:5 are analogous; both explain how a man shall live, i.e., partake of the real life which God gives to the one whom he regards as justified. But at the same time the two passages contradict one another, for the one says "by faith" and the other says "who keeps the commandments," i.e., "by works of the law." While the one passage corresponds to the promise which was given to Abraham who had faith, the other states the basic principle of the Law given at Sinai. Thus Paul must solve the problem of how it is possible to uphold the two passages which contradict one another so that each, promise and Law, can take the place which is due it according to Scripture. In accordance with the usual method of discussing contradictions between scriptural passages, Paul begins by determining which is valid (Gal. 3:13–18), in order that he may then explain how to resolve the

---

18. Like Gal. 2:16d, Gal. 3:11a is a paraphrase of Psalm 143:2. The apparent contradiction between this passage and Hab. 2:4 and Gen. 15:6 is resolved by means of an exegetical clarification: Psalm 143:2 is not to be taken absolutely, but means that "by works of the Law" or "in the Law" no one is justified before God. Cf. Rom. 1:17 and 3:20.

apparent contradiction (Gal. 3:19–25). Here I can only briefly present my interpretation of these much debated verses.

The key to the understanding of vv. 13–14 lies in the recognition that the words of 14a: "That the blessing of Abraham might come upon the Gentiles in Christ Jesus," are a paraphrase of God's oath to Abraham after the offering of his son Isaac: "In your offspring shall all the peoples of the earth be blessed" (Gen. 22:18). The expression "the blessing of Abraham" comes from Gen. 28:4, and the words "in Christ Jesus" have been inserted in place of "in your offspring."[19] The messianic interpretation of "offspring" derives from an analogy with Nathan's promise to David; in 2 Sam. 7:12 "your offspring" was understood as a designation of the Messiah.

The statement in v. 13 that Christ was made a curse on our behalf derives from a combination of the statement in Deut. 21:23 that the one who hangs on a tree is cursed with the report in Gen. 22 about the ram that was caught in a shrub and offered in place of Isaac. Here Paul makes use of an old Jewish Christian midrash which understood the crucifixion in light of Genesis 22. Paul's use of the midrash reveals his concern that the Law has not been arbitrarily set aside. Through Christ's vicarious bearing of the curse, a legal redemption has occurred. God's promise to Abraham has been fulfilled. The Gentiles have partaken of the blessing in Jesus Christ since they have received the Spirit through faith.[20]

In vv. 15–18 Paul asserts that the Law cannot make the promise invalid. As proof he uses an analogy with the law governing inheritance and wills. If the Law were a codicil added to God's covenant with Abraham, it would annul the validity of the whole covenant, and that cannot have been its intent. The analogy raises some legal questions, but it is clear

---

19. Already in Gal. 3:14 Paul presupposes the messianic interpretation of "Abraham's offspring," which he sets forth in 3:16. See chapter VIII note 12 and *The Crucified Messiah*, 153f.

20. By means of the appended clause in Gal. 3:14b, Paul blurs the distinction between "us," the Israelites, and the Gentile nations in 3:13–14a. He equates the blessing of Abraham with the Spirit which even Gentiles have received (cf. 3:5–9) and takes redemption from the curse of the Law to imply freedom from the Law itself (cf. 3:10–21; 4:5–6). Paul's whole argumentation in Galatians 3 is based upon two premises: 1. God's promises to Abraham, including the oath in Gen. 22:18, pertain to the crucified Christ, through whom Gentiles were made partakers of the promised blessing. 2. For this reason, the statements in Lev. 18:5 and Hab. 2:4 are mutually exclusive and must have different functions. On the basis of these presuppositions, Paul can draw the inference that only the covenantal curses, and not the blessings, apply to those who are under the Law (Gal. 3:10).

that Paul is asserting that the promise—and therefore also the words "by faith"—have an unconditional validity which the Law does not abrogate.

The real problem in discussing two contradictory scriptural passages is explaining how to interpret the other, differing statement. Paul addresses this problem when he asks: "Why then the law?" (v. 19). The answer is that it was given on account of transgressions, as a temporary provision "until the offspring should come, to whom the promise applies." Here again Paul seems to make use of a Jewish Christian messianic testimony. As was the case in v. 16 and even in v. 14, "offspring" is understood as a designation of the Messiah. The words *achris hou elthē . . . hō* (until the one should come . . . to whom) come from the oracle concerning Judah in Gen. 49:10, understood messianically, and read *'ad kî yābō' še-lô*.

In order to understand Paul's application of the phrase, however, it is even more important to note that similar formulations were used in connection with prescriptions and decrees which were in principle only provisional. They would be valid only "until a priest with Urim and Thummin should arrive" or "until a trustworthy prophet should arise" or "until the prophet and the anointed ones of Aaron and Israel come."[21]

What is radical in Paul's argument is that he understands the entire Law of Moses itself as such a provisional, interim arrangement, valid only for pre-messianic times. He further develops this understanding in Gal. 3:23-25 and 4:1-6. Paul stresses the provisional character of the Law when he says that it was given by angels through a mediator (v. 19c). This indicates that the Law was not an enduringly valid expression of God's will. But the text is completely misunderstood when, as some exegetes believe, the angels are thought to be hostile to God. The logical subject of the passive construction is God; he gave the Law.[22] Moses as mediator

---

21. See Neh. 7:65 (Ezra 2:63); 1 Macc. 14:41; cf. 4:46; 1 QS 9:10f.; cf. CD 6:10f.; 12:23f.; 20:1.

22. The interpretation of Gal. 3:20 remains difficult, but the context excludes interpretations that would make Paul deny that God is the ultimate originator of the Law. In that I agree with R. Bring, even if I am not able to follow the exegesis of Galatians 3 which he has set forth in several works, including *Commentary on Galatians* (Philadelphia: Muhlenberg, 1961) and "Der Mittler und das Gesetz," *KD* 12 (1966) 292-302. On the syntactical construction, see E. Bammel, "Gottes *diathēkē* (Gal. III.15ff.) und das jüdische Rechtsdenken," *NTS* 6 (1960) 317 n. 5; A. Giblin, "Three Monotheistic Texts in Paul," *CBQ* 37 (1975) 540-41. For a full survey of the discussion and a fresh proposal, see T. D. Callan, "The Law and the Mediator" (PhD diss., Yale, 1976). While Callan has not fully succeeded in solving the enigma, his proposal may point in the right direction, see esp. p. 214: "Thus Ga 3:20a is a parenthetical explicative comment on Moses' mediation of the Law seen in terms of Ex 32-4."

must take account of both parties—both God and the people. But if both the promise and the Law derive from the same God, then the idea that the Law is a provisional enactment does not give a satisfactory answer to the problem of the contradiction in Scripture. Paul sharply formulates this problem in the question: "Is the law then contrary to the promises?" (v. 21a).

Paul emphatically rejects the possibility of a conflict between the Law and the promises. He first inserts an explanatory observation: "If a law had been given which would make alive, then righteousness would indeed be from the law." In that case, Scripture would have contained two incompatible teachings about justification and life. But even as the Law cannot be understood as a restrictive clause added to the promise (v. 15–18), neither can it be understood as a provisional arrangement so that "by faith" would be valid for Abraham and for the time of the Messiah, while "by the Law" and therefore "by works of the Law" would be valid for the time between Moses and Christ. The unity of the will and purpose of the one God excludes such a duality.

Thus a real contradiction would have existed only if the Law had been able to lead to justification and life. Paul asserts that it was unable to do this and that this was never even God's intention for it. The Law served another purpose: "Scripture consigned all things to sin, that what was promised to faith in Jesus Christ might be given to those who believe" (v. 22). Thus Paul finds no contradiction here. Rightly understood, the Law is in harmony with the promises. It had a subordinate function which contributed to the realization of the promises.

It is important to note that it is not the Law, but rather Scripture which is the subject of the statement in v. 22. The Law is not a self-contained entity but rather a part of Scripture. It consigned all things to sin by ordaining the Law and demanding works (Lev. 18:51). In Romans, Paul explains more fully that the Law transformed sin into culpable transgression and in this way increased it. In Galatians he emphasizes that the function of the Law was subordinate to what was, according to Scripture, God's real aim—that the promise should be fulfilled and that those who belong to Christ should partake of it "by faith." The idea that the Law had an interim, negative, preparatory function is expressed in the statement that it was a *paidagōgos eis Christon* (custodian until Christ came); it is to be compared to guardians and trustees who watch over the heir until he come of age at some definite time. To assert the validity of the Law after Christ has come is, for Paul, not to uphold the Law, but rather to misuse it, to contradict the intention of the lawgiver. Though Paul goes on to apply the argument to the situation in Galatia (Gal. 3:23-4:6), I shall not follow the Apostle further, but will draw a few conclusions concerning our main problem.

Contradictions in Scripture are an old hermeneutical problem—discussed by the rabbis since Hillel. This problem was well known to Philo and to his predecessors, learned Jews of Alexandria. Paul is certainly not the first Christian exegete who concerned himself with it. But in connection with his doctrine of justification through faith, the problem received special emphasis. The argument in Gal. 3 follows in an independent way the usual pattern for the discussion of two scriptural passages which correspond to, yet contradict, one another. The promises to Abraham and the statement in Scripture that it is faith by which the righteous shall live are upheld uncurtailed. But the Law and its basic principle—that those who keep the commandments shall live by them—are also upheld. The Law was neither a clause added to the promise, nor a temporary substitute for it. In spite of the contradiction between the Law and the promise, or rather precisely because of this contradiction, the Law contributed to the fulfillment of the promise in Christ, "by faith" and not "by works of the Law." Precisely the necessity of preserving the freedom of the believer from the Law requires Paul to explain its role in Scripture.[23]

In no other place does Paul deviate more from the views of the rabbis. But in no other place is his style of argumentation more similar to that of the rabbis than in Galatians 3. After all, this follows logically; for if it is first proved that those who have been baptized in Christ and have received the spirit no longer stand under the Law, then the necessity for a halakic interpretation of individual commandments disappears.

Thus my investigation confirms Olof Linton's thesis that Paul used legal arguments precisely to assert freedom from the Law.[24] In recent years scholars, especially Germans, have discussed whether Paul in Gal. 3 (and Romans 4) outlines "salvation history" or gives an "existential interpretation" of the promise to Abraham.[25] This modern statement of alternatives is false. Paul is concerned not with a choice between objective

---

23. The ideas in Galatians 3 are, consequently, supplemented by what Paul says in Gal. 5:13-14, 18 and 23; cf. Rom. 8:4; 13:8-10.

24. "Paulus och juridiken," *STK* 21 (1945) 173-92. It is unfortunate that this important article on "Paul and law" (in the wide sense of the term) has never been made available to an international public.

25. On this problem see esp. G. Klein, "Individualgeschichte und Weltgeschichte bei Paulus," *Evangelische Theologie* 24 (1964) 126-65.

salvation history and the individual's understanding of his existence, but rather with a correlation between the situation in a mission congregation and the witness of Scripture. Events of the recent past and of the present— the coming of Jesus, his death and resurrection, the mission to the Gentiles and the outpouring of the Holy Spirit—are explained on the basis of Scripture, and Paul interprets Scripture in the light of these occurrences.

Since Paul as an apostle identifies the faith which is proclaimed in Scripture with faith in the crucified Messiah, Jesus Christ, he sees a contradiction between Christ and the Law, between faith and works, between Hab. 2:4 and Lev. 18:5. Jewish scholars especially have noted that in a passage like Gal. 3 Paul makes use of an idea of "the Law" which sharply deviates from the rabbinic understanding of the Torah as the life-giving revelation of God. From this, however, these scholars draw the incorrect conclusion that Paul cannot have been very familiar with the Jewish understanding of Torah.

Faith in the crucified Christ altered Paul's understanding both of the Law and of the promises. Because Paul understood it to be the antithesis to Christ and faith, the Law of Sinai was isolated from promise and covenant and understood one-sidedly, on the basis of Lev. 18:5, as saying that life is to be gained by keeping the commandments. In this way Paul could maintain that the Law, in spite of the contradiction between it and the fulfilled promise, nevertheless had its legitimate place in Scripture.[26]

The argument in Gal. 3 addresses the greatest problems faced by the early church in its mission, i.e., the relationship between Jews and Gentiles and the validity of the Mosaic Law for believers in Christ who were not of Jewish origin. These questions were discussed in a series of writings, some within and others outside the New Testament, and were resolved in various ways. Nevertheless, considerable agreement on Christian practice prevailed among the writings which have been accepted into the canon: believing Gentiles were acknowledged as brothers and full members of the church. It was not demanded that they let themselves be circumcised

---

26. This must be kept in mind in interpretations of Rom. 10:4: "Christ is the end (*telos*) of the law." In Rom. 10:4ff. Paul treats Lev. 18:5 and Deut. 30:12-14 as conflicting scriptural passages. He takes Lev. 18:5 to be a statement which Moses wrote in reference to the righteousness which is based upon the Law. The diverging statement in Deut. 30:12-14, that the word is near, is attributed to the righteousness based upon faith, and taken to refer to Christ who is proclaimed in "the word of faith." Since Deut. 30:12-14, no less than Lev. 18:5, refers to God's commandment, Paul would here seem to have made a distinction within the Old Testament concept of the Law. A similar distinction may, possibly, be presupposed in Rom. 3:27; cf. Gal. 6:2 and the variant reading in Gal. 3:19 (P46 and G d).

or that they keep the ritual laws. However, Israel's Holy Scriptures remain the Bible of the church and insofar as the Law is summarized in the commandment of love (or in the two great commandments), it remains the valid expression of the will of God. Disagreement in practical matters occurs only on particular points, such as eating meat offered to idols. In great measure the situation of the early church is similar to that which we find among the rabbis when, e.g., they almost unanimously accept Hillel's halaka concerning the paschal sacrifice, while they have different ways of supporting this view exegetically.

This is not without relevance for contemporary discussion of conflicts in Scripture and among the churches. It shows that agreement in matters of practice is not necessarily dependent on agreement about exegetical questions and hermeneutical principles.

With respect to the relationship between Jews and Gentiles in the church and to the freedom of Gentile Christians from the individual prescriptions of the Law, other early Christian theologians reached conclusions similar to Paul's but in different ways. What is characteristic of the teaching of Paul is that he comes to his interpretation through clarification of the relationship between promise and Law, so that justification by faith stands in contrast to the rule that he who keeps the commandments lives by them. Even if he has the concrete Law of Moses in view the whole time, he moves toward reduction of the Law to a principle of justification and life through works. Later Augustine and Luther moved further in this direction.[27]

For them the question of the validity of the Law of Moses was no longer so important. The question of how the relationship between the demand for works and the promise of grace in Scripture related to the salvation of the individual Christian was primary. But their concentration on the contrast between Law and gospel as the main point in the interpretation of Scripture was an extension of Paul's approach.[28]

27. The problem of contradiction in Scripture is also discussed in other contexts than that of law and gospel. Several Church Fathers are, like Philo and other hellenized Jews before them, concerned with the contrast between true knowledge of God and the anthropomorphic expressions in Scripture. It is noteworthy that this problem is hardly mentioned in the New Testament.

28. In his essay, "Trosrättfärdighet och lagens fullgörande," STK 45 (1969) 101-15, R. Bring criticized the original version of this study and restated his own interpretation of Galatians 3. He disputes that Paul sees a contradiction between Hab. 2:4 and Lev. 18:5. Without going into exegetical details, I will simply note that my interpretation of Gal 3:10-12 was not a result of, but rather the starting point for, my work on Jewish hermeneutics.

10

The One God of Jews and Gentiles (Romans 3:29–30)

IN HIS COMMENTARY ON the Epistle to the Romans, Ernst Käsemann has placed the short paragraph Rom. 3:27–31 under the heading: "Polemische Zuspitzung" (Polemical sharpening).[1] The formulation is typical for Käsemann, who has both provoked and stimulated his students and colleagues by his polemical sharpening of questions and opinions. His polemic has had two chief targets: on the one hand, any softening of Paul's doctrine that God justifies the ungodly, and on the other, a purely anthropological interpretation of the doctrine of justification. In both respects, Käsemann can draw support from the brief series of questions and answers in Rom. 3:27–31. Yet, his interpretation of the verses needs to be supplemented and corrected, mainly because Käsemann has failed to do justice to the target of Paul's polemic, the imagined spokesman of Judaism.

The formulation "Polemical Sharpening" summarizes the content of Rom. 3:27–31 in a correct but one-sided way. At the conclusion, Paul states that he does not abrogate but upholds the Law by his doctrine of justification. Käsemann himself understands this as a transition to Paul's interpretation of the story of Abraham in Rom. 4.[2] But the thesis in 3:27, that there is no longer room for boasting (*kauchēsis*), already points forward to chapter 4, where the treatment of the story of Abraham develops the theme. Abraham is also the chief example, whose story

---

1. *An die Römer,* 94.
2. Ibid., 97.

warrants the thesis that God justifies circumcised Jews and uncircumcised Gentiles in the same way, by faith. Just in doing so, God proves that he is the sovereign Creator who makes the dead alive.

As to the form, the questions and answers in Rom. 3:27-31 serve a double function. They comment on the preceding exposition of Paul's main thesis and prepare for the supporting argument from Scripture that follows. Even so, the verses sharpen what Paul has already stated in 1:16-17 and 3:21-26 by giving a polemical twist to his theses. This also applies to the concluding statement in 3:31. If Paul's contention that a person is justified by faith without works of the Law does uphold the validity of the Law, it follows *e contrario* that works of the Law do not (see Rom. 9:31). Käsemann is also right when he makes the following comment on Rom. 3:29-30: "Here the Apostle attacks Judaism on its own premises."[3] The question is whether Käsemann has given a correct description of those premises or not. The answer depends mainly on the meaning of some rabbinic passages. But before we turn to them, it may be useful to give a short, highly generalized sketch of Greek and Jewish monotheism.

GREEK AND JEWISH MONOTHEISM

In insisting that God is one, Christians were in agreement with many educated Greeks and Romans as well as with Jews. According to James 2:19 even the demons would agree. The formulation *heis theos* (one God) is well attested by inscriptions as well as in philosophical and theological literature. Erik Peterson, a learned scholar and one of Käsemann's teachers, has demonstrated that the formula can be used as an acclamation, in which the numeral has an elative meaning. It was possible to acclaim a god as being "one," i.e. unique, singular, without any denial of the existence of other gods.[4] In the Greek tradition, *heis theos* could also express a conceptual monotheism. This philosophical tradition can, at least, be traced back to the famous saying of Xenophanes (ca. 500 B.C.): "One God, greatest among gods and humans, in no way similar to mortals in either body or mind."[5]

---

3. Ibid., 96: "Der Apostel schlägt das Judentum von seinen eigenen Voraussetzungen aus."

4. E. Peterson, *HEIS THEOS: Epigraphische, formgeschichtliche und religionsgeschichtliche Untersuchungen* (FRLANT n.F. 24; Göttingen: Vandenhoeck & Ruprecht, 1926), esp. 216-21, 227-36, 304-5.

5. Quoted by Clement of Alexandria, *Strom.* V 109, cf. VII 22; H. Diels—W. Kranz,

The theme of unity and multiplicity pervades Greek philosophy from its beginnings. The one God, or the divine One, could be identified with the universe that encompasses all its parts, in some form of pantheism, or be identified with the hidden source and goal of all things. But the divine unity could also be contrasted with the diversity and the conflicts in the world of matter and of human beings. Occasionally, philosophical monotheism could have a polemical note, as when Xenophanes mocked the Ethiopians who made their gods snubnosed and black, or the Thracians who made theirs gray-eyed and red-haired, thus rejecting all anthropomorphic concepts and images. In general, however, philosophical monotheism was tolerant and coexisted with religious pluralism, polytheism, and worship of images. The one God of the philosophers left room for the many gods of civil religion and of cult associations. The traditional names of the gods could either be taken to refer to the one God, who had many names, or they could be interpreted as mythopoetic designations of the many powers, who were the agents of his rule. Commenting on the disagreements between the theologians of his day, the rhetorician Maximus of Tyre (2nd. cent. A.D.) states: "In all of this warfare and uproar and disagreement you can see on all the earth one generally accepted law and doctrine (*logos*), that there is one God, king and father, and many gods, children (*paides*) of God and co-rulers with God."[6]

If we turn to the Old Testament, we find a very different picture. The formulation "one God" is not in common use, even though it does occur, see Mal. 2:10: "Has not one God created us?" The classical statement of Jewish monotheism, the "Hear, O Israel" or *Shema*, does not speak of one God but of YHWH *ehad*, later read as "one Lord," in Greek *heis kyrios*. The original meaning may well have been: "YHWH is our God, YHWH alone."[7] The oneness of God is not an inference from the unity of the world, as it was among the Greeks. What is at stake is, much more, the exclusive sovereignty of YHWH, the God of Israel, who is the only God

---

Die Fragmente der Vorsokratiker (Berlin: Weidmann, 1959), I, 55, fr. 23. English translation, e.g., in J. M. Robinson, *An Introduction to Early Greek Philosophy* (Boston: Houghton Mifflin, 1968), 3.33 and 35. On monotheistic trends in Greek philosophy and religion, see, e.g., M. P. Nilsson, *Greek Piety* (H. J. Rose, trans.; Oxford: Clarendon, 1948), 115–24; A. J. Festugière, *La révélation d'Hermès Trismégiste*, II. *Le Dieu cosmique* (Paris: Gabalda, 1949).

6. See *Maximi Tyrii Philosophoumena* (ed. H. Hobein, Leipzig: Teubner, 1907), XI, 57b (p. 132, 2–6).

7. S. D. McBride, "The Yoke of the Kingdom: An Exposition of Deuteronomy 6:4-5," *Interpretation* 27 (1973) 273–306.

of his people and of the entire creation, and who does not tolerate that any other god is worshiped beside himself (see, e.g., Deut. 32:39; Isa. 44:6; 45:9). The tension between the monotheistic faith in God as the Creator of all mankind, and the specific, covenantal relationship between YHWH and his people, was resolved by means of the doctrine of election, which received its classical formulation in the book of Deuteronomy and in the oracles of Second Isaiah.[8]

With few exceptions, post-biblical Judaism retained exclusive monotheism without any compromise. A syncretistic identification of YHWH with other gods posed a threat at the time of radical Hellenization during the reign of Antiochus IV Epiphanes. After the crisis had been overcome, syncretistic theocracy (mixture of deities) was hardly more than a tangential phenomenon at the fringes of Judaism. Nonetheless, Greek and Jewish ideas did converge. Thus, it was *heis theos*, and not the *kyrios heis* of Deut. 6:4, that became the slogan of preaching, apologetics, and propaganda among Greek-speaking Jews.[9] Some Jewish writers, of whom only fragments have been preserved, quoted Greek thinkers and poets in support of their monotheistic faith, subjecting the sentences and verses to a Jewish interpretation. Such quotations were frequently altered, and new ones were produced.[10] The writings of Philo of Alexandria provide ample evidence for the degree to which it was possible to interpret and adapt the biblical concept of God to the presuppositions of Greek philosophy. Under these circumstances, it is not strange that the Jewish historian Josephus can claim that the doctrine of God set forth in the laws of Moses is in full harmony with the teaching of the wisest among the Greeks. He found the main difference to be that only a tiny minority of the Greeks had reached the insights that were common to all members of the Jewish people.[11]

As Greek monotheism is oriented toward the problem of unity and plurality, it was intimately bound up with cosmology. To Jews like Philo

---

8. Deut. 4:37ff.; 14:2; Isa. 41:8; 43:10; 44:1f. Cf. my article "Election and the People of God," in P. D. Opsahl and M. Tanenbaum, ed., *Speaking of God Today* (Philadelphia: Fortress, 1974), 31-38.

9. P. Dalbert, *Die Theologie der hellenistisch-jüdischen Missions-Literatur* (Hamburg-Volksdorf: H. Reich, 1954), 124-30.

10. On this literature, cf. A. M. Denis, *Introduction aux pseudépigraphes grecs d'Ancien Testament* (Leiden: Brill, 1970); E. Schürer, *The Literature of the Jewish People in the Time of Jesus*, ed. N. N. Glatzer, (New York: Schocken, 1972) 294-302.

11. *Against Apion*, II. 169.

and Josephus it was also a matter of course that the one God is the God of the whole universe and of all mankind. This does not mean that they have abandoned the idea that the Jewish nation has a peculiar relationship to God and, as a consequence, a unique role in the world. The idea of election is, however, no longer the main means of mediating between universal monotheism and Jewish particularism. Philo and Josephus stress much more that Moses was a wise lawgiver who made the true doctrine of God the basis for his legislation. Josephus used the term "theocracy" to describe the Jewish constitution; possibly he coined it himself.[12] Philo stresses, again and again, that the Mosaic legislation corresponds to the cosmic order after which it was modeled.[13] Common to both is the idea that a life conducted according to the Jewish laws is in full harmony with the order of the universe and the moral laws of nature. Slogans like "one law," "one temple," "one nation," which to the pagan world appeared as signs of intolerant exclusivity, become symbols of the universal oneness of God.[14]

SOME RABBINIC PASSAGES

In the Greco-Roman world, even the rabbis had to deal with the question of how the God of the whole world could be in some special sense the God of Israel. Drawing upon Billerbeck's collection of material, Käsemann in his commentary on Rom. 3:29 adduces a passage from the homiletic Midrash Exodus Rabba (29) as an example of the predominant rabbinic doctrine of God: "I am God for all who come into the world but I have associated my name with you alone; I am not called the God of the nations of the world but the God of Israel."[15] This passage can indeed

12. *Against Apion*, II. 165.

13. On Moses as the wise lawgiver in Philo and Josephus, see T. D. Callan, "The Law and the Mediator" (PhD diss., Yale, 1976), 79-130.

14. See, e.g., Philo, *Spec. leg.* I 67: "As God is one, there should only be one sanctuary;" *Sepc. leg.* IV 159: "The best constitution (*politeia*) and the same law and one God." Josephus, *Against Apion* II. 193: "One temple for one God, common to all for the God common to all, for what is like is always dear to everyone." Cf. also Josephus, *Ant.* IV. 200f.; Syr. Baruch 48:24; 78:4; 85:14 and, from a later period, Origen, *Against Celsus* V. 44; Hippolytus, *Refut.* IX. 18.1, and the Pseudo-Clementine letter from Peter to James 1:5. Contrast Eph. 4:4-6; 1 Clem. 46:6, etc. Cf. M. Dibelius, "Die Christianisierung einer hellenistischen Formel," *Botschaft und Geschichte* (Tübingen: Mohr, 1956) II, 14-29; Peterson, 254-56.

15. *An die* Römer, 96. Cf. (H. L. Strack &) P. Billerbeck, *Kommentar zum Neuen Testament aus Talmud und Midrash* (Munich: Beck, 1922-31), III, 185.

give the impression that the rabbis affirmed what Paul in Rom. 3:29f. denies, that God is only the God of the Jews and not also the God of the Gentiles. But the rabbis would not make that claim any more than Philo and Josephus did. Before we proceed, it is necessary to interpret the passage quoted and analogous statements on the presuppositions of rabbinic Judaism.

It is first of all necessary to observe that the rabbis treat almost all theological questions as problems of the right interpretation of Scripture. It was a basic presupposition that Scripture could not contradict itself, so that all apparent contradictions had some deeper meaning.[16] Especially within the school of Akiba it was also assumed that no single word of Scripture was superfluous but that even apparently negligible particles and repetitions had a special meaning. For this reason, scholars devoted a great deal of attention to phrases that seemed to be pleonastic or tautological. The passage which Käsemann adduced has a parallel in Ruth Rab. 1.1 and is ascribed to R. Shimeon b. Yohai, one of Akiba's students. It is a comment on the double name of God in Exod. 20:2: "I am YHWH your God" (*ʾānōkî YHWH ĕlōhêkā*). The same explanation is also used to explain Ps. 50:7. This passage is more striking than Exod. 20:2, since the same word for God is here repeated twice (*ĕlōhîm ĕlōhêkā ʾānōkî*). It would seem likely that the midrash was originally designed to interpret Ps. 50:7. In any case, it explains the double name of God by stating that God, who as such is the God of all mankind (*ĕlōhîm* or *YHWH*), is at the same time called the God of Israel (*ĕlōhêkā*), because he has associated his name with Israel alone or, better, with Israel in particular (*b y w t r*).[17] The concluding statement, "I am not called the God of the nations of the world but the God of Israel," does not in any way deny the universalistic monotheism which remains axiomatic. The point is that God has given his people a special honor by letting himself be called the God of Israel (by Scripture). As a matter of fact, the conclusion is lacking in earlier versions, found in tannaitic midrashim. It may well be a later, polemical addition, directed against Christians who claimed that the God of the Bible was their God.

16. See chapter IX above.

17. The version in Ruth Rab. Proem 1 reads: "I have not associated (*yyḥdty*) My name but with my people Israel." In rendering this and similar statements I have, in general, followed the translation in the Soncino Midrash Rabba (ed. H. Freedman—M. Simon, London 1939), see vol. VIII, *Ruth*, p. 3. For the tannaitic midrashim, I have consulted other existing translations without feeling bound by any one of them, as I have tried to render stereotyped phrases with some consistency.

In the tannaitic midrashim, Mekilta, Kaspa 4, and Sifre Deuteronomy § 31, the midrash on Ps. 50:7 is preceded by an analogous discussion of Exod. 34:23 and Deut. 6:4, or vice versa.[18] The problem in Exod. 34:23 is the apparently repetitious phrase: "Before the Lord YHWH, the God of Israel." The problem in Deut. 6:4 is caused by what the interpreters read as two independent nominal clauses: "YHWH is our God" and "YHWH is one," i.e. he is the God of Israel and at the same time the one God of the whole world. The Mekilta draws the conclusion which we have already encountered: "I have associated my name with Israel especially." The variant in Sifre has a slightly different wording: "His name was made to rest upon us (or upon Israel, or upon you) especially." This would seem to make the presence of God's name, i.e. of the revealed God, in Israel, the reason why he is called the God of Israel.

Sifre § 31 adds another explanation of the two parallel clauses in the *Shemaʿ*: "'YHWH is our God,' i.e. for us. 'YHWH is One,' i.e. for all who come into the world. 'YHWH is our God,' i.e. in this age. 'YHWH is One,' i.e. in the age to come, as it is written: 'On that day YHWH will be one and his name one' (Zech. 13:9)." This passage is of special interest in that it explicitly takes the confession *YHWH ʾeḥād* to imply the universality as well as the exclusive oneness of God. Eschatological hope resolves the tension between the universal and the particular components of Jewish monotheism.

Even the Mekilta parallel includes an addition, in this case inserted between the exegesis of Deut. 6:4 and Psalm 50:7:

> "Therefore thus says YHWH, the God of Israel." (2 Kings 21:12, Jer. 23:2, etc.).[19] But has it not also been said: "(I am YHWH,) the God of all flesh" (Jer. 32:27)? What, then, does Scripture

---

18. I have used J. Z. Lauterbach's edition of the Mekilta (I-III [1933–35] Philadelphia: Jewish Publication Society, 1949), and L. Finkelstein's edition of Sifre on Deuteronomy (1939, repr. New York: Jewish Theological Seminary, 5729/1969), 53f. The term translated with "especially" is *bywtr*, which is used adverbially to express a very high degree (of attachment). Lauterbach, III, 184f., on Kaspa 4, translates: "I have conferred my name particularly on my people Israel," but this translation tends to obscure the correlation between the comment and the designation "God of Israel" (or "your God"). In the Mekilta passage the term *bywtr* occurs twice, but it is absent from the comment upon Ps. 50:7, as in Ruth Rab. 1.1.

19. Lauterbach, III, 184 (on Kaspa 4) only gives the reference to 2 Kings 21:12, but the stereotyped formula of introduction occurs several times in the Hebrew Bible. Most likely, a passage from Jeremiah is meant. The later version in Midrash ha-Gadol on Deut. 6:4 reads: "Thus says YHWH Sabaoth the God of Israel." See S. Schechter, *Aspects of Rabbinic Theology* (1909, repr. New York: Schocken, 1961), 63 n. 2.

teach by saying: "The God of Israel"? Simply this: He associated his name with Israel especially.

Here the problem is not simply caused by the use of a double designation of God, as it was in the passages we have already discussed. The form is, rather, that of a midrash upon two apparently contradictory passages, one asserting that YHWH is the God of Israel, the other that he is the God of all mankind. The solution, however, is given in the stereotyped wording that is used throughout the catena in Mekilta Kaspa 4.

The solution is somewhat different in another series of apparently contradictory passages, discussed in Sifre Deuteronomy §40 (p. 80) on Deut. 11:12:

> "A land which YHWH your God cares for." Does he really care for it alone? Does he not care for all the lands, as it is written: "To bring rain on a land where no man is, . . . to satisfy the waste and desolate land" (Job 38:26f.). What, then, does Scripture teach by saying: "A land which YHWH your God cares for"? That he does not care but for this one, but because of the care with which he cares for it, he cares for all the lands together with it. In the same way, you read: "Behold, he who keeps (guards) Israel will neither slumber nor sleep" (Psalm 121:4). Does he not keep the whole universe, as it is said: "In his hand is the life of every living thing and the breath of all mankind" (Job 12:12)? What does Scripture teach by saying: "He who keeps Israel"? That he does not keep but Israel, but because of the keeping with which he keeps them, he keeps the universe together with them.

The midrash continues by contrasting 1 Kings 9:3 with Zech. 4:10b and Prov. 15:3. The solution is analogous to the other cases: because God's eyes and heart are in his house, they are in every place.

The book of Jeremiah does not only call YHWH "the God of all mankind" (*'ĕlōhê kōl bāśār*, Jer. 32:27) but also "King of the nations" (*melaek ha-gôyim*, i.e. "King of the Gentiles," Jer. 10:7). This latter designation is discussed in two fairly late midrashim, in both cases in the form of a short story. One of them occurs in the Midrash on the Psalms (93:1):

> "Who would not fear thee, O king of the nations"? The Holy One, blessed be he, said to Jeremiah: "You call me King of the nations? But am I not their (Israel's) king"? He said to Him: "Because thou hast called me prophet to the nations (Jer. 1:5), I too call thee King of the nations."[20]

20. Midrash Tehillim, Psalm 93.1 (ed. S. Buber, 1891, repr. Jerusalem) trans. W.

Another version of the story occurs in Exodus Rabba 29.9, a text that discusses the opening words of the Decalogue:

> "I am YHWH your God" (Exod. 20:2): It is written: "The lion has roared, who will not fear"? (Amos 3:8). This explains what is written: "Who would not fear thee, O King of the nations? For this is thy due." The prophets said to Jeremiah: "What do you mean by saying King of the nations? All the other prophets call him King of Israel, and you call him King of the nations." He answered them: "I heard him say to me: 'I appointed you a prophet to the nations' (Jer. 1:5), and I say: 'King of the nations.' If he does not spare his own children and his family, will he then spare others? As it is said: 'Terrible is God in his sanctuary'" etc. (Psalm 68:36; Jer. 10:7).

In this version, the point is that God, the king of the Gentile nations, will also judge them, just as he judges his own people.

Whether they deal with pleonastic or contrasting passages, all the texts which we have surveyed agree in affirming that God is the God of all mankind but especially the God of Israel. Both universalistic and particularistic statements in Scripture are upheld as valid, and a complete congruence between Scripture and reality is an axiom beyond discussion. Otherwise, the explanations are open to some variation. The most common opinion is that the God of all has given a special distinction to his people by letting himself be called the God of Israel or by letting his name rest upon his people. But the explanation can also be turned the other way round: the preservation of the world is a consequence of God's special care for Israel. Occasionally, the conclusion is drawn that the God who judges his own people will even more judge the other nations. But we have also encountered the opinion that the particular relationship between God and Israel exists in this age only; in the age to come he will manifest his kingship and be the one God of all mankind. Whatever the variations, there is a general consensus that God is not the God of Israel only but also the God of the Gentile nations—and yet there is a distinction.

Rabbinic tradition traces the methodical discussion of apparently contradictory or pleonastic passages back to Hillel.[21] The reliability of this tradition may be questionable, but the name of Hillel remains in any case a symbol for a type of exegetical research which originated

---

Braude, *Midrash on the Psalms* (New Haven: Yale University Press, 1959).

21. See chapter IX above, pp. 162-165.

among Jewish sages during the last century before the destruction of Jerusalem in 70 C.E. The earliest examples of such discussions do, however, deal with halakic antinomies. It would seem that it was only after the reconstruction of the rabbinic academies after 70 C.E. that the form became stereotyped and was also used in discussions of haggadic questions, including problems of theology. Yet, already at the time of Paul, the problem of God's relationship to mankind in general and to Israel in particular must have existed, even if the stereotyped forms for discussing it did not.

A passage from the Mekilta on the Song of Moses may serve to illustrate that the rabbis could discuss the problem without referring to any specific passage in support of their universal monotheism. The passage is a comment on Exod. 15:2:

> "YHWH is my strength and my salvation." Thou art a helper and supporter of all who come into the world but of me especially. "And my song is YHWH": Thou art the subject of song to all who come into the world but to me especially. He has proclaimed me of special distinction (*'myrh*) and I have proclaimed him of special distinction . . . (Deut. 26:18 and 17). But behold, all the nations of the world declare the praise of him by whose word the world came into being! Mine, however, is more pleasing (*n'ym*), as it is said: "But sweet (*n'ym*) are the songs of Israel" (2 Sam. 23:1).[22]

The impact of Greek philosophy is much less obvious in rabbinic writings than in Philo and Josephus. Yet, an apologetic note is discernible in the attempt to show that the concepts of election and covenant do not contradict universal monotheism. The rabbis could also defend the impartial justice of God by other means, e.g., by the concept of the noachic commandments which the Gentiles have failed to observe.[23] Of special importance was the idea that God had offered the Torah to all nations but that only Israel had accepted it.[24]

---

22. Shirata (or Shirta) 3, Lauterbach II, 23f. See also translation and comments in J. Goldin, *The Song at the Sea* (New Haven: Yale University Press, 1971), 109–11. The midrash continues by quoting other pairs of passages that illustrate the mutual relationship between God and Israel: Deut. 6:4 and 1 Chron. 17:21; Exod. 15:11 and Deut. 33:29; Deut. 4:7 and 8; Ps. 89:18 and Isa. 49:3.

23. Tos. Abod. Zar. 8:4, 6; B. T. Sanh. 56b; Sifre Deut. 343 on Deut. 33:2. Cf. Billerbeck, III, 36–38, 41f.

24. See, e.g., Mek. Bahodesh 5 on Exod. 20:2; Sifre Deut. 343 on Deut. 33:2. Cf. Billerbeck, III, 38–41, and, e.g., S. Aalen, *Die Begriffe 'Licht' und 'Finsternis' im Alten*

Whereas Philo and Josephus thought of Moses as the wise lawgiver who had modeled the constitution (*politeia*) of the Jews upon that of the universe, the rabbis identified the revealed Torah with the hypostatized Wisdom of God and thus with the beginning and principle of creation, with the cosmic world order itself.[25] When the rabbis stressed that the one God of all was in a special sense the God of Israel, they did not at all intend to separate God's saving action from his universal activity as the Creator and Judge of all mankind.[26] Their idea was, quite to the contrary, that God had acted as Creator and Judge when he gave the Torah to Israel, thereby claiming the world for himself, establishing his kingship and his law and order in the world which he had created. Accordingly, Israel's acceptance of the Torah was an event of cosmic significance. The righteous man (the *ṣaddîk*), who observes the commandments of the Torah, does not only care for his own salvation; he upholds the world.[27]

It is within this general context that we have to understand the rabbinic statements about the God of Israel who is also the God of the whole world, including the Gentile nations. Israel has received a mark of distinction, God being called her God, because it is by means of the Torah that God vindicates himself and his salvation, manifesting that he is the Creator and the Judge of the whole world. Only if we understand the rabbinic doctrine of God on its own premises does it become clear in what sense Paul turns against it "with unheard of boldness."[28]

Testament, Spätjudentum und Rabbinismus (Oslo: Norske Videnskapsakademi, 1951) 295f.

25. See, e.g., W. D. Davies, *Paul and Rabbinic Judaism*, 165-172; Aalen, 175-78, 183-95, 262-65, 272-79, 289; J. Jervell, *Imago Dei* (FRLANT n.F. 58; Göttingen: Vandenhoeck & Ruprecht, 1960) esp. 114-19. Cf. also my critical reviews of the books of Aalen and Jervell in *NovTT* 53 (1952) 61-84, and *NovTT* 61 (1960) esp. 87-90.

26. Commenting upon the passages from Exod. Rab. 29, Käsemann writes: "On the basis of the concept of the covenant, the saving action of God is here separated from the work of the Creator and Judge, as was indeed later (sic!) the case in Marcion's doctrine" (*An die Römer*, 96, my translation). This is a distortion.

27. Cf., e.g., Aalen, 282-289; R. Mach, *Der Zaddik in Talmud und Midrash* (Leiden: Brill, 1957).

28. "In unerhörter Kühnheit," *An die Römer*, 96.

CONCLUDING COMMENTS ON ROMANS 3:29-30

The series of short questions and answers in Rom. 3:27-31 (and 4:1-3) are typical of what is generally regarded as diatribe style.[29] A somewhat similar dialogical style also occurs in rabbinic midrashim, as illustrated by passages quoted earlier in this chapter, some of which were formal as well as material parallels to Rom. 3:28f., with the difference that the rabbinic texts included explicit quotations from the Bible. Considering the dates of the sources, we would do better not to assume that Paul made a creative use of the stereotyped rabbinic pattern. If there is more than a general similarity of style and content, the Pauline form, without quotations, is more likely to be an antecedent of the more elaborate rabbinic form than vice versa.[30]

In our context it is not necessary to pursue the question of Greek and of possible Jewish affiliations of the dialogical style in Rom. 3:27ff. It is more important to observe that not all of the direct questions are of the same nature. Some of them raise problems or objections (3:27 and 31), possibly attributed to an imaginary discussion partner (thus 3:31a, cf. 2:17). In Rom. 3:29, by contrast, Paul uses direct rhetorical questions to advance his own argument, in order to convince his dialogue partner and his audience: "Or is God (the God) of the Jews only? Is he not (the God) of the Gentiles also?" The answers are obvious. No Jew or Jewish Christian would deny that God, being one, is not only the God of the Jews but also the God of the Gentiles. The discussion partners agree in upholding a universal monotheism, as they also agree that salvation is effectuated by the grace of God (*sola gratia*).[31] Paul's "unheard of boldness" emerges only in the appended, attributive relative clause in 3:30: the one God is the one "who will justify the circumcised on the ground of their faith (*ek písteōs*) and the uncircumcised through their faith (*dia tēs písteōs*)." This means that, just as with respect to sin, there is no distinction with respect to salvation (see Rom. 3:22-23).

---

29. The definition of diatribe has proved to cause difficulties. Stan Stowers, a graduate student at Yale, is preparing a fresh investigation, with special attention to dialogical style in Romans.

30. If so, the development of the form would be analogous to that of enumeration of biblical examples, in which proof-texts are a "secondary and changeable part of the pattern." See W. S. Towner, *The Rabbinic "Enumeration of Scriptural Examples,"* (Leiden: Brill, 1973), 248f. etc.

31. Cf. Käsemann, *An die Römer*, 23: "Im sola gratia sind die Gegner sich einig" (the adversaries agree in [justification by] grace alone).

Within the context, Paul's reflection upon the oneness of God serves to support his doctrinal thesis that a human being—Jew or Greek—is justified by faith apart from works of the Law (Rom. 3:28). Paul has formulated this thesis as a summary of his interpretation of the gospel concerning Jesus Christ, the Son of God (see esp. 1:1-6, 16-17, and 3:21-26). His chief warrants he draws from the Old Testament (see esp. 3:21 and 4:1-25). By comparison, the argument from the oneness of God adds a secondary, more general and almost rational support: justification by faith, without any distinction between Jew and Greek, is in full harmony with the universal monotheism which the Jew also professes, but the radical consequence of which he fails to draw.

In drawing the consequence that radical monotheism excludes any distinction, Paul shows some affinity with Greek philosophical monotheism, which was universalistic and more or less cosmopolitan. Since Xenophanes, it could include polemic against religious particularism. Paul would seem to draw upon this tradition, whether he was conscious of it or not. Yet, he has given a very special twist to the ideas of the philosophers. In that respect, his remarks in Rom. 3:29-30 are similar to earlier passages in the letter.

In Rom. 1:19ff.; 2:14-15, 25-29 Paul makes use of ideas concerning a natural knowledge of God and of moral values and stresses the contrast between appearance and inner reality. Such ideas can be traced back to Greek philosophy.[32] Probably they were mediated to Paul by a Hellenized Judaism which used them for apologetic purposes, in order to prove that Jewish monotheism and the Jewish way of life were in full harmony with the insights of the best among the Greeks.[33] Paul reverses the perspective and uses the ideas polemically, in order to demonstrate that possession of the Mosaic Law does not make any fundamental difference.

Something very similar goes on in Rom. 3:29-30. Hellenized Jews had made an apologetic use of universalistic Greek monotheism, in order to prove the excellency of the Mosaic legislation and of the Jewish nation.[34] To the rabbis, the confession of the one, who alone is God, im-

---

32. Cf. Käsemann's commentary on the passages, with bibliographies. Esp. G. Bornkamm, "The Revelation of God's Wrath," (1935) in *Early Christian Experience* (trans. P. L. Hammer; New York: Harper & Row, 1969), 47-70; A. Fridrichsen, "Der wahre Jude und sein Lob. Röm. 2, 28f.", *Symbolae Arctoae (Osloenses)* 1 (1927) 39-49.

33. See, e.g., Bornkamm, 52-53 and my book, *Das Volk Gottes* (1941, repr. Darmstadt: Wissenschaftliche Buchgesellschaft, 1963), 72-73, 95-104, 109-119.

34. See, e.g., Philo, *Spec. leg.* II 164-166; Josephus, *Against Apion*, II. 165-192.

plied willingness to observe his commandments. Paul, on the contrary, gives a polemical twist to the monotheistic confession, turning it against the Jew who relies on the Law and boasts of his special relation to God. The oneness of God, the sovereign Creator of all, is demonstrated by the impartiality of his judgment and of his grace upon Jews and Greeks without any distinction. In the Pauline perspective, monotheism has become a warrant for the doctrine of justification, just as the recognition that all men are sinners, and that righteousness and glory belong to God alone, has become a criterion of genuine faith in the one God.

Ernst Käsemann has for good reasons stressed that Paul's doctrine of justification is a consequence of his Christology, and that Paul maintains the sovereignty of the Creator. But he seems to have failed to break radically with the common but simplistic notion of a contrast between Christian universalism and Jewish particularism. Jewish monotheism at the time of Paul was universalistic in its own way, and Christian monotheism remained exclusive. The condemnation of idolatry is an evidence of that (see, e.g., Rom. 1:18ff.). We would come closer to the truth by saying that both Jewish and Christian monotheism are particular as well as universal, specific as well as general. Paul's objections to the Jewish doctrines of God and of salvation are due to his faith in the crucified Christ. To Paul, it was not by giving the Torah at Sinai but by sending Jesus and raising him from the dead that God proved to be the Creator and Judge who claims the whole world for himself. The shift of the specific focus meant also that the universal aspect of biblical monotheism took on a new character. The universal law and order, embodied in the Torah, has been replaced by the universality of God's judgment, grace, and righteousness, revealed in the gospel for men and women who are all sinners, without any distinction.

The rabbis held that there was a distinction, but would not deny that God is the God of Gentiles also. Paul argues that there is no distinction but does not deny that God has associated himself especially with Israel, the people to whom he gave his promises. But when he elaborates on the privileges which God has granted to Israel, Paul does it in a very special way. Even when he brings salvation to his own people, God acts as he always does, justifying the ungodly and making the dead alive. That is how he is the one God of Jews and Gentiles.

PART II: INTRODUCTION TO THE LETTER TO THE EPHESIANS

Translator's Preface

For this monograph, I have benefited from help from David Adams and his wife Anne, whose German is far better than my own. I am grateful too for suggestions from Terry Callan. I have made no attempt to carry further the marvelous updating of *Introduction to Ephesians* by the editors of the volume from which this essay is taken, *Studies in Ephesians*, David Hellholm, Vemund Blomkvist, and Tord Vornberg. Their work is a magnificent tribute to their dedication and to the value of the scholarship of Nils Alstrup Dahl.

11

Introduction to the Letter to the Ephesians

1. QUESTIONS ABOUT COMPOSITION, STYLE, AND CHARACTERISTICS

1.1 Composition

TRADITION IDENTIFIES THE WRITING we will discuss as "The Letter of Saint Paul to the Ephesians." Today, every element of this traditional description is a matter for debate. We will return to the questions of authorship and audience, but first let's discuss whether or not the form and composition of the writing are those of a letter. Even that is controversial. The literary style is variously described as: "Testament of Paul,"[1] mystery dialogue, or a meditation on the mystery of Christ,[2] [a prayer letter[3]], a theological treatise . . . in the form of a letter,[4] a theological tractate,[5]

---

1. So for example R. Asting 1930 4-5, N. Sanders 1956, 9-20, especially 16.

2. So H. Schlier 1963, 21 and 22; [H. Marxsen 1978, 194]. Material in brackets in the notes and text indicates material inserted by the editors of *Studies in Ephesians*, unless they indicate a secondary separation within parentheses.

3. [So U. Luz 1989, 386, with reference to K. Usami, 1983, 150. Luz stresses that: "the author . . . does not want to write a liturgical text, but a Pauline letter," (ibid., 380) "prayer is an important link that holds together the dogmatic and the parenetic parts of Ephesians" (ibid., 386), so also now Luz 1998a, 107f., 118.]

4. So H. Conzelmann 1981a, 86; [Ph. Vilehauer 1975, 212f.; A. Lindemann, 1976, 240; H. Conzelmann/H. Lindemann 1995, 297; H. M. Schenke/K. M. Fischer 1978, 174].

5. [So Lindemann, 1976, 235 (= idem 1999, 211); idem 1979, 41; G. Strecker 1992,

an honorific preamble,⁶ a liturgical homily,⁷ a baptismal sermon in the form of a pastoral letter,⁸ or a Pentecost liturgy presented in the form of a letter,⁹ [a homily disguised as a letter,¹⁰ or a pastorally oriented letter.¹¹] The form can also be understood as an encyclical letter¹² (the view of most defenders of Pauline authorship), or as an imitation of a Pauline letter.¹³

The different attributions of form are not mutually exclusive, for the letter in antiquity had a broad array of uses. Proclamations, edicts and other legal documents could take the form of a letter.¹⁴ Further, scholarly and philosophical treatises, memoirs, etc., often took the form of letters. This was true both of authentic and of pseudonymous writings.¹⁵ For a person who is away, a letter can replace not just personal conversation, but a speech as well; the letters of Demosthenes to the senate and people of Athens are classic examples of this.¹⁶ The letter was also used in early Christianity in a variety of genres; see, e.g., The Letter to the Hebrews,¹⁷

71f.]

6. [So H. Hendrix 1988, 7; quoting Hendrix, also E. Mouton 1996, 288f.]
7. So J. Gnilka 1980, 33.
8. So W. Lueken, 1917, 359.
9. So J. C. Kirby 1968, 68ff., 123f., 150ff.
10. [So E. Best 1998, 62: "It seems best then to think of A. E. as intending to write a homily but, realizing that Paul normally wrote letters, deliberately disguising his homily as a letter. It is consequently a mixed genre."; similarly also T. Lincoln 1990, xli.]
11. [So R. Schnackenburg 1982, 19.]
12. [This view was first propounded by Th. Beza and H. Grotius, and then explicated by the Anglican Archbishop Usher (1664, 686) (A. Wirkenshauser/J. Schmid 1973, 485).]
13. So G. Johnston 1943, 111.
14. [See D. E. Aune 1987, 170.]
15. The lessons of Epicurus and Plutarch are examples. However, even in antiquity, the difference between a letter and a treatise could be pointed out; see Demetrius, *De Elocutione [Peri Hermeneias]*; [Text and translation of excerpts 233-35 by A. J. Malherbe 1988, 16-19;] also J. Strutris 1931, 185-220, especially 202-5; [M. L. Sirewalt, Jr 1993; D. Dormeyer 1993, 190-98; H. Görgemanns, 1997a, 1161-64; idem 1997b, 1166-69 and M. Zelzer 1997, 1164-66; R. Brucker 1997, especially 253-79; H. J. Klauck 1998].
16. See J. A. Goldstein 1968; [J. T. Reed 1997, 171-93].
17. [See W. G. Übelacker 1989, 18-26 *et passim*, also commentaries by H. Braun 1984, 1f.; H. Hegerman 1988, 1-4; H. W. Attridge 1989, 13f.; E. Grässer 1990, 15f.; H. F. Weiss 1991, 35-41.]

Pseudo-Barnabas,[18] the Revelation of John,[19] and the Martyrdom of Polycarp.[20]

The form of the Letter to the Ephesians is in any case that of a letter. The opening of the letter (1:1–2) follows the customary Pauline pattern;[21] only the absence of specific addressees in the text of the most ancient manuscripts stands out. At the end of the letter, the messenger, who apparently delivered the letter,[22] is recommended to its recipients (6:21–22; see Col. 4:7–9).[23] The closing deviates from standard Pauline form in that it doesn't address the recipients in the second person, but in the third (6:23–24).

The body of the letter (1:3–6:20)[24] opens with an encomium to God for God's blessing in Christ. Verses 1:3–14 develop the content of this encomium in various ways. This introductory encomium refers to the recipients becoming believers (see 1:13–14), and is followed by an assurance of Paul's thanksgiving and intercession for them (1:15ff.).[25] Thematic expressions indicate both the content of the intercession and the objective of the letter itself: it concerns the knowledge of God and what God's call entails (1:17b–19a). Then follows a demonstration of the power of God, manifested in Christ's resurrection and heavenly enthronement (1:19b–23). Believers are also made alive with Christ—through mercy (2:1–10).

The description of what the addressees have come to believe continues in verses 2:11–22. They are asked to consider what they once were as Gentiles and what they have now become in Christ Jesus: no longer estranged, but fellow citizens of the saints, the house and temple of God.

18. [See Vielhauer 1975, 601f., R. Hvalvik 1994/96, 71–86; F. R. Prostmeier 1999, 86–89.]

19. [See esp. M. Karrer 1986; J. Roloff 1984, 15f.; Aune 1997, lxxii–lxxv.]

20. [See G. Buschmann 1998, 47–49.]

21. [See F. Schnider/W. Stenger 1987, 3–41.]

22. [On the subject of carriers of letters, see M. M. Mitchell 1992, 641–62; see also D. J. Mosley 1973.]

23. [See Schnider/Stenger 1987, 112: "In the epistolary form of the Pauline school, information about third parties was an integral element of the postscript (see Col. 4:7–9 and Eph. 6:21f.) and served to buttress the fiction of a genuine letter."]

24. [So also Vielhauer 1975, 203f.; P. Pokorný 1992, 48; otherwise Hendrix 1988, 3; see 1st Thessalonians and commenting on it B. C. Johanson 1987, 60–67:1:1: Letter-Opening—1:2—5:24: Letter-Body—5:25–28: Letter Closing.] About the tripartite division of letters in antiquity, see H. Koskenniemi 1956, 155.

25. [See below Part III, Section IX; see also H. Krämer 1967, 34–46.]

The center of this important section is devoted to Christ's redemptive work:²⁶ Christ has overcome the separation between Jews and Gentiles and gives both free access to God.²⁷

The assurance of the intercession resumes in 3:1, but then is immediately broken off. An inserted section recalls the revelation given by God to Paul, and his mission and work as a servant of the gospel, through which God's formerly hidden plan of salvation has been realized (3:2–13).²⁸ Then the intercession is resumed and brought to a conclusion (3:14–19). The doxology in 3:20–21 with the introductory doxology frames the entire first major section of the letter (1:3–3:21).²⁹

The second major section (4:1–6:20) contains primarily instructions.³⁰ The opening exhortation connects to the thematic formulation in 1:18b. It concerns a way of living that is worthy of their call (4:1–16).

---

26. [So also Conzelmann 1981a, 98; H. Marxsen 1973b, 12; M. Barth 1974, 275. Best, 1998, 235f., however, states: "Since so many of the themes of the letter surface in 2.11–12 it has been termed its theological center . . . but this can only be true if we ignore the large final paraenetic section where Jewish-Gentile relations never surface. Indeed this and other sections might be regarded as preparation for the paraenesis. The whole letter hangs together in such a way that it is impossible to speak of a center or key passage."]

27. [Compare Usami 1983, 20ff.; Luz 1989, 388f., 391; E. Faust 1993, 221ff., 315–24; G. Sellin 1996, 293; see also below footnote 378 on page 268.]

28. [See Sellen 1996, 291: "This section is connected to the intercession as a digression on verse 3:1." For the definition of digression, see Quint, Inst., 4.3.14: "parekbasis . . . is a section outside the text's usual line of development, that serves an ancillary purpose;" compare also H. F. Plett 1975, 54: "An interruption of a thematically consistent text by an insertion that could stand alone, with a theme that could be complementary, unrelated, or even contrary to the theme of the surrounding text." The digression is related to the text around it in the same way that a parenthetical insertion is related to a sentence, or as the way the figure of speech hyperbaton disrupts the normal order of words;" here of course the digression is naturally complementary to the purpose of the text!; see also O. Linton 1964, 94: "Formally, verses 2–13 are a digression, but actually this section is intimately connected to the purposes of the Letter to the Ephesians;" U. Schnelle 1996, 349f., and Best 1998, 41–44, 293, 295, 300f.]

29. [Compare also Luz 1998a, 108.]

30. [See also Best 1998, 64: "4:1 connects the two (main elements); there is a change here from a prevailing indicative to a prevailing imperative . . . ;"] Barth 1974, 55–56 seeks to find three main sections: 1:15—2:22 (God's perfect work), 3:1—4:24 (God's ongoing revelation) and 4:25–6:20 (Attesting God's love). He stands pretty much alone in this analysis; the analogies to the other Pauline letters argue against it; see pages 203–4 below. [Sellin (1996, 297 note 110) also believes that the compositional structure of the letter is tripartite, though differently divided: 1. Epideictic section, 1:3–3:21. 2. Paraenetic section (exhortatio), 4:1–6:9, and 3. Peroratio, 6:10–20; similarly also Lincoln 1990, xliii–xliv in his "rhetorical outline."]

That is then restated in terms of the unity which has been bestowed and which is to be maintained.[31] All gifts, especially those of evangelists and leaders of the church, should serve to build up the body of Christ (4:7-16).

The paraenesis begins again with a new introductory formula: Christians should no longer wander like Gentiles, but rather—as they have learned—should put off the old man and put on the new (4:17-24). This gives an indication about the specific teaching which follows.[32] It is however rather loosely organized.[33] The instructions emphasize, often in antithetical phrasings, what is to be done and what is to be avoided, usually linked to their ethical foundations (4:25-5:14).[34] Exhortations to a virtuous life, followed by a thanksgiving in the name of Jesus, lead to a household code ("Haustafel") (5:15-21). Within the household code are broadly stated exhortations to wives and husbands, tied to the connection between Christ and his church (5:22-33).[35] The sections on children and fathers, and on slaves and masters, are shorter (6:1-9).

The concluding exhortation in 6:10-20 reconnects to the thematic formulation in 4:24. The argument is put in terms of the armor of God, and is presented as a battle against the powers of evil.[36] The invitation to prayer and intercession, especially for Paul, concludes the context of the letter, and leads to the note on the sending of Tychicus and to the concluding greeting (6:21-24).

Some have labelled the letter form of Ephesians "superficial" or "perfunctory."[37] But that is not actually true. Epistolary conventions occur not only in the prescript (1:1-2) and postscript (6:23-24), but also in transitions to new sections, e.g., 1;15f.; 4:1; 4:17.[38] The assumed setting is that the sender is physically separated from the recipients,

---

31. [Compare Sellin 1996, 295: "'Life in unity' is the highest ethical principle in the Letter to the Ephesians;" so also Luz 1989, 383; see also Luz 1998a, 151f.]

32. [So N.A. Dahl in an unpublished manuscript on the exegesis of verses 4:17-24; so also J. Jervell, 1960, 238.]

33. [Compare Sellin 1996, 296: "Organizing the following text is difficult."]

34. [See further page 213 below.]

35. [See J. P. Sampley 1971 and more recently G. W. Dawes 1998.]

36. [See Klauck 1998, 239: "(possibly with the military metaphors of 6:10-20 as a conclusion to the body of the letter)."]

37. So C. L. Minton 1951, 4; Gnilka 1990, 33. [Luz pointedly differs, 1989, 308.]

38. See J. A. Robinson 1904, 275-84; [See also Schnider/Stenger 1987; Klauck 1998].

and is personally unknown to them (1:15; 3:2). The letter clearly seeks to build a positive relationship between the apostle and the Gentile Christian recipients. The assurance of thanksgiving and intercession, indeed even the preceding benediction, are not directly liturgical, but have an epistolary function, to make clear the emotional involvement of the sender with the addressees.[39] The apostle's self-portrait and the entire letter seek to promote the growth of mutual esteem, intercession and solidarity (see esp. 3:13; 6:19-20). This confirms that Ephesians was conceptualized as a letter, real or fictitious.[40]

The theme of Ephesians is frequently described as "Christ and the Church."[41] There are indeed important and striking statements in the letter that support this view (see 1:22f.; 2:20-22; 3:9-10; 4:4-16; 5:22-33). Still, that description must be evaluated in the context of the entire content of the letter as well as of its compositional structure.[42] The verses within the letter that set out its themes do not confirm that description. Such thematic statements [that is, semantic meta-statements or abstractions] introduce new sections or form a transition.[43] They can also be the central statements of a section (2:5; 2:13). Verse 3:2 introduces the theme of the "stewardship of grace" given to Paul. Further, the thematic statements refer to that which the recipients have been given, or to what is expected of them. If we are forced to identify a primary theme, best is "God's call," or "called by God." In the first major section, the addressees are reminded of all that God's call implies (the hope to which he has called you ἡ ἐλπὶς τῆς κλήσεως αὐτοῦ, 1:18).[44] In the second, they are implored to live lives worthy of their calling (ἀξίως ... τῆς κλήσεως, 4:1).[45]

39. [See Luz 1989, 380f., 384f., 386-93.]

40. [So also Luz 1989, 380 et passim.]

41. See the title of Schlier's study of 1930: Christ and the Church in the Letter to the Ephesians; further, Schlier 1963, 15, 94ff., and Gnilka 1990, 33; Merklein 1973b; [H. Hubner 1997, 172-77, 189-90]. This assertion dates back at least to F. C. Baur 1845, 426f. [and idem 1867, 192 note 1]. "The main point is the Christology" (idem 1845, 256; "The basic idea of the two letters is actually the idea of the σῶμα Χριστοῦ (body of Christ) (idem 1845, 276).

42. [So also Luz 1998a, 108.]

43. See the thematic introductions in 1:3; 1:15; 4:1; 4:17; 5:15; 6:10f.; [6:21], and the transition statements in 1:20; 3:2; 4:22-24; 5:21. In 2:5 and 2:15 the thematic statements occur in the middle of a section. [On thematic or meta or abstract statements, see now D. Hellholm 1980; 1995a; 1995b; further, B. C. Johnason 1987; J. Holmstrand 1997.]

44. [Similarly Schlier 1963, 37; see also Vielhauer 1975, 212.]

45. [Similarly Schlier 1963, 177; see also Hübner 1993, 363: "He [the author of Ephesians] has above all conceived of his letter according to the Pauline division found

The form of expression alternates between appeals in the second person plural and more general statements, which are usually in the more inclusive first person plural. In that way, the author moves his area of concentration from the situation of the addressees to more general, theological, Christological, and ecclesiastical statements and back again. The general statements serve as explanation and incentive; they put the Christian life of the addressees in a broader context.[46] The proximity to "homily" and the presence of liturgical elements are not to be denied, but only prove that the letter is to be understood as a substitute for an address to the gathered community.[47] To what extent the epistolary form is real or fictitious can only be decided in connection with questions about the addressees and the author.[48]

If the first major section is predominantly "descriptive," while the second major section is predominantly "prescriptive" or, perhaps better, "preceptive," that corresponds to a pattern common both in letters and in speech, which can be infinitely varied. In all kinds of official documents, petitions, business letters, letters of recommendation, etc., essential information appears first, then recommendations, requests, entreaties, and so on.[49] Especially in friendly letters and diplomatic correspondence,

---

in Galatians and Romans, namely in one more theological section and in another more paraenetic section, which clearly also appears in Colossians;" idem 1997, 198f.; Best 1998, 64, 353.]

46. See esp. 2:1-8, 11-22; 3:2-13; 5:21-23, 25-33. Mitton 1951, 225-27 sees the change between "we" and "you" as an argument against the authenticity of the letter. G. Schille 1965, 17 (see diss. 1953; in addition, M. Dibelius/H. Greeven 1953, 112f.) sees the changes as devices for excerpts of elements of hymns, etc. The function of the change is in any case first to be understood in context; see Sampley 1971, 11f.

47. [See Seneca, *Ad Lucilium epistolae morales* 40:1 and 75:1ff.; Malherbe 1992, 285; Klauck 1998, 155-57, + 340, esp. 136. Cicero, *Philippica in M. Antonium* II. 4:7: *amicorum conloquias absentium*. Plett 1975, 17: "(Christian Weise [17TH CENTURY]) . . . *sermo absentis ad absentem* . . . ;" Dahl 1976b, 538-41; W. G. Müller 1994, 60-69; Mitchell 1998, 1757-60.]

48. [See L. R. Donelson 1986, 64f.: "The capacity of the Hellenistic letter to overcome the distance between friends and to make the absent present seems to be highlighted in pseudepigraphical letters. Moreover, in the pseudepigraphical letter, the letter is not an awkward and temporary substitute for an eventual meeting of sender and recipient, because such a meeting will never take place. The letter itself must carry the full and final presence of the sender;" further also Lincoln 1990, lxx-lxxiii.]

49. [Text with translation in J. L. White 1972 and idem 1986.] See also C.-H. Kim 1972; White 1972b; [idem 1984 and idem 1988;] C. J. Bjerkelund 1967; Hild. Cancik 1967, esp. 42-51, 60-66; [H. Cotton 1981; Malherbe 1992, 278-93; Hendrix 1988, 3-15; Sellin 1996, 292; otherwise Kl. Berger 1984, 1331].

another element appears: testimony to the sender's friendly disposition (φιλοφρόνησις) toward the recipients, which connects praise of the addressees with references to good relations in the past.[50] Nurturing good relations can be the primary purpose of a letter. Very often, however, the "friendship testimony," like the information, sets the background for polite but in part very strongly expressed requests that the addressees are expected to fulfill. The structure is easy to identify in the Pauline letters. The letter to Philemon serves as the simplest example. The assurance of thanksgiving, intercession and joy prepares for the request concerning the escaped slave Onesimos.[51] Paul expects that Philemon will receive Onesimos in a way that fully manifests the praise Paul has just expressed.[52]

In a certain respect, the composition of the letter to the Ephesians compares especially closely with that of 1 Thessalonians.[53] In 1 Thessalonians too the first major section is descriptive, framed by repeated thanksgiving and intercession (1 Thess. 1:3ff.; 2:13; 3:9-13).[54] The second major section is predominantly "preceptive," but also contains theological instruction (1 Thess. 4:13-17; 5:1-5; compare Eph. 4:7-16; 5:5, 23, 25-32).[55] In 1 Thessalonians as in Ephesians the paraenesis follows im-

50. Demetrius, *Peri Hermeneias/De Elucutione*. Discussing it, especially Koskenniemi 156, esp. 88-127; K. Thraede 1970, 17-25; Cancik 1967, 61-66; additional material in Dahl 1976b, 540f.

51. [See N. R. Petersen 1985, 83 note 66 with reference to Bjerkelund 1967, 123f. *et passim*: "I include in my understanding of the body of the Pauline letter the initial thanksgiving (*eucharisto*) section, which I also see as extending right up to the transition to the appeal or exhortation (*parakalo*). Thus I view the body of the Pauline letter as consisting of two main parts, which are linguistically introduced by thanksgiving and appeal formulas."]

52. See Bjerkelund 1967, 118-24; the expression of joy in v. 7 along with the assurance of thanksgiving in vv. 4-6 forms the background for the following request, see Weber 1970, 96-100. [That the letter to Philemon is not a private letter, but a Christian variation of an ancient letter of recommendation, that is to say, a public letter of recommendation, emphasizes especially M. Luetzsch 1994, 73-75 with notes 15-26, among other things with reference to "two other specifically named Christians, Apphia and Archippus, and furthermore an entire house church" (ibid., 74).]

53. [So already Bjerkelund 1967, 185-87; Vielhauer 1975, 204; Sellin 1996, 282, 290; on 1 Thess. See Johanson 1987, 67-69: "1 Thess. 1:2-3:13: A Predominant Expressive Function" (ibid. 67) . . . "1 Thess. 4:1-5:24: A Predominant Conative [[better: Persuasive (see *ibid.*, 65)-DH]] Function" (ibid., 72).]

54. [See now J. Lambrecht 2000a, 135-62.]

55. [See now J. Lambrecht 2000b, 163-78.]

*Translator's note: this is my attempt to render "anamnetische," which I will hereafter

mediately after the testimony to friendly relations and the recitation of the events in the addressees' coming to faith,* which serves to intensify the mutual connection between the sender and the recipients of the letter. In both letters, a polemical or theological section of the letter dedicated to a particular concern of the addressees' community (compare Romans 1:16–11:36) is missing.[56] This view relies too much on Romans in determining the "normal" structure of a Pauline letter. If a "normal" structure exists at all, it is to be found in Philemon and 1 Thessalonians. In the other letters, Paul varies the structure for various reasons and in different ways.[57] In Colossians, too, thanksgiving, intercession and recollections, etc., in 1:3–2:5, form the background for warnings and demands in 2:6–4:6. However, Ephesians does not closely resemble Colossians in structure.[58]

---

translate as "anamnetic," the English transliteration equivalent to the German.

56. On Ephesians see, e.g., Wikenhauser/Schmid 1973, 481; on 1 Thessalonians, P. Schubert 1939, 16–27, esp. 26; [now also Holmstrand 1997, esp. 71–74: I. Introduction (1:1-2); II. Corpus (1:2—5:25): 1. Thanksgiving (1:2—3:13); 2. Intercession and exhortation (4:1–5:25); III. Conclusion (5:26-28): "1 Thessalonians appears to be more uniform than is often claimed. The letter can be broken down into two parts, 1:2—3:13 and 4:1—5:25, which are distinct but nevertheless clearly related to one another" (ibid. 82); Klauck 1998, 267–81: I. Introduction (1:1-10): A. Prescript (1:1); B. Proömium (1:2-10); II. Corpus (2:1—5:11): A. Opening: Self Recommendation (2:1-12); B: Middle I: Desire to visit and the dispatch of a messenger (2:13-3:13); C. Middle II. Life before the endtime (4:1—5:11) D. Conclusion: Particular exhortations(5:12-22); III. Conclusion to the Letter (5:23-28): A. Epilogue: Benediction (5:23-24); B: Postscript (5:25-28); see R. W. Funk 1996, 270-71, and White 1972b, 70-72, 76-77, 86; Funk classifies 1 Thess. 2:1-12 as "the body." White distinguishes between "body-opening" (2:1-4), "body middle" (2:5-12 and 13:16) and "body-closing" (2:17—3:10). Applying this terminology, only Eph 2:11-22 constitutes the body of the letter, or rather its center.

57. In Romans, one can describe 1:16b—11:33 as a doctrinal exposition of the introductory part of the letter. In Galatians, the first part of the letter is not framed by thanksgiving and intercession, but rather by repeated expressions of disappointment (see 1:6-9; 3:1-5; 4:8-11). The demands begin in 4:12. Different from Ephesians, the mission and work of Paul appear first (1:11—2:20; compare Eph. 3:2-13), then the experiences of the reader (3:2-4:7; compare Eph. 1:13—2:22). [Best 1998, 353, however, stresses the structural proximity to Romans.]

58. [On the differing structure of Colossians, see now W. T. Wilson 1997, 259-54, who advances the theory that Colossians is organized in three parts on the model of Seneca's *Epistolae Morales* 16: "According to this interpretation, Colossians 1:2-2:7 (Section 1) constitutes paraenetic exhortation, 2:8-23 (Section II) paraenetic correction, and 3:1-4:6 (Section III) paraenetic exhortation, with 1:1-2 and 4:7-18 forming the text's epistolary framework."]

Structure of Ephesians[59]

[0. Προς Εφεσιους

1. Prescript (1:1-2)
2. Body: God's Call (1:3-6:20)
   2.1 First descriptive major section: the hope to which he has called you (ἡ ἐλπὶς τῆς κλήσεως) (1:3-3:21)[60]
       2.1.1. Introduction-Benediction (1:3-14)
   (Theme v. 3: God, who has blessed us with every blessing [Εὐλογητὸς ὁ θεὸς ... ὁ εὐλογήσας ἡμᾶς εν πάσῃ εὐλογίᾳ])
       2.1.2. Thanksgiving and Intercession (1:15-23)
   (Theme v. 15: I have heard of your faith and therefore I do not cease to give thanks for you as I remember you in my prayers [Διὰ τοῦτο κἀγὼ ἀκούσας τὴν καθ' ὑμᾶς πίστιν ... οὐ παύομαι εὐχαριστῶ ὑπὲρ ὑμῶν μνείαν ποιούμενος ἐπὶ τῶν προσευχῶν μου ...])
           2.1.2.1 Assurance of thanksgiving (1:15-16)
           2.1.2.2 Theme of the Intercession: Revelation of the knowledge of God (1:17-19a)
           2.1.2.3. Declaration of the manifestation of God's power through Christ's resurrection and heavenly enthronement (1:19b-23).
   (Transition v. 19f: for us who believe, according to the working of his great power, God put this power to work in Christ when he raised him from the dead. [πιστεύοντας κατὰ τὴν ἐνέργειαν τοῦ κράτους τῆς ἰσχύος αὐτοῦ. Ἣν ἐνήργησεν ἐν τῷ Χριστῷ])
       2.1.3. Soteriological gift of grace (2:1-10)
   (Theme v. 8: For by grace you have been saved [Χάριτί ἐστε σεσωσμένοι])[61]
       2.1.4. Recollection of God's call through Christ's work of reconciliation (2:11-22) Theme v. 11: (So then, remember

---

59. [What follows is an attempt to put the structure of Ephesians in tabular form based on Dahl's analysis above.]

60. [Sellin 1996, 281 and 282 note 11 (and idem 1999, 1345) structures the first indicative-prescriptive section as cyclic-concentric: A.

61. [On Hübner's hypothesis that this theme is an interpolation (1997, 162f.), see the citation in note 264 below.]

that at one time you Gentiles by birth. [Διὸ μνημονεύετε ὅτι ποτὲ ὑμεῖς τὰ ἔθνη ἐν σαρκί]...[62] v.13: But now in Christ Jesus you have been brought near by the blood of Christ [νυνὶ δὲ ἐν Χριστῷ Ἰησοῦ ὑμεῖς ... ἐγενήθητε ἐγγὺς ἐν τῷ αἵματι τοῦ Χριστοῦ])

    2.1.5.   The realization of God's plan of salvation through Paul's mission (3:1–13) (Transition v. 2: if indeed you have heard of the stewardship of God's grace given to me for you [εἴ γε ἠκούσατε τὴν οἰκονομίαν τῆς χάριτος τοῦ θεοῦ τῆς δοθείσης μοι εἰς ὑμᾶς])

    2.1.6   Intercession (3:14–19)

(Transition v. 14: for this reason, I bow my knees before the father [τούτου χάριν κάμπτω τὰ γόνατά μου πρὸς τὸν πατέρα])

    2.1.7   Doxology (3:20–21)

(Theme v. 20: To him who by the power ... be glory in the church [Τῷ δὲ δυναμένῳ ... αὐτῷ ἡ δόξα ἐν τῇ ἐκκλησίᾳ ...])

2.2 Second, preceptive major section: I beg you therefore ... to lead a life worthy of the calling (παρακαλῶ οὖν ὑμᾶς ... ἀξίως περιπατῆσαι τῆς κλήσεως) (4:1–6:20)[63] (Theme v. 1: I beg you therefore to lead a life [παρακαλῶ οὖν ὑμᾶς ... περιπατῆσαι])

    2.2.1   Exhortation to a way of life worth of God's call (4:1–16)

        2.2.1.1   Summons to preserve unity (4:2–6)

        2.2.1.2   Goal: growth of the body of Christ

    2.2.2   Exhortation to a change of way of life (4:17–16)

(Theme v. 17: Now this I affirm and testify in the Lord, that you must no longer live as the Gentiles do, in the futility of their minds. [τοῦτο οὖν λέγω καὶ μαπτύρομαι ἐν κυπίῳ, μηκέτι ὑμᾶς περιπατεῖν, καθὼς καὶ τὰ ἔθνη περιπατεῖ ἐν ματαιότητι τοῦ νοὸς αὐτῶν])

---

62. [See also Article 7, note 50, *Studies in Ephesians*.]

63. [Sellin 1996, 281 and 297 (also 1999, 1345) once again characterizes the second paraenetic section as cyclic-concentric:
A: 4:1–16 (Unity in diversity)
B: 4:17–24 (The old man and the new)
C: 4:25–32: (dually listed exhortations)
D: 5:1–2:(imitation of God with Christ as model)
C': 5:3–14 (dually listed exhortations)
B': 5:15–20 (the foolish life (of the old man) and the spirit-filled life (of the new man)
A': 5:21–6:9 (The family as the locus and image of unity).]

2.2.2.1   Forward/preface to specific instruction:[64] Exhortation to put off the old man and put on the new (4:17–24) (Transition vv. 22–24: Put off your old nature . . . and be renewed in the spirit of your minds, and put on the new nature [ἀποθέσθαι ὑμας . . . τὸν παλαιὸν ἄνθρωπον . . . ἀνανεοῦσθαι δὲ τῷ πυεύματι τοῦ νοὸς ὑμῶν καὶ ἐυδύσασθαι τὸν καινὸν ἄνθρωπον])

2.2.2.2   Specific instructions, often in formulations antithetical to the rationales (4:25–5:14)

2.2.3   The household code (5:15–6:9) (Theme v. 15: Be careful then how you live, not as unwise people but as wise [βλέπετε οὖν ἀκριβῶς πῶς περιπατεῖτε μὴ ὡς ἄσοφοι ἀλλ' ὡς σοφοι])

2.2.3.1.   Exhortation to the virtuous life (5:15–21) (Transition v. 21: Be subject to one another out of reverence for Christ [Ὑποτασσόμενοι ἀλλήλοις ἐν φόβῳ Χριστοῦ])

2.2.3.2.   Instructions for wives and husbands (5:22–33)

2.2.3.3.   Instructions for children, fathers, slaves and masters (6:1–9)

2.2.4   Concluding Exhortations (6:10–20)[65] (Theme v. 10: Finally, be strong in the Lord and in the strength of his power [τοῦ λοιποῦ, ἐυδυναμοῦσθε ἐυ κυρίῳ καὶ εν τῷ κράτει τῆς ισχύος αὐτοῦ])

---

64. [See above note 29. Schnelle 1996, 355 joins this concluding paraenesis to the conclusion of the letter.]

65. [Pokorný 1992, 48 classifies the concluding exhortations as the fourth part of the second major section; Sellin 1996, 291, 297 note 110 in contrast understands this section of the text as a third major section and thereby makes possible his cyclic-concentric structural analysis of the paraenetic major sections, see above note 63?; Lincoln 1990, xliii-xliv presents two structural analyses, an epistolary structure (like most interpretations), where the concluding exhortations are classified as the fourth part of the second major section, and a rhetorical structure, where the concluding exhortations are classified as a separate major section, a peroration (as by Sellin, ibid.); Klauck 1998, 238f. also sets out these same two structures, while R. E. Brown 1997, 621, however, presents first a "formal" structure, and then a "textual" structure. See also above note 24.]

3. Conclusion with Postscript[66]
   3.1 Epilogue (6:21–22)[67] (Theme v. 21: So that you may also know how I am and what I am doing. [ἵνα δὲ εἰδῆτε καὶ ὑμεῖς τὰ κατ' ἐμέ, τί πράσσω.])
   3.2 Postscript (6:23–24).[68]

1.2 Style and Characteristics

The structural similarity between Ephesians and 1 Thessalonians only brings the differences between the two letters into sharper focus. In 1 Thessalonians everything is true to life, concrete and personal. Paul reminds the Thessalonians of their own experiences, when they first heard the gospel message, of his own behavior among them and of his later desire, grief and consolation. The admonitions are indeed traditional, but refer to specific situations. In Ephesians, everything remains remarkably general, despite the letter form. 1 Thessalonians revives a temporarily suspended relationship, while Ephesians makes the first contact. The difference in timing is not enough to explain the contrasts between the two letters.[69] Romans and Colossians are also addressed to communities that Paul has not yet visited. In each of them, however, we find much more about the recipients and about their connection to Paul than we do in Ephesians.

The absence of specifics differentiates Ephesians from all the other letters ascribed to Paul. There is not a single mention of a place, not even, according to the most ancient manuscripts, in the address.[70] Apart from Paul, Tychicus and Jesus, not a single person is called by name. There are temporal references, but they are not to common experiences, but to the times before and after God's act in Christ and the coming to belief of the recipients, to the "evil day" (6:13) or to the "day of redemption" (4:30), to

---

66. [So too Vielhauer 1975, 204; Lincoln 1990, 461; Pokorný 1992, 48; see also above note 23.]

67. [See note 30 above.]

68. [When Best 1998, 613, notes that; "the five words with which AE begins ... form a ἵνα clause which does not add anything to the information given in the second ἵνα clause ... ," he has failed to see that the first ἵνα clause is meta-reference, which though admittedly different in content, is nevertheless analogous to other thematic sentences; see also note 80 below.]

69. [On the setting of Ephesians, see section 6 below.]

70. [More on this in section 5.1 below.]

the time before the foundation of the world, the age to come, and so on (e.g., 1:4, 21; 2:7). Specific conversion experiences are not mentioned.[71]

About the recipients of the letter, we know only that they were once Gentiles, but heard the gospel message, became believers and were sealed with the Holy Spirit (1:13f.; 2:11). It is taken for granted that they have heard of Paul without having known him personally (3:2). We can surmise that they live in Asia Minor only by comparing Ephesians 6:21 to Colossians 4:7-9.

What the letter says about Paul is also very general, basically only a retrospective on the revelation entrusted to him and on his work as proclaimer of the gospel message to the Gentiles (3:2-12). Additionally, we learn that he is imprisoned and that his sufferings, like his active ministry, benefit Gentile Christians (3:1, 13; 4:1). Imprisonment has not foreclosed the possibility of his preaching (6:19-20). Nothing is said about the reasons for his arrest, about the possibilities for release, about coworkers or about travel plans, etc. Nothing suggests that Ephesians, as is probably the case for Romans, is motivated more by the Apostle's plans than by the circumstances of the recipients.

In comparison to Colossians, it particularly stands out that the admonitions against false teaching are vague and general (4:14; 5:6). The unification of those who had been separated, Jews and Gentiles, is strongly emphasized (2:14-18; 3:5-6). However, the recipients appear all to have been of Gentile origin, and it is by no means clear that their relationship to Jews, either in their own community, or in their region, or indeed in Jerusalem, was a current problem.

The letter imparts no new information, but reminds the recipients of what they already know or should know. The only exceptions are the recommendation of Tychicus (6:21-22), and perhaps also the instruction about the correct interpretation of Genesis 2:24 and Psalm 68:19 [LXX 67:19] (Eph. 5:31f.: 4:8-11). Despite its epistolary form, Ephesians cannot be described as part of a dialogue.[72] Not only are familiar forms of

---

71. The only temporal adverbs in Ephesians are: ποτέ, νῦν, νυνί, μηκέτι, οὐκέτι, πάντοτε. Only μέχρι is used as a temporal conjunction (4:13), but neither ὅτε nor ὅταν.

72. According to Demetrius, Περὶ ἑπμηνείας /De Elocutione 223, the letter is τὸ ἕτερρον μέρος τοῦ διαλόγου (according to Artemon, the editor of Aristotle's letters). This analysis has as its model the style of a literary dialogue. The view that a letter is part of a conversation is prevalent among analysts in antiquity of epistolary form: e.g., Pseudo-Libanius (or rather Proclus), *Charactaeres epistolares*, Introduction, p. 14 (V. Weichert (editor) 1910 [or R. Foerster (editor) 1927; reproduced in Malherbe 1988, 66 [2]: Ἐπιστολὴ μὲν οὖν ἐστιν ὁμιλία τις ἐγγράμματος ἀπόντος πρρὸς ἀπόντα γινομένη

address like "(my) brothers and sisters," "beloved" and the like[73] missing, but also the allusions to questions, slogans, objections or opposing arguments, which make the interpretation of the other Pauline letters both fascinating and difficult. It is significant that Ephesians has no questions that demand an answer or that contain an accusation. The only direct question is rhetorical, or rather hermeneutical (4:9).[74]

Then absence of familiarity and warm affinity distinguishes Ephesians from the "short" Pauline letters (1 Thessalonians, Philippians, Philemon). The distance from the argumentative style of the chief letters, (Romans, 1 and 2 Corinthians, Galatians) is clearly even greater. Ephesians sets out no assumptions, from which to draw conclusions. It lacks not only the preceding conditional phrases, but also many of the conjunctions and particles that otherwise link the sentences together.[75] Problems are not posed and resolved. Neither is Ephesians an animated diatribe, with statements to often imaginary dialogue partners, questions, objections, emphatic denials and the like. Ephesians, unlike the chief letters, does not attack opponents or defend Paul. The letter exhorts the recipients to turn from evil and to do good; different possible grounds for decision are simply not discussed.[76]

The most positive characteristics of style we can group under the headings "plerophory" and "successive subordination."[77] Especially noteworthy are the many genitive constructions, that join two or more nouns

---

καὶ χρειώδη σκοπὸν ἐκπληροῦσα, ἐρεῖ δέ τις ἐν αὐτῇ ὥσπερ παρόν τις πρὸς παρόντα]). Compare Koskenniem 1956, 38-42, as well as Thraede 1970, 17-25; [more above in note 47].

73. See E. Schweizer 1963, 429; W. Bujard 1973, 208-10. The exhortations aimed at specific groups in the household code are of a different character. The lack of familiarity and warm affinity distinguishes Ephesians.

74. Direct questions are admittedly rare in the lesser Pauline letters, only in Phil. 1:18; 1 Thess. 2:19; 3:9f.; Col. 2:20-22. [On questions in the Pauline letters, see Dahl 1993.]

75. Ἄν, διότι, εἴπερ, ἐπεί, ἐπειδή, ἐφ' ᾧ (causal), μή (conj.), ὅπως, οὐδέ, οὔτε, οὐχί, πολλῷ μᾶλλον, ὥσπερ, ὥστε and others are all missing. Admittedly, Colossians has even fewer conjunctions, see Bujard 1973, 48-53.

76. Otherwise, e.g., 1 Cor. 7, 8-10 and Rom. 14. In Galatians, the main question is whether the Galatians will follow the teaching of the Judaizers or that of Paul. The tone of Galatians is unusually harsh, but on the whole the letter is more "deliberative" (or "symbouletic") than apologetic [so also Sellin, 1996, 294, note 92;]; otherwise, H. D. Betz 1974-75, 353-79 [= idem 1994, 63-97]; idem 1979, 14-25 [= idem 1988, 54-72].

77. Plerophory is commonly recognized; see already E. Percy 1946, 185-91; the designation "successive subordination" was introduced by H. Lester (1973, 111-19).

to each other.⁷⁸ Additional examples of the plerophoric style are coordinated synonymous nouns, other synonyms, appositions, parenthetical insertions, and a great many tightly connected clauses introduced by prepositions. Even rhetorical flourishes are in Ephesians an aspect of plerophory; they only rarely serve to make the style livelier.⁷⁹

The other main indication of style is successive subordination. The thematic sentences are almost without exception first.⁸⁰ From then on, the thought is more finely developed. Prepositional phrases, relative clauses, participial constructions and/or causal, comparative or subordinate clauses are joined to the thematic sentence or to each other. In general, one colon follows immediately after another. In this way, the compound sentences continue unbroken and almost without end.⁸¹

The combination of plerophory and successive subordination is especially notable where the thematic development advances cyclically, from an event to its cause and then from the cause to its result or its goal. This kind of cycle allows the original assertion to be revisited, and further developed from a new perspective. This type of cyclic, successive subordination is particularly conspicuous in chapter 1:3–13, but is also found elsewhere.⁸² Even without a completed cycle, an assertion can be developed initially and then taken up again and developed further (see 2:12ff., 19). There are also examples of anacoluthons in Ephesians.⁸³

The recurrence of the same or related phrasings has the result that sometimes small sections can be omitted without the reader noticing a break, or that something is missing. The relative clauses introduced with "in him" (ἐν ᾧ) in 1:7, 11, 13 could follow immediately after "in Christ" (ἐν Χριστῷ) in v. 1:3; they are not parallel with one another, but connect to the immediately preceding sentences. The development of themes in cyclic spirals is not unique to Ephesians. But in Romans, to name a single example, individual questions nearly always introduce digressions,

---

78. [At length on this point, see Sellin 1992, 85–107.]

79. The exception is Eph. 2:8–9; see footnote 300 and accompanying text.

80. Really noteworthy is only the prefix of a final clause in 6:21. In 6:8 the (conditional or relative) subordinate clause is inserted into the declarative sentence. Inserted subordinated clauses also occur earlier, e.g., 3:15; 5:3–4, 18; 6:2, 16.

81. See 1:3–14, 15–21; 2:1–3, 4–7, 15–18, 19–22; 3:2–7, 8–12, 14–19; 4:11–16; 5:17–23, 25–28.

82. See, e.g., 3:2–11; 5:25–33.

83. See esp. 2:1ff. and 2:5; 3:1ff. and 3:14. On the topic of Paul's entirely different use of anacoluthons, see G. Bornkamm 1961, 76–92.

which must be clarified before the main theme can be taken up again and brought to its conclusion.[84] In Ephesians, the thematic cycles more often develop the same theme in different ways. That is also true for larger sections. In chapters 1–2 appear three different aspects of the same salvation history (1:2–14; 1:18–23; 2:10–22). Two thematic introductions to the paraenesis present the same basic ideas (4:1 and 17–24).

The sentences setting out the paraenetic rules are shorter than elsewhere.[85] Asyndeta are more frequent, and positive and negative imperatives are coordinated with one another (see esp. 4:25–5:5). A justification regularly follows, why something is to be done or to be avoided, be it the cause, the result or the goal. A comparison to related demands in Colossians shows that the tendency to subordination appears even in Ephesians' paraenesis. Despite the stylistic differences within the letter, individual instances of style and syntax join to form an overall picture that harmonizes with the nature and overall organization of this singular letter.[86]

The style of Ephesians is characterized as "liturgical" or "hymnic." There are several reasons for that characterization. The succession "eulogy—thanksgiving—prayer—doxology" recurs with several variations in the text of prayers.[87] Several stylistic idiosyncrasies and individual phrases have marked parallels in Jewish and early Christian hymns and prayers.[88] But so far no one has been able to point to a liturgical text with an overall style really similar to that of Ephesians. The frequency of the relative clauses and participial constructions are not in themselves an indication of a hymnic style, especially since they are only rarely parallel with one another or are used as attributes of Christ. The observation that "the endless sequence of loosely connected very long sentences is also

---

84. See, e.g., J. Dupont 1955, 365–97; [also Hellholm 1997, 395, 404f., 408].

85. [See Best 1998. 353: "There is also a significant change of style in that, 4:11–16 apart, the long convoluted sentences of the earlier chapters disappear and are replaced by a crisper approach consisting mainly of brief sentences."]

86. The defenders of the authenticity of the letter have rightly stressed this point, see A. van Roon 1974, 205–12. The question, however, is whether or not the overall evidence points to a single author different from Paul, as for example Lester, 1973, 102–28 et passim [and now most exegetes] believe.

87. See Gnilka 1990, 26f. with reference to Dan. 3:26–45; Jub. 22:6–9, etc.

88. Examples quoted especially by Kirby, 1968, 132–38; S. Lyonnet 1961, 341–52; Percy 1946, 31 note 19; 39 note 33; 218–222; 480–81, 242.

found in the Qumran hymns"[89] doesn't help, since in the Qumran texts an overall coordination prevails that is missing in Ephesians.

Liturgical speech in Judaism and early Christianity was not limited to the sacramental realm. Praise and prayer were features of daily life, from morning to night (see Eph. 5:19f.). Praise was also customary on receipt of good news, and in important meetings. Praise of God for his blessings to human beings sometimes concludes these congratulatory messages.[90] Since the eulogy in Eph. 1:3-14 strikes the same note as the letter overall, one can with some justice describe Ephesians as a letter congratulating its recipients on their becoming believers. That is certainly not to say everything. The author explains and justifies—in order to convince. This is the purpose of the causative, consecutive, comparative, adversative, epexegetical and final connection of sentences and sentence elements.

If one classifies persuasive speech as "rhetorical" then one would describe the style of Ephesians as rhetorical rather than as "liturgical."[91] Admittedly, Ephesians has almost nothing in common with the forensic or deliberative (symbouletic) rhetorical genres.[92] Against that, one could with some justification assign Ephesians to the third rhetorical genre, "demonstrative" or "epideictic."[93] To this genre also belong panegyrics, eulogies for the living or dead, for gods and cities, and so on.[94] Ephesians is for long stretches a eulogy on God's power and mercy in Christ, on the privileges granted to the letter's recipients and to all Christians, and on the ministry of Paul. The greatness and glory of God's salvation event is stressed, by way of contrast to the reprehensible conduct of the Gentiles.

89. K. G. Kuhn 1960/61, 335.

90. [See Chapter VII in Studies in Ephesians.]

91. On the archetypes of rhetoric, see Aristotle, Ars rhetorica; Quintillian, Inst. Orat.; among modern handbooks, we should mention H. Lausberg 1973 [idem 1976; J. Martin 1974; G. Urding (ed.) 1992ff.; S. E. Porter (ed.) 1997.]

92. [Sellin 1996, 292 asserts that "the exhortatio belongs almost exclusively to the symbouletic rhetorical genus" and thus concludes that the second part of Ephesians must rather be classified as symbouletic.; so also idem 1999, 1345.]

93. [So with certain reservations with respect to the first part of Ephesians, Sellin also characterizes Ephesians as a whole as "a mixture of the epideictic and symbouletic rhetorical genres" (ibid., 1999, 1345). Sellin also observes with a reference to Brucker 1997, 181ff., "mixing of rhetorical genres and changes of style were not uncommon in ancient writings" (ibid., note 78). 1 Peter, related in other respects to Ephesians, also belong to the epideictic genre, see L. Thuren 1990.]

94. On eulogies for cities and constitutions, see D. L. Balch 1981, 23-59.

INTRODUCTION TO THE LETTER TO THE EPHESIANS 215

The entire argument is aimed at persuading the recipients to understand this and act accordingly.

The character of these "demonstrative" arguments presupposes an audience of baptized Gentiles. Past and future matter only to the extent that they are relevant to the present existence in Christ. Neither events of Israel's history nor eschatological events, such as the second coming of Jesus or the future resurrection, are discussed thematically. Christian existence in the present is set in a broader context of cause and goal. The perspective extends from the plan of God and his election from before the foundation of the world to the day of salvation and the coming age. The present as constituted by the Christ event always remains the center of attention. Some have contrasted this glorification of the present to Paul's theology, in that it lacks an eschatological aspect.[95] The contrast is not simply the result of a different theology.[96] It is in any event also a rhetorical difference, resulting from the different type of argumentation, and the dependence on hymnic language.[97]

The style taken as a whole shows that Ephesians is unique. In several places, the influence not only of the Septuagint, but also of Semitic sense of language, shine through. Both semiticisms and possibly Greek constructions are somewhat more frequent in Ephesians than in the other Pauline letters.[98] Successive subordination would be even more unusual in Hebrew or Aramaic than in Greek. Jewish Hellenism provides without any doubt the environment for the language, style and conceptual framework.[99] To the extent that a particular style is identifiable as the homiletic style of the Greek-speaking synagogue, 1 Peter, James, Hebrews and the Pastoral Epistles are much better examples than Ephesians.[100] A comparison to Colossians, 1 Peter and other early Christian literature shows that the common heritage has been reconfigured and stylistically integrated.

---

95. See esp. Conzelmann 1981a, 97; [idem 1965/74, 234/180 and idem 1979, 85–96; with respect to Ephesians, see Pokorný 1992, 16].

96. [See now M. Gese 1997.]

97. [On that point, see Lincoln, 1990, xli-xlvii; Hübner 1997, 22f.; Best 1997a (4), 51–68; idem 1998, 59–63.]

98. See J. H. Moulton/W. F. Howard 1929, 485; but esp. Kuhn 1960–61, 334–46 and Kl. Beyer 1962, 298.

99. See Van Roon 1974, 182–92; [so also Schnelle 1996, 358f.].

100. See A. Wifstrand 1967, 11–13, 30–32 [and further, for, among others, 1 Clement, 4 Maccabees, James, Hebrews, Didache 1–6, 16, Barnabas, see H. Thyen 1955, 11–26].

The style of Ephesians is also highly idiosyncratic when compared to that of the other Pauline letters. In Colossians too the style is plerophoric, and there too the compound sentences are excessively long. Phrases are much more often parallel with one another, so that H. Lester differentiates between the "appositional" style of Colossians, and Ephesians' "successive subordination."[101] Despite the differences, the Pauline corpus provides better and closer analogies to the idiosyncrasies of Ephesians than does any other literary corpus. One can assert that the literary uniqueness of Ephesians consists in the absence of some indications of Pauline style, while others appear more frequently than in the other Pauline letters. Scholars differ on the issue of whether or not Ephesians' uniqueness is consistent with Pauline authorship.

2. FROM THE HISTORY OF CRITICISM

The history of the canon of the New Testament shows that literary, historical and in part substantive biblical criticism were not entirely alien to the ancient church. Discussions about the Johannine writings, Hebrews and even about the short letter to Philemon prove this point. However, the Pauline authorship of Ephesians was not questioned in antiquity. To the extent it was discussed at all, the idiosyncratic style of Ephesians was ascribed to its catechetical character.[102] John Chrysostom noted as the special grandeur of Ephesians that in it Paul revealed things on which he was otherwise silent.[103] Only Marcion advanced a more radical critique; he tried to purify an underlying Pauline text from later interpolations. However, his treatment of Ephesians does not differ from that of the other Pauline letters he acknowledged as authentic. He spared only Philemon; the Pastoral Epistles he did not include in his Pauline canon.

Tertullian describes the address "To the Laodiceans" as Marcion's (whom he ironically describes as a "most diligent explorer") conjecture.[104] It is more likely, however, that Marcion found the title in a manuscript. The Ephesian address became generally accepted, apparently without

---

101. Lester 1973, 111-19.

102. See Euthalius, *Argumenta* MPG 85. 761 C; see also G. W. H. Lampe 1968, s.v. πρόγραμμα.

103. J. Chrysostom, *Sermons on Ephesians*, MPG 62.10.

104. Tertullian, *Adv. Marc.* V 17, MPL 2, 544-45; A. von Harnack 1924/85, 21-51; Beilage III 43*-56* *passim*.

much discussion. Where it was observed that the letter could not have been directed to a community in which Paul had stayed for a long time, the response was that the letter was sent before Paul went to Ephesus.[105] Theodor Beza was the first to hypothesize that the letter was a circular letter to several communities of Asia Minor.[106] Archbishop Ussher modified this thesis, to suggest that in the exemplar a space was left after the words "who are in" (τοῖς οὖσιν) that could be filled in with the names of the cities Tychichos was visiting.[107] Since then, discussion about the address of the letter, whether historical or fictional, has not ceased. A wide array of hypotheses have been advanced, but the most probable remain Ephesus, Laodicea or a broader circle of cities of Asia Minor. The history of criticism is defined not only by the issue of address, but also by the issue of authorship.

Erasmus was the first to voice critical doubts about the Pauline authorship of Ephesians. Doubts about authenticity generated by the idiosyncratic style have been overshadowed by those generated by content.[108] Only much later was the letter tradition attributed to Paul, held, along with Colossians, to be pseudepigraphical, but both by the same author, as far as we know first by the English Deist Evanson.[109] His arguments were mostly historical, based on a comparison with Acts. More methodical criticism dates from the beginning of the 19th century. After Schleiermacher and Usteri expressed the view that Paul had assigned the composition of the letter to an assistant, de Wette above all set out the arguments against the letter's authenticity: language, style, dependence on Colossians, connection with post-apostolic writings, and so on.[110]

De Wette's groundbreaking studies exerted far-reaching influence. His opinion, that Colossians was Pauline, but not Ephesians, never found general acceptance. Eichhorn attributed Ephesians to Paul,[111] Colossians

---

105. Theodore of Mopsuestia. *Commentary*, MPG 66, 911; similarly also Euthalius, MPG 85.761 [οὔπω μὲν ἑωπακως αὐτούς].

106. Theodor Beza 1598, 288.

107. J. Ussher 1654, 686.

108. Erasmus 1519/1705, 413/831: [Certainly the style differs so much from that of the other Pauline epistles, that the author could be viewed as someone else ... ; see Schlier 1963, 18 note 3 and Vielhauer 1975, 207 note 5.].

109. E. Evanson 1792, 26, 261-63.

110. F. Schleiermacher 1895, 8f., 165, 166 note 1, 194; L. Usteri 1824, 2ff., 256f., 269f.; W. M. L. de Wette 1847, 86-93; idem 1826/48, 256ff., 282-94.

111. [J. Eichhorn 1812, 279: Ephesians was a Pauline autograph; so later also

to an assistant.[112] E. Th. Mayerhoff went further, and tried to show by detailed arguments that Colossians was pseudepigraphical and dependent on Ephesians. He also doubted the authenticity of Ephesians, in his view the earlier letter. His work was largely ignored in later research on authenticity.[113]

F. C. Baur and his school contested the authenticity of both letters.[114] Generally, Colossians was considered the earlier letter; however, both letters could also be ascribed to the same author. For "Tendency Criticism" the common assignment of both letters to the history of ideas in the second century was important, and not only their "catholic" character but also their proximity to Gnosticism were stressed. Both the late dating and similar classification as inauthentic of all the shorter Pauline letters provoked counter arguments.

More complicated solutions were also proposed. The Dutch scholar S. Hoekstra believed that Ephesians, though later, was more "Pauline" than the earlier, pseudonymous, Colossians.[115] C. H. Weise[116] and F. Hitzig[117] tried to solve the problem by the hypothesis that Colossians in its original form was Pauline, but that there were later non-Pauline interpolations.[118] This hypothesis was set out in detail by H. J. Holtzmann, who used and improved the observations of his predecessors. The result of his detailed study was that Ephesians was dependent on Colossians, but also the reverse: Colossians was at some points dependent on Ephesians. The explanation offered for this hypothesis was that the author of Ephesians used an authentically Pauline version of Colossians, but inserted interpolations into the authentic text of Colossians.[119]

The work of de Wette, Mayerhoff, Baur and Holtzmann, and their critics, set out the basic data and explored the important alternatives. Holtzmann's work remained for more than two generations the most

---

P. Ewald 1910, 49: "I think it not unlikely that Ephesians alone of Paul's letters was written by his own hand."]

112. Eichhorn, *ibid.*, 278ff.: Timotheos!

113. E. Th. Mayerhoff 1838, esp. 143-47. Mayerhoff, who died as a young lecturer, was rehabilitated by Bujard 1973, 11 (see the Index under Mayerhoff).

114. Baur 1866-67; idem 1844, 385-92; A. Schwegler 1846, 330ff., 375ff.

115. S. Hoekstra 1868, 599-652; [see also below notes 164 and 166.]

116. [C. H. Weise 1867, 59.]

117. F. Hitzig 1870, 22-26.

118. See H. J. Holtzmann 1872, 24; Hitzig, ibid.

119. Holtzmann 1872, esp. pp. 148-93; see also P. W. Schmiedel 1885, 139f.

thorough investigation of the mutual relationship and origin of the two letters. Commentaries and introductions to the New Testament improved the evidence and refined to some degree the reasoning, but largely presented variants of the same solutions using variations of the same arguments.

Westcott, Hort and most English scholars adhered to the traditional attribution of both Colossians and Ephesians to Paul, as well as conservative Protestants,[120] and, for a long time, many Catholics.[121] The early and unanimous attestation of Ephesians supports the traditional view. The vindication of the authenticity of the seven letters of Ignatius and Zahn also supported the traditional attribution of Ephesians to Paul.[122]

From the nearly universally acknowledged authenticity of Philemon, some took another step to assert the authenticity of Colossians, and still another to assert the authenticity of Ephesians. One could counter critical objections by observing that vocabulary, style and content also varied widely in Paul's generally accepted letters. These scholars wished to reserve to Paul alone the combination of typically Pauline elements and creative originality.[123]

Conservative scholars have also been willing to take into account Paul's intellectual development, and that his state of mind and style might be influenced by his external circumstances, for example by his imprisonment in Caesarea (E. Haupt[124])—or in Rome or Ephesus. Critical scholars have generally assumed that Paul's teaching was more dogmatic and specific. Place, time and the reason the letter was written, and to whom, were discussed by defenders of its authenticity, without achieving a consensus. It is worth noting that [until recently] most scholarly

---

120. [E.g., Ewald, 1910, esp pp. 24-35; W. Michaelis 1954, 196-99 (Eph.) and 214-18 (Col.).]

121. [Most new Catholic commentaries no longer assert Pauline authorship, e.g., Gnilka 1990; F. Mussner 1982a see also idem 1992b; Schnackenburg 1982; so also J. Blank 1968, 19-22; Merklein 1973a, 19-54 and Klauck 1998, 238 and 242.]

122. [Th. Zahn 1873; J. B. Lightfoot 1889.]

123. Besides the defenders of authenticity in note 120, also: J. Hort, 1895 11-69; Zahn 1897-99, 347-68; see also L. Cerfaux 1960, 60-71 and Brown 1963, 373-79 [Brown has since cautiously changed his opinion; see note 140 below.]

124. E. Haupt 1902, esp. 70-83.

commentaries on Ephesians were written on the assumption that it was authentically Pauline.[125] [That is no longer the case.][126]

De Wette's intermediate position, that the letter to the Colossians was Pauline, but not Ephesians, is adopted by few commentators (but above all by Dibelius[127]), but more by the authors of excellent introductory treatises, including Goguel,[128] Moffat,[129] Mosbech,[130] McNeile,[131] Kümmel.[132] [A few commentators maintain that Colossians is not Pauline, but was written during Paul's lifetime by one of his students.[133] The introductions of, among others, Marxsen,[134] Vielhauer,[135] Schenke/Fischer,[136] Köster,[137] Conzelmann/Lindemann,[138] Schnelle[139] and Brown[140] describe both letters as deutero-Pauline.[141]]

In the first half of the 20th century, the view that Colossians was Pauline, but not Ephesians, became the consensus position. Various factors contributed to its popularity. Holtzmann's interpolation

125. B. F. Westcott 1906; Haupt 1902; Ewald 1910; T. K. Abbott 1897; J. A. Robinson 1904; Schlier 1963 [but see note 165 below]; Barth 1974.

126. [In addition to the Catholic commentaries mentioned in note 121, see Conzelmann 1981a; Lindemann 1985; Lincoln 1990; M. Bouttier 1991, Pokorný 1992; Hübner 1997; Luz 1998; so too V. P. Furnish 1992, 539-41; L. Hartman 1997b, 95 and 105.]

127. Dibelius/Greeven 1953.

128. M. Goguel 1926, 392-430, esp. 424 (Col.); 431-73, esp. 470 (Eph.)

129. J. Moffat 1918, 373-95.

130. H. Mosbech 1946-49, 512-26.

131. A. H. McNeile 1927, 154-63.

132. W. G. Kümmel 1963, 241-49, 257-62; idem, 1973, 298-305, 314-20; Kümmel gives a classic overview of the arguments. [Kümmel has since cautiously modified his view on Colossians, as on 2 Thessalonians, idem 1985, 483f: "One must acknowledge that Pauline authorship of the two letters is considered very unlikely."]

133. So, e.g., Schweizer 1976, 20-27; W. H. Ollrog 1979, 236-42; Hartman 1985, 200-01; see also idem 1997a, 169; Luz 1198b, 185-90 vacillates between a coworker's letter and pseudonymity.

134. [Marxsen 1978, 159-161, 169-171.]

135. [Vielhauer 1975, 196-200, 207-12.]

136. [Schenke/Fischer 1978, 165-67, 181-86.]

137. [H. Köster 1980, 701-09.]

138. [Conzelmann/Lindemann 1995, 289-90, 300.]

139. [Schnelle 1996, 239-35, and 349-52.]

140. [Brown 1997, 615-17 (if somewhat reluctantly), 626-30.]

141. [So too R. Kieffer in his *Theology* (1979, 172-80) and Strecker in his *Theology* (1996, 576-594, 595-606).]

hypothesis was too complicated to be believable. Hermann von Soden gradually limited the interpolation to Col. 1:15b–16; in this form, the hypothesis contributed little to understanding the relationship of the two letters.[142] The idiosyncratic terminology is used in Colossians to explain the religious conceptual framework of the opponents, but not in Ephesians.[143] The close connection to Philemon also ties Colossians to a specific place, while both the absence of a concrete context and a number of statements (among others, 2:20 and 3:6) point to a later time of composition for Ephesians.

The relationship to Colossians is generally regarded as the most important argument against the Pauline authorship of Ephesians. Particularly decisive was the "parallel terminology despite different concepts."[144] W. Ochel sought to demonstrate in detail his assertion of a reworking of Colossians in Ephesians, though he also presupposes Pauline authorship of Colossians.[145]

E. J. Goodspeed strongly advocated a particular form of this hypothesis, which was widely accepted, especially in the United States. J. Weiss had already hypothesized that the author of Ephesians was the collector of the Pauline letters, and had also inserted some catholicizing interpolations in the other letters (e.g., 1 Cor. 1:2b; 11:16; 14:36b).[146] This last hypothesis Goodspeed rejected, as well as Weiss's assertion that it was the lost letter to the Laodiceans, rather than Colossians, that was the prototype for Ephesians. He accepted the view that Ephesians was written as an introduction to the first collection of Pauline letters, and bolstered this theory with new arguments and additional hypotheses.[147] Most impressive was the argument that the author of Ephesians had access to the older letters, while all other writers who used Paul's letters knew Ephesians.[148] Goodspeed found in Ephesians 3:3 a reference to what was

---

142. See Herman von Soden 1885, 320–68, 497–542, 672–702; idem 1893a, 15, 28, 33.

143. Dibelius/Greeven 1953, 53, as well as the excursus, The Relationship between Colossians and Ephesians, 83–85; E. Lohmeyer 1964, 12–14; H. J. Chadwick 1954/55, 261–75; idem 1960, 145–53.

144. Dibelius/Greeven 1953, 84; [Vielhauer 1975, 209.]

145. W. Ochel 1934.

146. J. Weiss 1912, 2208–10; idem 1917, 108f., 553f. [challenged by, e.g., Vielhauer 1975, 215.]

147. E. J. Goodspeed 1933, 1–75.

148. *Ibid.*, 79–81; tabular presentation, 82–165; an extensive justification by A. E.

written in earlier letters.¹⁴⁹ Goodspeed's student John Knox explained the notable proximity to Colossians and Philemon by the hypothesis that the Onesimus [of Philemon] was the collector of the letters and the author of the introductory letter; he also identified Onesimus with the bishop of that name known from the Letter of Ignatius of Antioch to the Ephesians. Knox also tried to corroborate Goodspeed's hypothesis from later history of tradition.¹⁵⁰

In a very painstaking study, C. L. Mitton abandoned the highly hypothetical, nearly novelistic, components of Goodspeed's and Knox's reconstruction. More emphasis fell on the evidence that the author of Ephesians had used not only Colossians, but also other letters of Paul. The large number of more or less literal points of contact and especially the blending of phrases from various letters and contexts indicates that two different authors were at work.¹⁵¹ However, it is not merely superficial, literal, imitation. The author of Ephesians knew nearly all of Colossians, and memorable extracts of other letters of Paul, by heart, so that he could use them freely.¹⁵²

Mitton took the priority of Colossians as a given, but didn't prove it. J. Coutts was able to show that by the same kind of reasoning, one could arrive at the opposite conclusion, that Colossians used and conflated statements from Ephesians and other Pauline letters.¹⁵³ Independently of Mitton, F. C. Synge argued similarly: the form of the phraseological contacts points to two different writers. The common sentences and phrases fit together best in the context of Ephesians. Only this otherwise higher quality letter could therefore be written by Paul.¹⁵⁴

Barrett 1941.

149. [See Goodspeed 1933, 39-46.]

150. J. Knox 1935, esp. 46-57 [2ⁿᵈ Ed. 1959, 91-108]; idem 1942, 56-60, 172-76.

151. Mitton 1951, 138-58.

152. "The absence of identical sentences suggests that Ephesians is not the work of a writer who copied from a document open in front of him. It points rather to an author who knew the earlier writing so well that he was able to reproduce from memory [some] of its phrases and word-sequences." Mitton 1951, 243-44; see also 246-84.

153. J. Coutts 1957/58, 201-07; see idem 1956/57, 115-27. [See now also Hübner 1997, 144-45, Excursus: On the question of literary dependence: "The textual agreements thus show that the author of Ephesians apparently is dependent not only on Colossians, but on Philemon as well." So also E. Lohse 1968, 246-48, Schnelle 1996, 356f.]

154. F. C. Synge 1941, 69-76; idem 1958, 53-59.

Without discussing Ephesians, E. P. Sanders applied Mitton's methods to Colossians. Especially in Col. 1 and 2, he found examples of use and blending of Pauline formulations, but did not discount the possibility that a genuine letter of Paul was the exemplar.[155] In addition, the interpolation hypothesis was revived, usually for Colossians,[156] but also for Ephesians,[157] or for both letters.[158] Purely literary comparison has led neither to a decisive verification of de Wette's view, nor to a definitive refutation of the theories of Mayerhoff and Holtzmann.

Hilgenfeld, von Weiszäcker and Pfleiderer endorse Baur's rejection of the authenticity of both letters.[159] In the first decade of the twentieth century, this was the radical view of a minority. Some stated frankly that mediating hypotheses were unsatisfactory: one either accepted the authenticity of both letters, or considered both of them as pseudepigraphs.[160] That is the consensus view now. At the same time, partly but not entirely due to Bultmann's influence,[161] skepticism about Pauline authorship of Colossians has noticeably intensified.[162] Most maintained the priority of Colossians,[163] but to complete a description of the range

---

155. E. P. Sanders 1966, 28–46, esp. 28 and 44–45.

156. Ch. Masson 1950; idem 1953; J. Knox 1938, 146 n. 2; P. N. Harrison 1950, 268–94, esp. 272; idem 1964a, 595–604; idem 1964b, 65–78; E. P. Sanders 1966, 28, 44–45. For older conjectures, see Percy 19.

157. Goguel 1935, 254–85; idem 1936, 73–99.

158. W. Hartke 1961, 431–34; cf. J. Weiss 1912, 2207 and 2209.

159. A. Hilfgenfeld 1875, 659–81; C. von Weiszäcker 1902, 541–45; O. Pfleiderer 1890, 433–64; also P. Wendland 1912, 361–64.

160. Haupt 1902, 70: "Either both letters are non-Pauline or both are Pauline." K. and S. Lake 1937, 141: "Both or neither of these epistles may be genuine, but a 'straddle' which accepts one and not the other combines all the difficulties and solves none."

161. R. Bultmann 1965, 182, 486.

162. Examples include: Bornkamm 1966, 139–56; Lohse 1968, 253–57; [E. Käsemann 1959, 1727–28; Conzelmann 1981b, 176f.; Vielhauer 1975, 196–200; Schenke/Fischer 1978, 165–72; Lindemann 1983, 9–11; Pokorný 1987, 2–4, 8–17; M. Wolter 1993, 27–33; H. D. Betz 1995; Strecker 1996, 577f.; Hübner 1997, 9f., 272–277; A. Standhartibnger 1999]; among Catholics, Gnilka 1991, 19–26; [as authentic, J. Ernst 1990, 373]. Particularly remarkable is how the view of J. Schmid evolved over time: compare Schmid in Wikenhauser/Schmid 1973, 463–75 (Col.) and 479–96 (Eph.) with Schmid's much earlier work in 1928.

163. So for example Ewald, 1851, 409f.; [Lindemann 1985, 11–12; Pokorný 1992, 7–8; Hübner 1997, 17 *et passim*; see also note 166 below.]

of views, Conzelmann assumed that the author of Ephesians also made "Paulinizing" changes to the later Colossians.[164]

Twentieth century research has generally modified older hypotheses and supported them with additional evidence. New questions and conclusions have indeed appeared, but their usefulness for resolving the question of authenticity is uncertain. H. Schlier developed the hypothesis that Ephesians presupposes a Gnostic salvation myth, on the assumption that the letter was not Pauline. Later, he embraced the authenticity of the letter, without abandoning his history of religions reconstruction.[165] In both cases the conclusion is the same: both Ephesians and Colossians arose in the same history of religions environment. According to H. Merklein, a "cosmic Christology" was only later Paulinized in Ephesians and conformed to church structure in Colossians.[166] Above all, phraseological parallels to the Qumran writings have been documented. They have been cited as evidence both for and against Pauline authorship.[167] The suggestion has also been made that Paul used a former Essene as his scribe for Ephesians.[168]

With history of religions research, the search for exemplars, traditions and fixed patterns sometimes goes hand in hand. Such efforts, inspired initially by E. Norden and A. Seeberg and later primarily by M. Dibelius, achieved results with respect to Ephesians.[169] As earlier some saw Ephesians as a mosaic or anthology of texts from Colossians and other Pauline writings,[170] today one can view the letter as a mosaic of hymnic-liturgical and catechetical traditions.[171] If that's even approximately

164. Conselmann 1981a, 102; [so also note 115 above and note 166 below].

165. In Schlier 1930, Schlier obviously assumes that Paul is not the author (*ibid.*, p. 39 n. 1 and 75); differently Schlier 1957/63, 22-28. [However, Schnackenburg 1982, 21 n. 16 reports "based on oral conversations, [Schlier] had at the last doubts about Pauline authorship."]

166. Merklein 1973a, 24; idem 1973b, 84, 100f.; [Merklein 1981b, 37ff., 52-53, 58-62,; 1989, 380f.; so also Schenke/Fischer 1978, 176f.]

167. Kuhn 1961, 334-46; Mussner 1963, 185-98; [C. C. Caragounis 1977; Dahl, "Ephesians and Qumran," Studies in Ephesians.

168. J. Murphy O'Connor 1965, 1201-09.

169. E. Norden 1923, 240-308; A. Seeberg 1966, *passim*, but esp. 38, 80 and 239; Dibelius 1931, esp. 1-10; Dibelius/Greeven 1964, 14-23.

170. The word "mosaic" was first used by von Soden (1893b, 95): "like a work of mosaic." See Goodspeed 1933, 5-8; A. D. Nock 1937, 230; Johnston 1962 109. Mitton 1951, 99; Bjerkelund 1967, 184.

171. Käsemann 1980, 288-97; idem, 1958, 517-20; Sampley 1971, 1; [Best

true, the theory that the author was the editor of the Pauline corpus would be completely undermined. Even the relationship to Colossians must be viewed in a different light. The consequences for the question of authenticity remain ambiguous. Some researchers have argued that liturgical language and use of traditional forms and fragments make the traditional arguments against authenticity obsolete.[172] Others however have drawn the opposite conclusion: Ephesians is dependent on tradition in a completely different way from Paul, who showed his creative originality, even when he used tradition.[173]

E. Percy was the first to set out a linguistic-stylistic study that moved decisively beyond Holtzmann. He paid less attention to the overall character of the style than to its individual features. His demonstration that no other texts come as close to the style of Ephesians as some sections of the Pauline Epistles has not been refuted so far. In the end, Percy remained uncertain. He found that particularly in the paraenesis there could be literary dependence on Colossians.[174]

After Percy, A. van Roon in a detailed monograph has recently tried to prove the authenticity of Ephesians. He cites non-Pauline literature much less than Percy, but draws more than Percy on the overall composition and the subdivisions of sentence structure and meaning. He rightly recognizes the differences between the Pauline homologoumena and Ephesians, but he exaggerates the similarity between some extracts from the undoubted Pauline letters and Ephesians. To explain the relationship to Colossians, van Roon speculates that Paul and his assistant shared a common view and expressed it in somewhat different ways.[175]

Percy, van Roon and other defenders of authenticity have mainly dealt with stylistic features, which could be explained by the content and literary style of the letter. A systematic study of the small, unconscious habits of speech, most likely to expose a Pauline imitator, is not available. Studies that analyze the Pauline letters with electronic data processing statistical techniques are in their infancy.[176] [Since then, D. L. Mealand has in his multivariable analysis shown that "the distinctiveness of Colossians

---

1997a(4), 51–68].

172. Schille 1957, 325–34; see van Roon 1974, 440; also Barth 1974, 9–10, 41.

173. E.g., Käsemann 1958, 517–20.

174. Percy 1946, esp. 392–419.

175. van Roon 1974, esp. 91ff., and 426–31.

176. See K. McArthur 1968/69, 339–49 and the works referenced there of A. Q. Morton/J. McLeman 1964; later also Bujard 1973, 231–33.

and Ephesians emerged more clearly as the tests proceeded. The results of those tests do therefore tend to confirm the views of those who have argued that the letters are deutero-Pauline."[177] Walter Bujard's analysis of the style of Colossians was a substantial methodological advance.[178] At the same time, Hiram Lester presented a study of relative clauses in the Pauline homologoumena and antilegomena.[179] In these works appear the strongest objections so far to Pauline authorship of Colossians. The two have refuted the view of Percy shared by many, "one could almost say that Ephesians in terms of style relates to Colossians as Colossians does to the recognized Pauline letters."[180] [Vemund Blomkvist has recently refined Bujard's analytic method by segmenting the letters and found as a result that the language of Ephesians in the second main part approaches Paul's. This applies to the use of conjunctions, imperatives, infinitives and participles used as substantives. Thus we have more accurately described the intermediate position that, according to Bujard, Ephesians occupies in relation to Colossians and to the Pauline corpus. The Pauline character is connected to the paraenesis and thus does not apply to the letter as a whole.][181]

In the scholarly debate of the last century many of the same arguments have been made by both sides. Both the linkage of Pauline and non-Pauline characteristics, as well as the special relationship of Ephesians to Colossians, have been used repeatedly as arguments both for and against Pauline authorship. There are no definitive criteria for assessing the facts. It is therefore no wonder that the decision about authenticity has been largely dependent on the general picture which the scholars had of Paul and early Christianity. That their conservative or critical tendencies also play a role is obvious.[182] The letter's constant and notable attestation in Christian tradition supports authenticity;[183] the critical objections

---

177. [D. L. Mealand 1995, 86.]

178. Bujard 1973.

179. Lester, 1973, esp. 73.

180. So Percy 1946, 185; similarly already Haupt 1902, 56-57; against that view, Lester 1973, 73-77; see Bujard 1973, 76 and *passim*.

181. [V. Blomkvist 1993, 44—translated D. H.]

182. Only a few have so openly acknowledged the presuppositions for their judgment as Barth: "The burden of proof lies with those who question the tradition" (1974, 41); "It is advisable for the time being to still consider (sic) Paul its author" (ibid., 49).

183. See Holtzmann 1886, 290; Schmid 1928, 17 note 2; Wikenhauser/Schmid

rest on internal criteria. In order to attempt to explain the totality of the evidence, some scholars have suggested that Ephesians was written by one of Paul's assistants, or at least shaped by an assistant in important details.[184] Others described the "secretary" hypothesis as a stopgap or compromise solution.[185] One should nevertheless remember that some excellent scholars have left the question of authorship open.[186]

The debate about the authenticity of Ephesians continues. Some conclusions can nevertheless be drawn from the recent history of criticism:

1. In the present state of research, it is no longer possible to assume the Pauline authorship of Colossians, to argue from that either for or against the authenticity of Ephesians.[187]

2. Any satisfactory explanation has to take into account the overall state of affairs, not only the relationship of Ephesians to Colossians, but also the manner in which Ephesians not only differs more than Colossians from the acknowledged letters of Paul, but also agrees with them more than Colossians!

3. To explain both the similarities and the differences, one cannot confine the alternatives either to the identity of the author or to literary reminiscences. One must also take into account the possibility that the agreements are the result of more or less fixed traditions and conventions. Thus, the relationship of Ephesians to non-Pauline early Christian literature must also be examined.

1973, 486.

184. So already Schleiermacher 1895, 165f., 194; later, A. Wikenhauser 1953, 306-07; P. Feine/J. Behm 1950, 197; O. Roller 1933, 18ff.; M. A. Wagenführer 1941, 124-32; P. Benoit 1966, 195-211; idem 1963, 11-22; G. H. P. Thompson 1967, 5-6, 16; [van Roon 1974, 207f., 440; now also E. R. Richards 1991, esp. 169-98; Gamble 1995, 95f.]; against, Percy 1946 note 62 and 421f.

185. [Kümmel 1973, 315; Best 1998 criticizes Richards 1991: "Richards, 190, lists the explicit and implicit evidence for the use of secretaries, in respect of each letter; the only letters for which he finds no evidence are Ephesians and the Pastorals; despite this he asserts that Ephesians was "written with secretarial assistance" because it was written from prison where Paul might not have had the freedom to write; this, however, assumes Paul's authorship of the letter, which is precisely what is to be proved."]

186. E.g., A Jülicher/E. Fascher 193, 139-42; A. H. McNeile/C. S. C. Williams 1953, 185-87; H. J. Cadbury 1959-60, 91-102; B. Rigaux 1965, 145-50; [O. Kuss 1971, 28ff.].

187. On this point, I have gradually changed my own opinion, as one can see from my article "Colossians," Dahl 1962, 865, and from the observations in Dahl 1951, 241-64. [Otherwise already Dahl 1976a/81a, 268f.]

3. RELATIONSHIPS WITH EARLY CHRISTIAN LITERATURE

3.1 General

It has often been observed that the letter to the Ephesians, despite its special character, has remarkably many points of contact with other Pauline Epistles and early Christian writings. Not only the historical classification, but also the interpretation largely depends on how these "parallels" are assessed, whether as evidence of literary dependence or as evidence for the use of traditional material used in worship and teaching. A one-sided literary approach poses the risk, that comparing two documents with each other, one decides that one is dependent on the other, without sufficiently considering analogous formulations in other Christian and also non-Christian writings.[188] A form and tradition historical analysis can on the contrary lead to postulating the existence of hymnic, liturgical and catechetical "templates," when possession and editing by the author are neither provable nor refutable.[189]

Only a comprehensive collection and sifting of parallel materials can help resolve this dilemma. In a commentary, the material must be used in the interpretation of the relevant individual sections. But a brief overview may serve to clarify not only the scope but also the varying nature of the connections. The question, whether the connections occur because of literary dependence or not, is too restrictive. The relation to Ephesians is, for example, very different in the Odes of Solomon from that in Polycarp, although it is likely that Ephesians was known to both authors.

H. Schlier noted the proximity of the Odes of Solomon[190] to Ignatius of Antioch, as well as to canonical Ephesians.[191] In later research his observations have been neglected,[192] but largely solely because of the reaction against the theory of a fully developed, pre-Christian Gnosticism.

---

188. So in various ways Goodspeed 1933; Barnett in 1941; Mitton 1951.

189. E.g. Selwyn 1947; Schille 1965; [R. Deichgräber 1967; Kl. Wengst 1972; Vielhauer 1975, 9–57, with compilation of criteria (*ibid.*, 12); for hymns, now cautiously G. Kennel 1995, criticizing R. Brucker 1997].

190. [See now M. Franzmann 1991; M. Lattke 1995; the following is cited according to Lattke's transl.]

191. Schlier 1929; idem 1930, 14ff.

192. [Cf. However Fischer 1973, 60f.: in part pre-Gnostic; also Schenke/Fischer 1976, 183f.; Lindemann 1975, 61, 132.]

INTRODUCTION TO THE LETTER TO THE EPHESIANS

The relevance of Schlier's observations are however independent of his theory. We do not address here the extent to which the Odes are fairly described as "Gnostic."[193] A dichotomy within the Godhead does not seem to be presupposed. Rather, the Lord has made everything (Odes Sol 4:15, cf. Eph. 3.9). There is no Gnostic exegesis of Ephesians, as it is known mainly from the Valentinian school. The poet relies on inspiration, not on tradition. But he has apparently appropriated not only the language of the Old Testament Psalms, but also the language of Ephesians, and used each of them for his own purposes.

Shared religious-historical environment and linguistic conventions can explain most connections between the Odes and Ephesians, at least in part. Examples include contrasts between truth and error, darkness and light, the description of salvation using words for election, rescue, renewal, the concept of new life already achieved, and exaltation. Although the emphasis on the gift of knowledge is to be expected, the concept 'abundance' (πλήρωμα, *swmly'*) stands out, despite the different use.[194] Some metaphors and images are shared: seal, circumcision, foundation and dwelling, change of dress, groom and bride (cf. to Eph 1:13; 2:11ff., 20-22; 4:22-24; 5:22ff.). Most remarkable is the image of the Savior as the head and the redeemed as his limbs (Odes Sol 17:15, cf. 23:16, 18; 24:1).[195]

Correspondences in wording and phraseology can be illustrated best by a few examples:

"He has greatly blessed me" (28:4; cf. Eph. 1:3);

"Before the foundation of the world" (41:15; cf. Eph. 1:4);

"In the beloved" (8:.22; also 3:5, 7; cf. Eph. 1:6);

"As the amount of your love" (14:9; also 29:3; 42:16; cf. Eph. 1:7);

"The word of truth" (8:8; also 12,1.3; cf. Eph. 1:13);

"My eyes were enlightened" (11:14; cf. Eph. 1:18);

"That's why he had pity on me in his great mercy" (7:10; also 16:7; see Eph. 1:7; also 2.5);

"We live/rejoice in the Lord by his grace" (41:3; also 5:3; 9:5; 15:8; 25:4; see Eph. 2:7);

---

193. [See, e.g., H. Jonas 1964, 326-28; Vielhauer 1975, 750-56; K. Rudolph 1980, 34, 142, 238-40; Franzmann 1991, 6; Pokorný 1992, 22.]

194. [Schlier 1930, 42ff; idem 1963, 96-99; Haupt 1902, 44f. (Col.), 44f. (Eph.).

195. [On that point, Fischer 1973, 61.]

"They are my work" (8:18f.); also 7:9 and 11:20; cf. Eph 2.10);
"And I was close to him" (21:7; also 33:7; 36:6, 8; cf. Eph 2.13);
"I proclaim peace to you, his holy ones" (9:6; cf. Eph 2.17).
"And I will not be a stranger" (3:6; cf. Eph 2.19);
"So I knew him" (7:6; cf. Eph 4.20);
"I pulled out of the darkness, and I moved to light" (21:3; cf. Eph 4:22, 24; 5:8)

No single parallel proves that the letter to the Ephesians was known to the poet (or poets) of the Odes. The accumulation of parallels suggests, however, that this was the case. The shared language can also have been conveyed by common use of the literary forms recommended in Ephesians 5:18-19, psalms, hymns, and songs. Unlike the letter to the Ephesians, the Odes are in the first person, the speaker sometimes the Redeemed, sometimes the Redeemer. To the extent Ephesians uses the language of Old Testament Psalms, it is spiritualized and internalized. The language and style of inspired songs have become an essential part of the salvific experience. It lacks, however, the relationship to the salvation event, church community and mutual consideration which modified spiritualization in the letter to the Ephesians.

Polycarp[196] relates quite differently to the letter to the Ephesians in his letter to the Philippians. He appeals to sayings of the Lord, as well as to Paul's teaching. He cites the letter to the Ephesians (12.1) apparently as scripture.[197] The formula of introduction, attested only Latin, may reflect that Eph. 4:26a quotes the Septuagint's version of Psalm 4:5, to which the following exhortation in 4:26b is connected; this connection occurs outside Ephesians as well.[198] A reminiscence of Ephesians appears in Pol. 1:3: by grace you are saved, not by works (χάριτί ἐστε σεσωσμένοι, οὐκ ἐξ ἔργων) (cf. Eph. 2:5, 8, 9).[199] Other echoes of Ephesians appear (cf. Pol 2:1; 4:1.2; 8:2, 10:2; 11:2; 12.3). To what extent these formulations depend

---

196. [See Vielhauer 1975, 552-66]

197. [So C. M. Nielsen 1965, 199-216; Best 1998, 16.]

198. [See the interpretation ? in Lindemann 1979, 227f; now also the discussion in W. Bauer/ H. Paulsen1985, 125;] J. B. Bauer 1995, 69-71; but above all D. K. Rensberger 1981, 112 note 134 with reference to W. D. Stroker, 1970, 154-62: the elements at Eph 4:26 a and b have been combined and regarded as Scripture both before, and independently of, Ephesians.]

199. [Cf. Lindemann 1979, 222f.; Rensberger, 1981, 114f.; Bauer/Paulsen 1985, 115; J. B. Bauer 1995, 42; Best 1998, 16.]

on Ephesians, we cannot say, because the whole letter of the famous bishop is used for recapitulation of traditional doctrine, which is known both from written and oral tradition. He represents a type of Christianity like that of 1 Peter and especially of the Pastoral Epistles. What he has in common with Ephesians, is common Christian, especially paraenetic, material.

The letters of Ignatius,[200] in relation to Ephesians, as in other respects, occupy an intermediate position between the Odes of Solomon and Polycarp. The enthusiasm of the spirit-filled martyr connects to the catholicity of the church leader, who insists on unity and on the monarchical episcopate. The letters of the Apostle are considered unattainable role models for his own correspondence (cf. Ign. Rom 4:3). He calls the Christians of Ephesus "fellow initiates with Paul" who "mentions you in every letter" (Ign. Eph. 12.2). This confident assurance does not mean that Ignatius knew the Pauline letter "to the Ephesians" by that name.[201] Had he done so, he would have pointed out more, that Paul had honored the Ephesians through a special letter.[202] The many terminological echoes of the Pauline letter to the Ephesians in the Proömium of the Ignatian Letter to the Ephesians[203] suggest however that the Antiochean bishop could at least expect that Ephesians was known among the Christians in Ephesus.[204]

Ignatius to the Ephesians		Ephesians	
Prescript		1:3a	blessed (εὐλογητὸς)
to the blessed (... τῇ εὐλογημένῃ)		1:3b	who has blessed us with every spiritual blessing in the heavenly places (ὁ εὐλογήσας ἡμᾶς ἐν πάσῃ εὐλογίᾳ πνευματικῇ ἐν τοῖς ἐπουρανίοις ἐν Χριστῷ)
in greatness (ἐν μεγέθει)		1:19a	the immeasurable greatness (τὸ ὑπερβάλλον μέγεθος)

200. [See Vielhauer 1975, 540–52.]

201. [See Bauer/Paulsen 1985, 38; W. R. Schoedel 1985, 72 note 7.]

202. See 1 Clem. 47:1: Ἀναλάβετε τὴν ἐπιστολὴν τοῦ μακαρίου Παύλου τοῦ ἀποστόλου; Pol. 3:2: ὃς καὶ ἀπὼν ὑμῖν ἔγραψεν ἐπιστολάς.

203. [See also the synopsis by Schoedel 1985, 37.]

204. [See Schoedel 1985, 37: "It is tempting to think that . . . Ignatius felt it appropriate to address the Ephesians with language from an apostolic writing regarded as directed to them." [Lindemann argues against the literary dependency of Ign. Eph. on the Pauline Ephesians, Lindemann 1979, 205 as do Bauer/ Paulsen 1985, 21; Best states more cautiously: ". . . these [sc. parallels] taken together create a fair possibility that Ignatius knew our Ephesians." Best 1998, 15f.]

of God the Father (θεοῦ πατρός)	1:3a	the God and Father of our Lord Jesus Christ (ὁ θεὸς καὶ πατὴρ τοῦ κυρίου ἡμῶν Ἰησοῦ Χριστοῦ)
in the fullness (πληρώματι)	1:10a	of the fullness (... τοῦ πληρώματος ... [1:23b: τὸ πλήρωμα])
predestined (τῇ προωρισμένῃ)	1:5a	predestining us (προορίσας ἡμᾶς ...)
before the beginning of time (πρὸ αἰώνων)	1:4b	before the foundation of the world (πρὸ καταβολῆς κόσμου)
for glory (εἶναι ... εἰς δόξαν)	1:12a	might live for the praise of his glory (εἰς τὸ εἶναι ἡμᾶς εἰς ἔπαινον δόξης)
chosen (ἐκλελεγμένην ...)	1:4a	just as he chose us in him (καθὼς ἐξελέξατο ἡμᾶς ἐν αὐτῷ ...)
through the true passion (ἐν πάθει ἀληθινῷ)	1:7a	through his blood (... διὰ τοῦ αἵματος αὐτοῦ)
by the will of the Father and Jesus Christ (ἐν θελήματι τοῦ πατρὸς καὶ Ἰησοῦ Χριστοῦ ...)	1:5b	according to the good pleasure of his will (1:11b: according to his counsel and will) (κατὰ τὴν εὐδοκίαν τοῦ θελήματος αὐτοῦ) (1:11b: κατὰ τὴν βουλὴν τοῦ θελήματος αὐτοῦ)
and in blameless grace (καὶ ἐν ἀμώμῳ χαρᾷ)	1:4c	us to be holy and blameless (εἶναι ἡμᾶς ἁγίους καὶ ἀμώμους)

Ignatius quotes 1 Corinthians, also without acknowledgment (Ign. Eph. 16:1; Ign. Phld. 3:3; 18:1; Ign. Rom. 5:1). Ephesians at most provided the model for some statements. Most notable is to love their wives as the Lord the church. (ἀγαπᾶν τὰς συμβίους ὡς ὁ κύριος τὴν ἐκκλησίαν) (Ign. Pol. 5:1; cf. Eph. 5:25, 29).[205] The vocabulary and conceptual world of Ignatius show a special closeness to Ephesians. Ignatius used vocabulary that occurs in the New Testament only in Ephesians—*without God* (ἄθεος), *unity* (ἑνότης), *great* (μέγεθος), *good will* (εὔνοια) or is used there in a distinctive fashion (*mystery* (μυστήριον), *stewardship* (plan) (οἰκονομία), *fullness* (πλήπωμα), *bond* (σύνδεσμος). There are also expressions like *new man* καινὸς ἄνθρωπος, *imitators of God* (μιμηταὶ θεοῦ), *children of light* (τέκνα φωτός) and also metaphorical-mythological imagery: head, limbs, and body (Ign. Trall. 11:2; (Ign. Smyr. 1:2), building and temple (esp. Ign. Eph. 9:1) and armor (Ign. Pol. 6:2). In addition there appear, as also in

---

205. [Against Lindemann's view, that the similarities between Ignatius and the letter to the Ephesians reflect shared tradition (1979, 215), see Rensberger 1981, 66 note 12: "the source of Ephesians may be seen in Col 3:19, and it is precisely the characteristic alteration by Ephesians, "love your wives as Christ loved the church" that Ignatius reproduces"]

Polycarp, several parallels in instructions (for example, Ign. Eph. 16:1; Ign. Magn. 13:2, Ign. Trall. 2:1; 13:2; Ign. Phld. 3:3; Ign. Pol. 1:2; 4:3; 5:1). The connection to church tradition and the proximity to Gnosticism differ between Ignatius and Ephesians.[206] There is nonetheless a spiritual kinship, which is adequately explained neither by literary dependence nor by a common Pauline heritage.

Most of the apostolic fathers and also New Testament texts like Hebrews[207] and the Pastoral Epistles relate to the letter to the Ephesians as does Polycarp. Literary dependency is most likely, if anywhere, in the 1st and 2nd letters of Clement. In 1 Clem 46:6f. the expression *we are members one of another* μέλη ἐσμὲν ἀλλήλων (cf. Eph. 4:25; 5:30)[208] follows a unity formula (cf. Eph 4:25; 5:30). 2 Clem 14:2 says *the living church is the body of Christ* ἐκκλησία ζῶσα σῶμά ἐστιν Χριστοῦ (cf. Eph1:22). A quote from Gen 1.27 follows, and an exegetical explication which reflects Eph. 5:22–32, despite a different scriptural basis.[209] In Hermas the phrase "he grieves the Holy Spirit" λυπεῖ τὸ πνεῦμα τὸ ἅγιον is notable (Mand. X 3:2 [42:2]; cf. X 2:2f. [41:2] and III 4 [28:4]); but it doesn't need to depend on Eph. 4:30.[210]

In most cases, where Barnett and—more cautiously—Mitton consider dependence on Ephesians likely, it is common themes, related

---

206. H.W. Bartsch

207. [See A. Vanhoye, 1978, 216ff.]

208. [Against literary dependency Lindemann 1979, 189f. and idem 1992, 136; similarly, Rensberger 1981, 64f.; Best 1998, 15; H. E. Lona 1998, 50 note 3 and 493f.: "Without doubt, the same tradition appears [in 46:6] as in Eph. 4:4-6. Eph . . . But literary dependency is not proven, and the similarities can be explained by shared knowledge of Pauline usages;" see the synopsis in Lona 1998, 494. D. A. Hagner 1973, 222f., argues for literary dependence.]

209. [See Barnett 1941, 214f.; cf. Lindemann 1979, 267; idem 1992, 241: "The interpretation [in 14.2] is reminiscent of Eph. 5:21–33; but more clearly than there are Christ and the Church alike presented as pre-existent;" Rensberger 1981, 79f.: ". . . the statement that the church is Christ's body and that he is the male and the church the female, connected by a text from Genesis (1:27, however, not 2:24) are highly reminiscent of Eph. 5:22–33 . . . however, one can hardly exclude the possibility of a traditional origin for the imagery, with no direct dependence of 2 Clement on Paul;" Best 1998, 16 denies the dependency of the letter on Ephesians.]

210. [So also Lindemann 1979, 286f.; Best 1998, 16; see also Rensberger 1981, 84f.: ". . . Hermas, for whatever reason, does not quote books, authoritative or not . . . His treatment of Paul is merely a feature of this general usage, and tells us nothing one way or the other about his opinion of the Apostle and his letters." [See also N. Brox 1991, 45–49.]

phraseology and also paraenetic material, paraphrases of biblical texts, and more or less almost sermonic and liturgical linguistic patterns.

This applies particularly to the pastoral Epistles (see, e.g., Tit. 3:3-7 and Eph. 2:3-8). They have some vocabulary and themes in common with Ephesians. They stress for example that the precreation plan of God realized in Christ has been proclaimed by Paul (esp. 2 Tim 1:8-12; Tit 1:2-3; cf. 1 Tim 1:11-16; 2:3-7 and Eph. 3:2-12).[211] But terminology, syntax and style differ. There is no linear development from Paul to Ephesians to the Pastorals.[212]

An image of Paul adapted for use by a later church community and to some extent "domesticated" we find also in Acts.[213] Like Ephesians, and unlike in the Pastorals, the participation of the Gentiles in the salvation promised to Israel is a major theme. Similarities in vocabulary, phraseology and the use of Old Testament texts are not particularly noteworthy.[214] It is noteworthy, however, that the closest analogies appear mainly in two sections, Acts 20:18-36 and 26:16-18.

The "farewell speech at Miletus" shares many of its themes with Ephesians: the work and suffering of Paul, the Church as the object of Christ's saving acts, warning against heresy, pastoral ministry, working with one's own hands, in order to be able to help others.[215] There are also a few individual parallels: *with all humility* μετὰ πάσης ταπεινοφροσύνης (Acts 20:19; Eph. 4:2); *the purpose of God* τὴν βουλὴν τοῦ θεοῦ (Acts 20:27; cf. Eph. 1:11); see also Acts 20:28 and Eph. 1:7; Acts 20:32 and Eph. 1:18.

The recollection of Paul's divine commission at the end of his "speech before Agrippa" corresponds even more strongly to Ephesians. Almost every part of Acts 26:18 has a parallel in Ephesians:

to open their eyes ἀνοῖξαι ὀφθαλμοὺς αὐτῶν, cf. Eph. 1:18

from darkness to light ἀπὸ σκότους εἰς φῶς, cf. Eph. 5:8

and from the power of Satan to God καὶ τῆς ἐξουσίας τοῦ σατανᾶ ἐπὶ τὸν θεόν, cf. Eph. 2:2

---

211. [Cf. Roloff 1988, 85-87, 120f.]
212. [So also Pokorný, 1992, 15f.]
213. [Cf. Vielhauer 1965, 9-27; now also J. A. Fitmyer 1998, 145-47.]
214. Mitton 1951, 198-220.
215. [Cf. L. Aejmelaeus 1987, 127-28, 135-37, 161-64, 150-51; 171-75 *et passim*.]

that they may receive forgiveness of sins ποῦ λαβεῖν αὐτοὺς ἄφεσιν ἁμαρτιῶν, cf. Eph. 1:7

and a place among the sanctified καὶ κλῆρον ἐν τοῖς ἡγιασμένοις, cf. Eph. 1:11, 18

Parallels to Acts 26:18 appear also in Colossians, but there only in 1:12-14. The Qumran literature in particular shows that the common terminology is pre-Christian.[216] The complicated relationship Acts—Ephesians—Colossians—Qumran cannot be explained by the assumption of literary dependence.[217] It is rather more likely that Acts 20:18-35 and 26:16-18 use traditions of the Pauline school,[218] and in a form that relates more closely to Ephesians and, in part, to Colossians than to the Pastoral epistles.

The question whether there is literary dependence or a use of common tradition comes to a head in the much-discussed relationship between Ephesians and 1 Peter.[219] The similarity of the two introductory sections, Eph. 1:3-14 / 1 Pet. 1:3-12,220, is particularly noticeable,[220] but does not require literary dependence any more than the related ecclesiological statements in Ephesians 2:18-22/1 Pet. 2:4-10. More or less similar texts can be found in almost all parts of the two letters: Ephesians 1:18f. / 1 Pet. 1:3-5; Eph. 1:20-21/1 Pet. 3:22; Eph. 2:4 / 1 Pet. 1:3; Eph. 3:3-6/1 Pet. 1:10-12; Eph. 3:16/1 Pet. 3:4; Eph. 4:7/1 Pet. 4:10; Eph. 4:17f./ 1 Pet. 1:14f., 18; Eph. 4:25. 31/1 Pet. 2:1; Eph. 5:8/1 Pet. 2:9; Eph. 5:21ff. / 1 Pet. 3:1, 7; Eph. 6:5/1 Pet. 2:18; Eph. 6:11ff./1 Pet. 5:8; 1:13. In both letters, the recipients are reminded of the salvation they have received and exhorted to adopt a way of living that corresponds to it. Both letters emphasize the dichotomy between pagan past and newly bestowed privileges and obligations. Both the presentation of salvation history and ethical exhortations use patterns and formulations which were used in other settings, and which were probably already used

216. Lohse 1968, 66-77 on Col 1:12-14. [Cf. also Fitzmyer 1998, 760; Conzelmann 1963, 139 and Jervell 1998, 594f.: "Bekehrungssprache", Eph. 5:8; 1 Pet. 2:9; JosAs 8:9; 15:12; Col 1:12; 1 Thess. 1:9f.]

217. [So also Best 1998, 17f.; cf. also Dahl "Ephesians and Qumran,"*Studies in Ephesians*]; additionally, J. Knox 1966/80, 279-87; [Braun 1966, 167f., 219-22]; against Goodspeed 1933, 5-8, 82-165; Mitton 1951, 210-20.

218. [Cf. Deichgräber 1967, 78-87.]

219. [See L. Goppelt's summary, 1978, 48f.; P. J. Achtemeier 1996, 16-18, as well as Best 1998, 18f.]

220. [Barnett 1941, 54: a literary relationship is "a matter of practical certainty"]

in early Christian baptismal instruction. The assertions particularly characteristic of Ephesians do not appear again in 1 Peter. Instead, the hope for future deliverance and the present sufferings of Christians are much more strongly stressed.

The improbability of direct, literary dependence[221] is confirmed by the observation that comparison cannot determine whether Ephesians is dependent on 1 Peter[222] or the reverse.[223] Mitton observed that Ephesians was more closely related to 1 Peter than to Colossians, wherever the three letters are related.[224]

From the assumption Ephesians took the material common to the two letters from Colossians, the conclusion follows inexorably that 1 Peter is dependent on Ephesians, and not on pre-Colossian tradition.[225] However, it is a mistake to make that assumption in the first place. The close relation of Ephesians to 1 Peter proves that material that Ephesians has in commons with Colossians does not need to have been taken from Colossians.[226]

A comparison of Ephesians to the Johannine literature shows fully the inadequacy of a purely literary approach. A certain relationship with the Fourth Gospel was noticed long ago.[227] It is above all thematic in nature: the making alive of the dead is already present (John 5:21-26; Eph. 2:5-7). The Gentiles are united with the (true) Israelites, and all the elect are one in Christ (John 10:16; 11:50-52; 17:22-23; see Eph. 2:14ff.). Literary dependence is not to be seriously considered;[228] similar thoughts are expressed differently and the same terminology is used differently (cf., e.g., John 3:13/Eph. 4:9f.; John 3:20 / Eph. 5:13f.). The kind and degree of relationship occurs only secondarily through common literary

---

221. [So already J. M. Usteri 1887, 283-90; also Selwyn 1947, 426; Percy 1946, 440; recently, the commentaries on 1 Peter by Goppelt 1978, 49 and Achtemeier 1996, 17. So too the new commentaries on Ephesians by Mussner 1982, 19; Pokorný 1992, 18; Best 1998, 18f.]

222. So among others Schwegler II 1846, 58f.; J. Weiss 1912, 2209; J. Moffat 1918, 381ff.

223. Goodspeed 1933, 17; Mitton 1950, 73; idem 1951, 196; Schmid 1928, 333-62.

224. Mitton 1950, 71.

225. Mitton 1951, 176-97.

226. [K. Shimada 1991, 77-106, also criticizes Mitton on this point.]

227. [See Moffat 1918, 348f.; Abbott 1897, xxvii; Schmid 1928, 370f.; Kirby 1968, 166-68.]

228. [So also Best 1998, 18.]

INTRODUCTION TO THE LETTER TO THE EPHESIANS   237

influences. Ephesians relates in some ways to John, Ignatius and the Odes of Solomon, in other ways to 1 Peter, the Pastorals and Polycarp.

It has been conjectured that Ephesians was also known to the author of Revelation.[229] Though there are common themes, the contrast between Ephesians and the future eschatology of Revelation is more obvious (e.g., Rev. 3:21; 21:4/Eph. 2:6; Rev. 19:7; 21:2/Eph. 5:25FF.; Rev.21:14/ Eph. 2:20; Rev 10:7; 11, 18/Eph. 3:5; Rev. 18:4 / Eph. 5:12).[230] It is also uncertain whether a collection of Paul's letters to seven churches existed early enough to serve as an exemplar for the seven writings of Rev.2-3.[231] Especially worth noting is that the concluding greeting in Rev. 22:21 is, like that in Eph. 6:24, in the third person.[232]

Often, clear criteria for deciding whether there is literary dependence or not do not exist. One shouldn't expect anything else. In the Qumran literature, similar thoughts and expressions often occur, without any clear indication that one text is dependent on the other. Popular philosophers, moralists and rhetoricians of the early Roman Empire largely vary themes and topics, which they know from oral and written tradition, and only in favorable cases is it possible to determine literary dependence. The letter of Polycarp is the clearest example of such reproduction and variation of given tradition in early Christianity,[233] but 1 Peter[234] and Ephesians come very close.

We can frame the issue more generally. In a particularized environment like early Christianity, expression is not determined solely through vocabulary, morphology, and syntax. Phraseology and larger linguistic and thematic segments are available to the speaker or writer[235] [as a user of the argot of early Christianity (sociolect)][236] though the user

229. So R. H. Charles 1920, lxxxiiiff.; Barnett 1941, 41-51; [more cautiously, Mitton 1951, 170-173.]

230. [See Lindemann 1985, 14f.; Gnilka 1990, 19; Best 1988, 17.]

231. But see Gamble 1995, 61, .]

232. [The unusual third person formation Best also notes, 1998 619, though without reference to the parallel in Rev. 22:21.]

233. [See now J. B. Bauer 1995, *passim*, but especially the synopsis Pol and 1 Clem 28-30].

234. [See Selwyn 1947, 17-24; Goppelt 1978, 47-56; Achtemeier 1996, 12-23.]

235. [See, e.g., Pokorný 1992, 18: "most Parallels confirm only the influence a particular school tradition, developed within early Christianity, but those just mentioned confirm that the author of Ephesians knew several Pauline epistles . . . ".]

236. [On the concept "sociolect," see K.-H. Bausch 1980, 358-63; H. Kubczak 1979.]

has great flexibility about how to use them. Written attestation, especially in a somehow normative text, contributed to specifying a particular form of expression, and extending its temporal influence, even when it remains an open question how much a later author [in his personal habits of speech (idiolect)[237]] is dependent on an earlier text, if at all. Comparison of Ephesians to other early Christian literature strongly suggests the existence of more or less fixed, but flexible, forms of expression. However, analysis provides no support for the hypothesis that by excision of "glosses" and "interpretative material" one can reconstruct an exemplar, or that such an exemplar ever existed as a stand-alone text.

Some additional observations confirm this conclusion. Ephesians frequently reflects the language of early Christian liturgy, especially baptismal prayers and the accompanying rites of initiation. Without doubt, Ephesians is dependent on those liturgical formulations. However, one may assume that Ephesians used already existing expressions that echoed baptism terminology.[238]

It is still remarkable that some sentences of Ephesians could be cited later as "non-canonical words of Jesus." The most important occur in Eph. 4:26–30.[239] Other examples are less clear.[240] Apparently it is mostly with respect to sayings, which circulated independent of Ephesians and that were then attributed to the Lord, perhaps because it was thought that Paul quoted him. Ephesians does not contain clear allusions to the words of Jesus in the canonical Gospels. However, the Jesus tradition could have contributed indirectly to the selection and design of Ephesians paraenetic instructions.[241]

3.2. *The Letters of Paul*

The relationship of Ephesians to Colossians deserves special treatment. Ephesians has little in common with 2 Thessalonians. A comparison with Romans, 1 and 2 Corinthians, Galatians, Philippians, 1 Thessalonians,

---

237. [On the concept "idiolect," see G. Hammarström 1980, 428–33.]

238. *See* Dahl "THE CONCEPT OF BAPTISM IN EPHESIANS," STUDIES IN EPHESIANS

239. See A. Resch 1906/67: No. 70 (Eph. 4:28); No. 83 (Eph. 4:27); No. 92 (Eph. 4:30); No. 94 (Eph. 4:26).

240. Ibid.: No. 71 (Eph. 2:14); No. 89 (Eph. 3:15); No. 100 (Eph. 1:4) Very fragmentary are Nos. 96, 97, 104 and 192.

241. Cf. for example Eph. 4:2/Matt. 11:29; Eph. 4:28/Matt. 15:11; Eph. 4:32/Matt. 6:14; Eph. 6:14/Luke 12:35; Eph. 6:18/Mark 13:33; 14:38.

and Philemon shows, however, that some Pauline formulations that do not occur in Colossians reappear in Ephesians.[242] Mitton calculated that 29.1% of the words of words in Ephesians and Colossians (702 out of a total of 2,411, according to the text of Westcott and Hort) occur in the eight Pauline Epistles (including 2 Thessalonians) in similar phrases or contexts.[243] The number is not exact; one could make deletions (e.g., Romans 16:25–27), but one could also make additions. The numbers convey a reasonably accurate picture. The question is the extent to which recollections of the undoubted letters of Paul explain the relationships. Mitton himself does not assert dependence in every case, especially not where a similar phrase occurs several times either in Colossians or in the other letters. The percentage is reduced to 17.3% of the total text of Ephesians, to which should be added 26.5% of the text taken from Colossians.[244]

Further reductions are required. In some cases, more or less stereotyped phrases need not be explained by literary dependence (E.g., *the things about me* τὰ κατ' ἐμέ, *with fear and trembling* μετὰ φόβου καὶ τρόμου, *fragrant offering* ὀσμὴ εὐωδίας, *fullness of time* πλήρωμα τῶν καιρῶν, *children of light* τέκνα φωτός, *the inner man* ὁ ἔσω ἄνθρωπος, etc.). Correspondences in the letter form, doxologies, and other fixed forms prove little (cf. Eph. 1:1–2, 3a, 15–17; 3.20–21; 4.1; etc.). If Ephesians is not Pauline, we nevertheless have to conclude that Ephesians 1:15–17a is a free adaptation of Philemon 4–6. (*see* also Eph. 4:1; Phlm. 1:9).[245] The portions of the other undoubtedly Pauline letters which are the most likely to have echoes in Ephesians are:[246]

Romans	1:18–31; 2:11; 3:20–27; 5:1–2,10; (6:4–13; 8:28–30, 34–39;) 11:33, 36; 12:2–6; 13:11–14
1 Corinthians	2:6–10; 3:6–11, 16–17; 5:9–11; 6:9–10; 6:15–19; 8:6; 11:3; 12:46, 12–13; 24–28; 15:9–10; 15:24–28; 16:13
2 Corinthians	1:3; 1:22; 5:5; (5:17–20;) 6:14–16.
Galatians	1:12, 15–16; 2:16, 20; 3:14, 26–29; 5:19–23.
Philippians	1:9–11, 27; 2:9–11; 4:6–7.
1 Thessalonians	2:12; 4:11, 13; 5:4, 9.

242. [See esp. Mitton 1951, 98–158; Goodspeed 1933, 79ff.]
243. Mitton 1951, 104.
244. Mitton, 104–05.
245. [So also Hübner 1997, 144f.;] Best 1998, 27.]
246. [Cf. most recently the overview of "all possible references and allusions to 'recognized' Pauline Epistles," Gese 1997, 76–78, as well as the preceding exposition, ibid., 54–76; also J. Maclean 1995.]

Direct quotations do not appear.[247] Only rarely are short phrases repeated almost verbatim: *we are members of one another* (ἐσμὲν ἀλλήλων μέλη), Eph. 4:25; *see* Rom. 12:5; *the husband is the head of the wife* (ἀνήρ ἐστιν κεφαλὴ τῆς γυναικός), Eph. 5:23, *see* 1 Cor. 11:3. Neither can one speak generally of conscious editing or adaptation by an informed reader or listener (but see Eph. 2:8). In most cases, the candidates for dependence on the undoubted letters of Paul are intrinsically linked to the author's characteristic thinking and expressions. Mitton pointed out that most parallels are to especially striking segments of the undoubtedly genuine letters, and explains that fact by asserting that the text was imprinted in the memory of the author of Ephesians.[248] But that assertion overlooks the possibility that Paul himself in especially significant statements relied on traditional forms of expression.[249]

Other Ephesian parallels to Pauline letters refer ultimately to Old Testament texts: Eph. 2:14-18/Rom. 5:1-2/Isa. 57:19; 52:7; Eph. 2:20-22/1 Cor. 3:6-9, 16-17/Isa. 28:16; Eph. 4:7-12/1 Cor. 12/Ps. 68:18; Eph. 4:22-24/Rom. 6:6, 13, 14 (Col. 3:9-10)/Gen. 1:26f.; Eph. 5:2/Gal. 2:20/e.g., Ps. 40:7; Ex. 29:18. Ephesians also uses idiosyncratically texts which lie behind some parallels: Eph. 1:20-22/1 Cor. 15:24-28/Ps. 2; Ps. 110; Eph. 5:28-33/1 Cor. 6:15-16/Gen. 2:24; compare Lev. 19:18; Eph. 6:14-18/1 Thess. 5:8/Isa. 59:19; compare Isa. 11:4-5 and 52-7. Possible echoes of other Pauline letters are interwoven not only with each other, but also with Old Testament citations. The Old Testament references are not simply citations. It is entirely possible and in some cases verifiable that they have been taken over from pre-existing uses and interpretations (see, among others, Eph. 1:20-22; 2:20, 22).[250]

As Ephesians overall is much more general than the other Pauline letters, it is possible that the individual expressions themselves have been appropriated and generalized. Sometimes another explanation seems more likely, that Paul has used more or less firmly fixed traditional material in specific contexts to support his reasoning and arguments, which

---

247. [As noted also by Gese, 1997, 55.]

248. Mitton 1951, 136f. 247; [similarly Mitton 1976, 28: "It (sc. Ephesians) is written by one who had access to and knew intimately all these letters (sc. Pauline letters, and especially Colossians)"].

249. [So also Lindemann 1979, 122-30, esp. 125; Best 1998, 26; but on the contrary, see now Gese 1997, 54-85.]

250. [So too Best 1998, 26; see also Roloff 1999, 257-59 with reference to Ps. 118 (LXX 119); Isa. 28:16 and parallels in 1 Pet. 2:4-8; Luke 20:17f.; Mt. 21:42-44; Eph. 2:20 and Barn. 6:1-5.]

Ephesians uses in more traditional ways. The theme that willful ignorance of God, idolatry and moral decay are connected is used, e.g., in Rom. 1–3, to prove that there is no significant difference between Jews and Gentiles. In Eph. 4:17ff., however, the theme of willful ignorance is applied only to moral teaching. The warning against association with sinners in Eph. 5:7ff. lacks the clarification added in 1 Cor. 5:9–13 that the restriction applies only to sinners within the Christian community. Otherwise the assumption is obvious, that such formulations were not ad-hoc, but were used repeatedly by Paul, or even taken by him from traditional material (see, e.g., Eph. 1:13/2 Cor. 1:22; 2, 8f./Rom. 3:20–27 etc.; Eph. 3:3ff. / Gal. 1:12–15/1 Cor. 2:6f.; 4:5f.; 8:6).

As with the comparison of Ephesians to other early Christian literature, so too with its comparison to the authentic letters of Paul, one cannot make literary dependence or oral tradition mutually exclusive alternatives. When one takes into account factors determined by environment and tradition, it is hard to say whether a literary reminiscence is present or not in a particular text. Given the nature and number of the parallels, it is likely that the author of Ephesians knew not only Colossians and Philemon, but also 1 Corinthians and Romans, and possibly even Galatians.[251] The correlations to 2 Corinthians,[252] 1 Thessalonians, and Philippians, not to mention 2 Thessalonians, are too weak and too general to be able to prove that the author had at hand a whole Pauline corpus.

From the parallels discussed, one cannot argue conclusively for or against Pauline authorship of Ephesians. However, the comparison strengthens the impression that Ephesians is more traditional and less original in its characteristic formulations than Paul seems to be.[253] That most of the possible references are taken from 1 Corinthians or Romans coincides with the findings for other post-Pauline writings.

---

251. See Merkelin 1973a, 42; [Best 1998, 27].

252. [For 2 Corinthians, see on the one hand, the summary table in Pokorný 1992, 19 (1:1 to 13:9), on the other hand, the list above and Best 1998, 27: "it is interesting to note that all the more likely passages in 2 Corinthians which may have affected Ephesians come from its first nine chapters; AE may not have possessed the letter in the form we have it."]

253. Käsemann 1958, 520.

3.3. Colossians

The history of research has shown that the comparison of Ephesians to Colossians can be performed in various ways.[254] In a commentary, the parallels should be treated in sequence and in context; here, we can only give an overview of the overall relationship. Word counts don't tell us much. Out of a total word count of 529 words, Ephesians has 21 words in common with Colossians that are not found in any other Pauline letter. There are 3 others that Ephesians has in common only with one of the Pastoral Epistles. The count for Ephesians is somewhat higher than the comparable statistics for other letters: Romans, 16 in common with one letter, 4 with the Pastorals only; 1 Corinthians, 9 and 7; 1 Thessalonians, 10 and 0, and so on. However, the number is not especially striking, since Ephesians has 82 (83?) words unique to it, and 11 in common with the Pastoral Epistles as a group. The corresponding numbers for Colossians are 62 (68?) and 0 (3?).[255]

The correspondence in word sequence, phraseology and context is so great that the relationship between the two letters must be displayed synoptically. According to Mitton, one-fourth of Ephesians agrees more or less word for word with one-third of Colossians.[256] The distribution of the parallels between the two letters appears in the table below.

C4	C3	E2	E1	C1	C2	E3	E4
			1:1–2	1:1–2			
1:22, 14, 20; 1:9, 2 7.16	1:3	1:3–12					
1:12	1:5	1:13–14					

254. [See Schmid 1928, 384–457; Goodspeed 1933, 79–165; Ochel 1934; Percy 1946, 360–433; Mitton 1951, 55–158, 279–338; Merklein 1973a, 28–44; idem 1981a; idem 1981b; Van Roon 1974, 413–37; Coutts 1957–58; Benoit 1963; J. B. Polhill 1973; Schenke/Fischer 1978, 185; Schnackenburg 1982, 26–30; Lincoln 1990, xlvii–lviii; Pokorný 1992, 3–8; Furnish 1992, 536–37; Gese 1997, 39–54; Best 1997b; idem 1998, 20–25.]

255. See R. Morgentahler 1992, 173; the agreements with Philemon, mostly names, are excluded.

256. Mitton 1951, 57, 279–315; Wagenführer 1941, supplement [see further, e.g., Holtzmann 1872, 25f., 325–30; Abbott 1897, xxiii; Haupt 1902, 65–68; Goguel 1926, 460f.; Percy 1946, 384–418; van Roon 1974, 427–29; F. O. Francis/J. P. Sampley 1984, §§218–36, §§256–76; Lincoln 1990, xlix; Pokorný 1992, 3–5.]

INTRODUCTION TO THE LETTER TO THE EPHESIANS 243

C4	C3	E2	E1	C1	C2	E3	E4
	1:9		1:15f.	1:3f.			
					1:5–8	1:13	
			1:16f.	1:9f.		1:15f.	1:8f.
1:27, 12, 11	2:9f.		1:18–23	1:11–19		2:13–17	3:16
2:12; 1:29 3:1; 1:24							1:6f., 10, 2, 1f.
3:7, 6, 1; 1:10	2:13	2:1–10					
3:6f, 10f.	2:11, 14		2:11–16	1:20–22			2:1; 4:18; 1:4; 5:27
2:7, 19	2:10	2:17–22					
4:3; 2:2; 1:16			3:1–13	1:23–29			3:16f.; 1:2; 1:18; 4:13
1:11; 2:7, 9; 1:19	1:27, 23		3:14–19	2:1–3			
1:29, 26		3:20–21					
1:10	3:12–15	4:1–6					
1:28; 2:22		4,7–14					
1:18	2:19	4:15–16					
					2:4–5		5:6
1:21; 3:5			4:17–21	2:6–7			5:4
					2:8		5:6
					2:9–10	1:20–23	
					2:11–15	2:5–6, 11–15	1:19f.
					2:16–18		1:23 (?)
					2:19	4:15–16	
					2:20–23		
					3:1–4		2:5f.; 1:20

244 THE APOSTLE PAUL GUIDES THE EARLY CHURCH

C4	C3	E2	E1	C1	C2	E3	E4
					3:5-9a	4:25-31; 5:3-6	2:3
			4:22-24	3:9b-11			
4:6	3:8	4:25-31					
			4:32-5:1	3:12-13			
				3:14-15		4:2-4	
	3:5-8	5:3-6					
3:20; 5:4		5:7-18					
			5:19-20	3:16-17			
			5:21-22	3:18			
1:18		5:23-24					
			5:25a	3:19		5:28, 33	
1:28, 22		5:25b-33					
			6:1-9	3:20-4:1			
3:12; 1:11		6:10-17					
			6:18-20	4:2-4			
					4:5-6		5:15f.; 4:29
			6:21-22	4:7-9			
					4:10-17		
3:15		6:23					
			6:24	4:18			

The two middle columns, E1 and C1, set out extracts that appear in both letters in the same order, are functionally equivalent, and generally correspond in wording. The adjoining columns, E2 and C2, show the remaining parallels. Columns E3 and C3 present related semantic units, some of which include several verses, but which in the overall composition of the two letters are not in the same order. C3 thus provides parallels both to E1 and to E2, as E3 does to C1 and C2. The outermost columns E4 and C4 display scattered, mostly phraseological parallels.

The tabular overview shows that parallels are scattered throughout the two letters, but that even so there is a common structure. After the prescript (Eph. 1:1-2/Col. 1:1-2) follows an assurance of thanksgiving and intercession (Eph. 1:(3-14) 15-17/Col. 1:3-11. It proceeds to recollection of God's saving act in Christ and its significance for the recipients

(Eph. 1:18–23; 2:1–22/Col. 1:11–19, 20–22). Then follow statements about Paul and a return to intercession (Eph. 3:1–13, 14–21/Col. 1:23–29, 2:1–3 (or perhaps 2:1–5). Then comes the transition to admonitions and warnings (Eph. 4:1ff. and 17ff./ Col. 2:6ff.). The paraenesis is based on the theme of putting off the old person and putting on the new person (Eph. 4:22ff./Col. 3:5–15). The call to praise and thanksgiving leads into a household code (Eph. 5:19–20; 5:21–6:9/Col. 3:16–17; 3:18–4:1). Then follow concluding exhortations, a note about the bearer of the letter, and greetings (Eph. 6:10–20, 21–22, 23–24/Col. 4:2–6, 7–9, 10–17). These sections, arranged in the same order, thus follow the outline of a genuine Pauline letter.

However, the picture becomes more complex when we consider columns C3 and E3 or E4. Colossians 1:3–29 not only contains many parallels to Eph. 1:15 to 3:21, but even to Eph. 1:3–14. The next correlations with Eph. 1:20–2:22 occur in Col. 2:9–15, not in Col. 1:11–22. Eph. 4:22–5:6 and Col. 3:5–12 contain largely similar thoughts in related formulations, but the smaller units of meaning are arranged differently. Each letter uses common material in the context of an independent overall composition. In Ephesians the assurance of thanksgiving and intercession precedes the benediction. The intercession in Col. 1:9ff., unlike that in Eph. 1:17ff., is independent of the preceding thanksgiving. The prescriptive section in Ephesians has a two-fold introduction, in 4:1ff. and in 4:17ff.[257] In Colossians, the exhortations introduced by 2:6–8 (or 2:4–8) are broken off by weighty theological statements (2:9–15 and 19).[258] They provide the subject for further warnings and instruction that are connected without formulaic introduction. Thus the most important compositional factors are identified, which may explain the different organization of the material.

In addition to the common material one must also consider the material unique to each letter. In Colossians, but without parallels in Ephesians, are statements that refer to the congregation in Colossae and the local "philosophy," i.e., Col. 1:6–8, (2:3); 2:4–5, 8, 16–18, 20–23; 4:9a, 10–17. There are also more theological statements that have no counterpart in Ephesians cf. Col. 1:15–17a (Christ as the mediator of creation); 1:24 ("what is lacking in the suffering of Christ");2:12, 20; cf. 3:5 (dying with Christ); cf. also 2:3 and 3:11. It is harder to extract the material

---

257. Bjerkelund 1967, 185.
258. C. F. D. Moule 1957, 88; Bjerkelund 1967, 180–85; [Luz 1989, 377].

unique to Ephesians, because we can find a parallel in Colossians to each section in Ephesians, as the table above shows. There is material unique to Ephesians inserted within the framework of the household code (5:23-24, 25b-33; 6:2-3). Further, there are common themes that receive more extensive treatment in Ephesians (cf. Eph. 2:1-10/Col. 2:13; Eph. 2:11-22/Col. 1:20-22; 2:11, 14; Eph. 3:2-12/Col. 1:26-27; Eph. 4:25-31/ Col. 3:8-9). The special material of Ephesians consists largely of Old Testament citations, reminiscences, paraphrases and interpretations (Eph. 1:20b-22; 2:12-22; 4:8-11, 25-30; 5:18, 26-32; 6:2-3, 14-17.) Even the other statements without close parallels are not situational, but general (cf. Eph. 2:4, 7-9a; 4:5-7; 5:7-14; 6:11-13).

With respect to the parallels, that in context have a similar function, the correspondence in word order is in some cases slight (Eph. 1:18-23/ Col. 1:11-19; Eph. 3:14-19/Col. 2:1-3; Eph. 4:17-21/Col. Col. 2:6-7). There are other statements that partially overlap, although they are placed differently (Eph. 1:4b/Col. 1:22; Eph. 1:7/Col. 1:13; Eph. 4:2/Col. 3:12; Eph. 4:15b-16/Col. 2:19).[259] Several scattered parallels relate only in vocabulary and phraseology, but not in function or meaning.[260] Finally, we note that in some places in Ephesians different statements from Colossians appear to be linked ("conflation"),[261] but that conversely some parts of Colossians have parallels in various places in Ephesians and also in other Pauline letters (esp. Col. 1:9-29; 2:9-15).

The state of affairs is extremely complex. The relationship between Ephesians and Colossians resembles neither that between Romans and Galatians nor that between 2 Peter and Jude. The relationship between the two letters to the Thessalonians is a closer analog, but that relationship itself is a matter of continuing debate. Among the many conflicting opinions, one thing is fixed: the similarity between Ephesians and Colossians is based on more than common environment and common tradition. There is a historical and literary connection. The infrequently advanced assumption that Colossians is secondary and dependent on Ephesians does have some supporting arguments, but gives rise to more difficulties than it explains. The rule that the shorter text is the original indeed has some exceptions, but both within the household code and in other places the longer text of Ephesians obviously arises from

---

259. Percy 1946, 372-379.
260. Percy 1946, 379-418.
261. [Mitton 1951, 138-58.]

interpretive expansion (cf. Eph. 5:23-24, 25b-33; 4:16). With respect to the overall composition, it is even more difficult to derive the structure of Colossians from Ephesians than vice versa (Cf., e.g., Eph. 1:3-14 or Col. 2:9-15, 19, with parallels).[262]

The advocates of the view that Colossians is secondary (or interpolated) have insisted rightly that deriving the formulations of Ephesians from corresponding statements in Colossians is sometimes impossible, or at least quite forced. A few examples will suffice. In Colossians' household code, the section on slaves is disproportionately long (Col. 3:22-25). This seems to be due to a special influence, perhaps Philemon. The sentence *there is no partiality* (προσωπολημψία οὐκ ἔστιν) has its natural place in the admonitions to masters, where it is in Eph. 6:9. That the author of Ephesians did not rely only on the structure of Colossians is confirmed by the commandment to honor parents, because instructions similar to household codes in Hellenistic Judaism included that commandment.[263]

Eph. 2:1-10 broadens and "Paulinizes" the concept that those previously dead because of their sins have been made alive again in Christ in connection with the preceding Christological statements inspired by Psalms 110:1 and 8:7 (cf. esp. 2:5b, 8-10).[264] Jewish prayer language appears especially in 2:4. In Colossians 2:13, the same idea is used almost only incidentally and is in some tension with the preceding statement in 2:12, which speaks not of death in sin, but as in Romans 6 of burial with Christ. One could if pressed explain Col. 2:9-15 as a compilation from Eph. 3:19; 1:21-23; Rom. 2:29; Eph. 2:11; Rom. 6:4; Eph. 1:19; 2:1, 5; 1:6, 7; 2:14-15 and 1:21. By contrast, one cannot identify Col. 2:13 as the exemplar for Eph. 2:1-10.

262. [So also Lindemann 1985, 11.]

263. [See Philo, *Decal.* 106-34, 165; *Spec.* II 225-27; *Deus* 17; *Mos.* II. 198; *Mut.* 40; *Plant.* 146; *Ebr.* 17; LAB 11:9; *Ps-Phokyl.* 175-227. Cf. J. E. Crouch 1972, 74-83; D. C. Balch 1981, 51-59; P. W. van der Horst 1978, 187-202; Strecker 1989, 349-75; J. Thomas 1992, 378-91; Wilson 1994, 7-9, 134-45. With respect to the household codes, see additionally: K. Thraede 1980, 359-68; D. Lühmann 1980, 83-97; P. Fiedler 1986, 1063-73; K. O. Sandnes 1994; C. Osiek/D. L. Balch 1997; H. Moxnes (ed.) 1997; S. K. Stowers 1998, 287-301.]

264. [Cf. Hübner 1997, 274, who advances the hypothesis: "*by grace you have been saved* χάριτί ἐστε σεσῳμένοι in 2:5 and *For by grace you have been saved through faith* τῇ γὰρ χάριτί ἐστε σεσῳμένοι διὰ πίστεως, etc., in 2:8, together with *not the result of works, so that no one may boast* οὐκ ἐξ ἔργων, ἵνα μὴ τις καυχήσηται in 2:9 are later glosses, and in fact the glosses of an interpolator who wished to explain the Pauline doctrine of justification."]

Related phrases are often better organized in Ephesians than they are in Colossians. The sentence *In him we have redemption through his blood, the forgiveness of our tresspasses* ἐν ᾧ ἔχομεν τὴν ἀπολύτρωσιν, διὰ τοῦ αἵματος αὐτοῦ, τὴν ἄφεσιυ τῶν παραπτωμάτων fits stylistically and substantively in the Ephesians opening eulogy (1:7). With few deviations (*through his blood* διὰ τοῦ αἵματος αὐτοῦ is missing and *of sins* τῶν ἁμαρτιῶν appears instead), the same sentence appears in Col. 1:14. There it transitions from the self-contained and cohesive section 1:12–13 to the hymn to Christ in 1:15–20. The statement that Christ is the head, from which the whole body grows, appears both in Eph. 4:15b–16 and in Col. 2:19. In Ephesians the statement forms the crowning conclusion of a section, which several shorter phrases reference (*as each part is working properly* ἐν μέτρῳ ἑνὸς ἑκάστου μέρους, *in building itself up* εἰς οἰκοδομὴν ἑατοῦ; *in love* ἐν ἀγάπῃ; *to knit together* συναπμολογούμενον, cf. Eph. 2:21, *according to the working* κατ' ἐνέργειαν, 1:19). The corresponding sentence in Col. 2:19 is shorter and seems to be original. However, it is not anchored in the context, but is attached only by the participle phrase *and not holding fast to the head* καὶ οὐ κρατῶν τὴν κεφαλήν to the previous warning against false teachers. Substantively, it belongs much more with the earlier statement in 2:10 about Christ as the head of all rule and dominion. The explanation is this: the statement in Col. 2:19 is not fashioned for this application, but comes from a hymn about Christ as the head of the world, used in Colossians as part of the antiheretical polemic, but in Ephesians it is more consistently harmonized with church structure and conformed to Pauline teaching.[265]

The relationship of Ephesians to Colossians cannot be explained without making the author of Ephesians' knowledge of Colossians a necessary precondition, but that doesn't by itself provide an adequate explanation of Ephesians. The author of Ephesians is the inheritor of a broader range of traditions, as a comparison of Ephesians to the other Pauline letters, to 1 Peter and to other early Christian literature shows.[266] Further, his use of Scriptural statements is largely traditional. Ephesians' author must have had independent access to more or less fixed expressions used in Colossians. In addition to individual observations, that we find the parallels generally in the context of fixed stylistic forms or structures supports this hypothesis: eulogies (or *beraka*, 1:3–14),

265. Percy 1946, 413–16; Merklein 1973a, 30, 89–99; H. J. Gabathuler 1965, esp. 125–31, 143; [Schenke/Fischer 1978, 176].

266. [See above sections 3.1 and 3.2.]

hymnic expressions (1:20ff., maybe even 2:14ff.), the soteriological contrast between "Once" and "Now" "(2:1–10, 11–22), the structure "hidden—revealed" (3:4–10?), catalogues of vices and virtues (4:31; 5:35), household codes (5:21 ff.). Liturgical and catechetical traditions cannot however explain the agreements in epistolary form, the self-description of the sender or the overall composition (cf. Eph. 1:1–2, 15–17; 3:1–14; 6:18–20, 21–22).

As Gnilka correctly recognized, no simplistic explanation is sufficient: "the relationship of Ephesians to Colossians demands that Colossians is the exemplar, but that the author of each was immersed in a complex matrix of traditions that each one drew upon independently."[267] This conclusion is tenable only on the view that "traditions" are not—or only rarely—regarded as fixed and transmitted as self-contained unities. This is indicated by the many, sometimes purely phraseological, individual parallels. There are also some similarities in style and language that are explained neither by literary nor by historical tradition. Here it suffices on the one hand to point to the parallels noted by many, especially from the Qumran literature,[268] and on the other hand to the terminology which gave rise to a "Gnostic" interpretation.[269] Whether one might better speak about religious and philosophical syncretism than about Gnosticism[270] is irrelevant in this context. It would be more than odd, if a writer who uses the language of esoteric wisdom revelation and religious cosmology, should have adopted and reinterpreted concepts from Colossians such as *body* σῶμα and *head* κεφαλή, *fullness* πλήρωμα and *be filled* πληροῦσθαι, *mystery* μυστήριον and *stewardship, plan* οἰκονομία;[271] one will rather have to conclude that the author of Ephesians was not only familiar with Colossians and with the traditions used therein, but was also at home in the same linguistic and theological milieu.

Some consider it more likely that the two letters shared a common template or a first draft.[272] This hypothesis explains the overall picture no

267. Gnilka 1990, 13; [now also Schnelle 1996, 350, 356 f.]

268. On Colossians, see Lohse 1968, 69–73 and *passim*; on Ephesians, see Kuhn 1961, 334–46; Mussner 1963, 185–98; Gnilka 1990, 123–25 [as well as Dahl with many bibliographical references in Article II in *Studies in Ephesians*].

269. Schlier 1930; Käsemann 1933; Vielhauer 1939/79; Pokorný 1965; [Fischer 1973, esp. 173–200; Schenke 1973, 223–25.]

270. [Cf. Vielhauer 1975, 214:

271. Dibelius/Greeven 1953, 83–85; Mitton 1951, 82–97.

272. Cf. van Roon 1974, 205.

better than an interpolation hypothesis does. One must ask the question whether or not the theories have become so complicated, and must take into account so many unknown factors, that the traditional assumption that Paul wrote both letters becomes in the end the most likely, because it offers the simplest explanation. In fact, one must conclude that Paul wrote both of the letters or neither of them.[273] The evidence for a post-Pauline composition is to be sure somewhat greater for Ephesians (see, e.g., 2:20; 3:6; 4:7ff.). But in some respects Ephesians resembles the undoubted letters of Paul more closely.[274] If Colossians were genuine, but not Ephesians, a later editor would have worked to "Paulinize" an authentic Pauline letter! The authenticity of Colossians has some support in Philemon (see Col. 4:9-17, perhaps also 3:22-25).[275] The idiosyncratic terminology could be explained by the assumption that Paul addresses the concepts of philosophy seeking "to the Gnostics to be a Gnostic."[276] Conversely, however, the style of Ephesians is easier to explain as belonging to the category of a "catholic" letter, while the situation in Colossae demanded argumentation and polemics, not merely positive portrayals, warnings and reminders.

Dibelius thought that the relationship of Ephesians to Colossians "provided the key to decide the question of authenticity."[277] That assertion is true only to the extent "that correspondences in terminology despite conceptual differences" argue against common authorship of both letters.[278] As examples, we can mention in addition to *head* κεφαλή and *body* σῶμα, *mystery* μυστήριον and *reconcile* ἀποκαταλλάσσειν also *fullness* πλήρωμα, *stewardship, plan* οἰκονομία or *bond* σύνδεσμος with the genitive. In addition, we need to add Ephesians' interpretive expansions of common good. To assert Pauline authorship of Colossians, one must also assert that the situation in Colossae required arguments from Scripture. As is well known, Thessalonians and Philippians contain no scriptural

---

273. [See above note 160.]

274. [See above note 181.]

275. Knox 1938, 144-60; idem 1959, 34-55.

276. Dibelius/Greeven 1953, 53 and 83; Chadwick 1954-55, 270-75, esp. 271.

277. Dibelius/Greeven 1953, 83.

278. Dibelius/Greeven 1953, 84. [Vielhauer 1975, 209; see already W. Bousset 1921/65, 287, note 2: "A comparison between Ephesians and Colossians from the perspective of the theme ἐκκλησία proves beyond doubt that the two letters have different authors. Ephesians is in a conceptual sphere completely different from that of Colossians."]

citations and fewer scriptural allusions than 1 and 2 Corinthians, Romans and the Galatians. However, Ephesians refers to the Old Testament much more frequently than Colossians! Despite all their correspondences, each letter has its own characteristic style.[279] To maintain Pauline authorship of both letters, one must at the least concede that he used different assistants.

4. THE AUTHOR

"Introductions" to Ephesians have generally discussed the question of authorship as part of the background. This has often, though not always, led to methodological errors, in two different ways: (1) the writer highlights distinctive features, and uses them uncritically to argue against the authenticity of the letter, without sufficiently taking into account how greatly Paul can vary his style and even his themes according to circumstances.[280] (2) The writer can demonstrate that the distinctive features reflect the literary and rhetorical style and the special occasion, purpose and content of the letter and concludes, uncritically, that the distinctive features do not therefore exclude Pauline authorship.[281] To avoid such errors, I postponed, other than in the discussion of the history of research, the question of authorship until I had made the attempt to describe impartially the idiosyncratic features of the letter and its relationship to writings both within and outside the Pauline corpus. With this overall picture of the letter as context, I now return to the question of the identity of the author.

Paul himself is not responsible for the literary and linguistic form of the letter. This view best explains both the general character of Ephesians and also its relationship to the Colossians.[282] A number of specific observations support this conclusion:

---

279. [See now esp. Best 1997b, 72–96.]

280. [Schlier 1963, 23: ". . . the often uncritical and superficial approach of several so-called critics."]

281. Typical are Schlier 1963, 27; Barth 1974, 41–50; Percy 1946, 191–99, 202–52; van Roon 1974, esp. 438–40 *et passim*; [see already Haupt 1902, 80–82, although somewhat hesitantly.]

282. See above sections 3.2 and 3.3. [Lexically, Ephesians has some idiosyncrasies: "Ephesians has 35 words unique to it in the New Testament [ed.: Aland 1978, 456], of particular importance: ἑνότης (Eph. 4:3, 13), κοσμοκράτωρ (Eph. 6:12), μεσότοιχον (Eph. 2:14) and πολιτεία (Eph 2:12)." (Schnelle 1996, 349). In syntax, the Pastoral

1. Ephesians uses the term *the devil* ὁ διάβολος, while Paul uses *Satan* σατανᾶς and other synonyms.²⁸³ This is hardly a coincidence, because Ephesians also differs otherwise from Paul in demonology. Only in Ephesians is there a direct relationship between the devil and the cosmic powers and principalities.²⁸⁴

2. Ephesians uses the expression *in the heavenly places* ἐν τοῖς επουρανίοις five times, while Paul says *in heaven* ἐν οὐρανῷ or *in the heavens* ἐν (τοῖς) οὐρανοῖς. This again is not an isolated phenomenon, because Ephesians presupposes generally a cosmology different from Paul's.²⁸⁵

3. Ephesians contains multiple, often cosmological designations for God, which do not occur in Paul: in God who created all things ἐν τῷ θεῷ τῷ τὰ πάντα κτίσαντι (3:9); before the Father, from whom every family ... takes its name πρὸς τὸν πατέρα, ἐξ οὗ πᾶσα πατριὰ ... ὀνομάζεται (3:14f.); one God and Father of all, who is above all εἷς θεὸς καὶ πατὴρ πάντων. ὁ ἐπὶ πάντων κτλ. (4:6).²⁸⁶

4. Only Ephesians speaks of "the coming age" or "the coming ages" (1:21; 2:7). Even otherwise, the author of Ephesians does not use Pauline expressions for the future eternity or for the time before

---

Epistles differ less than Ephesians and Colossians from the undoubted letters of Paul; see Lester 1973, 72-82: "After comparing and contrasting the stylistic similarities and differences within the natural groupings of the Antilegomena ... one can safely assert that, in terms of relative distance from the style of the Homologoumena the Antilegomena can be arranged as follows: Homologoumena—II Thess.—II Tim.—Tit.—I Tim.—Eph/Col" (*ibid.*, 82).

283. Διάβολος: Eph. 4:27; 6:11; See also 2:2; In the undoubted letters, however, ὁ σατανᾶς: Rom. 16:20; 1 Cor. 5:5; 7:5, etc.; l Thess. 3:5; cf. ὁ ὀλοθρευτής: 1 Cor. 10:10; ὁ πονηρός: 2 Thess. 3.1.

284. Eph. 6:11f.; cf. also 2:2f.; on that, B. Noack 1948; [now also highlighting the importance of the cosmic "powers" C. E. Arnold 1989, *passim*].

285. *In the heavenly places* Ἐν τοῖς επουρανίοις: Eph. 1:3, 20; 2:6; 3:10; 6:12. Cf. 1:20-23; 2:.2-3; 3:18; 4:8 10. Ephesians seems to presuppose a three level view of the universe instead of a spherical view. [See Dahl 1965, 63-75; for more on the worldview, cf. Gnilka 1990, 63ff.; Lindemann 1985, 121-23. Hübner 1997, 260-63.)

286. There are also other names of God without full equivalents in Paul: 1:17: *the God of our Lord Jesus Christ* ὁ θεὸς τοῦ κυρίου ἡμῶν Ἰησοῦ Χριστοῦ (cf. 1:3b), *the Father of glory* ὁ πατὴρ τῆς δόξης; 1:11: *the one working all things* τοῦ τὰ πάντα ἐνεργοῦντος κτλ.; 3:20: *to the one being able* τῷ δὲ δυναμένῳ; 5:20: *to God the Father* τῷ θεῷ καὶ πατρί.

Creation.²⁸⁷ As in the previous case, the terminology may be "liturgical"; however, that fails to explain why throughout Ephesians differs from Pauline expressions for eternity.

5. Ephesians introduces two citations with *it is said* διὸ λέγει, while Paul uses other introductions, e.g., *as it is written* καθὼς γέγραπται or *scripture says* λέγει ἡ γραφή. However, the formula *it is said* διὸ λέγει used in Eph. 4.8 and 5.14 appears in non-Pauline writings.²⁸⁸ Further, Ephesians' exegetical terminology differs from Paul's: *now the... what is it, if not* τὸ δὲ ... τί ἐστιν, εἰ μὴ ... (4:9); *this is a great mystery, but I take it to mean* τὸ μυστήριον τοῦτο μέγα ἐστίν, ἐγὼ δὲ λέγω εἰς ... (5:32); cf. also 6:2, 17.

6. Especially notable is the use of the expression "in Christ" and variations on it. The determinate form *in Christ* "ἐν τῷ Χριστῷ" appears in Ephesians 1:10, 12, 20, but otherwise only in 1 Cor. 15:22 and 2 Cor. 2:14. The expressions *in the Lord Jesus* ἐν τῷ κυρίῳ Ἰησοῦ (1:15); *in Christ Jesus our Lord* ἐν τῷ Χριστῷ Ἰησοῦ τῷ κυρίῳ ἡμῶν (3:11); *in the beloved* ἐν τῷ ἠγαπημένῳ (1:6) and *in Jesus* ἐν τῷ Ἰησοῦ (4:21) are unique to Ephesians. The pronominal form *in him* ἐν αὐτῷ occurs more frequently in Ephesians and Colossians than in the other letters.²⁸⁹ *In whom* Ἐν ᾧ (in this sense) appears only in Ephesians and Colossians.²⁹⁰ Only in Ephesians is a relative clause with *in whom* ἐν ᾧ added to an "in Christ" at the end of the preceding sentence (Eph. 1:6f., 10f., 12f.; 3:11f.) In similar constructions in Romans 5:2, 11, Paul repeats the preposition *through* διά.

The different use of a Pauline formula like *in Christ* ἐν Χριστῷ and variations argues more strongly against Pauline authorship of Ephesians than the use of non-Pauline expressions does. Ephesians uses the formula in statements in which God is the actor, Christ the intermediary, and

---

287. 3:21: *to all generations of ages of ages* εἰς πάσας τὰς γενεὰς τοῦ αἰῶνος τῶν αἰώνων; 4:6: *who is above all and through all and in all* ὁ ἐπὶ πάντων καὶ διὰ πάντων καὶ ἐν πᾶσιν; 1:4: *before the foundation of the world* πρὸ καταβολῆς κόσμου; 3:10f.: *in accordance with the eternal purpose* κατὰ πρόθεσιν τῶν αἰώνων.

288. [Heb. 3:7; James 4:6.]

289. *In him* Ἐν αὐτῷ: Eph. 1:4, 9(?), 10; 2:15, 16(?); in Col. 7 or 8 times; in the homologoumena only 5 times; *in whom* ἐν ᾧ: Eph. 1:7, 11, 13; 2:21, 22; 3:12; and by analogy 4:30; in Col. 3 or 4 times. The frequency of the remaining variations is not especially striking: *in Christ* ἐν Χριστῷ: 1:1; 2:5 (P⁴⁶ B D G); 2:6, 7(B pl); 2:10, 13; 3:6, 21; *in the Lord* ἐν κυρίῳ

290. See Lester 1973, 187.

Christians the ones affected by the action, as for example in 1:3: *who has blessed us in Christ* ὁ εὐλογήσας ἡμᾶς ... ἐν Χριστῷ. In Paul, there are only partial analogies to this type of expression.[291] Without analogy in Paul is the use of *in him* ἐν αὐτῷ in a sentence with Christ as the subject: 2:15. Ephesians is also unique in its use of *in him* ἐν αὐτῷ in a statement about election (1:4) and in a doxology (3:21). When one considers both the frequency and use of Ephesians' formulaic expressions, one must conclude that the author was strongly influenced by Paul, but varies from him and is not Paul himself.

The deviations from Pauline usage noted above in items 1–6 cannot explain Ephesians' literary character, the reason the letter was written, its content or its specific style. The deviations show that the author uses terminology different from that of Paul and also uses expressions typical of Paul in ways different from Paul. Other observations can be added,[292]

291. "In Christ" designates Christ as the representative of God and/or as the intermediary of salvation in various constructions. (1) God is subject, the predicate a transitive verb with a personal pronoun object, usually *us* ἡμᾶς: Eph. 1:3: *blessed* εὐλογήσας; 1:4: *chose* ἐξελέξατο; 1:6: ἐχαρίτωσεν *graced;* cf. 2:5 συνεζωοποίησεν *made alive with;* 2:6: *raised us up with and made us sit with* συνήγειρεν καὶ συνεκάθισεν; cf. 1:10; 2:15 and with a dative object 4:32: *forgave us* ἐχαρίσατο ὑμῖν. There is no exact analogy to this construction in the Pauline homologoumena. The closest are Rom. 8:2(?); 2 Cor. 2:14; 5:17; 1 Pet. 5:10; Col. 2:15(?). Also Col. 1:19; 2:9. (2) God is the logical subject of a passive verb: 1:11: *we were chosen* ἐκληρώτημεν; 1:13: *you were sealed* ἐσφραγίσθητε; 2:10: *created* κτισθέντες; (2:22: *are being built into* συνοικοδομεῖσθε); 4:21: *were taught* ἐδιδάχθητε (?). Analogues: Col. 2:10, 11, 12(?); cf. 1:16; 1 Cor. 1:4, 5; 15:22; Gal. 2:17. (3) God is the subject, the predicate a transitive verb with a direct object: 1:19: *made known to us the mystery* γνωρίσας ὑμῖν τὸ μυστήριον; 1:20; (2:7); 3:11. There are no analogies to this construction. (4) Statements about what Christians have or have become "in Christ" (1:7; 3:12; 2:13; 3:6; 5:8). Similar constructions also appear in Paul (Rom. 15:17; 1 Cor 15:31; Gal. 2:4; Philemon 8; cf. Col. 1:14; Rom. 12:5; 1 Cor. 1:30; 2 Cor. 5:21). It is certainly somewhat striking that "in the Lord" appears in Eph. 5:8; one would have expected in Paul "in Christ;" cf. Schmauch 1935, 175.

292. Some theological terms are used differently in Colossians and in the Pauline homologoumena, e.g., *head* κεφαλή and *body* σῶμα, *church* ἐκκλησία, *fullness* πλήρωμα, *fill* πληροῦν, *reconcile* ἀποκαταλλάσσειν, *mystery* μυστήριον, *inheritance* κληρονομία; see above section 3.2, section 3.3 and Merklein 1973a, 29–35; additionally, P. L. Hammer 1960, 267–72; J. D. Hester 1968. On the question of authorship, even linguistic details can be important. For example, Ephesians uses the form ἅ as the neuter plural of the relative pronoun (5:4; similarly Col. 2:18, 23; 2 Tim. 2:20; Tit. 1:11); Paul always uses ἅτινα. Ephesians and Colossians append epexegetical relative clauses with ὅ ἐστιν, while Paul uses τοῦτ' ἔστιν (Eph. 1:14, 3:13) in contrast to Philemon 12; Rom. 1:12, etc. (but Phil. 1:28 differs, ἥτις ἐστίν, like Eph. 6:2). Cf. F. Blass/A. Debrunner/F. Rehkopf 1976, §132:2; Lester 1973, 64. Μᾶλλον δέ appears in Eph. 4:28 and 5:11 as a transition from a positive contrast to a preceding negative exhortation, different from Rom. 8:34;

but only a full analysis and statistical processing of linguistic features would be able to assure a conclusive result. Instead, here I will try to characterize the author with the help of some individual observations. If a convincing overall picture emerges, we will have achieved a positive result that confirms the negative result that the author was not Paul.

It should first be noted that the author was a personal student of the Apostle's.[293] This assumption best explains the combination of Pauline and non-Pauline elements in language, style and thought that some scholars advance as an argument for, and others as an argument against, Pauline authorship.[294] Situational and polemical statements in the undoubted Pauline letters have few echoes in Ephesians. The parallels to Ephesians are rather in the conventional form of the letter and in particular in sections which reflect more general topics of preaching, instruction and worship. One must conclude that the author was familiar not only with the Apostle's literary corpus, but also with the oral form of its language. Different observations make probable that the author of Ephesians was one of the Apostle's coworkers.

In some cases it is evident, in others likely or at least possible, that Ephesians is not dependent on the text of the undisputed letters of Paul, but instead directly on older shapes and patterns of preaching and on the language of worship which the received texts also reflect.[295] In this context it is quite unimportant whether this material is in a strict sense "pre-Pauline tradition," or whether Paul was himself actively involved in shaping the material.[296] In any case, Ephesians uses the older material in a fairly traditional way, without the particular applications and modifications which characterize the genuine Pauline letters. A few examples will suffice here.[297]

---

1 Cor. 14:1, 5; Gal. 4:9. Only Ephesians uses both διὰ τοῦτο (1:15, 17) and διὰ ταῦτα (5:6), ἀντί τούτου (5:31; [LXX has: ἕνεκεν τούτου] and τούτου χάριν (3:1, 14) specifying a reason. For additional idiosyncrasies in vocabulary phraseology and style, see, e.g., Moffat 1918, 385-89; Schmid 1928, 131ff.; Percy 1946, 179-252; Merklein 1973a, 19-25; Lester 1973; van Roon 1974, 100-212; [J. H. Moulton/N. Turner 1976, 84f.; Lincoln 1990 lxv-lxvi; Best 1998, 27-32].

293. Differing, Vielhauer 1975, 212; see also Conzelmann/Lindemann 1995, 300.]
294. [See note 170 above.]
295. [Cf. Schille 1965, 15-20; Fischer 1973, 109-47; Best 1998, 75-83.]
296. Cf J. Becker 1989, 110.
297. See Käsemann 1958, 518f.; Schille, 1965.

The benediction in 2 Cor. 1:3ff. reflects the circumstances of the letter and refers to an event in the life of Paul. The structure of the benediction in Eph. 1:3-14 is shaped by an exemplar from Judaism. In 2 Cor. 1:21f. and 5:5, Paul relies on confirmation by the Holy Spirit to establish his credibility and assurance about a controversial situation. The similar formulations in Eph. 1:13f. and 4:30 remind baptized Gentiles about their experience in very simple way.[298]

Interpretive paraphrases of Psalms 8:7 and 110:1 appear both in Eph. 1:20-23 and in 1 Cor. 15:22-28. In 1 Cor. 15, Paul carefully distinguishes between different features of the eschatalogical drama; the enemy forces, including death, have not yet been subjected to Christ. Thus, Paul corrected an eschatological enthusiasm [cf. 1 Cor 12:28F.] that might arise from Christological enthronement hymns.[299] The hymnic style did not differentiate between realized and future aspects of the enthronement. The author of Ephesians is not dependent on 1 Cor. 15, but on the style and wording of pre-Pauline or early Pauline enthronement hymns. One could go further and suggest that the concept that the baptized were already raised and enthroned with Christ was known to the Corinthian enthusiasts (cf. Eph. 2:5-7; 1 Cor. 4:8). In any case it is likely that the chronologically later testimony in Ephesians 2:5-7 reflects an older layer in the history of tradition than the later stage of baptismal teaching in Romans 6, where Paul speaks only of crucifixion and burial with Christ, while he deliberately omits the analogous statement about resurrection with Christ.[300]

It may here suffice to provide another particularly clear example. In Eph. 5:3-14, there is a warning against associating with notorious sinners, who are excluded from the Kingdom of God and of Christ. Similar warnings are also known from Judaism, particularly from Essene piety. The text in Ephesians 5 relates especially closely with 1 Cor. 5:9, 11; 6:9f. However, in 1 Cor. 5 Paul clarifies what he had written in a previous

---

298. See Dahl, "Benediction and Congratulations" and "The Concept of Baptism in Ephesians" *Studies in Ephesians*.

299. Cf. D. Lührmann 1965, 118f.; J. C. Hurd 1965/83, 195-200; [On 1 Cor. 15 see now among others Conzelmann 1981c, 319-21; K.-G. Sandelin 1976; Sellin 1986; J. H. Ulrichsen 1995, 781-99; W. Verburg 1996; N. Walter 1998, 109-127].

300. It is also likely that the term *the old man* ὁ παλαιὸς ἄνθρωπος was connected traditionally with clothing symbolism (Eph. 4:22-24; Col. 3:9-11). However, the idea of the crucifixion of the old man with Christ (Rom. 6:5) may be specifically Pauline. See also Eph. 2:5-8; [On the clothing metaphor, see Dahl, "Kleidungsmetaphern: der alte und der neue Mensch" *Studies in Ephesians*].

letter. His warning against community with fornicators, the greedy, idolaters, etc., refers only to people within the community. There is no trace of clarification or indeed of correction in Ephesians. The author of Ephesians writes rather about the same things Paul must have written about in the lost letter to the Corinthians that antedates what we know as 1 Corinthians. It is apparently a piece of both Pauline and universal early Christian moral teaching.[301] What is provable in this case, is also likely more generally: the author is in same stream of tradition as Paul, but concerns himself little if at all with the specific interpretations and applications of the common tradition that appear in the surviving letters of Paul.[302]

The author is nevertheless certainly a "Paulinist." At any rate, at one point he even goes beyond Paul. The statement that Christ has abolished the law (Eph. 2:15) doesn't exist in the letters written by Paul himself and contradicts at least in this form Paul's assertion that he through his teaching does not abolish the law, but rather upholds it, i.e., that his function isto bring the law to its intended fruition (Rom. 3:31; cf. Gal. 3:21f). The author calls circumcision "so-called" and "in the flesh" and "made with hands" (2:11), and used a more denigrating terminology than Paul, despite Rom. 2:26-29, Gal. 5:12 and Phil. 3:2-3. Eph. 2:8-9 lacks the polemical climax on the works of the law in its contrast between grace and works, but the final clause *so that no one may boast* ἵνα μή τις καυχήσηται shows that the author brings out the specific Pauline doctrine.[303]

The presentation of Paul in Ephesians 3:2-12 speaks both positively and negatively about Paul's self-understanding. In 1 Cor. 15:9 Paul calls himself *the least of the apostles* ὁ ἐλάχιστος τῶν ἀποστόλων, in Eph. 3:8

---

301. Cf. Dahl 1963, 65-77.

302. One can find almost everywhere more or less stereotyped preaching paradigms: the "revelation" paradigm: "once hidden—now revealed" (3:4-6, 9-11; cf. 1:4-6, 9-11); the "soteriological contrast" paradigm: "once you were ... but now you are ... (2:11-22; 5:8; see 2:1-10); the "conformance paradigm" (4:32; 5:2; see 5:25f.—at the same time "teleological"; cf. 2:14-16); "lists of offenders" who do not inherit the Kingdom of God, but are struck by the anger of God (5:5, 6; see 1 Cor. 6:9f.; Gal. 5:19-21; also Eph. 4:17-19 and Rom. 1:18ff.); "household codes" (5:21-6:9); "virtue or spiritual goods as weapons" (6:11-17; cf. 1 Thess. 5:8). On the first mentioned paradigms, see Dahl, 1954-57, 3-9 [see now also Wolter 1987, 287-319 and Hellholm 1998, 333-48].

303. [Hübner 1997, 274 however, here assumes a later interpolation, see the quote above in note 264.]

I am the least of all the saints ἐμοὶ τῷ ἐλαχιστέρῳ πάντων ἁγίων. The increased use of some Paulinisms fits into the overall picture.³⁰⁴

The author combines in the letter which he wrote in the name of the Apostle pre-Pauline material with Pauline and even post-Pauline elements. Nevertheless, the overall perspective shows that he belongs to a later generation than that of Paul. Equality of Gentiles with Jews is not a controversial question, but a revealed mystery, the greatness of which the former pagans need to recall (2:11-22; 3:5-7). Paul is understood primarily as an intermediary of the revelation of the mystery (3:2-12).³⁰⁵ The self-portrait of the Apostle is described with the same, strangely stylized, lofty language, as the more liturgical sections of the letter. The unity of the church is a central idea of the letter,³⁰⁶ but we learn nothing about its actualization beyond the boundaries of the local community. For the author, the "holy" apostles and the prophets form the foundation of the church (2:20; see 3:3). One can debate the extent to which such formulations were possible only in the post-Pauline period.³⁰⁷ But one gets the impression that our writer looks at the apostles and prophets as ideals, rather than as people of flesh and blood (cf. by way of contrast Gal. 1:16f; 2:6-10).

Compared to the charismatic teaching of Paul (1 Cor. 12, Rom. 12:3-8), Eph. 4:7-16 highlights more strongly the special function of the servant of the word. The warning against false teachers (4:14) is quite stereotypical. In this, as in other respects, the letter to the Ephesians is close to the Apostolic Fathers and to the later writings of the New Testament. One cannot on that basis make any hasty conclusions on chronology. Both these concepts and their linguistic formulation can have existed long before their initial attestation in the extant literature, and people living at the same time can have belonged to different theological generations. The author of Ephesians must have been a man of the transitional period: he belonged to the Pauline circle, but still shares many traits with Christian teachers and leaders at the end of the first century.

304. See above *passim* and Lester 1973, esp. 102-28.

305. [Cf. Best 1998, 293, 295, 300f.]

306. [See Sellin 1996, 295: "Life in 'unity' is the overriding principal for the ethics of Ephesians."]

307. The designation attested in Gal. 2:9 "στῦλοι" allows one to conclude that this view was possible even while Paul lived; cf. also Matt 16:18 and Rev. 21:14.

The letter to the Ephesians should clearly be assigned to the trajectory leading from Paul to so-called "Early Catholicism".[308] One should not overlook, however, that there is also a trajectory leading from Paul through Ephesians to the Christian Gnostics of the second century. Different approaches to this development already exist within Ephesians itself: the revelation of hidden wisdom and knowledge of God is for the author an essential aspect of Christianity (Eph. 1:8f, 17ff.; 3:2ff., 14ff.).[309] People who were dead in their sins, have been raised with Christ (2:5–8; cf. 5:14). The writer refers to specific situations less often than Paul, but has instead expanded the doctrine of salvation through the inclusion of cosmological terminology. A similar reinterpretation of cosmological ideas took place in Gnostic circles, but one need not assume that Ephesians presupposes the fully developed, anti-cosmic dualism of later Gnostic systems.[310]

Although later development led in different directions, there is no tension within Ephesians between "early Catholic" and "Gnosticizing" tendencies. Rather, the grace of God proclaimed in the gospel and the full participation of the Gentiles in salvation is presented as the highest, inscrutable mystery. The author uses terms that would otherwise be familiar for secret revelations, esoteric knowledge, religious cosmology, and theosophy to present the common belief of Christians in the language of these categories. In this, he follows a widespread trend in later antiquity. Philosophizing mystagogues and religious philosophers, as well as Jews both in Palestine and in Alexandria, described their own teachings as revealed knowledge, in order to lead their followers to the path of redemption. Even where no religious syncretism took place, the same terminology was used. In comparison with Paul, Ephesians represents greater accommodation of the religious syncretistic language of the Hellenistic environment, without thereby becoming less Jewish.[311]

308. Käsemann agrees: 1980; [Fischer 1973;] and Merklein 1973a; the radical difference concerns the assessment of "Early Catholicism" inside and outside of the New Testament. [See now also Schenke/Fischer 1978, 178f.; Hübner 1993, 370f.]

309. [Cf. now Hellholm 1998 240–42.]

310. I pointed out the adoption and reframing of cosmological terminology in Ephesians in 1946 in my review of Percy in Dahl 1947, 366–74. It is now pretty generally accepted: cf. for example the works of C. Colpe 1960, 173–87; Hegermann 1961; Merklein 1973a; Fischer 1973; [similarly recently also Pokorný 1992, 22–24, esp. 23 with note 22; additionally now also Faust 1993].

311. Cf. Dahl, 1975, 57–75; also in particular M. Hengel 1973, 381–94 (excursus No. 4: "Higher wisdom by revelation"); E. H. Pagels 1975, 115–33.

The author reaches back over and over again to the Old Testament, alluding to, paraphrasing and also interpreting it.[312] Comparison to Colossians and the other letters shows that the references to Scripture are frequently part of Ephesians' "special material," material idiosyncratic to it. Ephesians uses the Old Testament like the smaller Pauline letters and, as the exegetical terminology shows, somewhat differently from the "main letters." In many cases, it is clear that author knew not only the Old Testament texts, but also the associated early Christian and Jewish traditions.[313] One cannot attribute everything to pre-existing tradition. The author must also have been a trained exegete. In 5:28-33 he combines paraphrases of the command to love in Lev 19:18 with an interpretation of Gen 2:24 that he contrasts with other interpretations.[314] In 4:8-12, he cites Ps. 68:19 in a form known from the Targum, which goes back to the Hebrew text. His exegesis presupposes the association of the Psalm verse with Moses, to which he appends a Christological interpretation.[315]

The terminology of the letter can be traced back to Greek as well as to Jewish sources. In addition to Stoic material, one should not ignore Platonic elements in the philosophical and religious syncretism of the time.[316] The author certainly did not have the philosophical education of someone like Philo of Alexandria. At some points, however, Philo's writings offer particularly remarkable parallels, for example to the idea of the cosmic head and its body.[317] The author was exposed to these elements of Greek philosophy through the medium of Hellenistic Judaism.

In Eph. 2:11f., the author calls the addressees "you Gentiles" and reminds them of the privileges given them in Christ, paraphrasing Is. 57:9 and using the language of Jewish proselytism. That may reflect that

312. [Cf. now T. Moritz 1996.]

313. Cf. esp. Eph. 1:20-22 (+ 2:5-7); 2:13-17, 20-22; 4:7-12, 25-30; 5:2, (14), 17, 25-33; 6:2-3, 13-17. [For comparison to Colossians, see section 3.3 above.]

314. See Sampley 1971, esp. 139ff., 158ff.; see also Dawes 1998, 106f., 168-91.

315. [Cf. P. Billerbeck 1926, 596—99. For more information, see, e.g., Schlier 1963, 192: "to explain this reference to Christ and indeed to the exalted Lord is obviously the intention of the parenthetical insertion in verses 9 and 10"; Kirby 1968, 61-69, 138f., 146; in addition, Schnackenburg 1982, 179-82; Gnilka 1990, 206-10; Lincoln 1990, 243f.; Pokorný 1992, 169-72; Hübner 1997, 205:" . . . He (the author of Ephesians) has also made a statement about God in Christ"; Best 1998, 378-88.]

316. This, oddly, is rarely emphasized; but cf. Chadwick1960, 150f.; see also Eph. 1:18; 2:14; 3:17; 5:1.

317. See esp. Colpe 1960, 172-87; Hegermann 1961, 9-87 [see now also Luz 1998a, 126-30.]

he is writing in Paul's name. Speaking and writing as if someone else (*fictio persona; προσωποποιΐα*) was a form used in rhetoric of the classical period.[318] However, one gets the impression that the author himself was an Israelite. Quite a few researchers, whose perspectives about Ephesians otherwise diverge, nevertheless believe that the author was a Jewish Christian.[319] In addition to the use of the Old Testament, the particularly close connection to Hebrew phraseology known from the synagogue liturgy and the hymns of Qumran (esp. Eph. 1:13ff.; 2:5ff.) shows that this view is more than a conjecture.[320] Ephesians speaks differently from Paul about *sons of men* τοῖς υἱοῖς τῶν ἀνθρώπων (3:5). Expressions like *children of wrath* τέκνα ὀργῆς or *of light* φωτός (2:3 or 5:8) or *in the sons of men* ἐν τοις υἱοῖς τῶν ἀνθρώπων (2:2), the connections of the genitive of some abstract nouns and other constructions show that the language of Ephesians is somewhat more strongly Semitic in form than that of Paul. One may draw the conclusion that the author was bilingual or trilingual, and was at home not only in the Judaism of the Greek-speaking diaspora, but also in Hebrew, and Aramaic-speaking circles.

If our attempt to describe the author is generally correct, we have to look for the author within a very limited circle. Gentile Christians such as Onesimos or Tychicus are not possibilities. Timothy we may also exclude, especially since in Ephesians, unlike in Colossians and Philemon, Timothy is not named as co-sender.[321] We rule out Paul's older coworkers, Barnabas, Silas/Silvanus, Apollos or Prisca and Aquila. If we're on the right track, the author belonged to the generation after Paul's, but was a

---

318. See, e.g., Lausberg 1973, 411–13 (§§ 826–29); [J. Martin 1974, 292f., esp. Quintilian, *Inst. orat.* 9.2.31; see S. K. Stowers 1995, 180–202: "Cicero, Quintilian und die Progymnasmata ... of Theon, Hermogenes und Aphthonius provide the best evidence from the rhetorical tradition for προσωποποιΐα in the early empire" (*ibid.*, 180).]

319. See, e.g., F. W. Beare 1953, 601; Käsemann 1958, 520; Bjerkelund 1967, 187; Murphy-O'Connor 1965; 1201–09; [Kirby 1968, 165; Kümmel 1973, 322; Schenke/Fischer 1978, 187; Best 1998, 8 and 91f.; as a possibility, also Ernst 1974, 261; Pokorný 1992, 40. Mitton argues for a Gentile Christian, Mitton 1951, 264; idem 1976, 30; as does Lindemann 1976, 247.]

320. Lyonnet 1961, 341–53; Kirby 1968; Kuhn 1960–61, 334–46; [see also above note 98, as well as Dahl "Ephesians and Qumran," Studies in Ephesians.]

321. Schleiermacher early suggested Tychicus as the actual author: Schleiermacher 1895, 165f., 194; later also, e.g., [Goguel 1926, 174; cf. also idem 1935/36; W. L. Knox 1939, 203;] Mitton 1951, 268 and unfortunately I myself, see Dahl, 1966, 14. About the hypothesis of Onesimos as the author (Goodspeed 1933; J. Knox 1935/59; Harrison 1964a), see above. Eichhorn 1812, 278ff. thought Timothy was the author.

Jew who converted to Christianity in its Pauline form and who was also a personal assistant of the apostle's. He must have been an unusual and important man. One would assume that his work was not limited to drafting Ephesians, and that he would not have been completely forgotten.

Colossians can help at this point. In it, greetings are conveyed from three men, Aristarchus, Mark and Jesus Justus. They are described as the only of Paul's coworkers "of the circumcision," and as having been a comfort to him (Col. 4:10–11). If the writer of Ephesians was a Jewish Christian, and if he wrote the letter during Paul's lifetime and on his behalf, he would have had to be one of these three. In this case, the other coworkers would have drafted the letters to the Colossians and to Philemon at the same time.[322]

In Acts, we learn that Aristarchus was a Macedonian from Thessalonica; He was with Paul in Ephesus and accompanied him on the trip to Macedonia (and Corinth) and later on the voyage to Rome (Acts 19:29; 20:4; 27:2). Probably he was one of the delegates who followed Paul to Jerusalem to present the collection. His name is Greek and it is not sure whether or not he was of Jewish origin.[323] Mark is described as a cousin of Barnabas, and is apparently also known as John Mark (cf. Acts 12:12, 25; 13:5, 13; 15:37, 39). Jesus Justus is known only from Col. 4:11.[324]

John Mark und Jesus Justus have both a Hebrew and a Latin name, like Saul/Paul.[325] They will have had therefore the connections both to a Hebrew-Aramaic and a Greek environment, which we have presupposed for the author of Ephesians. In favor of Mark, one can cite the acquaintance

---

322. [Cf. Best 1998, 621; "It (sc. Ephesians) was probably written not by Paul but by someone strongly under his influence who had also been associated with the author of Colossians. Probably they both belonged to a continuing group of Paul's disciples."]

323. According to Herm. Von Soden 1893, 70 the reference in Col. 4:11 is only to Mark and Jesus Justus; Lohse 1968, 242 disagrees.

324. Of those named in Col 4:10ff., only Jesus Justus doesn't appear in Philemon. Otherwise, however, if Zahn's (1897, 321) and E. Amling's (1909, 261f.) conjecture is right, that one should read Philemon 23–24 not as ἐν Χριστῷ Ἰησοῦ, Μᾶρκος, etc., but as ἐν Χριστῷ, Ἰησοῦς, Μᾶρκος, etc. [so also W. Foerster 1938, 286; J. Knox 1959, 35, note 2; Lohse 1968, 242 with note 8; *ibid.*, 288 with note 2; Ollrog 1979, 49 note 229; Pokorný 1987, 162f; Standhartiger 1999, 81 note 85; However, against that view P. Stuhlmacher 1975, 55; Gnilka 1982, 92; Lindemann 1983, 74; Wolter 1993, 281; 39; assessed by Hübner as questionable, 1997, 39; see also the discussion in Schweizer 1976, 24; cf. also P. Lampe 1998, 230f., where in the translation, "Jesus" is left out and ignored in comment].

325. See V. A. Tcherikover 1957, 28 with note 69; Lohse 1968, 242 note 7: "the name Justus was more common among Jews."

INTRODUCTION TO THE LETTER TO THE EPHESIANS   263

with non-Pauline and early Pauline traditions. Ephesians and 1 Peter are so closely related that the mention of Mark in 1 Peter 5:13 is not a difficulty. The author of the Gospel of Mark cannot be the same as the author of Ephesians. It is however questionable whether or not the Gospel is correctly attributed. I deem the otherwise unknown Jesus Justus as the one most likely to be the author of Ephesians. Since he is mentioned only in Colossians, we may assume that he was one of the youngest coworkers of Paul and therefore a figure in the transition to the next generation.[326] Entirely hypothetically, one might speculate that the remark that he had become a consolation to Paul refers to his involvement in the drafting of Ephesians, while Mark, according to the parenthesis in Col. 4:10, had another task. We of course know so little about Jesus Justus that we can neither fully prove nor disprove the hypothesis that he is the unknown writer of Ephesians.

If Ephesians and Colossians were not written during Paul's lifetime, but only several decades after his death, then there are additional uncertainties. But even in that case, the two letters arose in the same environment, most likely within a Pauline 'school' in Ephesus.[327] Further, by the year 80 or 90, a Jewish steward of Pauline tradition would have been a very atypical situation.[328] It is also worth noting that the list of greetings in Col. 4:10-14 is more extensive than that in Philemon 22-24. If that suggests that Colossians is later than Philemon, the author of Colossians must nevertheless have intended to recommend the people in the list to his readers.[329] He added the name Jesus Justus probably because Jesus Justus was a recognized, Jewish member of the Pauline school. Even if Colossians, and then necessarily Ephesians, were not written until after

326. [Cf., independent of Dahl, also Vielhauer 1975, 212: "the author was a—probably not personally—student of Paul's and younger than the author of Colossians, who knew well the teachings of the Apostle and independently developed them further" and Tavern/Fischer 1978, 186: "the author of Ephesians is . . . not Paul, but a student of Paul's, but a younger (emphasis added—DH) student, to be distinguished from the senior students of Paul who wrote Colossians".]

327. [See esp. Conzelmann 1979, 88-96; Schenke 1974-75, 505-18, esp. 516; Tavern/Fischer 1978, 233-47; Pokorný, 1992, 15-21; Best 1998, 36-40; also Gamble 1975, 403-18.]

328. [cf. Lohse 1968, 242f.; Lindemann 1983, 74; Pokorný 1987, 163; Hübner 1997, 119.]

329. [cf. Wolter 1993, 217: "that the author of Colossians alludes to the greeting list of Philemon, though he expanded it, provides some evidence for an independent tradition of the names of Paul's coworkers;" further also Pokorný 1987, 163.]

the death of the Apostle,[330] it would not diminish the probability that the author of Ephesians is among the Jewish Christians named in Col. 4:10–11, most likely Jesus Justus.

One might characterize the attempt to give a name to the writer of Ephesians as idle guesswork. This thought experiment has nevertheless not been in vain. It in any case establishes that the letter to the Ephesians was the work of a single man. This man was born a Jew and was a younger student of Paul's. We have shown that, though there were only a few, there were some people who fit this personal description. That man or someone like him, a coworker of Paul's in his later years, could have written Ephesians two decades later. The question of whether Paul personally commissioned the letter or whether it was pseudonymous becomes less important, through it remains nevertheless difficult to answer.

The author has apparently sought to compose a letter of Paul. But even though he did not write as he probably would have written a letter in his own name, he accepts the role of author. He therefore bears full responsibility for the design of the text. We cannot say whether or not Paul was involved in any way in the composition of Ephesians.[331] Under these circumstances, we conclude that the author wrote Ephesians on his own initiative and not on Paul's behalf. It is admittedly not more than slightly more probable. Our efforts to identify the author exclude only the literary but not the representative authenticity of Ephesians. Given what we know, it is also difficult to say whether it is more likely that a coworker wrote the letter with Paul's approval, or only after Paul's death, naming Paul as the author.[332] A decision regarding these two alternatives can be made, if at all, only taking into account the circumstances of the composition of Ephesians and the purpose of the letter.

---

330. [Cf. Best 1995, 507–18.]

331. On the participation of assistants (or friends) in drafting letters, see above notes 184 and 185 and the literature cited in them.

332. [In the lifetime of Paul: Ollrog 1979, 219–33; Schweizer 1976, 26f.; Hartmann 1997a, 169; after the death of Paul: the majority of researchers; on pseudepigraphy, see, among others, W. Speyer 1971; K. von Fritz (ed.) 1972; N. Brox (ed.) 1977; K. Aland 1980; D. G. Meade 1986; Donelson 1986, 7–66; Standhartinger 1999, 29–59.]

5. ADDRESS

5.1 Title and Setting

The title "to the Ephesians" is first attested in Irenaeus,[333] but can be found in all later church fathers[334] and in the surviving manuscripts and translations. A generation before Irenaeus Marcion in his revised edition of the Pauline epistles named the letter "to the Laodiceans." It is probable that Marcion found this title in an edition of the Pauline letters which included the Pastoral Epistles. The remaining letters seem to have been described as letters of Paul to seven churches. The letter to Philemon might have been attached to Colossians.[335]

In the oldest editions of the Pauline corpus "to the Ephesians" appeared only in the title. The place of residence of the recipients was not specified in the text of the letter. The words *in Ephesus* ἐν Ἐφέσῳ are missing in the oldest manuscripts. Marcion and the pre-Marcion edition certainly had no place names in the text.[336] One can thus conclude that the two titles "to the Ephesians" and "to the Laodiceans" go back to an editor and that there once circulated a version of Ephesians without a specific address.[337] That would not be without a parallel, because in the

---

333. [*Adv. Haer.* V. 3:3; 8:1; 14:3; 24:4.]

334. [E.g., Tertullian, *Adv. Marc.* V. 11:12; 17:1; Clement of Alexandria, *Strom.* IV. 8; *Paed.* I. 5.]

335. That Marcion's ordering goes back to an earlier edition is clear from the partial agreement with the Seven Letter edition. [See, in particular, Dahl "Welche Ordnung der Paulusbriefe wird vom Muratorischen Kanon vorausgesetzt?" "The Particularity of the Pauline Epistles as a Problem in the Ancient Church" and "The Origin of the Earliest Prologues to the Pauline Letters," *Studies in Ephesians* with bibliographical references. Also now Gamble 1995, 60f. and 273f. notes 82–84.]

336. [Otherwise Lindemann 1976/99, 239/215: "In the second case a reason would have to be found, why Marcion changed the original reading. And this reason can in fact be identified: Marcion realized as well as later B* and A*, that Ephesians could not have been written by Paul to Ephesus. So he changed the address in a way suggested by Col. 4:16."]

337. [Cf. D. Trobisch 1994, 41f.: "... the three oldest manuscripts of the Ephesian letter—P46, Codex Vaticanus (B 03) and Codex Sinaiticus ([ℵ] 01)—donot name recipients in the text of the Eph 1.1. And yet even these manuscripts have "to the Ephesians" in the title. One need not be a specialist, to understand that a scribe could have taken the address from the title and inserted it at the appropriate place in the text. That is to be seen in Codex Vaticanus (B 03) and Codex Sinaiticus ([ℵ] 01): there the address has been entered as a correction in the text. In contrast, it is difficult to name a sensible reason why a writer should have deleted the address from the text, but left it in the title. From this consideration, it seems clear that the oldest form of the text of

textual tradition of Romans there are traces that suggest that there was once a version of Romans 1–14, in which the references in Rom. 1:7 and 15 to the recipients were deleted.[338] This "catholicizing" version was apparently prompted by the desire to have an epistle of Paul's addressed to all Christians.[339]

The text without the place name in Eph. 1:1 could be original under the assumption of pseudonymity.[340] But in this case, it would be a generalizing but clumsy imitation of the address of other Pauline letters (cf. Col. 1:2; Rom. 1:7 and Phil. 1:1)[341] [or a catholicizing imitation directly dependent on to Col 1:2[342]]. Final greetings are missing from Ephesians, both the commission to deliver a greeting as well as its content.[343] The concluding blessings in Eph. 6:23-24 show that the author was able to vary freely standard forms of Paul's letters.[344] The note about sending Tychicus in 6:21-22 presupposes that the letter was intended

---

Ephesians did not contain an address".]

338. Cf. Dahl 1962, 261–71, esp. 267f. ["The Particularity of the Pauline Epistles as a Problem in the Ancient Church," *Studies in Ephesians* and above all H. Y. Gamble 1977, esp. 116–117 [cf. already H. Lietzmann 1933/71, 27; but otherwise Lambert 1976/99, 237/ 213 note 10: "the tendency to 'catholicize' the letters would probably have been more common in the manuscripts; and in any case the findings in Romans are different from those in Ephesians (Codex Boernerianus and its Latin tradition strike ἐν Ῥώμῃ but retain ἐν Ἐφέσῳ)."

339. [See, e.g., Trobisch 1989, 73; Gamble 1995, 98ff., with note.]

340. Benoit 1966, 195–211, who advocates the secretary hypothesis, wonders whether or not the reading of P46 might be original. [Cf. Best 1997a(2), 22; idem 1998, 100f. 1928, who proposes (following Schmid, 1928, 125ff.; Goguel 1935, 254ff.; idem 1936, 73ff.; P. Dacquino 1955, 102–10; Kirby 1968, 170) the conjecture: τοῖς ἁγίοις καὶ πιστοῖς ἐν Χριστῷ Ἰησοῦ; so also Pokorný 1992, 49; Faust 1993, 18: "In the letter itself, the address cannot read ἐν Ἐφέσῳ, because the letter was intended for Gentile Christians throughout the region". Similarly, Arnold 1989, 13–14, 38–39.]

341. [Cf. Lindemann 1976.]

342. [so Sellin 1998, 176–78;] This under two conditions: "the phrase εἶναι πιστὸς ἐν Χριστῷ Ἰησοῦ is . . . equivalent to: "believe" or "have faith" or "be a believer in Jesus Christ" and the "καί reinforces . . . only the explicative, epexegetical function of the participial apposition (ibid., 177). "This 'catholic' address has an echo in the thanksgiving in 1:15: ἡ καθ' ὑμᾶς πίστις ἐν τῷ κυρίῳ Ἰησοῦ (your faith in the Lord Jesus Christ). This καθ' ὑμᾶς has the same function as the participial formulation with εἶναι in 1:1" (ibid., 178); idem 1999, 1346: "according to the model of Col. 1:2 this address is to be read: 'to the Gentiles, (who are) believers in Christ Iesus' . . . Ephesians is therefore in fact a 'catholic' Pauline letter."]

343. [See Schnider/Stenger 1987, 119–135, esp. 119 and 126.]

344. [See Schnider/Stenger 1987, 131–135, esp. 132; see also Pokorný 1992, 250f.]

for a specific audience.³⁴⁵ One must therefore conclude that the letter originally contained an indication of the address, which was lost in an early stage of the textual tradition, before the first complete edition of the letters of Paul.³⁴⁶

We don't know what the original address was. The address of Ephesus most probably migrated from the title to the text.³⁴⁷ Only a few scholars accept the possibility that Ephesus could original.³⁴⁸ The Laodicean address attested by Marcion could be original, although the words "in Laodicea" do not appear in any text of the title of the letter.³⁴⁹ The comment about the letter "from Laodicea" in Col. 4:16 provides only weak support for the hypothesis. It does not explain why all references to the circumstances of a specific community are missing from Ephesians, unlike Colossians.³⁵⁰ The hypothesis that the text originally had the words

345. [Cfl. Bouttier 1991, 271: "καὶ ὑμεῖς, you also, would suggest that other communities had received this information. This is an argument in favor of a circular letter sent with a copy, after others, intended for Ephesus."]

346. [Cf. Schenke /Fischer 1978, 182: "Originally a concrete location stood in the address of the epistle, which is totally lost. It might somehow have seemed offensive. The offense was eliminated in three different ways: 1) by simply omitting the questionable location; (2) by the theory, this letter is the letter to the Laodiceans mentioned in Col. 4:16; by comparison of 6:21f. to Col. 4:7ff. (Tychicus is deemed the bearer!); 3) by replacing the old location with ἐν Ἐφέσῳ, prompted by 2Tim 4:12." Additionally, the comment about the emergence of the Ephesian address by Vielhauer 1975, 215: "However, the emergence of the Ephesian address seems clearly connected to the collection of the Pauline Epistles; combining the note about Tychicus in 6:21f with the reference in 2 Tim. 4:12: "Tychicus I sent to Ephesus" seemed to enable the missing location to be added; so Ephesus was added to a letter of Paul's which the Church accepted as the 'letter to the Ephesians;'" see already Dibelius/Greeven 1953, 57; also G. Lüdemann 1996, 126.]

347. See the citation from Trobisch 1994, 41f. note 337 above.

348. Barth 1974, 11 and 67 [following Ch. G. Neudecker 1840, 502] plays with the thought, that the letter could be addressed to Gentiles, who were baptized in Ephesus after the departure of Paul. Gnilka 1990, 2-7 thinks that ἐν Ἐφέσῳ in 1:1 could be an original part of the letter, assuming that the letter is pseudonymous. In that case, the author would have had a completely different view from that of Acts about the relationship between Paul and the church of Ephesus. That is conceivable, but the text-critical findings are scarcely consistent with the hypothesis. [Decidedly for the originality of the Ephesians address, above all for syntactical reasons, Lindemann 1976/99, 235-51/211-27; see also Blass/Debrunner/Rehkopf 1976, 413, 4.]

349. [See now Standhartiger 1999, n. 47: "... this tradition is not entirely unlikely, but there is no additional evidence to support it.... The letter from Laodicea mentioned in Col. 4:16 is in my opinion a fiction."]

350. The Laodicea hypothesis, [first advanced by J. Mill in 1707, Proleg. note 71-79

in Colossai ἐν Κολοσσαῖς³⁵¹ is perceptive. But it is based on a one-sided assessment of Ephesians as a reworking or "revised edition" of Colossians.

A comparison with Colossians shows quite clearly where we have to place the addressees (cf. Eph. 6:21f.; Col. 4:7-9). Col. 2:1-3 describes Paul's strivings (in prayer) at the time of the letter's composition, not only for Christians in Colossae, but also for those in Laodicea, and for all who didn't know him by sight. Col. 4:13 states in a similar way about Epaphras, "that he has worked hard for you and for those in Laodicea and in Hierapolis." It is a small step to use these two statements to identify the addressees of the Ephesians.³⁵² The letter is obviously not just for a single community, but still requires that we place the addressees in Asia Minor and that we conclude that they did not know Paul personally.³⁵³ If the letter was actually sent with Tychicus, it was apparently intended for the Christian communities in Laodicea and Hierapolis, perhaps for those in other cities of Asia Minor as well. Ephesians is then probably the letter "from Laodicea." But even if the letter to the Ephesians is pseudonymous, its relationship to the texts cited from Colossians remains. The author of Ephesians could from Col 2:1-3, 4; 4:12-13 and 4:16 have inferred the existence of a letter to communities of Asia Minor in addition to Colossians. The letter to the Ephesians would then be an attempt to replace the letter believed lost.³⁵⁴

---

and then adopted by, among others, J. J. Wettstein; see Wikenshauser/Scmid 1973, 484], has gained many adherents, such as, e.g., Lightfoot 1893, 375-96; von Harnack 1910, 696-701 and later G. Zuntz, 1953, 228 note 1; [Masson 1953, 141, 227]. For more, Schmid 1928, 69-93.

351. Ochel 1934, 17 (following a suggestion by Hans von Soden). However, this hypothesis does not explain the analogy to the text problem in Rom. 1:7, 15. It is also not clear why a collection could not contain two letters of Paul to the Colossians.

352. Particularly noteworthy is the correspondence between Ephesians and the intercessory purpose set out in Col.2:2: *that their hearts may be encouraged as they are knit together in love, to have all the riches of assured understanding* ἵνα παρακληθῶσιν αἱ καρδίαι αὐτῶν συμβιβασθέντες ἐν ἀγάπῃ καὶ εἰς πᾶν πλοῦτος τῆς πληροφορίας τῆς συνέσεως; see esp. van Roon 1974, 246ff.

353. [cf. Gamble 1977, 115-24; idem 1995, 98: "Ephesians is addressed to a concrete historical situation, but not a purely local one."]

354. The apocryphal letter to the Laodiceans (transl. and literature in W. Schneemelcher 1989a, 41-44) is a similar attempt. It is possible, however, that the existence of a Laodicean letter could be inferred apart from Col. 4:16 One could have known that a Laodicean letter had circulated once in the church, without realizing that it was identical with the letter to the Ephesians. About other reconstructions of lost letters, see Speyer, 1971, [136-39, esp. 137].

Thus, Ephesians' author's intent was to draft a letter of Paul's to the Christians in Laodicea, Hierapolis, and maybe in other cities of Asia Minor. To that extent, the hypothesis of a circular letter is plausible.[355] The assertion that the original left a space after *who are in* τοῖς οὖσιν for place names, goes too far; there is no evidence from antiquity of such a practice.[356] Further, the hypothesis of scribal error is not credible.[357] Of the many hypotheses, two deserve serious consideration: (a) the letter could have been issued in several copies, each with a place name. When Ephesians was later copied for broader circulation, for example in the church of Ephesus, the copyist could have deleted each place name.[358] This hypothesis presupposes that the letter was really delivered by Tychicus to the communities which received it. (b) Perhaps more likely is the proposal by A. van Roon, that the original was: *to the saints in Hieropolis and Laodicea, faithful in Christ Jesus* τοῖς ἁγίοις τοῖς οὖσιν ἐν Ἱεραπόλει καὶ Λαοδικείᾳ, πιστοῖς ἐν Χριστῷ Ἰησοῦ. The enigmatic καὶ before *faithful* πιστοῖς remained, when the place names were deleted.[359]

All hypotheses about the original addresses of Ephesians remain uncertain. That the context is the sending of a letter is however quite clear, whether the letter was actually sent along with Colossians or merely just gives that impression. In both cases, the presupposition is that Paul first came into direct contact with the addressees through a letter, to win them to support of his mission and of his understanding of the Gospel. It harmonizes the composition and the content of the letter, which can be summarized under the keywords baptism and baptismal traditions and instruction. From this perspective, the conclusion that the letter was intended for newly established Christian communities is reasonable; however, there is evidence for a later date, not least the summary warning against all kinds of heresies in Eph. 4:14.[360]

355. [So now also Luz 1998a, 108: "... a circular or circular letter"].

356. [Roller 1933, 199–212, 520–525; Luz argued again for a text gap, 1998a, 108.]

357. R. Batey 1963, 101ff., suspected τοῖς οὖσιν was originally τοῖς Ἀσίας (sic). According to Santer 1969, 247–48, the original text was: τοῖς ἁγίοις καὶ πιστοῖς τοῖς οὖσιν ἐν Χριστῷ Ἰησοῦ. The words καὶ πιστοῖς were omitted due to haplography, then later added in the margin, and later still reinserted in the text in the wrong place.

358. In Dahl 1951, 241–64, I tried to justify this hypothesis. The practice this assumes is well attested, see 1 Macc. 15:16–24 and also Roller 1933, 199–212.

359. [Cf. Van Roon 1974, 72–85; Lincoln 1990, 3f.; to the contrary, Best 1997a(1), 13; idem 1998, 99.]

360. Cf. Dahl 1951 and the criticism against the hypothesis there by Kirby 1968, 40–44 and Gnilka 1990, 1–7.

5.2. Heresy

The warning against heresy in Eph. 4:12-14 is very general and unspecific.[361]

(12) *to equip the saints for the work of ministry, for building up the body of Christ, (13) until all of us come to the unity of the faith, and of the knowledge of the Son of God, to maturity, to the measure of the full stature of Christ. (14) We must no longer be children, tossed to and fro and blown about by every wind of doctrine, by people's trickery, by their craftiness in deceitful scheming.*

(v. 12) πρὸς τὸν καταρτισμὸν τῶν ἁγίων εἰς ἔργον διακονίας, εἰς οἰκοδομὴν τοῦ σώματος τοῦ Χριστοῦ, (v. 13) μέχρι καταντήσωμεν οἱ πάντες εἰς τὴν ἑνότητα τῆς πίστεως καὶ τῆς ἐπιγνώσεως τοῦ υἱοῦ τοῦ θεοῦ, εἰς ἄνδρα τέλειον, εἰς μέτρον ἡλικίας τοῦ πληρώματος τοῦ Χριστοῦ, (v. 14) ἵνα μηκέτι ὦμεν νήπιοι, κλυδωνιζόμενοι καὶ περιφερόμενοι παντὶ ἀνέμῳ τῆς διδασκαλίας ἐν τῇ κυβείᾳ τῶν ἀνθρώπων ἐν πανουργίᾳ πρὸς τὴν μεθοδείαν τῆς πλάνης . . .

One can with some difficulty connect these verses to false teachings found elsewhere among Christians, which could also be found among the letter's recipients. But my suspicion is that the author wants to correct an already existing error. One must reckon with the possibility that the author actually faced a situation in which neither the "unity of the spirit" nor loyalty to Paul were present, as the author of Ephesians would have wanted.[362]

---

361. [cf. Fischer 1973, 196: "perhaps 4.14 refers, where Ephesians warns against false teaching, to Gnostic speculation, but the author does not specifically say that. His theological thinking is not polemical, but reconciliatory;" Hübner 1997, 209: "that according to [v.] 14 the target community is in a very vulnerable position, namely tempted by false teaching, is symptomatic that the Ephesians must grow in their knowledge of Christ so that they are resistant to false teaching;" Luz 1998a, 152: "V. 14 mentions in striking detail the dangers that threaten the Church . . . the text is best explained by the hypothesis, that the author of Ephesians knows of heresies among the addressees. Then, it is also understandable why he reduced the list of Pauline charisms so conspicuously in v. 11 to preaching and teaching and why he in v. 13 takes up again the key phrase 'unity of belief.'"

362. [Cf. Köster 1980, 708; Pokorný 1992, 181: "in the time of the Apostle Paul, heresy was a future possibility, at the time of the author of Ephesians, it was already a real threat. This confirms our earlier observations (article 3, b [4:1-6]), according to which the addressees were threatened by false doctrine, even if the false teachers did not reject their Pauline heritage, but only sought for a supposedly higher unity (4:20, cf. Col 2:18f.)"]

INTRODUCTION TO THE LETTER TO THE EPHESIANS 271

Apart from Eph. 4:14, there is some evidence that Ephesians, despite its non-polemical form, has an anti-heretical purpose. The interpretation of the "great mystery" of Gen 2:24 is contrasted in Eph. 5:31 f. to other interpretations.[363] The author relates the citation to Christ and the Church, but in a way that does not exclude its application to earthly marriage; rather, marriage is seen as an image of the relationship between Christ and the church.[364] In the context of the letter, the Christological-ecclesiological "mystery teachings" serve the purpose of explaining and justifying practical rules for married people. One should not reverse the structure of the text and suppose that the traditional household code gave the author a welcome opportunity to develop from a different perspective his thoughts on the mystery of Christ and the Church.[365] Instead, he cited a particularly profound mystery at this point because he could use it to teach and deepen the marriage ethic of the household code. Thus he could oppose, even without direct polemics, an encratic (but also Gnostic) rejection of (or contempt for) marriage,[366] which, in turn, was most likely based on an allegorizing interpretation of the statements about men and

---

363. [See above note 315 and its bibliographical references; also Bornkamm 1942, 829f.; Dibelius/Greeven 1953, 95; Sampley 1971, 56f.; Best 1998, 552f., 555f.: Philo has allegorically interpreted Gen 2:24 (LA II. 49; Gig. 65) and Ps. Philo (LAB 32, 15) has interpreted it typologically.]

364. [So with reference to the polemic against Gnosticism also Köster 1980, 709: "In the interpretation of the household code, the writer tries to understand the obligations of the spouses as an image of heavenly reality. The relationship between man and woman corresponds to the relationship of the celestial figures of Christ and the Church. These designs are specifically anti-Gnostic; because Gnosticism generally saw in the rejection of marriage an attestation of belonging to the heavenly world; so already J. Belser 1908, 178; M. Meinertz 1931, 98; see also Dahl "The Concept of Baptism in Ephesians," *Studies in Ephesians* page 422 with note. See also Pokorný 1992, 228-32: "Excursus: Christ and the Church as husband and wife;" T. Karlsen Seim 1995, 179: ". . . the similarities are not ontological but relational;" for various interpretations, see Lincoln 1990, 380-83; Best 1998, 552-57.]

365. [So older scholars like F. A. von Henle 1908, 304f.; Ewald 1910, 241ff.; Haupt 1902, 223f. as well as Schmid 1928, 166, 330f.; so also recently Strecker 1996, 598: "The relationship of the Church to Christ was explained by the image of marriage. The 'mystery' of Gen. 2:24 is interpreted with reference to Christ and the Church. The connection by love of Christ to the Church is like a marital partnership (5, 31f.)," and also Gese 1997, 103f.; cf. also below note 404. [Schnackenburg, 1982, 260ff. explicitly rejects this interpretation.]

366. [See particularly Fischer 1973, 195: "Early Gnosticism is hostile to marriage, and Eph. 5 can be seen as a correction of the Gnostic mystery;" in addition, Bouttier 1991, 247-51.]

women in Genesis 1–3.³⁶⁷ [It is not an example of a Gnostic syzygy pair, as is *ExAn* (NHC II, 6) 132:21–133:11, where the Old Testament text refers to the unification of the fallen soul with her brother.]³⁶⁸

The statement in Eph. 2:14 *he has made both groups into one* ὁ ποιήσας τὰ ἀμφότερα ἕν should be considered along with the interpretation of Gen 2:24 (*and the two become one flesh* ἔσονται οἱ δύο εἰς σάρκα μίαν). The author varies a common formula, that spoke of the overcoming of fragmentation and the restoration of unity. While the formula in its historical context was used principally with reference to the duality of male and female, in Ephesians it refers only to the separation and enmity between Jews and Gentiles. This suggests in turn an indirect polemic against a belief that associated salvation with overcoming sexuality.³⁶⁹

The author has appropriated the concept that Christians have already been delivered from death into true life, and from the mundane world to a heavenly existence (2:1–10). He understands this experience as a sharing in the resurrection and enthronement of Christ. That would also have been possible for ascetic spiritualists and mystics. However, in Ephesians the assertion, probably originating in hymnic language statements, receives a Pauline interpretation: becoming alive with Christ is understood as salvation by grace, not by works, as a new creation, which manifests itself in good works (Eph. 2:8–10).³⁷⁰ The prescriptive part of the letter, chapters 4–6, makes clear the nature of these good works: it is to live as a Christian in the everyday world.

367. [See W.A. Meeks 1974, 193–97; Fischer 1973, 192f.; Pagels 1983, 151f.]

368. [See above note 314; also Schlier 1930, 65f.;] idem 1963, 262; Dibelius/Greeven 1953, 95; Lincoln 1982, 33; Bornkamm 1942, 830; Köster 1980 above note 364.]

369. See the omission of male and female in 1 Cor 12:13 and Col. 3:11; see Jervell 1960, 294f.; D. C. Smith 1973.34–54; [in addition, now including W. Schrage 1999, 207f. with note 558, 216–218; Lindemann 1983, 58f.; see also the quotation from Köster 1980, 709 note 364 above; and Fischer 1973, 195 note 366 above; see also notes 36, 37, and 38 on page 422. Also Dahl, "Kleidungsmetaphern: der alte und der neue Mensch" *Studies in Ephesians* note 33. Recently Standhartinger 1999, 233 note 218, maintains, referring to among others the Greek-Latin bilingual (D *), (F), (G), the minuscule 629 and the old Latin tradition that the text "neither male nor female" is possibly original: "should Colossians have been written in Rome after Paul's death, the predominantly Latin tradition would suggest that the possibility that this reading is original cannot be ruled out;" for the meaning of the bilingual, see Dahl "0230 (= PSI1 306) and the Fourth-Century Greek-Latin Edition of the Letters of Paul," *Studies in Ephesians*.]

370. Cf. Hübner's interpolation hypothesis, set out above in note 264.

If this analysis is correct, we can understand what is going on in Ephesians. The author opposes the view that emphasizes revelation of a higher wisdom and salvation as deliverance from an earthly, bodily existence, through which the actual 'self' (whether *soul* ψυχή, *mind* νοῦς or *spirit* πνεῦμα) is able to rise (or return) to the higher, celestial spheres. Symbolic rituals, ascetic exercises and mystical experiences were important means of obtaining otherworldly salvation, but by no means always played the same role. In manifold variations, this type of piety was too widespread to be considered a preliminary stage of Gnosticism. A redemptive piety of this kind found its way into ancient Judaism, probably in Palestine.[371] It was manifested and flourished above all in Christian monasticism.

These tendencies were present in the Pauline communities as well, as, among other things, the esteem accorded to wisdom, to glossalia, and to sexual abstinence in Corinth, attest (cf. 1 Cor. 1–4; 7; 12–14).[372] Even the denial of the future resurrection (1 Cor. 15) probably belongs in this context.[373] Colossians shows that a somewhat different variation of ascetic mystical salvation piety was also present in the historical setting of Ephesians.[374]

It is nowhere clear that Ephesians combatted a particular heresy. We can only see general tendencies that were also, but by no means only, present in the Colossian "philosophy." Based on Eph. 4:14, one might rather suggest that many teachings claimed to reveal hidden wisdom and promised salvation from the earthly world and from the fragmentation that is marked by sexuality.[375] We may suppose that these teachings were presented as interpretations of the mysteries contained in the Holy

---

371. [see, e.g., G. G. Scholem 1946; idem 1965; W. C. Van Unnik 1978, 65–86; Tröger 1980 155–68; Strecker 1980, 261–82; Hegermann 1961, 26–46, 52ff.; Colpe 1960 182ff.; Faust 1993, 19–41.]

372. [Cf. commentaries by J. Weiss 1910/70, *ad loc.*; Conzelmann 1981c, *ad loc.*; G. D. Fee 1987, *ad loc.*; Schrage1991, *ad loc.*; idem 1995, *ad loc.*; idem 1999, *ad loc.*; Ch. Wolff 1996, *ad loc.*; additionally, Dahl 1967, 313–35; L. Schottroff 1970, 170–200; B. A. Pearson 1973; A. C. Wire 1990; M. M. Mitchell 1991; W. Deming 1995; Ch. Forbes 1997.]

373. [Cf. in addition to the commentaries cited in the previous note also Schottroff 1970, 115–69; Sandelin 1976; Sellin 1986; Ulrichsen 1995, 781–99; Verburg 1996.]

374. [Cf. for example recently Hartmann 1995, 25–39; Hübner 1997, 94–97, as well as the research overview in Standhartinger1999, 16–27.]

375. [Cf.above note 369.]

Scriptures and in Christian tradition.[376] Whether or not the author invoked Paul must, however, remain open. The author of Ephesians sees in all such higher teachings error at work, which prevents Christians from attaining the "unity of the faith and of the knowledge of the son of God" (Eph. 4:12f.).

Our author is not arguing as Paul did, apologetically, polemically, or ironically. He doesn't quote the slogans of heresy, to warn against them, as Colossians does (2:16, 18, 20-23). Ephesians counters heresy simply by surpassing it. The author proclaims that the truth that various doctrines distort is all present in the Gospel message, whose servant Paul was, whom Gentile Christians heard and believed. This Gospel is the true doctrine (*the word of truth* ὁ λόγος τῆς ἀληθείας) [1:13]), the revelation of the hidden mystery and of God's plan from all eternity. There is no spiritual blessing in the heavenly places that not has been already been given in Christ, to those who have received a share of this mystery. Paul is portrayed as an intermediary of this revelation.[377] Through the Gospel, whose servant he was, the hidden mystery has been made known to humankind. Through the church, in which Gentiles are joined to Jews in one body, the manifold wisdom of God is known even to the heavenly powers and forces, because the unification in Christ of those who were separated is the eternal and universal plan of God (Eph. 3:2-12; cf. 1:8-10). The Paul of Ephesians prays that Christians continue to grow in knowledge, as in love, but the purpose of revealed wisdom is not esoteric teaching, but the hope given with God's call and the greatness of his power in Christ. What is important to acknowledge is not the inscrutable dimensions of the universe, or other cosmic mysteries, but the love of Christ, which cannot be limited (cf. Eph. 1:16ff.; 3:14-19).

But a positive observation is more important: the statement (2.14-15) *having made both groups into one . . . that he might make the two . . . into one new humanity* ὁ ποιήσας τὰ ἀμφότερα ἕν . . . ἵνα τοὺς δύο κτίσῃ . . . εἰς ἕνα καινὸν ἄνθρωπον refers in the context to the unification of Jews and Gentiles in Christ.[378] That may stand in opposition to a widespread

---

376. [See, e.g., the *Acta Pauli*; [on this, Schneemelcher 1989b, 193-214 with lit].

377. [See esp. Best 1998, 293, 295, 300f.;] Hellholm 1998, 242; in addition, also Luz 1989, 386-93.]

378. [So, e.g., Schlier 1963, 134; Vielhauer 1975, 214; Gnilka 1990, 138-42; Lincoln 1990, 139-46. Meeks 1974, 204; idem 1977, 215; idem 1983, 168, 180, 187. Luz 1989, 388f.; 391; esp. now Faust 1993, 111-50; Hübner 1997, 169-172, 181; Best 1998, 250-59. Disputed especially by Lindemann 1975, 173; idem 1976/99, 247/223f.,

view, for which redemption from alienation and fragmentation lay in overcoming the male/female dichotomy.[379] If that is true, not only Eph. 5:21-33, but also Eph. 2:14-18, tacitly oppose an ascetic mystical piety of which the "philosophy" in Colossae is only one example among many.[380] Only detailed exegesis can assess the overall extent to which the latent anti-heretical tendency is present.

The letter to the Ephesians speaks effusively not only about the revelation, but also about the salvation, which all the baptized have received. It is sufficient to recall the two first chapters of the letter. The whole plerophoristic, encomiastic style is purposeful if its purpose is to overwhelm heretical claims. Much more than the vain imaginings of heresy has been given in Christ to those who have heard the Gospel and believed, who have been sealed by baptism with the Holy Spirit: revelation of hidden wisdom, unity instead of divisiveness and fragmentation, life from death, elevation to the heavenly spheres. The members of the church need only hold on to what already has been given to them, to grow and mature.[381]

Since Ephesians describes heretical teachings only as background for praise of true revelation and real salvation and is otherwise silent about them, the differences are difficult to determine. Without more information, we do not know how monistic and dualistic, anthropological and cosmological ideas, or even space and time, future and present, natural and historical concepts were connected to one another in the heretical teachings about salvation. It would be too simple to assume that Ephesians had taken over terminology and formulations of the "opponents" and critically interpreted them.[382] We need rather to consider that the author and those whom he summarily denounces as false teachers used substantially the same language. The letter to the Ephesians represents

---

also idem 1985 15, 52f. On the issue of an underlying (gnostic or apocalyptic) hymn or creed, see Schlier 1930, 18-26; idem 1963, 129-34; Schille 1965, 24-31; J. T. Sanders 1965, 216-18; 1972, 181-86; Fischer 1973, 131-37; Lindemann 1975, 156-59; idem 1985, 47; Gnilka 1990, 147-52; Lincoln 1990, 127-31; as well as Hübner 1997, 180f. Deichgräber 1967, 165-69 doubts there is an underlying hymn; D. C. Smith 1970, esp. 8-43, denies a gnostic hymn is implied in the context; Best 1998, 247-50, stresses the Old Testament reference, and Faust 1993, ibid., highlights the political implications.]

379. [So Dahl 1965, 74 note 45; as a possibility also Meeks 1977, 215.]

380. [On that point, see, e.g., F. O. Francis 1973, 163-95, 209-18; Meeks/F. O. Francis (eds.) 1973 209-18; Hartmann 1995, 25-39.]

381. [Cf. Hübner 1997, 198.]

382. Pokorný 1965, 125-30. [Bultmann 1966, 183-95;] [Schottroff 1970: for John as for Paul.]

more than Paul does a Hellenistic/late antiquity religiosity, which considered its own teachings as revealed wisdom and salvation as detachment from the world, but without the idea of the return of the entire universe to its original unity. According to the letter to the Ephesians, revelation and salvation are only given in Jesus Christ. But perhaps even the proponents of heresy would have said as much as that. The author of Ephesians insists, however, that revelation and redemption are available only in the publically proclaimed gospel, through which Gentiles were called to faith and baptism, and were sealed with the Holy Spirit.

The sublime, mystical language conveys in Ephesians the reward of belief in the Pauline Gospel and profession of the faith common to all the baptized. Eph. 1:5 gives adoption as children of God (υἱοθεσία) as the first, emphatic, example of "every spiritual blessing in the heavenly places." Eph. 1:7 (cf. Col. 1:14) identifies redemption with the forgiveness of transgressions in substantial agreement with Christian thought both before and contemporaneous with Paul. Correspondingly, the prior state of "death" is interpreted as "dead" "in your sins and transgressions," not as "dead" because of the actual corporeal death of the soul.[383] Precisely at these points, the rejected teachings are positioned differently: they are more esoteric, mystical and encratistic. This clear contrast affected, as we have seen, the assessment of marriage and of sexuality. The analogy with the Colossian "philosophy" makes it likely that the heresies of Ephesians also linked disdain for marriage with ascetic practices.[384] Fasting and self-mortification were often prerequisites for revelations and mystical experiences. If we may assume similarities to the heresies of Ephesians, then not only the prescriptions for spouses, but also the entire paraenesis have great value for determining the concerns and overall composition

383. [As in Gnosticism, see Dahl, "Kleidungsmetaphern: der alte und der neue Mensch," *Studies in Ephesians*.]

384. [In contrast, Ephesians is completely supportive of marriage; cf. Hübner 1997, 177: "the author of Ephesians does not share the hostility to the body and the antihistorical understanding of existence, as it manifested itself in some writings of Plato, Philo, and Gnosticism. The author's esteem for marriage in Ephesians 5:22ff is enough by itself to make that clear!" So also M. Y. MacDonald 1996, 231: "In contrast to 1 Corinthians 7, however there is no hint in Ephesians 5:21–33 that celibacy is preferred for those who can stave off temptation. Nowhere in Paul's letters does the significance of marriage receive the same detailed attention as it does in this Deutero-Pauline work, dating probably from the last third of the first century"; Luz 1998a, 110: "The only exception to his loyalty to Paul is his understanding of marriage (5, 22–33), which in my opinion goes directly against the Pauline position"; See also ibid., 171, 173. Also see Dahl, "The Concept of Baptism in Ephesians," Studies in Ephesians notes 38–42.]

of the letter. The prescriptions are sometimes remarkably elementary: Christians should love each other, tolerate and forgive, and also otherwise behave themselves, not lying, working honestly, etc. (cf. 4:25–6:9). This elementary presentation of community, everyday ethics, is especially appropriate, when it serves to reinforce instructions for the newly converted, in silent, but emphatic, opposition to esoteric rites, on which teachers of heresy insisted.[385]

The only clear warning against false teaching appears in the section about the unity of the Church and the diversity of the gifts of Christ (4:1–16). From this section alone, one is easily able to deduce something about the situation which Ephesians addresses. However, efforts to do that have led to contradictory results. K. M. Fischer says that Ephesians was written at a time when the risk of the fragmentation of the church threatened individual, disparate local churches: "Ephesians attempted to uphold the structure of Pauline mission, while all other surviving writings of that time try to establish the office of bishop everywhere."[386] H. Merklein in contrast places Ephesians in a line of development, which leads from Paul to the full formation of ecclesiastical office in the Pastorals. The "shepherds" in Ephesians 4:11 are identified with the bishops of other writings.[387] However, questions about "office" and "structure" are not intrinsic to Ephesians, but are imported into it; that makes understandable that one can answer them in opposite ways as Fischer and Merkleindo.[388]

---

385. [For the meaning of the parenesis in Ephesians, see esp. Luz 1989, 376–96, which however emphasizes more strongly the contrast to Colossians, because "In particular the situational section Col. 2 . . . is hardly taken up in Ephesians;" "yet the author remains interested in Colossians' paraenesis" (ibid., 377).].

386. Fischer 1986, 201.

387. Merklein 1973a, 57–117, 393–98 [like Merklein, now also Hübner 1993, 370f.].

388. [Cf. the probably mediating position in Santiago in 1996, 598–605: "In Colossians municipal offices are not mentioned. . . . In contrast, Eph 4:11 with its list of apostles, prophets, evangelists, pastors and teachers indicates an advanced stage of church organization. Paul also knows a sequence in the ordering of community functions, with apostles and prophets in the first place (1 Cor. 12:18). However, his structure of offices is charismatically determined, but Ephesians makes a clear distinction. Apostles and prophets belong to the 'foundation' (θεμέλιον) of a previous generation of the Christian Church, while the community now sees evangelists, pastors and teachers discharging the offices of preaching, leadership and teaching. Unlike Pauline tradition, that assumes divine appointment, Ephesians attributes the appointment of community officeholders to the Risen Christ. The dominant power

The exegetical issue in Eph. 4:7–16 is mainly that though Ephesians emphasizes the "measure" given to each believer(4:7–16), the "gifts of Christ" are nevertheless identified with specific preachers and leaders. Both thoughts are thus linked, that the function of special "gifts" is seen as providing structure for the entire body of Christ, with all its individual parts (4:10, 16; cf. οἱ πάντες in v. 13). In this context, it is a matter of relative indifference, whether the preachers and leaders are designated charismatically or by appointment to church positions, and also, whether their service was to the whole church or limited to the local community. The contrast emphasized is that between, on the one hand, the Apostles, prophets, evangelists and teachers, who are dedicated to building up the body of Christ, and on the other, the proponents of heresy, whose esoteric teachings destroy the unity of the community.

The central section 2:11–22 is more important than 4:7–16 in determining the purpose of Ephesians and the situation the letter addresses. Older exegetes largely found here an echo of Paul's struggle for freedom from the law. But Hermann von Soden early suggested that the section was rather directed against a "centrifugal individualism" in Gentile Christians, and adds: "That tendency may have blended with a conviction of superiority on the part of those born Jews."[389] According to Käsemann, the letter is addressed to Gentile Christians, who were about to sever the connection to Jewish Christianity.[390] The hypothetical situation described by Paul in Rom. 11:17ff. had actually occurred. The problem with this hypothesis is that nowhere in Ephesians is it evident that the relationship of Gentile Christians to Jews and Jewish Christians was a problem. The paraenesis urges only preserving unity among church members (cf. Eph. 4:1–6, 13–16). One must also keep in mind that the emphasis in Eph. 2:11–13 and 19–22 is on the changed situation of the former pagans. Accordingly, Eph. 2:14–18 stresses that pagans have access to salvation equal to Jews. The full equality of Jews in the Church would of course have been self-evident to the author, but we cannot find any practical consequences of that view in the text of the letter.

The letter to the Ephesians takes up the idea of God's people, to remind Gentile Christians of the privileges given to them, and to guide them to a right ecclesial self-understanding. The author also seeks to save

---

of the cosmic Christ is made concrete in his supervision of the church community.]

389. Herman von Soden 1893, 85f.

390. Käsemann 1958, 517; [similarly also Mitton 1976, 30.]

the Church from impending fragmentation. No Gentile Christian at the time of the Ephesians has rejected the Old Testament. But Scripture could be spiritualized allegorically. In contrast, the author of Ephesians holds firmly to the "political" relationship of the promises to a community of citizens and fellow citizens.[391] The latent anti-heretical tendency comes here above all to light, in the assertion that estrangement of existence lies not in the difference of gender, but in the separation of Jews from Gentiles, overcome only in Christ.

6. TIME AND SETTING OF EPHESIANS

In view of the characteristics of Ephesians, the state of critical research and the relationship of the letter to Colossians and the other Pauline Epistles, we have drawn the conclusion that Paul himself did not write the letter, but that it is possible that a coworker of the Apostle's wrote it on his behalf.[392] We have identified the author as a younger, Jewish Christian disciple of Paul, who wrote the letter during Paul's lifetime or after his death, so either around the year 60 or around the year 80. The sending of the letter to Christians in various cities of Asia Minor could be fact or fiction. The question, when the letter was written, is so far left unanswered. A decision is difficult, because fixed chronological clues are missing and there are arguments worth considering both for and against pseudonymous authorship.

Both the good external attestation and the likelihood that Ephesians had a history before its incorporation into a collection of Pauline letters support the assertion that the letter is "authentic," at least in the broader sense of "authorized."[393] But also the complicated relationship between Ephesians and the epistles to the Colossians and to Philemon would be most easily explained by assuming that all three letters were in fact written at the same time and sent with Tychicus and Onesimus. Paul had a direct part in the letter to Philemon (cf. Philemon 19). With respect to the two other letters, one would have to assume that he supervised the work of two different coworkers.[394]

391. [On this point, esp. Faust 1993, 221–483.]

392. [See above note 112 as well as note 132 for some suggestions about the composition of Colossians.]

393. [see *Studies in Ephesians* and note 52.]

394. Cf. Van Roon 1974 esp. 911–94 and 426–31.

There are a few, very weak, connections between Philemon and Ephesians.[395] Colossians, however, has a close relationship with the two other letters. Ephesians presupposes not only Colossians, but must also have arisen in the same environment, either at the same time or slightly later. One can only clarify the setting of Ephesians with the assistance of Colossians. On the other hand, the connections between Colossians and Philemon are so tight that one must assume a fairly sophisticated fiction to suggest that the setting for Colossians is not real.[396] However, if Colossians was really sent by Paul to Colossae, then Ephesians could have been written and sent at the same time. The main advantage of this solution is that it does not need to deal with unknown factors, because coworkers who might have been the actual authors of the letters were with the Apostle at the time of his imprisonment (cf. Philemon 1 and 23-24; Col. 1:1, 4:10-14).[397]

But the question is whether the simplest solution is in this case correct, or whether the letter to the Ephesians is better understood as pseudonymous. First of all we must consider the absence of a concrete reference to the location of the recipients of the letter. If pressed, one can suggest that the letter was sent to multiple communities, but that would be natural in a pseudonymous letter. Further, the question of where the letter was written poses difficulties. If one considers Philemon alone, its composition in Ephesus seems most likely. Onesimos would most likely have sought and found Paul, and from there, Paul could hope to be able to visit Philemon in a short time (Phlm. 22).[398] If the composition of Ephesians was during Paul's lifetime, it had to have been much earlier than Paul's final imprisonment in Rome. The whole issue of the time and place of the captivity Epistles is too complicated to permit a definitive conclusion.

395. See esp. the similarity of the Thanksgiving period, Philemon 4ff. and Eph. 1:15f.; [see also the Hellenistic examples in Lohse 1968, 40f.]

396. In addition to the naming of Onesimos and Archippos in Col. 4:9 and 17 and the common names in the greeting lists (Col. 4:10-14; Philemon 23f.) Col. 3:22-24 stands out. The elaborateness and style of the exhortation to slaves could be connected to the case of Onesimos, see esp. J. Knox 1935/59, chap. 3, note 23 and idem 1938, 144 60. [See Lohse 1968, 246f. and now the considerations in Standhartinger 1999, 81–85.]

397. I was long myself in favor of this proposed solution, cf. esp. Dahl 1945, 85–103; idem 1956, 1100–02; cf. on this Percy 1946, 354 note 24, 447; Kirby 1968, 40-44. [Otherwise however Dahl 1976a/81a, 268f.]

398. Cf. esp. Lohse 1968, 264; [Stuhlmacher 1975, 21; Gnilka 1982, 4-6; Wolter 1993, 237f.].

The most important arguments for a pseudonymous writing are less precise and relate to the overall understanding of the letter. There is first of all the question of whether or not it is credible that Paul gave his staff such great freedom to write his letters as one would have to accept both for Colossians and for Ephesians. Drafting by two different coworkers would in any case significantly qualify the tradition of Pauline authorship. The rule, questionable in any case, that in doubtful case one should hold to tradition, cannot be applied to Ephesians.[399] One must simply look for the higher degree of historical probability. Crucial is whether or not the letter actually presupposes a setting different from that reconstructed by combining Eph. 6:21f. with details from Colossians. That requires special attention to the spread of heresy.

Only the almost casual remark in Eph. 4:14 warns explicitly, as we have observed, against false teachings. The context in Eph. 4:16 presents variations on the theme of one body and many members, but presupposes a different setting and probably a later time than the Pauline teachings about spiritual gifts (cf. 1 Cor. 12; Rom. 12:3-8).[400] But it is doubtful that the letter is aware of controversy over the organization of the church or takes a position on the relationship in the church of charism to office.[401] It seems that Eph. 4:8-13 identifies gifts of the Risen Christ with particular servants of the Word and leaders of the church. The author

---

399. Otherwise, e.g., Barth 1974, 41.

400. [Cf. Fr. W. Horn 1992, 87 note 87; Luz 1989, 392: "In the entire paraenesis of the letter, but especially in 4:1-16, similarities to Romans 12 are evident.... There are in Ephesians to no other Pauline text so many similarities in so compact a section as there are to Romans 12." [Note 60: These similarities to Romans 12 are much closer than those often advanced for 1 Cor. 12.]

Eph. 4:1/ Rom. 12:1 (παρακαλῶ οὖν ὑμᾶς)
Eph. 4:4/Rom. 12:4 (ἕν σῶμα)
Eph. 4:7/Rom 12:3 (χάρις, δίδωμι, ἕκαστος)
Eph. 4:11f./Rom. 12:6f. (prophets, teachers, ministers)
Eph. 4:12f., 16/Rom. 12:3f. (μέτρον, σῶμα)
Eph. 4:23/Rom. 12:2 (ἀνανεοῦσθαι, τοῦ νοός)
Eph. 4:28/Rom. 12:8, 14 (μεταδιδόναι, χρεία)
Eph. 5:17/Rom. 12:2 (τί τὸ θέλημα τοῦ)
Eph. 4:25/Rom. 12:5 (ἀλλήλων μέλη)
Eph. 5:11/Rom. 12:2 (δοκιμάζειυ τί εὐάρεστον).]

401. As we saw above, on this assumption Fischer 1973, 33-48 and Merklein 1973a, 57-117, 393-98, reach different conclusions. According to Fischer, Ephesians tries "to remain faithful to the structure of the Pauline mission" (*ibid.*, 201). According to Merklein, Ephesians legitimizes the development of church offices; [so too Hübner 1993, 370f.]

stresses however their duty to provide for the building up of the body of Christ and the spiritual growth of all its members. It is a matter of relative indifference in this context whether they are seen as charismatics or as office holders. There is no contrast to an alternative church organization, but an emphatic contrast to the structure and activities of heresy, whose destructive influences could destroy unity of belief and of understanding. One can hardly avoid the conclusion that Ephesians was aimed at a setting where the author believed that heresy was already widespread.[402]

The exhortations to the married in Eph. 5:22–33 show the kind of heretics the author was fighting. The author deepens and anchors the exhortations given in the household code by reference to the relationship between Christ and the church. Neither the wording nor the overall composition allow us to reverse this state of affairs,[403] as though the traditional structure of the author provided an opportunity to present his ecclesiology.[404] The explanation of the "great mysteries" in Eph. 5:13f. in truth assigns special value to earthly marriage. The interpretation provided for Gen. 2:24 contrasts to other interpretations (see esp. 5:32 *but I say* ἐγὼ δὲ λέγω).[405] The letter therefore consciously takes a position against contempt for, or rejection of, marriage, even if without a direct polemic. We can conclude from that position that the heresies against

---

402. [See above Section 5.2.]

403. R. P. Martin 1967/68, 296–302, recognized that correctly. The theory of Luke as possible author is clearly impossible.

404. [So also recently Dawes 1998, 168–91, who indeed affirms the dual reference, but concludes that "Up until now the parallel between husband wife and Christ and the Church was made by way of an explicit analogy. Here we move towards an implicit metaphorical identification of the two unions, insofar as the union of Church and Christ is described in words drawn from the bodily union of husband and wife" (*ibid.*, 185); see also note 365 above.]

405. [So especially in connection with M. Smith 1951 esp. 28 and Sampley 1971, 89.] Lindemann understands the formulation differently 1985, 105: "I interpret . . . that 'but' does not imply a contradiction, as if author wants to distance himself from other interpretations; it is rather a 'but' which highlights the weight which the author attaches to following explanatory statement (cf. in Paul Rom. 3:22; 1 Cor. 10:11; Phil. 2:8)." On the basis of the opinion that the author of Ephesians does not intend to cite Gen. 2:24, Dawes 1998, 182 (following Abbott 1897/1985, 175) understands ἐγὼ δὲ λέγω not as a distancing feature, but as a personal statement: 'I am speaking'. The appropriate translation of v. 32b would then be: 'I am speaking, however, about Christ and the Church', or (more specifically), "It is Christ's relationship with the Church which I amdescribing as a 'great mystery.'"]

which Eph. 4:14 warns represented a widespread encratic-mystical [and Gnostic] piety, of which the Colossian "philosophy" was one example.[406]

If we conclude based on Eph. 4:12–14 and 5:31f. that an anti-heretical tendency plays a bigger role in Ephesians than is initially apparent, it is reasonable to assume that we can find it elsewhere as well. Exegesis has to ask to what extent the plerophoristic rhetoric in Eph. 1:3 is proof that the revelation and redemption given in Christ surpasses everything false teachers pretended was esoteric revelation and otherworldly—or even cosmic—redemption. The central section Eph. 2:11–22 is relevant in this context. In the foreground is the call to former pagans, to bear in mind the greatness of the privileges they share with the Israelites (cf. esp. 2:11, 13, 19–22). Older commentators often also found an echo of the fight for the freedom of Gentile Christians from the law and for their equality with Jewish Christians.[407] Today, the view is quite common that the section is addressed to Gentile Christians who were in danger of losing their connection to Jewish Christianity.[408] If the relationship of Gentile Christians to Jews and Jewish Christians was a practical, current problem, we would expect the paraenesis would return to it, but that does not happen. Instead, the unity of pagans and Jews in the church is understood in Eph. 3:2–12 as a revelation of the hidden wisdom of God. Accordingly, the concept of Eph. 2:11–22, that the eternal plan of God for reconciliation of the universe was accomplished in Christ, when Christ made pagans and Jews one, is important.[409] Eph. 2:14ff. differs from the widespread view

---

406. [For references, see note 380 above.]

407. [See, e.g., Ch. Core 1898, 107ff.; J. A. Robinson 1904, 60ff.]

408. Cf. already Herm. von Soden, 1893, 85f.; later esp. Schlier 1963, 27; Käsemann 1958, 517, and following him Fischer 1973, 16, 79–94; also Sampley 1971, 3, 160 *et passim*. Cf. also Barth 1959a and idem 1959 b; in his commentary, Barth expresses himself cautiously; see idem 1974, 282–91; [so also Fischer 1973, 86–94.]

409. [See Dahl "Gentiles, Christians, and Israelites in the Epistle to the Ephesians," *Studies in Ephesians*; see also Linton 1964, 84ff.; Luz 1989, 391: "When it comes in 2:11–22 to the unity of the Church, Christ has unified Jews and Gentiles through the apostolate of Paul, and the paraenesis requires the church to affirm Christ's gift of unity in its daily life, to be a church that corresponds to that reality. In that way, the church continues the unity affirming mission of the Apostle Paul;" similarly Hübner 1997, 162–171, 181–83; Sellin 1999, 1347: "2:11–22 is central to Ephesians: the linkage both of the symbols death/blood/cross and the unity of Jews and Gentiles to the realized plan of a new humanity, in which peace and reconciliation will be manifested." To the contrary, Lambert, 1985, 15 and especially 46: "it (sc. v. 13) shows that the topic of vv. 11–13 is not 'Jews and Gentiles', but rather: 'past pagan existence without Christ—current existence in Christ'".]

that overcoming the division between the sexes was a feature of redemption.[410] The interpretation of Gen. 2:24 in Eph. 5:31f. makes it likely that such a view was present in the immediate environment of Ephesians. In Eph. 4:11–22 as well, the author takes a stand, albeit indirectly, against an encratic/mystical piety.[411]

Traces of an anti-heretical tendency in Ephesians are not in themselves an argument for pseudonymous authorship. That would also be possible in Paul's lifetime.[412] That the tendency is only indirectly expressed is, however, more understandable under the assumption that we have to distinguish between a fictitious setting for the letter and the real situation at the time of its composition.[413] The serious differences between the two positions can be summarized in the following points:

1. The literary fiction is that the letter is addressed to newly converted Gentile Christian communities, with which Paul had earlier had a personal relationship. Spatial separation is in fact a disguise for temporal separation.

2. Apparently the letter reminds the newly converted Christians of their transition from paganism to Christianity, in order to explain to them everything that their conversion entailed. In reality, the author consciously falls back on the foundational experiences of the Gentile Christian mission in Asia and therefore stresses the mission and work of Paul, their first hearing of the gospel, baptism, etc.

3. The paraenetic rules are in general fairly elementary. "There are exhortations that are obvious to all but the newly converted."[414] The author wants to stress that Christian love and everyday ethics are the marks of a lifestyle worthy of their calling, not rejection of marriage and other ascetic practices.

4. The message of Ephesians is both clear and simple; it deals with the content and the consequences of a single, common Christian faith.

---

410. Material in D. C. Smith 1973, 34–54. In a later essay, Smith (1977, 78–103) stated that the "heretics" were pagans, who had been converted first to a mystical form of Judaism and later to Christianity. [Against that view, now Best 1988, 67.]

411. [See above and notes 366 and 384.]

412. Dacquino 1958, 338–49 on the contrary finds in the contrast to heresy an argument for the authenticity of Ephesians.

413. [See especially Dahl 1977, 305–15. Sellin 1999, 1345f. expresses this as the distinction between the "implied writer" and the "real author."]

414. Dibelius/Greeven 1953, 92.

That message is, however, presented in language and in a rhetorical form that seeks to surpass all heretical claims for the revelation of higher wisdom and salvation.

5. According to the literary fiction, heresies are a threat, against which the recipients are being warned in advance. In the actual setting of the author, "heresy" is widespread and only a minority of the Christians of Asia Minor remains loyal to Paul and his gospel, as Ephesians understands it.[415]

6. The form is completely non-polemical, but the letter is nevertheless full of indirect polemic against a type of revelation and salvation religion widespread in the Hellenistic period and Late Antiquity that was adopted also in Judaism and Christianity.

7. From the note about Tychicus at the end of the letter and probably also from the original address, Ephesians was sent to a localized audience. However, the content was intended for all Gentile Christians in Asia Minor and beyond.

Both opponents and defenders of the authenticity of Ephesians have had trouble finding a satisfactory answer to the questions of its purpose and of the circumstances of its composition. This difficulty was largely caused by the failure to distinguish clearly enough between literary fiction and de facto situation. When one does consider both literary fiction and actual situation, individual details and the letter as a whole are more comprehensible.[416] This gives a plausible explanation to the juxtaposition of non-Pauline and Pauline elements and of "pre-Pauline" traditions and "post-Pauline" perspectives. Further, pseudonymity is also easier to understand. It was not only and not primarily a means whereby the author could claim Apostolic authority and revelatory significance for his own

---

415. Eph. 4:14 should be compared in this case to passages such as Acts 20:29f and 1Tim. 4:1–5. Percy 1946, 325f. and 447 has realized that Eph. 4:14 gives rise to serious problems for the assumption that the letter is directed to newly converted communities, but he tried to overcome them. Fischer 1973, 17f., correctly asks: "Is the author perhaps not in the position of the stronger party, but rather of the weaker, someone who would be risking his last chance to be able to exert more influence on future development by engaging in polemic." [See the similar situation regarding the Apocalypse of John and on this see esp. H. Räisänen 1995, 151–66.]

416. To the contrary A. Jülicher 1931, 142: "Many details in the letter are more easily understood on the assumption that a student of the Apostle—who in many ways approached the master!—was the author; but the letter as a whole remains enigmatic."

contemporizing interpretation of Pauline teaching.[417] The drafting of a letter supposedly from Paul gave the author the opportunity to refer to the foundational beginnings of Gentile Christianity in Asia Minor and at the same time to combat the heretics of his own day, without alienating through direct polemics people that he hoped to win over to his position.

If it can be shown independently that Colossians was only written after the death of Paul, it follows from that, that Ephesians is also pseudonymous.[418] But the opposite conclusion is also inevitable: if Ephesians is pseudonymous, then the setting of Colossians must also be a fiction, because it is scarcely believable that a letter written in the lifetime of the Apostle should in many ways be less "Pauline" than the later, pseudonymous letter. To explain the emergence of the two letters, and indeed that of the Pastoral Epistles, it is necessary to postulate the persistence, in otherwise unknown circumstances, of a Pauline school in Asia Minor.[419]

Our knowledge of the history of Christianity in Asia Minor in the period between Paul and Ignatius is very fragmentary. It is however quite clear that Pauline influence, if it was ever dominant, was later overshadowed by other influences.[420] The Pastoral Epistles show clearly that encratic/mystical tendencies continued to exist (see esp. 1 Tim 4:1-5; 2 Tim 2:18).[421] The Apocalypse of John shows that "orthodox" teaching was by no means always Pauline,[422] and even Ignatius has to warn against heresy.[423] Ephesians fits easily in this context. This confirms the conclusion based on analysis of the letter and of the location of its author: the assumption of pseudonymity, although more complicated than the "secretary hypothesis," is nevertheless historically more likely, because it is able to explain all the facts.

417. So esp. Merklein 1973a 215f., 220-22, 230f.

418. Synge; see above note 154.

419. On this Schenke 1974-75, 505-18; (and esp. Conzelmann 1965-74, 231-44/177-90, idem 1979, 85-96;) H. Ludwig 1974; P. Müller 1988; L. Alexander 1992, 1005-11; eadem, 1995, 60-83; Standhartinger 1999, 277-89.]

420. See W. Bauer, 1934/64 and Köster 1971, 107-46; idem 1980, 698-746.

421. [Cf. M. Dibelius/H. Conzelmann 1966, 52-54; Roloff 1988, 228-39; L. Oberlinner 1994, 171-86; idem 1995, 98-101; I. H. Marshall / P. H. Towner 1999, 50f.; in addition, D. R. MacDonald 1983; M. Y. MacDonald 1988, 181-83; eadem 1996, 161-65.]

422. On the Nicolaitans, see E. Schüssler Fiorenza 1973, 567-74; [now also Räisänen 1995, 151-66; further Klauck 1994, 115-43].

423. [On this, among others, W. Bauer 1934/64, 65-80; E. Molland 1970, 17-23; Bauer/Paulsen 1985, 64f.; Ch. Trevett 1980; eadem, 1983, 1-18.]

The distinction between literary fiction and factual situation improves the exegesis of Ephesians. Otherwise, it makes no real difference whether a Jewish Christian student of Paul's wrote the letter around the year 60 or around the year 80. Attempts to fill in the gaps of our knowledge through hypothesis and speculation have only a limited value. It is much more important to note the general social and historical situation in which the letter was created. From the second century onwards, the letter to the Ephesians has been read and interpreted under changing conditions. The situation and thus also the assumptions and the issues were different in later times than at the time of the letter's composition. That realization is an essential prerequisite for evaluating the many, contradictory interpretations. A few observations must suffice here.

1. Ephesians is sufficiently close in time to the founding mission that the author can remind Christians of their pagan past. The contrast between "once" and "now" permeates the entire letter. Especially in a pseudonymous letter, this would only have been possible at a time when some church members had personally experienced conversion from idolatry.[424] Most writings of the early second century show that the situation was different by then. Ignatius, for example, relies much less than Ephesians on the transition marked by baptism; he invokes rather the Eucharist and the bishop, as preservers of the unity of the Church.[425] Later interpretations of Ephesians, and general theological systems, differ in the way in which they deal with the contrast between "once" and "now". The solutions differed, precisely because the contrast remained theologically significant, even if it was no longer anchored in actual experience.

2. Ephesians addresses the recipients as "holy" and "believing" and assumes that they are all members of the body of Christ. Ephesians, unlike the Pastorals and several contemporaneous writings, does not view the church as a "mixed body," which contains true and false brethren.[426] In this respect, Ephesians holds to Paul's teaching. In Paul, too, harsh judgments about a community could stand along a recollection of the sanctification and justification in the name of Jesus Christ given in the

---

424. Similarly, 1 Peter; [cf. Vielhauer 1975, 581 f.: "... they (sc. the addressees) often are addressed as newly baptized (especially 2:2, but also 1:3, 12, 23; 2:10, 25; 3:21) ... "; Goppelt, 1978, 56–64; Brox 1979, 24–34; B. Olsson 1982, 19f., 83f.; Achtemeier 1996, 50–58; Schnelle 1996, 460–63;] see also Barnabas [and on it Vielhauer 1975, 601–07 and, if very little to the question of the addressees, Prostmeier 1999, 111–34.]

425. [On Ignatius, cf. Bauer/Paulsen 1985, 29–31; Schoedel 1985, 21.]

426. Cf., e.g., 2 Tim. 2:20; Matt. 7:21f.; 13:47–50 etc.; John 8:31; 1 John.

spirit (cf. esp. 1 Cor. 6:1–11).[427] The letter to the Ephesians, however, is silent about the existence of unworthy or even apostate Christians. Issues of church discipline and Christian penance are not addressed.

3. It is one-sided to regard ecclesiology as the central theme of Ephesians. However, Ephesians' statements about the Church do in fact go beyond anything we find in other New Testament writings. The word ἐκκλησία refers always to the entire church, unlike Paul, never to a specific local community. Any related explanations and instructions concern the common life of Christians who have a mutual, personal relationship. We hear nothing about connections among local churches comparable to the Pauline collection for Jerusalem. When Paul wrote to the "church of the Thessalonians" or "the church of God in Corinth", the addressees knew what group of people was meant, and others could have known it. In Ephesians, the extent to which the church is at all comprehensible in sociological categories remains uncertain. In any case, if the letter is pseudonymous, it must at the time of its composition already have been hard to specify exactly where the Church, which is the body of Christ, was to be found. In the second century, Gnostics, church fathers and others differed about the identity of the Church, to which the ecclesiology of the Ephesians was related.[428] That also explains, more than particular exegetical issues do, later controversies about "high" and "low" church, pietism, spiritualism, etc.

4. Ephesians is emphatically universalistic, not only because it emphasizes the unity of Jews and Gentiles, but also because the letter looks forward to the reconciliation of the entire universe in Christ and sees the Church as the core of that renewed universe.[429] The church of the letter to the Ephesians was still a tiny minority in the Roman Empire, which almost like a sect distanced itself from its environment (cf. Eph 4:17 20; 2:1–3; 5:5–14). This universalism of a particular group could not be maintained in the Church, especially after Constantine, in the long run. Where that has been renewed in special groups, it has been the result of distancing from other baptized Christians, so in opposition to the overall ecclesiastical concerns of Ephesians.

427. [Cf. Conzelmann 1981c, 131–37; Schrage 1991, 402–36.]

428. [It is probably no coincidence. that "as far as the RS (sc. revelation schema) is concerned . . . among the Gnostics Eph. 3:3–5 is the NT text most frequently referred to and quoted . . . ;" cf. only Hippol. *Ref.* 35, 1–2 (Hellholm 1998, 242).]

429. [On the universalism of Ephesians, see also Mitton 1976, 29; Gnilka 1990, 47 with note 5; Köster 1980. 707f.; Strecker 1996. 598f.; Sellin 1999, 1346.]

5. The observations in items (2) to (4) all lead to the conclusion that the ecclesiology of Ephesians is somewhat utopian.[430] Paul consciously presents the contrast between the power of God manifested in Christ and the weakness of Christians as a paradox.[431] The power of Christ is effective in weakness (cf. 1 Cor. 1:18–2:5; 2 Cor. 12:9; 13:3f. etc.). Also the letter to the Ephesians knows that those who are already resurrected and exalted with Christ must still endure struggle and suffering (cf. Eph. 3:13; 6:10ff.). But the paradoxes "life in death" and "strength in weakness" are missing in Ephesians. Precisely because Ephesians is more utopian than paradoxical, in later times one could understand and explain the letter in different ways. Ephesians' particularly clear contrast between salvation already realized in Christ and existing world reality was lost on the Gnostics, who explained the corporeal world as an unreal semblance. As the Church gained influence, the ecclesiology of Ephesians, understood very differently, could be used in fact as the ideological basis for claims of ecclesiastical power.[432] It was however in turn possible to find in Ephesians consolation for the anxious conscience. Ephesians spoke of the forgiveness of the sins of baptized members of the church, along with forgiveness, salvation and life. Movements that sought renewal and the unity of the churches were not infrequently especially inspired by Ephesians, with which they sometimes also shared a utopian element. Only relatively slowly has the realization dawned, that Ephesians might inspire not only a charismatic church structure, but a radical critic of a church, in which new dividing walls between Christians and Jews and between nations, races and social classes, have been erected.

6. What applies to all writings is especially true of Ephesians: understanding depends not only on what has been written, but on the presuppositions of the readers.[433] That this is particularly clear in the case of Ephesians is related to its utopian element. But it is also due to the literary nature of this letter. The letter calls Christians to remember what has been given to them in Christ. A commemorating recollection however presupposes previous experience, which though it can be clarified and deepened, cannot be created by the exhortation to remember alone. With some justification, one could describe Ephesians as a letter

---

430. Meeks 1977, 209–21 and Fischer 1973 have understood the utopian elements of Ephesians better than Merklein 1973a. Cf. also Chadwick 1960, 147.

431. [Cf. Bultmann 1965/84, 102ff.; Hübner 1997.]

432. E.g., Beare 1953, 607, wrongly charged Ephesians with its later use.

433. [Cf. Mouton 1996, 280–307.]

of congratulations, addressed to Gentiles who had become Christians.[434] How one understands a congratulatory message is no less determined by the presuppositions of those congratulated than by the words of the person congratulating them. The words of Ephesians can be heard with humble gratitude, but there is also the danger that they encourage an ecclesial triumphalism.

7. BIBLIOGRAPHY

Abbott, T. K. 1897. *A Critical and Exegetical Commentary on the Epistles to the Ephesians and to the Colossians*. ICC. Edinburgh: T. & T. Clark.

Achtemeier, Paul J. 1996. *1 Peter: A Commentary on First Peter*. Hermeneia. Minneapolis: Fortress.

Aejmelaeus, Lars. 1987. *Die Rezeption der Paulusbriefe in der Miletrede (Apg 20:18–35)*. AASF B 232. Helsinki: Suomalainen Tiedeakatemia.

Aland, Kurt, ed. 1978. *Vollständige Konkordanz zum griechischen Neuen Testament. Band II: Spezialübersichten*. Berlin: de Gruyter.

———. 1980. "Noch einmal: Das Problem der Anonymität und Pseudonymität in der christlichen Literatur der ersten beiden Jahrhunderte." In *Pietas: Festschrift für Bernhard Kötting*, edited by Ernst Dassmann and K. Suso Frank, 121–39. JAC Erg. 8. Münster: Aschendorff.

Alexander, Loveday C. A. 1992. "Schools, Hellenistic." In *ABD*, 5:1005–11.

———. 1995. "Paul and the Hellenistic Schools: The Evidence of Galen." In *Paul in His Hellenistic Context*, edited by Troels Engberg-Pedersen, 60–83. Minneapolis: Fortress.

Allen, John A. 1958/59. "The 'In Christ' Formula in Ephesians." *NTS* 5:54–62.

Amling, Ernst. 1909. "Eine Konjektur im Philemonbrief." *ZNW* 10:261–62.

Arnold, Clinton E. 1989. *Ephesians: Power and Magic*. SNTSMS 63. Cambridge: Cambridge University Press.

Asting, Ragnar K. 1930. *Die Heiligkeit im Urchristentum*. FRLANT 29. Göttingen: Vandenhoeck & Ruprecht.

Attridge, Harold W. 1989. *The Epistle to the Hebrews*. Hermeneia. Philadelphia: Fortress.

Aune, David E. 1987. *The New Testament in Its Literary Environment*. LEC. Philadelphia: Westminster.

———. 1997. *Revelation 1–5*. WBC 52. Dallas: Word, 1997.

Balch, David L. 1981. *Let Wives Be Submissive: The Domestic Code in I Peter*. SBLMS 26. Atlanta: Scholars.

Barnett, Albert E. 1941. *Paul Becomes a Literary Influence*. Chicago, IL: University of Chicago Press.

Barth, Markus. 1959a: *Israel und die Kirche im Brief des Paulus an die Epheser*. TEH 75. Munich: Kaiser.

———. 1959b: *The Broken Wall: A Study of the Epistle to the Ephesians*, Chicago: Judson.

---

434. [See Dahl, "Benediction and Congratulation," Studies in Ephesians; idem 1951, 241–64.]

———. 1974. *Ephesians*, 2 vols. AB 34. Garden City, NY: Doubleday.
Bartsch, Hans-Werner. 1940. *Gnostisches Gut und Gemeindetradition bei Ignatius von Antiochien*. Beiträge zur Förderung christlicher Theologie 2/44. Gütersloh: Bertelsmann.
Batey, Richard. 1963. "The Destination of Ephesians." *JBL* 82:101.
Bauer, Johannes Bapt. 1995. *Die Polykarpbriefe*. KAV 5. Göttingen: Vandenhoeck & Ruprecht.
Bauer, Walter. 1934/64. *Rechtgläubigkeit und Ketzerei im ältesten Christentum*. 2nd ed., with an afterword by Georg Strecker. BHTh 10. Tübingen: Mohr/Siebeck 1964 [1st ed., 1934].
Bauer, Walter, and Henning Paulsen. 1985. *Die Briefe des Ignatius von Antiochia und der Polykarpbrief*. HNT 18: Die Apostolischen Väter 2. Tübingen: Mohr/Siebeck.
Baur, Ferdinand Christian. 1844. "Kritische Miscellen zum Epheserbrief." *Theologische Jahrbücher* 3: 378–95.
———. 1845. *Paulus, der Apostel Jesu Christi*, Stuttgart: Becker & Müller.
———. 1866–67. *Paulus, der Apostel Jesu Christi*, besorgt von E. Zeller, 2 vols. Leipzig: Fues/Reisland.
———. 1866. *Vorlesungen über neutestamentliche Theologie*. Leipzig: Fues/Reisland.
Bausch, K.-H. 1980. "Soziolekt." In *Lexikon der Germanistischen Linguistik*, edited by Hans Peter Althaus et al., 2:358–63. 2nd ed. Tübingen: Niemeyer.
Beare, F. W. 1953. "Ephesians." In *The Interpreters Bible*, 10:597–749. Nashville: Abingdon-Cokesbury.
Becker, Jürgen. 1989. *Paulus: Der Apostel der Völker*. Tübingen: Mohr/Siebeck.
Belser, Johannes. 1908. *Der Epheserbrief des Apostels Paulus*. Freiburg: Herder.
Benoit, Pierre. 1961. "L'horizon paulinien de l'Épître aux Éphésiens." In *Exégèse et Théologie II*, 53–96. Paris: Cerf.
———. 1963. "Rapports littéraires entre les épîtres aux Colossiens et aux Éphésiens." In *Neutestamentliche Aufsätze: Festschrift für Josef Schmid*, edited by J. Blinzler et al., 11–22. Regensburg: Pustet.
———. 1966. "Éphesiens." In *DBS* VII, Paris: Letouzey & Ané 1966, 195–211.
Berger, Klaus. 1984. "Hellenistische Gattungen im Neuen Testament." In *ANRW* II.23.2, 1031–432. Berlin: de Gruyter.
Best, Ernest. 1997a. *Essays on Ephesians*. Edinburgh: T. & T. Clark.
———. 1997a(1). "Ephesians 1.1." In 1997a, 1–16.
———. 1997a(2). "Ephesians 1.1 Again." In 1997a, 17–24.
———. 1997a(4). "The Use of Credal and Liturgical Material in Ephesians." In 1997a, 51–68.
———. 1997b. "Who Used Whom? The Relationship of Ephesians and Colossians." *NTS* 43 (1997) 72–96.
———. 1998. *A Critical and Exegetical Commentary on Ephesians*. ICC. Edinburgh: T. & T. Clark 1998.
Betz, Hans Dieter. 1974–75. "The Literary Composition and Function of Paul's Letter to the Galatians." *NTS* 21:353–79. [Reprinted in Betz 1994: 63–97.]
———. 1979. *Galatians*. Hermeneia. Philadelphia: Fortress.
———. 1988. *Der Galaterbrief: Ein Kommentar zum Brief des Apostels Paulus an die Gemeinden in Galatien*. Ein Hermeneia-Kommentar. Munich: Kaiser 1988.
———. 1994. *Paulinische Studien: Gesammelte Aufsätze III*. Tübingen: Mohr/Siebeck 1994.

---. 1995. "Paul's 'Second Presence' in Colossians." In *Texts and Contexts: Biblical Texts in Their Textual and Situational Contexts: Essays in Honor of Lars Hartman*, edited by Tord Fornberg and David Hellholm, 507-18. Oslo: Scandinavian University Press.

Beyer, Klaus. 1968. *Semitische Syntax im Neuen Testament. I. Satzlehre*. 2nd ed. StUNT 1. Göttingen: Vandenhoeck & Ruprecht.

Beza, Th. 1598. *Novum Testamentum Graece et Latine*. Genf: Vignon.

Billerbeck, Paul, and Hermann L. Strack. 1926. *Kommentar zum Neuen Testament aus Talmud und Midrasch*. Vol. 3: *Die Briefe des Neuen Testaments und die Offenbarung Johannis*. Munich: Beck.

Bjerkelund, Carl J. 1967. *Parakalô: Form, Funktion und Sinn der parakalô-Sätze in den paulinischen Briefen*. BTN 1. Oslo: Universitetsforlaget.

Blank, Josef. 1968. *Paulus und Jesus: Eine theologische Grundlegung*. SANT 18. Munich: Kösel.

Blass, Friedrich, Albert Debrunner, and Friedrich Rehkopf. 1975. *Grammatik des neutestamentlichen Griechisch*. 14th ed. Göttingen: Vandenhoeck & Ruprecht.

Blomkvist, V. 1993. *Stilen i Efeserbrevet sammenlignet med Kolosserbrevets: Et bidrag til for-fatterspørsmålet*. Hovedoppgave i Kristendomskunnskap. Det teologiske fakultet, Universitetet i Oslo.

Bornkamm, Günther. 1942. "μυστήριον." In *ThWNT* 4:809-34. Stuttgart: Kohlhammer.

---. 1961a. "Paulinische Anakoluthe im Römerbrief." In *Das Ende des Gesetzes: Paulusstudien. Gesammelte Aufsätze*, 1:76-92. BEvTh 16. 3rd ed. Munich: Kaiser.

---. 1961b. "Die Häresie des Kolosserbriefes." *Das Ende des Gesetzes: Paulusstudien. Gesammelte Aufsätze*, 1:139-56. BEvTh 16. 3rd ed. Munich: Kaiser.

Bousset, Wilhelm. 1921/65. *Kyrios Christos: Geschichte des Christusglaubens von den Anfängen des Christentums bis Irenaeus*. 2nd ed. Göttingen: Vandenhoeck & Ruprecht, 1921 [5th ed., 1965, with a foreword by Rudolf Bultmann].

Bouttier, Michel. 1991. *L'Épître de saint Paul aux Éphésiens*. CNT 2/9B. Genf: Labor & Fides.

Braun, Herbert. 1966. *Qumran und das Neue Testament*. Vol. 1. Tübingen: Mohr/Siebeck.

---. 1984. *An die Hebräer*. HNT 14. Tübingen: Mohr/Siebeck.

Brown, Raymond E. 1963. "Ephesians among the Letters of Paul." *RevExp* 60:373-79.

---. 1997. *An Introduction to the New Testament*. ABRL. New York: Doubleday.

Brox, N., ed. 1977. *Pseudepigraphie in der heidnischen und jüdisch-christlichen Antike*. WdF 484. Darmstadt: Wissenschaftliche Buchgesellschaft.

---. 1979. *Der erste Petrusbrief*. EKK 21. Neukirchen-Vluyn: Neukirchener.

---. 1991. *Der Hirt des Hermas*. KAV 7. Göttingen: Vandenhoeck & Ruprecht.

Brucker, Ralph. 1997. *'Christushymnen' oder 'epideiktische Passagen'? Studien zum Stilwechsel im Neuen Testament und seiner Umwelt*. FRLANT 176. Göttingen: Vandenhoeck & Ruprecht.

Bujard, W. 1973. *Stilanalytische Untersuchungen zum Kolosserbrief als Beitrag zur Methodik von Sprachvergleichen*. SUNT 11. Göttingen: Vandenhoeck & Ruprecht.

Bultmann, Rudolf. 1966. *Das Urchristentum im Rahmen der antiken Religionen*. Rowohlts deutsche Enzyklopädie 157/158. Munich: Rowohlt 1966.

— 1984. *Theologie des Neuen Testaments*. NTG. 6th ed. Tübingen: Mohr/Siebeck.

Buschmann, G. 1998. *Das Martyrium des Polykarp*. KAV 6. Göttingen: Vandenhoeck & Ruprecht.

Cadbury, H. J. 1959-60. "The Dilemma of Ephesians." *NTS* 5 (1959-60) 91-102.
Cancik, Hildegard. 1967. *Untersuchungen zu Senecas epistulae morales.* Spudasmata 18. Hildesheim: Olms 1967.
Caragounis, Chrys C. 1977. *The Ephesian Mysterion: Meaning and Content.* CBNT 8. Lund: Gleerup 1977.
Cerfaux, L. 1960. "En faveur de l'authenticité des épîtres de la captivité." *RechBib* 5 (1960) 60-71.
Chadwick, H. J. 1954-55. "All Things to All Men." *NTS* 1:261-75.
———. 1960. "Die Absicht des Epheserbriefes." *ZNW* 51:145-53.
Charles, R. H. 1920. *A Critical and Exegetical Commentary on The Revelation of St. John.* Vol. 1. ICC. Edinburgh: T. & T. Clark.
Colpe, Carsten. 1960. "Zur Leib-Christi-Vorstellung im Epheserbrief." In *Judentum, Urchristentum, Kirche: Festschrift für Joachim Jeremias*, edited by Walter Eltester, 172-87. BZNW 26. Berlin: de Gruyter.
Conzelmann, Hans. 1963. *Die Apostelgeschichte.* HNT 7. Tübingen: Mohr/Siebeck.
———. 1965/74. "Paulus und die Weisheit." *NTS* 12:231-44. Reprinted in *Theologie als Schriftauslegung: Aufsätze zum Neuen Testament*, 177-90. BEvTh 65. Munich: Kaiser 1974.
———. 1979. "Die Schule des Paulus." In *Theologia Crucis, Signum Crucis: Festschrift für Erich Dinkler zum 70. Geburtstag*, edited by C. Andresen and G. Klein, 85-96. Tübingen: Mohr/Siebeck.
———. 1981a. "Der Brief an die Epheser." In J. Becker et al., *Die Briefe an die Galater, Epheser, Kolosser, Thessalonicher und Philemon*, 86-124. NTD 8. Göttingen: Vandenhoeck & Ruprecht.
———. 1981b. "Der Brief an die Kolosser." In J. Becker et al., *Die Briefe an die Galater, Epheser, Kolosser, Thessalonicher und Philemon*, 176-202. NTD 8. Göttingen: Vandenhoeck & Ruprecht.
———. 1981c. *Der erste Brief an die Korinther.* 2nd ed. KEK 5. Göttingen: Vandenhoeck & Ruprecht.
Conzelmann, Hans, and Andreas Lindemann. 1995. *Arbeitsbuch zum Neuen Testament.* 11th ed. UTB 52. Tübingen: Mohr/Siebeck.
Cotton, Hannah. 1981. *Documentary Letters of Recommendation in Latin from the Roman Empire.* BKP 132. Königstein: Hain.
Coutts, J. 1956-57. "Ephesians 1:1-14 and 1 Peter 1:3-13." *NTS* 3:115-27.
———. 1957-58. "The Relationship of Ephesians and Colossians." *NTS* 4:201-7.
Crouch, James E. 1972. *The Origin and Intention of the Colossian Haustafel.* FRLANT 109. Göttingen: Vandenhoeck & Ruprecht.
Dacquino, P. 1955. "I destinatari della lettera agli Efesini." *RivBib* 6:102-10.
———. 1958. "Interpretatio Epistolae ad Eph. in luce finis intenti." *VD* 36:338-49.
Dahl, Nils Alstrup. 1947. "Ernst Percy, 'Die Probleme der Kolosser- und Epheserbriefe'." *SvTK* 23:366-74.
———. 1951. "Adresse und Proömium des Epheserbriefes." *ThZ* 7:241-64.
———. 1954/57. "Formgeschichtliche Beobachtungen zur Christusverkündigung in der Gemeindepredigt." In *Neutestamentliche Studien für Rudolf Bultmann*, edited by Walter Eltester, 3-9. Berlin: Töpelmann, 3-9.
———. 1956. "Epheserbrief." In *EKL*, 1:1100-2. 2nd ed. Göttingen: Vandenhoeck & Ruprecht.

———. 1962. "Kolosserbrief." in *EKL*, 2: 865–66. 2nd ed. Göttingen: Vandenhoeck & Ruprecht.

———. 1963. "Der Epheserbrief und der verlorene Erste Brief des Paulus an die Korinther." In *Abraham unser Vater: Juden und Christen im Gespräch über die Bibel. Festschrift für Otto Michel zum 60. Geburtstag*, edited by Otto Betz et al., 65–77. Leiden: Brill.

———. 1965. "Das Geheimnis der Kirche nach Eph. 3,8–10." In *Zur Aufbauung des Leibes Christi: Festschrift Peter Brunner*, edited by E. Schlink and A. Peters, 63–75. Kassel: Stauda.

———. 1966. *Et Kall. Bibelstudium over Efeserbrevet*. Oslo: Land og Kirke.

———. 1967. "Paul and the Church at Corinth according to 1 Corinthians 1–4." In *Christian History and Interpretation: Studies Presented to John Knox*, edited by W. R. Farmer et al., 313–35. Cambridge: Cambridge University Press.

———. 1975. "Cosmic Dimensions and Religious Knowledge (Eph. 3:18)." In *Jesus und Paulus: Festschrift für Werner Georg Kümmel zum 70. Geburtstag*, edited by E. E. Ellis and Erich Grässer, 57–75. Göttingen: Vandenhoeck & Ruprecht.

———. 1976a/81a. "Ephesians, Letter to the." In *IDBSup*, 268–69.

———. 1976b/81b. "Letter." In *IDBSup*, 538–41.

———. 1977. "Interpreting Ephesians: Then and Now." *Theology Digest* 25:305–15.

———. 1982. "Dåpsforståelsen i Efeserbrevet." In S. Pedersen (Hrsg.), *Dåben i Ny Testamente: Festschrift Hejne Simonsen*, Århus, 141–60.

———. 1993. "Når Paulus spør." In *Kirken i tiden—Troen i folket: Festskrift til biskop Georg Hille*, 47–59. Oslo: Verbum.

Dawes, Gregory W. 1998. *The Body in Question: Metaphor and Meaning in the Interpretation of Ephesians 5:21–33*. Biblical Interpretation Series 30. Leiden: Brill.

Deichgräber, Reinhard. 1967. *Gotteshymnus und Christushymnus in der frühen Christenheit: Untersuchungen zu Form, Sprache und Stil der frühchristlichen Hymnen*. SUNT 5. Göttingen: Vandenhoeck & Ruprecht.

Deissmann, Adolf. 1892. *Die neutestamentliche Formel "in Christo Jesu."* Marburg: Elwert.

Deming, Will. 1995. *Paul on Marriage and Celibacy: The Hellenistic Background of 1 Corinthians 7*. SNTSMS 83. Cambridge: Cambridge University Press.

De Wette, Wilhelm Martin Leberecht. 1826/48. *Lehrbuch der historisch-kritischen Einleitung in die kanonischen Bücher des Neuen Testaments*. Berlin: Reimer, 5th ed. 1848.

———. 1847. *Kurze Erklärung der Briefe an die Colosser, an Philemon, an die Epheser und Philipper*. KEHNT 2/4. Leipzig: Weidmann.

Dibelius, Martin. 1931. "Formgeschichte zum Neuen Testament (außerhalb des Evangeliums)." *ThR* 3:207–42.

———. 1921. *Der Brief des Jakobus*. 7th ed. KEK 15. Göttingen: Vandenhoeck & Ruprecht, 1921.

Dibelius, Martin, and Hans Conzelmann. 1966. *Die Pastoralbriefe*. 4th ed. HNT 13. Tübingen: Mohr/Siebeck.

Dibelius, Martin, and Heinrich Greeven. 1953. *An die Kolosser, Epheser, an Philemon*. 3rd ed. HNT 12. Tübingen: Mohr/Siebeck.

———. 1964. *Der Brief des Jakobus*. 11th ed. KEK 15. Göttingen: Vandenhoeck & Ruprecht.

Donelson, Lewis R. 1986. *Pseudepigraphy and Ethical Argument in the Pastoral Epistles.* HUT 22. Tübingen: Mohr/Siebeck.
Dormeyer, Detlev. 1993. *Das Neue Testament im Rahmen der antiken Literaturgeschichte: Eine Einführung.* Die Altertumswissenschaft. Darmstadt: Wissenschaftliche Buchgesellschaft.
Dupont, J. 1955. "Le problème de la structure littéraire de l'épître aux Romain." *RB* 62:365-97.
Eichhorn, Johann Gottfried. 1804-27. *Einleitung in das Neue Testament.* Leipzig: Weidmann.
Erasmus von Rotterdam. 1519/1705. *Annotationes in Novum Testamentum.* Basel: Froben, 1519 [= "Annotationes in Novum Testamentum." In *Opera Omnia*, Vol. VI, Luguduni Batavorum 1705].
Ernst, Josef. 1974. *Die Briefe an die Philipper, an Philemon, an die Kolossser, an die Epheser.* RNT. Regensburg: Pustet.
———. 1990. "Kolosserbrief." In *TRE* 19:370-76. Berlin: de Gruyter.
Evanson, Edward. 1792. *The Dissonance of the Four Generally Received Evangelists and the Evidence of Their Respective Authenticity Examined.* Ipswich: Jermyn.
Ewald, Paul. 1910. *Die Briefe des Paulus an die Epheser, Kolosser und Philemon.* 2nd ed. KNT 10. Leipzig: Deichert.
Faust, Eberhard. 1993. *Pax Christi et Pax Caesaris: Religionsgeschichtliche, traditionsgeschichtliche und sozialgeschichtliche Studien zum Epheserbrief.* NTOA 24. Göttingen: Vanden-hoeck & Ruprecht.
Fee, Gordon. D. 1987. *The First Epistle to the Corinthians.* NICNT. Grand Rapids: Eerdmans.
Feine, Paul, and Johannes Behm. 1950. *Einleitung in das Neue Testament.* Heidelberg: Quelle & Meyer.
Fiedler, P. 1986. "Haustafel." In *RAC*, 13:1063-73. Stuttgart: Hiersemann.
Fischer, Karl Martin. 1973. *Tendenz und Absicht des Epheserbriefes.* FRLANT 111. Göttingen: Vandenhoeck & Ruprecht.
Fitzmyer, Joseph A. 1998. *The Acts of the Apostles.* AB 31. New York: Doubleday 1998.
Foerster, R., ed. 1927. *Libiani opera.* Vol. 9. Leipzig: Teubner.
Foerster, W. 1938. "Ἰησοῦς." In *TWNT*, 3:284-94.
Forbes, Christopher. 1997. *Prophecy and Inspired Speech: In Early Christianity and Its Hellenistic Environment*, Peabody, MA: Hendrickson 1997.
Foster, Ora Delmar. 1913. "The Literary Relations of the 'First Epistle of Peter.'" Transactions of the Connecticut Academy of Arts and Sciences 17, 363-538. New Haven: Yale University Press.
Francis, Fred O. 1973. "Humility and Angelic Worship in Colossae." In Meeks and Francis, eds., 1973:163-95.
Francis, Fred O., and J. Paul Sampley. 1984. *Pauline Parallels.* Foundations and Facets. Philadelphia: Fortress.
Franzmann, M. 1991. *The Odes of Solomon: An Analysis of the Poetical Structure and Form.* NTOA 20. Göttingen: Vandenhoeck & Ruprecht.
Fritz, K. von, ed. 1972. *Pseudepigraphia I. Pseudopythagorica - Lettres de Platon - Littérature pseudépigraphique juive.* Fondation Hardt pour l'étude de l'antiquité classique. Entretiens Tome 18. Vandœuvres-Genève: Hardt.

Funk, Robert W. 1966. *Language, Hermeneutic, and the Word of God. The Problem of Language in the New Testament and Contemporary Theology.* New York: Harper & Row.

Furnish, Victor Paul. 1992. "Ephesians, Epistle to the." In *ABD*, 2:535-42.

Gabathuler, H.-J. 1965. *Jesus Christus: Haupt der Kirche, Haupt der Welt.* ATANT 45. Zurich: Zwingli.

Gamble, Harry Y. 1975. "The Redaction of the Pauline Letters and the Formation of the Pauline Corpus." *JBL* 94:403-18.

———. 1977. *The Textual History of the Letter to the Romans: A Study in Textual and Literary Criticism.* StD 42. Grand Rapids: Eerdmans.

———. 1995. *Books and Readers in the Early Church: A History of Early Christian Texts*, New Haven: Yale University Press.

Gese, M. 1997. *Das Vermächtnis des Apostels: Die Rezeption der paulinischen Theologie im Epheserbrief.* WUNT 2/99. Tübingen: Mohr/Siebeck.

Gnilka, Joachim. 1982. *Der Philemonbrief.* HTK 10/4. Freiburg: Herder.

———. 1990. *Der Brief an die Epheser.* 4th ed. HTK 10/2. Freiburg: Herder.

———. 1991. *Der Brief an die Kolosser.* 2nd ed. HTK 10/1. Freiburg : Herder.

Gore, Charles. 1898. *St. Paul's Epistle to the Ephesians: A Practical Exposition.* New York: Scribner.

Görgemanns, H. 1997a. "Epistel A-F." In *Der Neue Pauly. Enzyklopädie der Antike*, edited by H. Cancik and H. Schneider, 3:1161-64, Stuttgart – Weimar: Metzler.

———. 1997b. "Epistolographie." In *Der Neue Pauly. Enzyklopädie der Antike*, edited by H. Cancik and H. Schneider, 3:1166-69. Stuttgart: Metzler.

Goguel, Maurice. 1922-26. *Introduction au Nouveau Testament.* Vols. I-IV.2. Paris: Leroux.

———. 1935/36. "Esquisse d'une solution nouvelle du problème de l'épître aux Éphésiens." *RHPR* 111:254-85; 112:73-99.

Goldstein, Jonathan A. 1968. *The Letters of Demosthenes.* New York: Columbia University Press.

Goodspeed, Edgar J. 1933. *The Meaning of Ephesians.* Chicago: University of Chicago Press.

Goppelt, Leonhard. 1978. *Der Erste Petrusbrief.* KEK 12/1. Göttingen: Vandenhoeck & Ruprecht.

Grässer, Erich. 1990. *An die Hebräer (Hebr 1-6).* EKK 17/1. Neukirchen-Vluyn: Neukirchener.

Hagner, Donald A. 1973. *The Use of the Old and New Testament in Clement of Rome.* NT.S 34. Leiden: Brill 1974.

Hammarström, G. 1980. "Idiolekt." In H. P. Althaus/H. Henne/H. E. Wiegand (Hrsg.), *Lexikon der Germanistischen Linguistik*, Band 2, 2. Aufl., Tübingen: Niemeyer, 428-33.

Hammer, P. L. 1960. "A Comparison of κληρονομία in Paul and in Ephesians." *JBL* 79:267-72.

Harnack, Adolf von. 1910. "Die Adresse des Epheserbriefes des Paulus." *SPAW* 37:696-709.

———. 1924. *Marcion: Das Evangelium vom fremden Gott. Eine Monographie zur Geschichte der Grundlegung der katholischen Kirche.* 2nd ed. Leipzig: Heinrichs. Reprint, Darmstadt: Wissenschaftliche Buchgesellschaft, 1985.

Harrison, P. N. 1950. "Onesimus and Philemon." *ATR* 32:268-94.

———. 1964a. "The Author of Ephesians." In F. L. Cross (Hrsg.), *Studia Evangelica, Vol. II, Part I: The New Testament Scriptures*, edited by F. L. Cross, 595-604. TU 87. Berlin: AV.

———. 1964b. *Paulines and Pastorals*. London: Villiers.

Hartke, W. 1961. "Vier urchristliche Parteien und ihre Vereinigung zur apostolischen Kirche." In *Studia Patristica*, Vol. II, edited by F. L. Cross, 431-34. TU 79. Berlin: AV.

Hartman, Lars. 1985. *Kolosserbrevet*. KomNT 12. Uppsala: EFS.

———. 1995. "Humble and Confident: On the So-Called Philosophers in Colossae." In *Mighty Minorities? Minorities in Early Christianity—Positions and Strategies. Essays in Honour of Jacob Jervell on His 70th Birthday 21 May 1995*, edited by David Hellholm et al., 25-39. Oslo: Scandinavian University Press.

———. 1997a. "On Reading Others' Letters." In *Text-Centered New Testament Studies: Text-Theoretical Essays on Early Jewish and Early Christian Literature*, edited by David Hellholm, 167-77. WUNT 102. Tübingen: Mohr/Siebeck 1997.

———. 1997b. *'Into the Name of the Lord Jesus': Baptism in the Early Church*. Studies of the New Testament and Its World. Edinburgh: T. & T. Clark.

Haupt, Erich. 1902. *Die Gefangenschaftsbriefe*. KEK 8/9. 8th ed. Göttingen: Vandenhoeck & Ruprecht.

Hendrix, Holland. 1988. "On the Form and Ethos of Ephesians." *USQR* 42:3-15.

Henle, F. A. von. 1908. *Der Epheserbrief des hl. Apostels Paulus*. 2nd ed. Augsburg: Huttler 1908.

Hegermann, Harald. 1961. *Die Vorstellung vom Schöpfungsmittler im hellenistischen Juden-tum und Urchristentum*. TU 82. Berlin: AV.

———. 1988. *Der Brief an die Hebräer*. ThHK 16. Berlin: EVA.

Hellholm, David. 1980. *Das Visionenbuch des Hermas als Apokalypse. Formgeschichtliche und text-theoretische Studien zu einer literarischen Gattung I: Methodologische Vorüberlegungen und makrostrukturelle Textanalyse*. CBNT 13. Lund: Gleerup.

———. 1995a. "Enthymemic Argumentation in Paul: The Case of Romans 6." In *Paul in His Hellenistic Context*, edited by T. Engberg-Pedersen, 119-79. Minneapolis: Fortress.

———. 1995b. "Substitutionelle Gliederungsmerkmale und die Komposition des Matthäusevangeliums." In *Texts and Contexts: Biblical Texts in Their Textual and Situational Contexts. Essays in Honor of Lars Hartman*, edited by Tord Fornberg and David Hellholm, 11-76. Oslo: Scandinavian Univeristy Press.

———. 1997. "Die argumentative Funktion von Römer 7.1-6." *NTS* 43:385-411.

———. 1998. "The 'Revelation-Schema' and Its Adaptation in the Coptic Gnostic Apocalypse of Peter." *SEÅ* 63:233-48 [= Festschrift für Birger Olsson].

Hengel, Martin. 1973. *Judentum und Hellenismus: Studien zu ihrer Begegnung unter besonderer Berücksichtigung Palästinas bis zur Mitte des 2. Jh.s v. Chr*. 2nd ed. WUNT 10. Tübingen: Mohr/Siebeck.

Hester, James D. 1968. *Paul's Concept of Inheritance: A Contribution to the Understanding of Heilsgeschichte*. Scottish Journal of Theology Occasional Papers 14. Edinburgh: Oliver & Boyd.

Hilgenfeld, A. 1875. *Historisch-Kritische Einleitung in das Neue Testament*. Leipzig: Fues.

Hitzig, F. 1870. *Zur Kritik der paulinischen Briefe*. Leipzig: Hirzel.

Hoekstra, S. 1868. "Vergelijking van de brieven aan de Efez. en de Coloss. vooral uit het oogpunt van beider leerstellige inhoud." *Theologisch Tijdschrift* 2:599–658.

Holmstrand, Jonas. 1997. *Markers and Meaning in Paul: An Analysis of 1 Thessalonians, Philippians and Galatians.* CBNT 28. Stockholm: Almqvist &Wiksell.

Holtzmann, Heinrich Julius. 1872. *Kritik der Epheser- und Kolosserbriefe auf Grund einer Analyse ihres Verwandtschaftsverhältnisses.* Leipzig: Engelmann.

Horn, Friedrich Wilhelm. 1992. *Das Angeld des Geistes: Studien zur paulinischen Pneumatologie.* FRLANT 154. Göttingen: Vandenhoeck & Ruprecht.

Horst, P. W. van der. 1978. "PsPhokylides and the NT." *ZNW* 69:187–202.

Hort, F. J. A. 1895. *Prolegomena to Saint Paul's Epistles to the Romans and to the Ephesians*, London: Macmillan.

Hurd, J. C., Jr. 1965. *The Origin of 1 Corinthians.* London: SPCK. Reprinted, Macon, GA: Mercer 1983.

Hvalvik, Reidar. 1994/96. *The Struggle for Scripture and Covenant: The Purpose of the Epistle of Barnabas and Jewish-Christian Competition in the Second Century.* Oslo: Det teologiske Menighetsfakultet 1994. [= WUNT 2/82. Tübingen: Mohr/Siebeck 1996.]

Hübner, Hans. 1993. *Biblische Theologie des Neuen Testaments.* Vol. 2, *Die Theologie des Paulus und ihre neutestamentliche Wirkungsgeschichte.* Göttingen: Vandenhoeck & Ruprecht.

———. 1997. *An Philemon, An die Kolosser, An die Epheser* (HNT 12), Tübingen: Mohr/Siebeck.

Jervell, Jacob. 1960. *Imago Dei: Gen 1,26f. in Spätjudentum, in der Gnosis und in den paulinischen Briefen.* FRLANT 76. Göttingen: Vandenhoeck & Ruprecht.

———. 1998. *Die Apostelgeschichte.* KEK 3. Göttingen: Vandenhoeck & Ruprecht.

Johanson, Bruce C. 1987. *To All the Brethren: A Text-Linguistic and Rhetorical Approach to I Thessalonians.* CBNT 16. Stockholm: Almqvist & Wiksell.

Johnston, George. 1943. *The Doctrine of the Church in the New Testament.* Cambridge: Cambridge University Press.

———. 1962. "Ephesians." In A. Buttrick et alii (Hrsg.), *The Interpreter's Dictionary of the Bible*, Vol. II, Nashville: Abingdon, 108–14.

Jonas, Hans. 1964. *Die Mythologische Gnosis: Mit einer Einleitung zur Geschichte und Methodologie der Forschung.* FRLANT 51. 3rd ed. Göttingen: Vandenhoeck & Ruprecht.

Jülicher, Adolf, and Erich Fascher. 1931. *Einleitung in das Neue Testament.* 7th ed. Grundriss der theologischen Wissenschaften 3/1. Tübingen: Mohr/Siebeck.

Käsemann, Ernst. 1933. *Leib und Leib Christi.* BHTh 9. Tübingen: Mohr/Siebeck.

———. 1958. "Epheserbrief." In *RGG*, 2:517–20. 3rd ed. Tübingen: Mohr/Siebeck.

———. 1959. "Kolosserbrief." In *RGG*, 3: 1727–28. 3rd ed. Tübingen: Mohr/Siebeck, 1727–28.

———. 1980. "Ephesians and Acts." In *Studies in Luke–Acts*, edited by Leander E. Keck and J. Louis Martyn, 288–97. Philadelphia: Fortress.

Karrer, Martin. 1986. *Johannesoffenbarung als Brief: Studien zu ihrem literarischen, histor-ischen und theologischen Ort.* FRLANT 140. Göttingen: Vandenhoeck & Ruprecht.

Kennel, Gunter. 1995. *Frühchristliche Hymnen? Gattungskritische Studien zur Frage nach den Liedern der frühen Christenheit.* WMANT 71. Neukirchen-Vluyn: Neukirchener.

Kieffer, René. 1979. *Nytestamentlig Teologi*. 2nd ed. Lund: Verbum.
Kim, Chan-Hie. 1972. *Form and Structure of the Familiar Letter of Recommendation*. SBLDS 4. Missoula, MT: Scholars.
Kirby, John C. 1968. *Ephesians, Baptism and Pentecost: An Inquiry into the Structure and Purpose of the Epistle to the Ephesians*. London: SPCK.
Klauck, Hans-Josef. 1994. "Das Sendschreiben nach Pergamon und der Kaiserkult in der Johannes-offenbarung." In idem, *Alte Welt und neuer Glaube. Beiträge zur Religionsgeschichte, Forschungsgeschichte und Theologie des Neuen Testaments*, 115–43. NTOA 29. Göttingen: Vandenhoeck & Ruprecht.
———. 1998. *Die antike Briefliteratur und das Neue Testament: Ein Lehr- und Arbeitsbuch*. UTB 2022. Paderborn: Schöningh.
Knox, John. 1935/59. *Philemon among the Letters of Paul*. Chicago: University of Chicago Press. [Rev. ed., Nashville, TN: Abingdon 1959].
———. 1938. "Philemon and the Authenticity of Colossians." *JR* 18:144–60.
———. 1942. *Marcion and the New Testament: An Essay in the Early History of the Canon*. Chicago: University of Chicago Press, 1942.
———. 1966/80. "Acts and the Pauline Letter Corpus." In *Studies in Luke–Acts: Essays Presented in Honor of Paul Schubert*, edited by Leander E. Keck and J. Louis Martyn, 279–87. New York: Abingdon. [Reprinted, Philadelphia: Fortress 1980.]
Knox, Wilfred L. 1939. *St. Paul and the Church of the Gentiles*. Cambridge: Cambridge University Press.
Köster, Helmut. 1971. "GNOMAI DIAPHOROI: Ursprung und Wesen der Mannigfaltigkeit in der Geschichte des frühen Christentums." In Helmut Köster and James M. Robinson, *Entwicklungslinien durch die Welt des frühen Christentums*, 107–46. Tübingen: Mohr/Siebeck.
———. 1980. *Einführung in das Neue Testament im Rahmen der Religionsgeschichte und Kulturge-schichte der hellenistischen und römischen Zeit*. GLB. Berlin: de Gruyter.
Koskenniemi, Heikki. 1956. *Studien zur Idee und Phraseologie des griechischen Briefes bis 400 n. Chr.* AASF. Ser B 102.2. Helsinki: Akateminen Kirjakauppa.
Krämer, H. 1967. "Zur sprachlichen Form der Eulogie Eph. 1,3–14." *WuD* 9:34–46.
Kubczak, Hartmut. 1979. *Was ist ein Soziolekt? Überlegungen zur Symptomfunktion sprachlicher Zeichen unter besonderer Berücksichtigung der diastratischen Dimension* Sprach-wissenschaftliche Studienbücher. Heidelberg: Winter.
Kümmel, Werner Georg. 1963. *Einleitung in das Neue Testament*. 12th ed. Heidelberg: Quelle & Meyer 1963.
———. 1973. *Einleitung in das Neue Testament*. 17th ed. Heidelberg: Quelle & Meyer.
———. 1985. "L'exégèse scientifique au XXe siècle: le Nouveau Testament." In *Le monde contemporain et la Bible*, edited by Claude Savart and Jean-Noël Aletti, 473–515. Bible de Tous les Temps 8. Paris: Beauchesne.
Kuhn, Karl Georg. 1960–61. "Der Epheserbrief im Lichte der Qumrantexte." *NTS* 7:334–46.
Kuss, Otto. 1971. *Paulus: Die Rolle des Apostels in der theologischen Entwicklung der Urkirche*. Regensburg: Pustet.
Lake, Kirsopp, and Silva Lake. 1937. *An Introduction to the New Testament*. New York: Harper..
Lambrecht, Jan. 2000a. "Thanksgivings in 1 Thessalonians 1–3." In *The Thessalonians Debate: Methodological Discord or Methodological Synthesis?*, edited by Karl P. Donfried and J. Beutler, 135–62. Grand Rapids: Eerdmans, 2000.

———. 2000b. "A Structural Analysis of 1 Thessalonians 4–5." In *The Thessalonians Debate: Methodological Discord or Methodological Synthesis?*, edited by Karl P. Donfried and J. Beutler, 163–78. Grand Rapids: Eerdmans, 2000.
Lampe, G. W. H. 1968. *A Patristic Greek Lexicon*. 2nd printing. Oxford: Clarendon.
Lampe, Peter. 1998. *Der Brief an Philemon*. NTD 8/2. Göttingen: Vandenhoeck & Ruprecht.
Lattke, Michael. 1995. *Oden Salomos: Übersetzt und eingeleitet*. FC 19. Freiburg: Herder.
Lausberg, Heinrich. 1973. *Handbuch der literarischen Rhetorik: Eine Grundlegung der Literatur-wissenschaft*. 2 vols. 2nd ed. Munich: Hueber.
———. 1976. *Elemente der literarischen Rhetorik*. 5th ed. Munich: Hueber.
Lester, Hiram J. 1973. "Relative Clauses in the Pauline Homologoumena and Antilegomena." PhD diss., Yale University.
Leutzsch, Martin. 1994. *Die Bewährung der Wahrheit: Der dritte Johannesbrief als Dokument urchristlichen Alltags*. Stätten und Formen der Kommunikation im Altertum II; BAC 16. Trier: Wissenschaftlicher Verlag Trier.
Lietzmann, Hans. 1933. *An die Römer*. HNT 8. 4th ed. Tübingen: Mohr/Siebeck. [5th ed., 1971.]
Lightfoot, J. B. 1889. *The Apostolic Fathers*. Part 2. S. Ignatius, S. Polycarp. Vol. 2. 2nd ed. London: Macmillan.
———. 1893. "The Destination of the Epistle to the Ephesians." In *Biblical Essays*, London: Macmillan, 375–96.
Lincoln, Andrew T. 1990. *Ephesians*. WBC 42. Dallas: Word.
Lindemann, Andreas. 1975. *Die Aufhebung der Zeit: Geschichtsverständnis und Eschatologie im Epheserbrief*. StNT 12. Gütersloh: Mohn.
———. 1976/99. "Bemerkungen zu den Adressaten und zum Anlass des Epheserbriefes." ZNW 67:235–51. [Reprinted in: *Paulus, Apostel und Lehrer der Kirche: Studien zu Paulus und zum frühen Paulusverständnis*, 211–27. Tübingen: Mohr/Siebeck 1999.]
———. 1979. *Paulus im ältesten Christentum: Das Bild des Apostels und die Rezeption der paulinischen Theologie in der frühchristlichen Literatur bis Marcion*. BHTh 58. Tübingen: Mohr/Siebeck.
———. 1983. *Der Kolosserbrief*. ZBK 10. Zürich: TVZ.
———. 1985. *Der Epheserbrief*. ZBK 8. Zürich: TVZ.
Linton, Olof. 1964. *Pauli mindre brev*. Tolkning av Nya Testamentet 9. Stockholm: SKDB.
Lohmeyer, Ernst. 1964. *Die Briefe an die Philipper, Kolosser und an Philemon*. KEK 9. 8th ed. Göttingen: Vandenhoeck & Ruprecht.
Lohse, Eduard. 1968. *Die Briefe an die Kolosser und an Philemon*. KEK 9/2. Göttingen: Vandenhoeck & Ruprecht.
Lona, Horacio E. 1984. *Die Eschatologie im Kolosser- und Epheserbrief*. FzB 48. Würzburg: Echter.
———. 1998. *Der erste Clemensbrief*. KAV 2. Göttingen: Vandenhoeck & Ruprecht.
Lüdemann, Gerd. 1996. *Heretics: The Other Side of Early Christianity*. Translated by John Bowden. London: SCM.
Lührmann, Dieter. 1965. *Das Offenbarungsverständnis bei Paulus und in paulinischen Gemeinden*. WMANT 16. Neukirchen-Vluyn: Neukirchener.
———. 1980. "Neutestamentliche Haustafeln und Antike Ökonomie." *NTS* 27:83–97.

Ludwig, Helga. 1974. "Der Verfasser des Kolosserbriefes—Ein Schüler des Paulus." Theol. diss., University of Göttingen.
Lueken, Wilhelm. 1917. "Die Briefe an Philemon, an die Kolosser und an die Epheser." In *Die Schriften des Neuen Testaments*, edited by Johannes Weiss, et al., 2:358–83. 3rd ed. Göttingen: Vandenhoeck & Ruprecht.
Luz, Ulrich. 1989. "Überlegungen zum Epheserbrief und seiner Paränese." In *Neues Testament und Ethik: Für Rudolf Schnackenburg*, edited by Helmut Merklein, 376–96. Freiburg: Herder.
———. 1998a: *Der Brief an die Epheser*. NTD 8/1. Göttingen: Vandenhoeck & Ruprecht, 105–80.
———. 1998b: *Der Brief an die Kolosser*. NTD 8/1. Göttingen: Vandenhoeck & Ruprecht, 181–244.
Lyonnet, Stanislas. 1961. "La bénédiction de Eph 1,2–14 et son arrière-plan judaique." In *A la rencontre de dieu: Mémoriale A. Gelin*, 341–52. La Pay: Mappus.
MacDonald, Dennis Ronald. 1983. *The Legend and the Apostle: The Battle for Paul in Story and Canon*, Philadelphia: Westminster.
MacDonald, Margaret Y. 1988. *The Pauline Churches: A Socio-Historical Study of Institutionalization in the Pauline and Deutero-Pauline Writings*. SNTSMS 57. Cambridge: Cambridge University Press.
———. 1996. *Early Christian Women and Pagan Opinion: The Power of the Hysterical Woman*. Cambridge: Cambridge University Press.
Maclean, Jennifer Kay Berenson. 1995. "Ephesians and the Problem of Colossians: Interpretation of Texts and Traditions in Eph 1,1—2,10." PhD. diss., Harvard University.
Malherbe, Abraham J. 1988. *Ancient Epistolary Theorists*. SBLSBS 19. Atlanta: Scholars.
———. 1992. "Hellenistic Moralists and the New Testament." In *ANRW* II 26.1, 267–333. Berlin: de Gruyter.
Marshall, I. Howard, and Philip H. Towner. 1999. *A Critical and Exegetical Commentary on the Pastoral Epistles*. ICC. Edinburgh: T. & T. Clark.
Martin, Josef. 1974. *Antike Rhetorik: Technik und Methode*. HAW II.3. Munich: Beck.
Martin, Ralph P. 1967–68. "An Epistle in Search for a Life-Setting." *ExpT* 79:296–302.
Marxsen, Willi. 1978. *Einleitung in das Neue Testament*. 4th ed. Gütersloh: Mohn.
Masson, Charles. 1950. *L'Épître de Saint Paul aux Colossiens*. CNT(N) 10. Neuchâtel: Delachaux & Niestlé.
———. 1953. *L'Épître de Paul aux Éphésiens*. CNT(N) 9. Neuchâtel: Delachaux &Niestlé.
Mayerhoff, Ernst Theodor. 1938. *Der Brief an die Colosser mit vornehmlicher Berücksichtigung der drei Pastoralbriefe*. Edited by J. L. Mayerhoff. Berlin: Schultze.
McArthur, Harvey K. 1968–69. "καὶ Frequency in Greek Letters." *NTS* 15:339–49.
McNeile, A. H. 1927. *An Introduction to the Study of the New Testament*. Oxford: Oxford University Press.
McNeile, A. H., and C. S. C. Williams. 1953. *An Introduction to the Study of the New Testament*, 2nd ed. Oxford: Oxford University Press.
Meade, David G. 1986. *Pseudonymity and Canon*. WUNT 39. Tübingen: Mohr/Siebeck.
Mealand, David L. 1995. "The Extent of the Pauline Corpus: A Multivariate Approach." *JSNT* 59:61–92.
Meeks, Wayne A. 1974. "The Image of the Androgyne: Some Uses of a Symbol in Earliest Christianity." *HR* 13:165–208.

———. 1977. "In One Body: The Unity of Human Kind in Colossians and Ephesians." In *God's Christ and His People: Studies in Honour of Nils Alstrup Dahl*, edited by Jacob Jervell and W. A. Meeks, 209-21. Oslo: Universitetsforlaget.

———. 1983. *The First Urban Christians: The Social World of the Apostle Paul*. New Haven: Yale University Press.

Meeks, Wayne A., and Fred O. Francis, eds. 1973. *Conflict at Colossae*. SBLSBS 4. Missoula, MT: Scholars.

Meinertz, Max. 1931. *Der Epheserbrief.* HSNT 7. 4th ed. Bonn: Hanstein.

Merklein, Helmut. 1973a. *Das kirchliche Amt nach dem Epheserbrief.* StANT 33. Munich: Kösel.

———. 1973b. *Christus und die Kirche: Die theologische Grundstruktur des Epheserbriefes nach Eph 2,11-18*. SBS 66. Stuttgart: KBW.

———. 1981a. "Eph 4,1-5. 20 als Rezeption von Kol 3,1-17." In *Kontinuität und Einheit: Für Franz Mussner*, edited by Paul-Gerhard Müller und Werner Stenger, 194-210. Freiburg: Herder.

———. 1981b. "Paulinische Theologie in der Rezeption des Kolosser- und Epheserbriefes." In *Paulus in den neutestamentlichen Spätschriften*, edited by K. Kertelge, 25-69. Freiburg: Herder.

Michaelis, Wilhelm. 1954. *Einleitung in das Neue Testament*. 2nd ed. Bern: Haller.

Mill, J. 1707. *Novum Testamentum Graece*. Oxford: Oxford University Press..

Mitchell, Margaret M. 1991. *Paul and the Rhetoric of Reconciliation: An Exegetical Investigation of the Language and Composition of 1 Corinthians*. HUTh 28. Tübingen: Mohr/Siebeck.

———. 1992. "New Testament Envoys in the Context of Greco-Roman Diplomatic and Epistolary Conventions: The Example of Timothy and Titus." *JBL* 111:641-62.

———. 1998. "Brief. I. Form und Gattung; II. Schrifttum." In *RGG*, 1:1757-62. 4th ed. Tübingen: Mohr/Siebeck.

Mitton, C. Leslie. 1950. "The Relationship between I Peter and Ephesians." *JTS* N.S. 1:67-73.

———. 1951. *The Epistle to the Ephesians: Its Authorship, Origin and Purpose*. Oxford: Clarendon.

———. 1976. *Ephesians*. NCB. London: Oliphants.

Moffat, James. 1918. *An Introduction to the Literature of the New Testament*. 3rd ed. International Theological Library. Edinburgh: T. & T. Clark.

Molland, E. 1954/70. "The Heretics Combatted by Ignatius of Antioch." *JEH* 5:1-6. [Reprinted in *Opuscula Patristica*, 17-23. BTN 2. Oslo: Universitetsforlaget 1970.]

Morgenthaler, Robert. 1992. *Statistik des neutestamentlichen Wortschatzes*. 4th ed. Zurich: Gotthelf.

Moritz, Thorsten. 1996. *A Profound Mystery: The Use of the Old Testament in Ephesians*. NovTSup 85. Leiden: Brill.

Morton, A. Q. 1964. *Christianity and the Computer*. London: Hodder & Stoughton.

Mosbech, Holger. 1946-49. *Nytestamentlig Isagogik*. Copenhagen: Gyldendal.

Mosley, D. J. 1973. *Envoys and Diplomacy in Ancient Greece*. Historia: Einzelschriften 22. Wiesbaden: Steiner.

Moule, C. F. D. 1957. *The Epistles of Paul the Apostle to Colossians and to Philemon*. Cambridge: Cambridge University Press.

Moulton, J. H., and W. F. Howard. 1929. *A Grammar of New Testament Greek*. Vol. II, Edinburgh: T. & T. Clark [= Nachdruck 1986].

Moulton, J. H., and Nigel Turner. 1976. *A Grammar of New Testament Greek*. Vol. IV, Edinburgh: T. & T. Clark.
Mouton, E. 1996. "The Communicative Power of the Epistle to the Ephesians." In *Rhetoric, Scripture and Theology: Essays from the 1994 Pretoria Conference*, edited by Stanley E. Porter and Thomas H. Olbricht, 280–307. JSNTSup 131. Sheffield: JSOT Press.
Moxnes, Halvor. 1997. *Constructing Early Christian Families: Family as Social Reality and Metaphor*. London: Routledge.
Müller, Peter. 1988. *Die Anfänge der Paulusschule: Dargestellt am zweiten Thessalonicherbrief und am Kolosserbrief*. ATANT 74. Zurich: TVZ, 1988.
Müller, W. G. 1994. "Brief." In *Historisches Wörterbuch der Rhetorik*, edited by G. Ueding, 2:60–76, Darmstadt: Wissenschaftliche Buchgesellschaft.
Murphy-O'Connor, Jerome. 1965. "Who Wrote Ephesians." *The Bible Today* 18:1201–9.
Mussner, Franz. 1963. "Beiträge aus Qumran zum Verständnis des Epheserbriefes." In *Neutestamentliche Aufsätze: Festschrift für Prof. Josef Schmid zum 70. Geburtstag*, edited by J. Blinzler et al., 185–98. Regensburg: Pustet.
———. 1982a. *Der Brief an die Epheser*. ÖTK 10. Würzburg: Echter.
———. 1982b. "Epheserbrief." In *TRE*, 9:743–53, Berlin: de Gruyter.
Neudecker, Christian Gotthold. 1840. *Lehrbuch der historisch-kritischen Einleitung in das Neue Testament: mit Belegen aus den Quellenschriften*. Leipzig: Breitkopf.
Neugebauer, Fritz. 1961. *In Christus = En Christōi: Eine Untersuchung zum Paulinischen Glaubensver-ständnis*. Göttingen: Vandenhoeck & Ruprecht.
Nielsen, Charles M. 1965. "Polycarp, Paul and the Scriptures." *ATR* 47:199–216.
Noack, Bent. 1948. *Satanás und Sotería: Untersuchungen zur neutestamentlichen Dämonologie*. Copenhagen: Gad 1948.
Nock, Arthur Darby. 1937. *St. Paul*. New York: Harper.
Norden, Eduard. 1923. *Agnostos Theos: Untersuchungen zur Formengeschichte religiöser Rede*. 2nd ed. Stuttgart: Teubner 1923.
Oberlinner, Lorenz. 1994. *Die Pastoralbriefe: Erste Folge: Kommentar zum Ersten Timotheusbrief*. HThK XI.2/1. Freiburg: Herder.
———. 1995. *Die Pastoralbriefe. Zweite Folge: Kommentar zum Zweiten Timotheusbrief*. HThK XI.2/2. Freiburg: Herder.
Ochel, W. 1934. "Die Annahme einer Bearbeitung des Kolosser-Briefes im Epheser-Brief in einer Analyse des Epheser-Briefes untersucht." Diss. Marburg, Würzburg: Triltsch.
Ollrog, Wolf-Henning. 1979. *Paulus und seine Mitarbeiter: Untersuchungen zu Theorie und Praxis der paulinischen Mission*. WMANT 50. Neukirchen-Vluyn: Neukirchener.
Olsson, Birger. 1982. *Första Petrusbrevet*. KomNT 17. Stockholm: EFS.
Osiek, Carolyn, and David L. Balch. 1997. *Families in the New Testament World. Households and House Churches*. The Family, Religion, and Culture. Louisville: Westminster John Knox.
Pagels, Elaine H. 1975. *The Gnostic Paul. Gnostic Exegesis of the Pauline Letters*. Philadelphia: Fortress.
———. 1983. "Adam and Eve, Christ and the Church." In *The New Testament and Gnosis*, edited by A. H. B. Logan and A. J. M. Wedderburn, 146–75. Edinburgh: T. & T. Clark.

Pearson, Birger A. 1973. *The Pneumatikos-Psychikos Terminology in 1 Corinthians: A Study in the Theology of the Corinthian Opponents of Paul and Its Relation to Gnosticism*. SBLDS 12. Missoula, MT: Society of Biblical Literature.
Percy, Ernst. 1946. *Die Probleme der Kolosser- und Epheserbriefe*. Acta reg. Societas Humanorum Litterarum Lundensis 39. Lund: Gleerup 1946.
Petersen, Norman R. 1985. *Rediscovering Paul. Philemon and the Sociology of Paul's Narrative World*. Reprinted, Eugene, OR: Wipf & Stock, 2008.
Pfleiderer, Otto. 1890. *Der Paulinismus*. 2nd ed. Leipzig: Reisland.
Plett, Heinrich F. 1975. *Einführung in die rhetorische Textanalyse*. 3rd ed. Hamburg: Buske.
Pokorný, Petr. 1965. *Der Epheserbrief und die Gnosis: Die Bedeutung des Haupt-Glieder-Gedankens in der entstehenden Kirche*. Berlin: EVA.
———. 1987. *Der Brief des Paulus an die Kolosser*. ThHK 10/1. Berlin: EVA.
———. 1992. *Der Brief des Paulus an die Epheser*. ThHK 10/2. Leipzig: EVA.
Polhill, John B. 1973. "The Relationship between Ephesians and Colossians." *RExp* 70:439–50.
Porter, Stanley E., ed. 1997. *Handbook of Classical Rhetoric in the Hellenistic Period 330 B.C.–A.D. 400*. Leiden: Brill.
Prostmeier, Ferdinand-Rupert. 1999. *Der Barnabasbrief*. KAV 8. Göttingen: Vandenhoeck & Ruprecht.
Räisänen, Heikki. 1995. "The Clash between Christian Styles of Life in Revelation." In *Mighty Minorities? Minorities in Early Christianity—Positions and Strategies. Essays in Honour of Jacob Jervell on His 70th Birthday 21 May 1995*, edited by David Hellholm et al., 151–66. Oslo: Scandinavian University Press.
Reed, J. T. 1997. "The Epistle." In S. E. Porter, ed., 1997:171–93.
Rensberger, D. K. 1981. "As the Apostle Teaches: The Development of the Use of Paul's Letters in Second-Century Christianity." PhD diss., Yale University.
Resch, Alfred. 1906/67. *Agrapha: Außerkanonische Schriftfragmente*. 2nd ed. Leipzig: Hinrichs. Reprint, Darmstadt Wissenschaftliche Buchgesellschaft, 1967.
Richards, E. Randolph. 1991. *The Secretary in the Letters of Paul*. WUNT 2/42. Tübingen: Mohr/Siebeck.
Rigaux, Béda. 1964. *Paulus und seine Briefe: Der Stand der Forschung*. BiH 2. Munich: Kösel.
Robinson, J. Armitage. 1904. *St. Paul's Epistle to the Ephesians*. 2nd ed. London: Macmillan.
Roller, Otto Konrad. 1933. *Das Formular der paulinischen Briefe: Ein Beitrag zur Lehre von antiken Briefen*. BWANT 58. Stuttgart: Kohlhammer.
Roloff, Jürgen. 1984. *Die Offenbarung des Johannes*. ZBK 18. Zurich: TVZ.
———. 1988. *Der erste Brief an Timotheus*. EKK 15. Neukirchen-Vluyn: Neukirchener.
———. 1999. "Zur matthäischen Deutung der Winzerparabel (Mt 21, 42–44)." In *Das Urchristentum in seiner literarischen Geschichte: Festschrift für Jürgen Becker zum 65. Geburtstag*, edited by Ulrich Mell und Ulrich B. Müller, 247–62. BZNW 100. Berlin: de Gruyter.
Roon, A. van. 1974. *The Authenticity of Ephesians*. NTSup 39. Leiden: Brill 1974.
Rudolph, Kurt. 1980. *Die Gnosis. Wesen und Geschichte einer spätantiken Religion*, 2nd ed. Göttingen: Vandenhoeck & Ruprecht.
Sampley, J. Paul. 1971. *"And the Two Shall Become One Flesh": A Study of Traditions in Eph 5:21–33*. SNTSMS 16. Cambridge: Cambridge University Press.

Sandelin, K.-G. 1976. *Die Auseinandersetzung mit der Weisheit in 1. Korinther 15*. MSÅÅ 12. Åbo: Åbo Akademi.
Sanders, E. P. 1966. "Literary Dependence in Colossians." *JBL* 85:28–45.
Sanders, J. N. 1956. "The Case for the Pauline Authorship." In *Studies in Ephesians*, edited by F. L. Cross, 9–20. London: Mowbray.
Sanders, Jack T. 1965. "Hymnic Elements in Ephesians 1–3." *ZNW* 56:214–32.
Sandnes, Karl Olav. 1994. *A New Family: Conversion and Ecclesiology in the Early Church with Cross-Cultural Comparisons*. Studien zur Interkulturellen Geschichte des Christentums 91. Bern: Lang.
Santer, Mark. 1969. "The Text of Ephesians i.1." *NTS* 15:247–48.
Schenke, Hans-Martin. 1973. "Die neutestamentliche Christologie und der gnostische Erlöser." In *Gnosis und Neues Testament: Studien aus Religionswissenschaft und Theologie*, edited by Karl-Wolfgang Tröger, 205–29. Berlin: EVA.
———. 1974–75. "Das Weiterwirken des Paulus und die Pflege seines Erbes durch die Paulus-Schule." *NTS* 21:505–18.
Schenke, Hans-Martin, and Karl Martin Fischer. 1978. *Einleitung in die Schriften des Neuen Testaments. I: Die Briefe des Paulus und Schriften des Paulinismus*. Berlin: EVA.
Schille, Gottfried. 1957. "Der Autor des Epheserbriefes." *ThLZ* 82:325–34.
———. 1965. *Frühchristliche Hymnen*. Berlin: EVA.
Schleiermacher, Friedrich. 1895. *Einleitung in das Neue Testament*. Sämtliche Werke I. Berlin: Reimer.
Schlier, Heinrich. 1929. *Religionsgeschichtliche Untersuchungen zu den Ignatiusbriefen*. BZNW 8. Berlin: Töpelmann.
———. 1930. *Christus und die Kirche im Epheserbrief*. BHTh 6. Tübingen: Mohr/Siebeck.
———. 1963. *Der Brief an die Epheser: Ein Kommentar*. 4th ed. Düsseldorf: Patmos.
Schmauch, Werner. 1935. *In Christus: Eine Untersuchung zur Sprache und Theologie des Paulus*. NTF Paulusstudien 1/9. Gütersloh: Bertelsmann.
Schmid, Josef. 1928. *Der Epheserbrief des Apostels Paulus, seine Adresse, Sprache und literarischen Beziehungen*. BSt 22/3–4. Freiburg: Herder.
Schmiedel, P. W. 1885. "Kolossae II." In *Allgemeine Encyclopädie der Wissenschaften und Künste, IIe Section, 37er Theil*, edited by J. S. Ersch and J. G. Gruber, 139ff. Leipzig: Brockhaus.
Schnackenburg, Rudolf. 1982. *Der Brief an die Epheser*. EKK 10. Neukirchen-Vluyn: Neukirchener.
Schneemelcher, Wilhelm. 1989a. "Der Laodicenerbrief." In Schneemelcher, ed., 41–44.
———. 1989b. "Paulusakten." In Schneemelcher, ed., 1989, 193–214.
Schneemelcher, Wilhelm, ed. 1989. *Neutestamentliche Apokryphen. II. Band: Apostolisches, Apokalypsen und Verwandtes*, 5th ed. Edited by Edgar Hennecke. Tübingen: Mohr/Siebeck.
Schnelle, Udo. 1996. *Einleitung in das Neue Testament*. UTB 1830. 2nd ed. Göttingen: Vandenhoeck & Ruprecht.
Schnider, Franz, and Werner Stenger. 1987. *Studien zum neutestamentlichen Briefformular*. NTTS 11. Leiden: Brill.
Schoedel, William R. 1985. *Ignatius of Antioch*. Hermeneia. Philadelphia: Fortress.
Scholem, Gershom. 1946. *Major Trends in Jewish Mysticism*. New York: Schocken.

———. 1965. *Jewish Gnosticism, Merkabah Mysticism, and Talmudic Tradition*. 2nd ed. New York: Jewish Theological Seminary.
Schottroff, Luise. 1970. *Der Glaubende und die feindliche Welt: Beobachtungen zum gnostischen Dualismus und seiner Bedeutung für Paulus und das Johannesevangelium*. WMANT 37. Neukirchen-Vluyn: Neukirchener.
Schrage, Wolfgang. 1991. *Der erste Brief an die Korinther (1 Kor 1,1—6,11)*. EKK 7/1. Neukirchen-Vluyn: Neukirchener.
———. 1995. *Der erste Brief an die Korinther (1 Kor 6,12—11,16)*. EKK 7/2. Neukirchen-Vluyn: Neukirchener.
———. 1999. *Der erste Brief an die Korinther (1 Kor 11,17—14,40)*. EKK 7/3. Neukirchen-Vluyn: Neukirchener.
Schubert, Paul. 1939. *Form and Function of the Pauline Thanksgivings*. BZNW 20. Berlin: Töpelmann.
Schüssler Fiorenza, Elisabeth. 1973. "Apocalyptic and Gnosis in Revelation." *JBL* 92:567–74.
Schwegler, Albert. 1846. *Das nachapostolische Zeitalter in dem Hauptmoment seiner Entwicklung*. 2 vols. Tübingen: Fues 1846.
Schweizer, Eduard. 1963. "Zur Frage der Echtheit des Kolosser- und des Epheserbriefes." In *Neotestamentica*, 429. Zurich: Zwingli.
———. 1976. *Der Brief an die Kolosser*. EKK 12. Neukirchen-Vluyn: Neukirchener.
Seeberg, Alfred. 1966. *Der Katechismus der Urchristenheit*. With an introduction by F. Hahn. ThB 26. Munich: Kaiser.
Seim, T. Karlsen. 1995. "A Superior Minority? The Problem of Men's Headship in Ephesians 5." In *Mighty Minorities? Minorities in Early Christianity—Positions and Strategies*, edited by David Hellholm, 167–81. Oslo: ScUP.
Sellin, Gerhard. 1986. *Der Streit um die Auferstehung der Toten: Eine religionsgeschichtliche und exegetische Untersuchung von 1 Korinther 15*. FRLANT 138. Göttingen: Vandenhoeck & Ruprecht.
———. 1992. "Über einige ungewöhnliche Genitive im Epheserbrief." *ZNW* 83:85–107.
———. 1996. "Die Paränese des Epheserbriefes." In *Gemeinschaft am Evangelium: Festschrift für Wiard Popkes zum 60. Geburtstag*, edited by Edwin Brandt et al., 281–300. Leipzig: EVA.
———. 1998. "Adresse und Intention des Epheserbriefes." In *Paulus, Apostel Jesu Christi: Festschrift für Günter Klein zum 70. Geburtstag*, edited by Michael Trowitzsch, 171–86. Tübingen: Mohr/Siebeck.
———. 1999. "Epheserbrief." In *RGG*, 2:1344–47. 4th ed. Tübingen: Mohr/Siebeck.
Selwyn, Edward Gordon. 1947. *The First Epistle of St. Peter*. 2nd ed. London: Macmillan.
Shimada, K. 1991. "Is 1 Peter Dependent on Ephesians? A Critique of C. L. Mitton." *AJBI* 17:77–106.
Smith, Derwood C. 1970. "Jewish and Greek Traditions in Ephesians 2:11–22." PhD diss., Yale University.
———. 1973. "The Two Made One." *OJRS* 1:34–54.
———. 1977. "The Ephesian Heresy and the Origin of the Epistle to the Ephesians." *OJRS* 5:78–103.
Smith, Morton. 1951. *Tannaitic Parallels to the Gospels*. JBLMS 6. Philadelphia: SBL.
Soden, Hermann von. 1885. "Der Kolosserbrief." *JPT* 11:320–68, 497–542, 672–702.
———. 1893a: *Der Brief an die Kolosser*. HC 3. 2nd ed. Leipzig: Mohr/Siebeck.

———. 1893b: *Der Brief an die Epheser* (HC 3), 2nd ed. Leipzig: Mohr/Siebeck.
Speyer, Wolfgang. 1971. *Die literarische Fälschung im heidnischen und christlichen Altertum*. HAW I.2. Munich: Beck.
Standhartinger, Angela. 1999. *Studien zur Entstehungsgeschichte und Intention des Kolosserbriefes*. NovTSup 94. Leiden: Brill.
Stirewalt, M. L., Jr. 1993. *Studies in Ancient Greek Epistolography*. SBLSBS 27. Atlanta: Scholars.
Stowers, Stanley K. 1995. "7.7–25 as a Speech-in-Character (προσωποποιία)." In *Paul in His Hellenistic Context*, edited by T. Engberg-Pedersen, 180–202. Minneapolis: Fortress.
———. 1998. "A Cult from Philadelphia: Oikos Religion or Cultic Association?" In A. J. Malherbe/F. W. Norris/J. W. Thompson (Hrsg.), *The Early Church in Its Context: Essays in Honor of Everett Ferguson*, edited by Abraham J. Malherbe et al., 287–301. NovTSup 90. Leiden: Brill.
Strecker, Georg. 1980. "Judenchristentum und Gnosis." In *Altes Testament, Frühjudentum, Gnosis*, edited by Karl-Wolfgang Tröger, 261–82. Gütersloh: Mohn.
———. 1989. "Die neutestamentlichen Haustafeln (Kol 3,18—4,1 und Eph 5,22—6,9)." In *Neues Testament und Ethik: Für Rudolf Schnackenburg*, edited by H. Merklein, 349–75. Freiburg: Herder.
———. 1992. *Literaturgeschichte des Neuen Testaments*. UTB 1682. Göttingen: Vandenhoeck & Ruprecht.
———. 1996. *Theologie des Neuen Testaments*. Edited and expanded by F. W. Horn. GLB. Berlin: de Gruyter.
Stroker, William D. 1970. "The Formation of Secondary Sayings of Jesus." PhD diss., Yale University.
Stuhlmacher, Peter. 1975. *Der Brief an Philemon*. EKK. Neukirchen-Vluyn: Neukirchener.
Sykutris, J. 1931. "Epistolographie." In *RE Suppl.* 5:185–220. Stuttgart: Metzler.
Synge, F. C. 1941. *St. Paul's Epistle to the Ephesians: A Theological Commentary*. London: SPCK.
———. 1958. *Philippians and Colossians: Introduction and Commentary*. TBC. 2nd ed. London: SCM.
Tcherikover, Victor A. 1957. *Corpus Papyrorum Judaicarum*. Vol. 1. Cambridge: Harvard University Press.
Thomas, Johannes. 1992. *Der jüdische Phokylides: Formgeschichtliche Zugänge zu Pseudo-Phokylides und Vergleich mit der neutestamentlichen Paränese*. NTOA 23. Göttingen: Vandenhoeck & Ruprecht.
Thompson, G. H. P. 1967. *The Letters of Paul to the Ephesians, to the Colossians, and to Philemon*. CBC. Cambridge: Cambridge University Press.
Thraede, Klaus. 1970. *Grundzüge griechisch-römischer Brieftopik*. Zetemata 48. Munich: Beck.
———. 1980. "Zum historischen Hintergrund der 'Haustafeln' des NT." In *Pietas: Festschrift für Bernhard Kötting*, Ernst Dassmann und K. Suso Frank, 359–68. JAC.E 8. Münster: Aschendorff.
Thurén, Lauri. 1990. *The Rhetorical Strategy of 1 Peter: With Special Regard to Ambiguous Expressions*. Åbo: ÅAP.
Thyen, Hartwig. 1955. *Der Stil der Jüdisch-Hellenistischen Homilie*. FRLANT 65. Göttingen: Vandenhoeck & Ruprecht.

Trevett, Christine. 1980. "Ignatius and His Opponents in the Divided Church in Antioch." PhD diss., University of Sheffield.
———. 1983. "Prophecy and Anti-Episcopal Activity: A Third Error Combatted by Ignatius?" *JEH* 34:1–18.
Trobisch, David. 1989. *Die Entstehung der Paulusbriefsammlung: Studien zu den Anfängen christlicher Publizistik*. NTOA 10. Göttingen: Vandenhoeck & Ruprecht, 1989.
———. 1994. *Die Paulusbriefe und die Anfänge der christlichen Publizistik*. KT 135. Gütersloh: Kaiser 1994.
———. 1996. *Die Endredaktion des Neuen Testaments. Eine Untersuchung zur Entstehung der christlichen Bibel*. NTOA 31. Göttingen: Vandenhoeck & Ruprecht.
Tröger, Karl-Wolfgang. 1980. "Gnosis und Judentum." In *Altes Testament, Frühjudentum, Gnosis: Neue Studien zu "Gnosis und Bibel,"* edited by Karl-Wolfgang Tröger, 155–68. Berlin: EVA.
Übelacker, Walter G. 1989. *Der Hebräerbrief als Appell. I. Untersuchungen zu exordium, narratio und postscriptum (Hebr 1–2 und 13,22–25)*. CBNT 21. Stockholm: Almqvist & Wiksell.
Ueding, Gert, ed. 1992ff.: *Historisches Wörterbuch der Rhetorik*. Vol. 1, 1992; Vol. 2, 1994; Vol. 3, 1996; Vol. 4, 1998. Darmstadt: Wissenschaftliche Buchgesellschaft.
Ulrichsen, Jarl Henning. 1995. "Die Auferstehungsleugner in Korinth: Was meinten sie eigentlich?" In *Texts and Contexts: Biblical Texts in Their Textual and Situational Contexts. Essays in Honor of Lars Hartman*, edited by Tord Fornberg and David Hellholm, 781–99. Oslo: Scandinavian University Press.
Unnik, W. C. van. 1978. "Gnosis und Judentum." In *Gnosis: Festschrift für Hans Jonas*, edited by Barbara Aland, 65–86. Göttingen: Vandenhoeck & Ruprecht.
Usami, Kôshi. 1983. *Somatic Comprehension of Unity: The Church in Ephesus*. AnBib 101. Rome: Biblical Institute Press.
Ussher, J. 1654. *Annales Vesteris et Novi Testamenti II*. London: Crook.
Usteri, Johann Martin. 1887. *Wissenschaftlicher und praktischer Commentar über den ersten Petrusbrief*. Zurich: Hohr.
Usteri, L. 1824. *Entwicklung des paulinischen Lehrbegriffs mit Hinsicht auf die übrigen Schriften des Neuen Testamentes*, Zurich: Orell, Füsli.
Vanhoye, Albert. 1978. "L'épître aux Éphésiens et l'épître aux Hébreux." *Bib* 59:198–230.
Verburg, W. 1996. *Endzeit und Entschlafene: syntaktisch-sigmatische, semantische und pragmatische Analyse von 1 Kor 15*. FzB 78. Würzburg: Echter.
Verner, David C. 1983. *The Household of God: The Social World of the Pastoral Epistles*. SBLDS 71. Chico, CA: Scholars.
Vielhauer, Philipp. 1975. *Geschichte der urchristlichen Literatur: Einleitung in das Neue Testament, die Apokryphen und die Apostolischen Väter*. GLB. Berlin: de Gruyter.
Wagenführer, Max Adolf,. 1941. *Die Bedeutung Christi für die Welt und Kirche: Studien zum Kolosser- und Epheserbrief*. Leipzig: Wigand 1941.
Walter, N. 1998. "Leibliche Auferstehung? Zur Frage der Hellenisierung der Auferweckungs-hoffnung bei Paulus." In *Paulus, Apostel Jesu Christi: Festschrift für Günter Klein*, edited by Michael Trowitzsch, 109–27. Tübingen: Mohr/Siebeck.
Webber, Robert D. 1970. "The Concept of Rejoicing in Paul." PhD diss., Yale University.
Weichert, Valentinus. 1910. *Demetrii et Libanii qui ferunter Τύποι Ἐπιστολικοί et Ἐπιστολιμαῖοι Χαρακτῆρες*. Leipzig: Teubner.

Weiss, Hans-Friedrich. 1973. "Gnostische Motive und antignostische Polemik im Kolosser- und Epheserbrief." In *Gnosis und Neues Testament: Studien aus Religionswissenschaft und Theologie*, edited by Karl-Wolfgang Tröger, 311–24. Berlin: EVA.
———. 1991. *Der Brief an die Hebräer*. KEK 13. Göttingen: Vandenhoeck & Ruprecht.
Weiss, Johannes. 1910/70. *Der erste Korintherbrief*. 9th ed. KEK 5. Göttingen: Vandenhoeck & Ruprecht.
———. 1912. "Literaturgeschichte, Urchristlich." In *RGG*, 3:2208–10. 1st ed. Tübingen: Mohr/Siebeck.
———. 1917. *Das Urchristentum*. Göttingen: Vandenhoeck & Ruprecht.
Weisse, Christian Hermann. 1867. *Beiträge zur Kritik der paulinischen Briefe a. d. Gl., R., Eph. und Kol.* Edited by E. Sulze. Leipzig: Hirzel.
Weiszäcker, Carl von. 1902. *Das apostolische Zeitalter der christlichen Kirche*. 3rd ed. Tübingen: Mohr/Siebeck.
Wendland, Paul. 1912. *Die urchristlichen Literaturformen*. HNT 1.3. Tübingen: Mohr/Siebeck.
Wengst, Klaus. 1972. *Christologische Formeln und Lieder des Urchristentums*. StNT 7. Gütersloh: Mohn.
Westcott, B. F. 1906. *Saint Paul's Epistle to the Ephesians*. London: Macmillan.
Wettstein, J. J. 1751–52/1962. *Novum Testamentum Graecum*. 2 vols. Amsterdam: Dommerian. Reprint, Graz: Akademische Druck- und Verlagsanstalt 1962.]
White, John L. 1972a: *The Form and Function of the Body of the Greek Letter: A Study of the Letter-Body in the Non-Literary Papyri and in Paul the Apostle*. SBLDS 2. Missoula, MT: Scholars.
———. 1972b: *The Form and Structure of the Official Petition: A Study in Greek Epistolography*. SBLDS 5. Missoula, MT: Scholars.
———. 1984. "New Testament Epistolary Literature in the Framework of Ancient Epistolography." In *ANRW* 25.2:1730–56. Berlin: de Gruyter.
———. 1986. *Light from Ancient Letters*. Foundations and Facets. Philadelphia: Fortress.
———. 1988. "Ancient Greek Letters." In *Greco Roman Literature and the New Testament*, edited by David E. Aune, 85–105. SBLSBS 21. Atlanta: Scholars.
Wifstrand, Albert. 1967. *Die alte Kirche und die griechische Bildung*. Dalp Taschenbücher 388 D. Munich: Francke.
Wikenhauser, Alfred. 1953. *Einleitung in das Neue Testament*. Freiburg: Herder.
Wikenhauser, Alfred, and Josef Schmid. 1973. *Einleitung in das Neue Testament*. 6th ed. Freiburg: Herder.
Wilson, Walter T. 1994. *The Mysteries of Righteousness: The Literary Composition and Genre of the Sentences of Pseudo-Phokylides*. TStAJ 40. Tübingen: Mohr/Siebeck.
———. 1997. *The Hope of Glory: Education and Exhortation in the Epistle to the Colossians*. NovTSup 88. Leiden: Brill.
Wire, Antoinette C. 1990. *The Corinthian Women Prophets: A Reconstruction through Paul's Rhetoric*. Reprint, Eugene, OR: Wipf & Stock, 2003.
Wolff, Christian. 1996. *Der erste Brief des Paulus an die Korinther*. THK 7. Leipzig: EVA.
Wolter, Michael. 1987. "Verborgene Weisheit und Heil für die Heiden. Zur Traditionsgeschichte und Intention des 'Revelationsschemas.'" *ZTK* 84:297–319.
———. 1993. *Der Brief an die Kolosser. Der Brief an Philemon*. ÖTK 12. Würzburg: Echter.
Zahn, Theodor. 1873. *Ignatius von Antiochien*. Gotha: Perthes.

———. 1897–99. *Einleitung in das Neue Testament.* Leipzig: Deichert.
Zelzer, M. 1997. "Epistel G-H." In *Der Neue Pauly: Enzyklopädie der Antike*, edited by H. Cancik and H. Schneider, 3:1164–66. Stuttgart: Metzler.
Zuntz, Günther. 1953: *The Text of the Epistles: A Disquisition upon the Corpus Paulinum.* Schweich Lectures of the Britisch Academy 1946. London: Oxford University Press.

General Bibliography

THIS BIBLIOGRAPHY INCLUDES WORKS for which the footnotes will list only author and page number (except in those cases where the author has more than one book on this list). The bibliography also includes some general works on Paul, which are recommended to the attention of students, even though I have not frequently referred to them.

Bjerkelund, Carl J. *Parakalo: Form, Function und Sinn der parakalō-Sätze in den paulinischen Briefen.* Bibliotheca theologica Norvegica 1. Oslo: Oslo University Press, 1967.
Bornkamm, Günther. *Paul.* Translated by D. M. G. Stalker. New York: Harper & Row, 1971.
Bultmann, Rudolf. *The Theology of the New Testament.* 2 vols. Translated by Kendrick Grobel. New York: Scribner, 1951-55.
Dahl, Nils A. *The Crucified Messiah and Other Essays.* Minneapolis: Augsburg, 1974.
———. *Jesus in the Memory of the Early Church.* Minneapolis: Augsburg, 1976.
Davies, W. D. *Paul and Rabbinic Judaism.* London: SPCK, 1948. 2nd.ed. 1958.
Farmer, William R. et al., eds. *Christian History and Interpretation: Studies Presented to John Knox.* Cambridge University Press, 1967.
Fridrichsen, Anton. *The Apostle and His Message.* UUÅ, 1947, 3. Uppsala: Almqvist & Wicksell, 1947.
Hurd, J. C., *The Origin of I Corinthians.* New York: Seabury, 1965.
Käsemann, Ernst. *An die Römer.* HNT 8A. Tübingen: Mohr/Siebeck, 1973. 2nd ed., 1974. 4th ed., 1980.
———. *Commentary on Romans.* Translated and edited by Geoffrey W. Bromiley. Grand Rapids: Eerdmans, 1980.
———. *New Testament Questions of Today.* Philadelphia: Fortress, 1969.
———. *Perspectives on Paul.* Translated by Margaret Kohl, Philadelphia: Fortress, 1971.
Knox, W. L. *St. Paul and the Church of the Gentiles.* Cambridge: Cambridge University Press, 1939.
Kümmel, Werner Georg. *Introduction to the New Testament.* Rev. ed. Translated by Howard Clark Kee. Nashville: Abingdon, 1975.

Malherbe, Abraham J. *Social Aspects of Early Christianity*. 1977. Reprint, Eugene, OR: Wipf & Stock, 2015.
Meeks, Wayne A., ed. *The Writings of St. Paul*. New York: Norton, 1972.
Munck, Johannes. *Paul and the Salvation of Mankind*. Translated by Frank Clarke. Richmond: John Knox, 1959.
———. *Christ & Israel: An Interpretation of Romans 9–11*. Translated by Ingeborg Nixon. Philadelphia: Fortress, 1967.
Ridderbos, Herman. *Paul: An Outline of His Theology*. Translated by John Richard DeWitt. Grand Rapids: Eerdmans, 1975.
Rigaux, Béda. *The Letters of St. Paul: Modern Studies*. Translated by Stephen Yonick. Herald Scriptural Library. Chicago: Franciscan Herald, 1968.
Roetzel, Calvin J. *The Letters of Paul*. Atlanta: John Knox, 1975.
Sanders, E. P. *Paul and Palestinian Judaism*. Philadelphia: Fortress, 1977.
Schoeps, Hans-Joachim. *Paul: The Theology of the Apostle in the Light of Jewish Religious History*. Translated by Harold Knight. Philadelphia: Westminster, 1961.
Schubert, Paul. *The Form and Function of the Pauline Thanksgivings*. BZNW 20. Berlin: Töpelmann, 1939.
Schweitzer, Albert. *Paul and His Interpreters*. Translated by W. Montgomery. New York: Macmillan, 1951.
———. *The Mysticism of Paul the Apostle*. Translated by W. Montgomery. New York: Macmillan, 1955.
Stendahl, Krister. *Paul among Jews and Gentiles, and Other Essays*. Philadelphia: Fortress, 1976.

Index

OLD TESTAMENT

Genesis

1–3	272
1:3	127n5
1:26–27	127n5
1:26f	240
1:27	134, 134n14, 165, 233, 233n209
2:24	165, 210, 233n209, 240, 260, 271, 271n363, 271n365, 272, 282, 282n405, 284
3:15	131n12
4:25	131n12
6:6–8	169
6:6–7	169
12:3	133, 170
15	135, 170n17
15:6	80, 108, 109, 130, 133, 170, 171n18
15:6 LXX	108
15:7	130
15:13	170n17
15:18	130
19:32	131n12
22	132, 172
22:13	132
22:16–18	133
22:18	132, 172, 172n20
22:18 LXX	132
28:4	132, 172
49:10	131, 131n12, 132n13, 173

Exodus

9:16	164
12	145, 146n28
12:5	164
12:15	163, 163n5, 164
12:21	163n6
12:41	164
15:2	170n17
15:11	187
16:18	187n22
20:2	28n22
20:5–6	183, 186, 187n24
20:22	91, 152n39
29:18	164n8
32–34	240
33:19	173n22
34:1	145
34:6–7	127n5
34:23	91, 152n39
34:33 (35)	184
34:34	139n3
	139, 139n3

Leviticus

13:37	163n6
18:5	136, 149, 162, 170, 171, 172n20, 176, 176n26, 177n28

Leviticus (continued)

18:51	174
19:18	240, 260
23:10–16	163n6
26:11	128n6

Numbers

7:89	163n5
12:7–8	127n5
15:17–21	152n40
23:19	167, 168, 169

Deuteronomy

	164, 181
4:7	187n22
4:8	187n22
4:37ff	181n8
6:4	181, 184, 184n19, 187n22
8:5	167, 168, 169
9:4	149
11:12	185
14:2	181n8
16	164
16:2	163
16:8	163n6
16:12	164n8
21	133
21:23	132, 172
24:1	165
26:17	187
26:18	187
27:15–26	134n16
27:26	133, 171
28:1–14	171
28:15–68	134n16
29:3 MT	151n37
29:4	151n37
30:11ff	149
30:11	149
30:12–14	149, 176n26
30:12f	149n34
30:14	148n32, 149
31:6	150n36
32	150n35
32:21	150, 150n35, 151, 154n46
32:39	181
32:43	123n1
33:2	187n23, 187n24
33:29	187n22

Joshua

1:5	150n36

1 Samuel

12:22	150n36

2 Samuel

7	129
7:10	131n12
7:12ff	131n12
7:12–14	128
7:12	131n12, 172
7:14	128n7, 129n9
23:1	187

1 Kings

9:3	185

2 Kings

21:12	184, 184n19

1 Chronicles

17:21	187n22

2 Chronicles

35	163

Ezra

2:63	173n21

Nehemiah

7:65	173n21
9:8	129

Job

12:12	185
15:8	157n54
38:26f	185
41:3	157n54
41:3 MT	157n54

Psalms

	97, 230
2	240
4:5	230
8:7	247, 256
18(17):49	123n1
22:7	94n31
31(32):1f LXX	108
40:7	240
50:7	183, 184, 184n18
51:4	129
67:19 LXX	210
68:18	240
68:19	210, 260
68:36	186
69	151n37
69:23–24	151n37
69:29	94n31
69:30	94n31
73:2	94n31
89:18	187n22
94:14	150n36
106 (107):26 LXX	149
110	240
110:1	247, 256
112:9	37
117(116):1	123n1
118	240n250
118:22	148n32
119 LXX	240n250
121:4	185
143:2	171n18
143:2 (LXX 142:2)	106

Proverbs

8	149n34
15:3	185

Isaiah

1:9	147
6:9–10	151n37
8:14	148, 148n32
10:5	146n27
10:22–23	147
11:4–5	240
11:10 LXX	123n1
11:16	153n41
11:52–57	240
13:5	146n27
27:9	154
28:16	148, 148n32, 149, 240, 240n250
29	151n37
29:10	151n37
29:16	145n26
41:3	157n54
41:8	181n8
43:10	181n8
44:1f	181n8
44:6	181
45:9	145n26, 181
49:3	187n22
49:9	66
52:7	142n17, 149, 240
52:11	128n6
52:15	142n17
53:1	142n17, 149
55:10	37
57:9	260
57:19	240
59:19	240
59:20–21	154
59:21	154n47
65:1–2	150

Jeremiah

	185
1:5	185, 186
10:7	185, 186
18:1–6	145n26
21:34f	128n6
23:2	184
27:25 LXX	146n27
27(50):25 LXX	146n28
31	154
31:31–34	127n5

Jeremiah (continued)

31:33	127n5
31:37	150n36
32:27	184, 185
50:25	146
50:25 MT	146n27

Ezekiel

36:26	127n5
37:27	128n6

Daniel

3:26–45	213n87
9:11	134n16

Hosea

	147, 148
1:10	147n29
1:10 MT	147n29
2:1	147n29
2:1 MT	147n29
2:23	147n29
2:25 MT	147n29
10:12	37

Joel

2:32	148n32
3:5 (2:32)	149
3:5 MT	148n32

Amos

3:8	186

Habakkuk

2:4	107, 109, 134, 136, 162, 171, 171n18, 172n20, 176, 177n28
2:4 LXX	107

Zechariah

4:10b	185
13:9	184

Malachi

1:2–3	145
2:10	180

NEW TESTAMENT

Matthew

5:39f	26n16
6:14	238n241
7:21f	287n426
10:9	32n32
10:9–14	32n33
11:29	238n241
13:47–50	287n426
15:8f	151n37
15:11	238n241
16:18	258n307
19:3–9	165
21:42–44	240n250
24:14	155n50
24:47	23n6
25:35–36	48
27:40	151n37

Mark

	263
6:8–11	32n33
12:35–37	162
13:10	155n50
13:33	238n241
14:38	238n241

Luke

6:27–29	49
9:3–5	32n33
10:4–11	32n33
10:7	32n32
11:21	23n6
12:33	23n6
12:35	238n241
18:14	101
20:17f	240n250
24:48	72n5

INDEX 317

John

	161n2, 237
1:1ff	149n34
3:13	236
3:20	236
5:21–26	236
8:31	287n426
10:16	236
11:50–52	236
17:22–23	236

Acts

	6, 26, 34, 35, 42, 72n5, 217, 235, 262, 267n348
2:32	72n5
2:44–47	29n25
3:15	72n5
4:36–37	35n41
5:30f	132
5:32	72n5
6:1–6	29n25
9	72n5
10:39	72n5
10:39f	132
10:41	72n5
12:12	262
12:25	262
13:5	262
13:13	262
13:31	72n5
13:33	122
13:38f	96
15:37	262
15:39	262
16:15	26n18
17	1
18	2
18:3	34n38
18:8	26n18
19:29	262
20:4	262
20:17	234
20:18–36	234
20:18–35	235
20:19	234
20:28	234
20:29f	285n415
20:32	234
22	3, 72n5
22:3	3n3
22:28	35n40
23:16–22	35n40
26	72n5
26:16–18	234, 235
26:18	234, 235
27:2	262

Romans

	70–85, 96, 139, 141, 143, 174, 203n45, 205, 205n57, 209, 210, 211, 212, 238, 241, 242, 246, 251, 266n338
1–14	266
1–11	158
1–8	140, 142, 144
1–4	81, 89, 140
1–3	241
1–2	80n18, 88
1:1–7	74
1:1–6	72n5, 128, 142n17, 190
1:1–3	128
1:1–2	128
1:2–6	78, 87
1:2–4	131
1:2	129n10
1:3–4	128, 129, 129n9
1:7	266, 268n351
1:7a	75
1:8–17	78
1:8	141n9
1:9–15	142n17
1:10	76n13
1:12	76, 77, 254n292
1:13–14	75
1:13	76, 141n15, 142n16
1:14	78
1:15–18	78

318 INDEX

Romans (*continued*)

1:15	77, 141n15, 266, 268n351
1:16—15:13	82
1:16—11:36	205
1:16—5:21	81
1:16ff	82
1:16-18	78, 79
1:16-17	78, 129, 179, 190
1:16	79, 82, 87, 140, 142
1:16b—11:33	205n57
1:17—8:39	141
1:17-18	82
1:17	79, 80, 98, 107, 129n10, 171n18
1:18—3:26	158n56
1:18—3:20	79, 85
1:18—2:11	56, 80
1:18ff	191, 257n302
1:18-31	239
1:18	78
1:19ff	190
1:19-32	79
1:24ff	84
1:29	21n1
1:32	79
2:1—3:9	141n14
2:1-5	79
2:1	79
2:6-11	79
2:11	80n18, 239
2:12-29	79, 80
2:13	80
2:14-16	80
2:14-15	190
2:17ff	84
2:17-24	80
2:17-20	135
2:17	189
2:25-29	80, 190
2:26-29	257
2:29	247
3:1-8	80, 140n6
3:1-5	140
3:1-4	85
3:1	80
3:4-8	83
3:5	129
3:7-8	85, 140n7
3:8	45n18
3:9-20	80
3:19-20	85
3:20-27	239, 241
3:20-24	94n31
3:20	92, 106, 140n7, 171n18
3:21—4:25	92
3:21ff	79
3:21-26	80, 81, 91, 179, 190
3:21	79, 80, 129, 149, 190
3:22-23	15, 189
3:22	282n405
3:22b-23	66n11, 79, 84n27
3:23—4:6	83n25
3:24-26	102, 103n9, 130n11
3:24	132
3:25-26	130
3:25	102, 130
3:26	129
3:27ff	189
3:27-31	80, 141n14, 178, 179, 189
3:27	176n26, 189
3:28f	189
3:28	96, 190
3:29-30	80, 158n55, 178-91
3:29f	110
3:29	182, 189
3:30	189
3:31	83, 85, 92, 140n7, 179, 189, 257
3:31a	189
4	12, 80, 91, 92, 130, 142n21, 175, 178
4:1-25	129n10, 190
4:1-3	189
4:3-8	108
4:5	80, 109, 147
4:9-16	108
4:11-12	80

4:13–15	92, 108, 140n7	6–8	81, 92, 140
4:13	130	6:1—7:6	82n23, 140n7
4:14–15	131	6–7	80, 92
4:15–16	140n6	6	82, 83, 92, 247, 256
4:16–18	141n13		
4:16	124	6:1ff	23n7, 82, 83, 92
4:17ff	80n19	6:1	82
4:17–22	130	6:3ff	83
4:17	80, 130, 147	6:4–13	239
4:21	122	6:4	247
4:23	124	6:5	256n300
4:24–25	80, 82	6:6	240
4:24	130	6:7	83, 101
4:25	102, 103n9	6:9	257n302
5–8	80, 82	6:11–13	86
5	81, 82, 92	6:13	86, 240
5:1–11	81, 81n22, 82, 85, 88–90, 91, 140	6:14	82, 240
		6:15ff	82, 83
5:1–2	89, 92, 239, 240	6:15	82
5:1	88	6:17ff	83
5:2	88, 253	7	12, 82, 94, 94n31, 95, 112
5:3–4	89, 140n7		
5:3	88	7:1–6	95
5:4	88	7:1–4	83
5:5	89	7:1	141n15
5:6–10	89	7:4	141n15
5:6–8	147	7:5—8:4	140n7
5:6	89	7:5–6	82, 83, 84
5:7	89	7:6b	84n27
5:8	89	7:7—8:4	135
5:9–11	82	7:7ff	82
5:9	89	7:7–25	82n23, 84n26, 85, 94
5:10	239		
5:11	92, 253	7:7–12	84
5:12—7:25	90	7:7	82, 84
5:12ff	82, 91	7:12	82
5:12–21	82n23, 91–92	7:13ff	82
5:12–19	81	7:13	82, 84
5:12	92	7:14–25	84, 93–95
5:13–14	91	7:14–15	84
5:15	91, 152n39	7:14	93, 94n31
5:16	91	7:15	93
5:17	91	7:16	93
5:20–21	82, 85, 92, 108, 135, 140n7, 158n56	7:17	93
		7:18–19	84
		7:18	93
5:20a	140n6	7:19	93
5:21	83, 257n302	7:20	93

Romans (continued)

7:21	93
7:22–23	84
7:22	93
7:23	93
7:24–25a	84, 94
7:24	93
7:25	93
7:25a	82
7:25b	66n11, 84n27
8	81, 82, 84, 85, 88–89, 90, 92, 103, 112
8:1ff	82
8:1–39	81n22, 88–90
8:1–17	140n7
8:2	89
8:2–17	83
8:2(?)	254n291
8:4–13	136
8:4	89, 114, 175n23
8:9	89
8:9–11	89, 95
8:9ff	23n7
8:10	89
8:11	89, 129n9
8:12	141n15
8:13–17a	89
8:13b	89
8:15–17	108
8:17–39	140n7
8:17–30	130
8:17	89
8:17a	89
8:17b	82, 88
8:18ff	82
8:18–39	137
8:18	88
8:20	88
8:21	88
8:23	89, 95, 134n15
8:24–25	88
8:25	88
8:25b	84
8:26–27	89
8:28–30	89, 239
8:29–30	88
8:29f	103, 103n9
8:30	88, 89
8:31–34	89
8:31–32	89
8:31–39	89, 140
8:33–34	89
8:33	88, 89, 103, 148n32
8:34–39	239
8:34	89, 254n292
8:35–39	89
8:35–37	88
8:35	89
8:38–39	18
8:39	89
9–11	13, 80, 82, 85, 138, 139, 140, 141, 142, 143, 144, 144n25, 150n35, 156, 157, 158
9	144, 144n24, 150
9:1ff	141
9:1–5	144
9:1–3	141, 148
9:1	141
9:3	141n11
9:4–5	141
9:4	123
9:5	142n21
9:6–33	141n14
9:6–16	142n21
9:6–11	147
9:6	144, 150, 156
9:6a	85
9:6b	85, 145
9:7–13	85
9:7	85
9:7a	145
9:14ff	85
9:14	145
9:17	146, 146n28
9:19ff	85
9:20	151n37
9:21ff	146
9:22–29	85
9:22–24	146
9:22–23	146
9:24–26	147

9:24	147	11:1-2	147n30
9:25-29	147	11:1	150
9:25-26	147n29	11:2-6	150
9:26	147	11:2	150
9:27-29	145, 150	11:5-7	150
9:29	150n35	11:5-6	142n19
9:30	148	11:8-10	151, 151n37
9:30—10:21	144, 150n35	11:11-14	154n46
9:30—10:4	144n25	11:11-12	141n14, 153n43
9:30-33	85, 85n28, 144n24, 148, 151n38	11:11	150n35, 153
		11:12	151, 155, 155n48
		11:13-14	151
9:31	148, 179	11:13f	142n18
9:32-33	129n10	11:13	142
9:33b	149	11:15-24	142n19
10	144, 144n24, 144n25, 150	11:15-16	153n43
		11:15	147, 151, 155
10:1ff	141	11:16	152
10:1-17	85	11:17ff	278
10:1-3	85n28	11:17-24	153
10:1	144n24	11:18ff	86
10:2	141	11:19-24	141n14
10:4ff	176n26	11:20	86
10:4-21	141n14	11:21	151
10:4-17	149	11:23-24	153n43
10:4	85n28, 149, 176n26	11:23	153
		11:24-26	138n1
10:5	107	11:24	153
10:6ff	129n10, 149n34	11:25-36	142n21
10:6-17	108	11:25-26	153
10:8-21	151n38	11:25	139
10:11-13	148n32	11:25b	154
10:12f	110	11:26-27	154, 154n47
10:15	142n17	11:28-36	140
10:16-21	85	11:28-32	147
10:16	85n28	11:28f	152
10:17—11:36	156n52	11:30-32	158n56
10:17	66n11, 84n27, 85n28, 142n17	11:30-31	154
		11:33-36	142n18, 157, 158
10:18-20	148	11:33	239
10:19	150n35, 151, 154n46	11:36	239
		12:1—15:13	86
11	138, 139, 142, 144, 148, 150n35, 152, 156	12-13	140
		12	281n400
		12:1	86, 141n15, 281n400
11:1-10	85		
11:1-7	141n14	12:1-2	86
11:1-6	145	12:2-6	239

INDEX 321

Romans (continued)

12:2	86, 281n400
12:3–8	258, 281
12:3f	281n400
12:3	86, 281n400
12:4	281n400
12:5	240, 254n291, 281n400
12:6f	281n400
12:7	29n23
12:8	29n23, 281n400
12:13	22n5
12:14	49, 281n400
12:16	86
13:1–7	22n3
13:8–10	114, 136, 175n23
13:11–14	239
13:11–13	23n7
14:1—15:6	86, 87
14	211n76
14:1	87
14:6	17n14
14:14	17n14
15	142
15:3	151n37
15:4	124
15:7–13	82, 87, 140
15:8–12	129n10, 131
15:8–10	129n9
15:8–9	123
15:8	122, 124, 126
15:9–12	87
15:10	147n30
15:14	76, 86, 141n15
15:15–33	76
15:15–22	111
15:15–21	142n17, 142n18
15:16	72, 86
15:17	254n291
15:19–23	155n49
15:20–21	75
15:21	142n17
15:22–31	142n20
15:23	5, 76
15:24	77
15:25–33	140, 142n21
15:25	36
15:26–32	6
15:26	36
15:27–31	31n29
15:27	23n8, 36, 142n19
15:28	36
15:29	77n14
15:30–33	48n21
15:30–32	77
15:30	141n15
15:31f	77
15:31	36
16	63n3, 77n15
16:1–2	27n20
16:3–5	27n20
16:3–4	141n13
16:5	152n40
16:7	141n11
16:11	141n11
16:17	141n15
16:20	252n283
16:21	141n11
16:23	27
16:25–27	239

1 Corinthians

	7, 25n13, 41, 42, 43, 44, 54n32, 55, 60, 60n47, 102, 211, 232, 238, 241, 242, 251, 257
1–4	40, 41, 42, 43, 43n13, 44, 45, 46, 48n21, 52, 55, 57, 58, 60, 61, 61n50, 113, 273
1–2	43
1:2b	221
1:4ff	52
1:4–9	141n10
1:4	254n291
1:5	254n291
1:8	73n7
1:9	142n18
1:10—4:21	40–61, 61n50
1:10–13	46
1:10	46, 51, 52n28
1:11–12	47

1:12f	49	3:16–17	239, 240
1:12	40, 42, 49	3:18	54n31
1:13–17	47	3:18–21	46, 47
1:13–15	53n30	3:19f	54
1:13	47	3:21	47, 56n35
1:14—3:2	53	3:21–23	46, 53, 53n30, 54
1:14–17	53	3:22	50
1:14	48	4:2–5	54, 61n50
1:16	26n18	4:3	48
1:17—3:2	46	4:3–4	47
1:17	48	4:4	94, 101, 112
1:18—2:5	289	4:4–5	56n39
1:18–25	47, 53	4:5	58
1:19f	54	4:5f	241
1:20	54n32	4:6	47, 50, 54, 56n35
1:23–25	151n38	4:7	56n35
1:24	15	4:7–10	46, 47
1:26	26n17	4:8ff	58
1:26–31	47, 53	4:8–13	47
1:30	103, 254n291	4:8	48, 256
1:31	54	4:9–13	46, 55
2:1	48	4:11–13	48
2:1–5	1n1, 47, 53	4:13–18	56n39
2:4	48	4:14–21	47, 48n21
2:6—3:2	53	4:14–15	46
2:6–10	239	4:14	57
2:6–16	47	4:16–17	46
2:6f	241	4:16	46, 51
2:9	54	4:17	141n13
2:14—3:4	58	4:18–21	61n50
3:1	48	4:18f	55
3:1–2	47	4:18	45, 49, 57
3:2	48	4:19–21	46
3:2c–4	47	4:19–20	56n39
3:3	53	4:19f	56n35
3:3–4	45, 46, 47	4:19	45n17, 56n35
3:5—4:6	46	4:21	45n17
3:5–9	50	5–16	42, 44
3:5–11	53n30	5	44, 56, 256
3:5–17	53	5:1	56n35
3:6	54	5:1–6	57
3:6–9	240	5:3–4	55n33
3:6–11	239	5:3	56n35
3:10	54	5:5	252n283
3:10–11	47, 53	5–6	55, 56n39, 57
3:10–17	54	5:9ff	57
3:11–15	58	5:9–13	56, 241
3:16	68n13	5:9–13a	57n40

1 Corinthians (continued)

5:9–11	42, 56, 57n40, 63, 63n3, 239
5:9–10	56
5:9	256
5:10f	21n1
5:10	56
5:11	56, 256
6	44
6:1–11	25n15, 56, 104, 288
6:1–8	56
6:2	23n9
6:3	23n8
6:5	57
6:9–11	56
6:9–10	56, 239
6:9f	256, 257n302
6:10	21n1
6:11	102, 103n9
6:12–20	56
6:15–19	239
6:15–16	240
7–8	8
7	56n39, 59, 211n76, 273, 276n384
7:5	252n283
7:9	55n33
7:17ff	25n13
7:20	25n13
7:21b	25n14
7:23	18
7:24	25n13
7:29–31	24n11
7:31	18
7:40b	55n33
8–10	211n76
8:6	239, 241
9	31n31
9:3ff	33n35
9:3–18	49
9:4	32n33
9:6–14	32n32
9:6	32n33
9:8	54n32
9:9	54n32
9:11	23n8
9:14	32n32
9:15–18	32n34
9:18	32n33, 33
9:19	18
9:22	9
10–11	124
10:1–13	59
10:1	142n16
10:10	252n283
10:11	23n7, 282n405
10:23—11:1	48n21
10:23–30	17n14
11:1	31n31
11:2–15	59
11:2	50n25
11:3	239, 240
11:16	55n33, 221
11:17–34	55n34
11:17–24	27n19
11:18	52n28
11:33–34	48n21
11:34b	55n33
12–14	56n39, 59, 273
12	240, 258, 281, 281n400
12:1	142n16
12:4–6	239
12:12–13	239
12:13	272n369
12:18	277n388
12:24–28	239
12:25	52n28
12:28f	256
12:28	29n23
12:31	59n44
13	8
13:3	22, 23n6
14:1	59n44, 255n292
14:5	255n292
14:12	59n44
14:21	54n32
14:34–35	59
14:34	54n32
14:36b	221
14:37–38	55n33
14:39	59n44

15	56n39, 58, 256, 256n299	1:19–22	127
		1:19	126
15:1	141n13	1:20	126
15:1–2	55n33	1:21f	23n7, 256
15:3–11	72n5	1:22	134n15, 239, 241
15:9–10	239	1:23—2:11	126n4
15:9	257	1:23–24	141n10
15:10	55n33	1:23	67, 141n9
15:11	50, 72	2:4	63n3, 67
15:12	45n18	2:5ff	57n41
15:22–28	156n51, 256	2:5–11	38
15:22	253, 254n291	2:8f	241
15:24–28	239, 240	2:14	253, 254n291
15:31	254n291	2:15–16	65, 68n13
15:34	45n18	2:17	67
16:1	36	3:1—4:6	127
16:2	29n25, 36	3	127, 139
16:3	36	3:1–3	127n5
16:5–7	45n17, 55	3:1	45n18, 60n47, 66
16:5	152n40	3:3	127n5
16:12	50	3:4—4:16	127n5
16:13	239	3:4	68n13
16:15–16	51	3:9ff	68n13
16:15	36	3:12	68n13
16:17–18	51	3:13–15	139n3
16:19	27n20	3:13a	139n3
16:24	55	3:13b–15	139n3
		3:16–18	139n3

2 Corinthians

	38, 39, 43, 45, 55n33, 60, 64, 64n8, 65, 68, 68n13, 69, 73n7, 74, 126, 128, 211, 238, 241, 241n252, 251	3:16	138, 139, 139n3
		3:17–18	139, 139n3
		4:1–6	126n4
		4:1–2	67
		4:1	68n13
		4:3–6	68n13
		4:3–4	65
		4:3f	128
1–9	38–39	4:4–6	72n5
1–7	38, 67, 68, 126n4	4:5	72
1:3ff	256	4:7	68n13
1:3	239	5:1	68n13
1:8	142n16	5:5	23n7, 134n15, 239, 256
1:10	141n13		
1:12	67, 126n4, 141n9	5:11–13	126n4
1:15ff	49	5:11–12	67
1:15–22	9, 126n4	5:11	66
1:15–18	126n4	5:12	60n47, 66
1:17	67	5:14–21	83n25
		5:14–20	66

2 Corinthians (*continued*)

Reference	Pages
5:14	35
5:17–21	72n5
5:17–20	239
5:17–19	66n11
5:17	23n7, 254n291
5:20	66n11, 67
5:21	66n11, 84n27, 96, 254n291
6:1-2	64n7
6:1	66, 67
6:3–10	64n7, 66, 67
6:6–8	67
6:11—7:4	65, 68
6:11–13	62
6:13—7:2	128
6:13–14	65n10, 66
6:13	64
6:14—7:1	39, 56, 62–69, 63n3, 63n4, 64n8, 67n13, 68n14, 128, 128n8
6:14ff	63n5, 64n7, 66
6:14–16	239
6:16	68n13, 128n6, 147n30
6:17	128n6
6:18	128n7
7	39
7:1	68, 68n13, 127
7:2	62, 64, 67
7:4	38, 39, 141n10
7:5	39
7:7–13	38
7:12	57n41
7:15–16	38
7:16	141n10
8	30n28, 38, 39
8:1	36
8:2	30, 36
8:3	141n12
8:4	36, 37
8:5	30
8:6	36, 68n13
8:7	36, 37
8:8–15	28n22
8:8	37, 38
8:9	30, 36
8:10	38
8:11	37, 68n13
8:12	37
8:14	36
8:16–24	39
8:16–23	31n30
8:16	37
8:17	37
8:18	68
8:19	36, 37
8:20–21	31
8:20	36
8:22	68
8:23	68
8:24	36, 37, 38
9	30n28, 38, 39
9:1	39
9:2	37
9:3–5	39
9:3	37
9:4ff	38
9:4	37
9:5	36
9:6	36, 37
9:7	29
9:8	22n4, 22n5, 37
9:9	37
9:10–14	31n29
9:10	37
9:11	36
9:12	36
9:13	36, 38
9:14	36
9:15	142n18
10–13	40, 60, 61n50, 63n3, 68
10	39
10:2	45n18
10:7	41, 42, 49, 53n30
10:10	2n1, 60n47
10:12–16	32n33
10:12	45n18
10:13–16	75
11:1–4	53n30
11:2–4	68
11:2	72
11:3	128

INDEX   327

11:4	53n30	2:10	30
11:7–12	33n35	2:11ff	110
11:7–11	49	2:11–21	135
11:8	33n36	2:15ff	13
11:9	33n36	2:15–21	112
11:10	32n34, 141n8	2:16–21	83n25
11:12–15	32n33	2:16	106, 239
11:14	68	2:16d	171n18
11:17–33	43n13	2:17	254n291
11:17	37	2:19–20	72, 95
11:23–25	48	2:20	239, 240
11:23	49, 53n30	3	12, 135, 142n21, 148, 169, 170, 172n20, 173n22, 175, 175n23, 176, 177n28
12:9	289		
12:11–15	32n33		
12:13	33, 33n36, 49		
12:14–18	33n35		
12:14–16	31n30	3:1–12	171
12:18	68	3:1–5	108, 133, 134, 170, 205n57
12:19	60n47, 68n13		
12:21	68	3:2—4:7	205n57
13:3f	289	3:5–9	172n20
13:5–10	38	3:6–9	133
		3:6	108, 133, 170

Galatians

	96, 109, 143n22, 174, 203n45, 205n57, 211, 211n76, 238, 241, 246, 251	3:7	133
		3:8–9	133, 170
		3:8	170n17
		3:10–21	172n20
		3:10–12	134, 177n28
		3:10	171, 172n20
1–2	61n50	3:11	107
1	2	3:11a	171n18
1:4	10, 23n7	3:12	107
1:6ff	72n5	3:13–19	134
1:6–9	205n57	3:13–18	171
1:7	45n18	3:13–14	132, 133, 172
1:11—2:20	205n57	3:13f	132
1:11–16	72	3:13–14a	134, 172n20
1:12–15	241	3:13	172
1:12	239	3:14	108, 132, 133, 172n19, 173, 239
1:15–16	239		
1:16f	258	3:14a	132, 172
1:20	141n8	3:14b	134, 172n20
1:23–24	72n5	3:15–18	108, 135, 170n17, 172, 174
2:4	254n291		
2:6–10	258	3:16	131, 170n17, 172n19, 173
2:7–9	72n5		
2:9	258n307	3:17	170n17
		3:18–23	108

INDEX

Galatians (continued)

3:19–25	172
3:19–20	135
3:19	131, 132n13, 173, 176n26
3:19c	173
3:20	135n17, 173n22
3:20a	173n22
3:21–29	135
3:21f	257
3:21	135
3:22	134, 170n17, 174
3:23—4:6	175
3:23–25	173
3:26–29	134, 239
3:28	15, 110, 134
4:1–6	173
4:3	17
4:4–6	23n7
4:5–6	172n20
4:6–11	170
4:6–7	133, 134
4:6f	108
4:8–11	205n57
4:9	255n292
4:21ff	129n9
4:21–31	108, 142n21
4:23	129n9
4:29	129n9
5:2ff	8
5:6	110
5:12	257
5:13–23	136
5:13–14	175n23
5:14–15	114
5:18	175n23
5:19–23	239
5:19–21	56, 257n302
5:23	175n23
6:2	176n26
6:6–10	22n5
6:6	32n33
6:10	25
6:11–17	48n21, 142n21
6:15	23n7, 110

Ephesians

	16, 17n13, 72n5, 158n57, 197–290, 205n56, 206n59, 209n69, 210n71, 214n92, 214n93, 215n95, 217n111, 218n111, 222n152, 227n185, 230n198, 231n204, 232n205, 233n209, 236n221, 240n248, 241n252, 249n268, 250n278, 252n282, 254n292, 255n292, 259n310, 262n392, 263n326, 265n336, 265n337, 266n337, 266n338, 266n342, 267n348, 268n352, 268n353, 268n354, 270n361, 270n362, 276n384, 277n385, 277n388, 281n400, 281n401, 282n405, 288n429, 289n430, 289n432
1–2	213
1:1–2	199, 201, 206, 239, 242, 244, 249
1:1	253n289, 265n337, 266, 266n342, 267n348
1:2–14	213
1:2	243
1:3—6:20	199, 206
1:3—3:21	200, 200n30, 206
1:3–14	199, 206, 212n81, 214, 235, 244, 245, 247, 248, 256
1:3–13	212
1:3–12	242
1:3	132, 202n43, 229, 252n285, 254, 254n291, 283
1:3a	231, 232, 239
1:3b	231, 252n286
1:4–6	257n302

INDEX 329

1:4	210, 229, 238n240, 243, 253n287, 253n289, 254, 254n291	1:15f	201, 243, 280n395
		1:15	202, 202n43, 206, 253, 255n292, 266n342
1:4a	232	1:16ff	274
1:4b	232, 246	1:16f	243
1:4c	232	1:16	254n291
1:5	276	1:17–19a	206
1:5a	232	1:17b–19a	199
1:5b	232	1:17ff	245, 259
1:6f	243, 253	1:17	252n286, 255n292
1:6	229, 247, 253, 254n291	1:18–23	213, 243, 245, 246
		1:18f	235
1:7	212, 229, 234, 235, 246, 247, 248, 253n289, 254n291, 276	1:18	202, 229, 234, 235, 243, 260n316
		1:19	247, 248, 254n291
		1:19a	231
1:7a	232	1:19b–23	199, 206
1:8–10	274	1:19f	206, 243
1:8f	243, 259	1:20—2:22	245
1:9–11	257n302	1:20ff	249
1:9	253n289	1:20–23	243, 252n285, 256
1:10f	253	1:20–22	240, 260n313
1:10	243, 253, 253n289, 254n291	1:20–21	235
		1:20	202n43, 243, 252n285, 253, 254n291
1:10a	232		
1:11	212, 234, 235, 252n286, 253n289, 254n291	1:20b–22	246
		1:21–23	247
1:12f	253	1:21	210, 247, 252
1:12	253	1:22f	202
1:12a	232	1:22	233
1:13—2:22	205n57	1:23	243
1:13ff	261	1:23b	232
1:13–14	134n15, 199, 242	2:1ff	212n83
1:13f	210, 256	2:1–22	245
1:13	212, 229, 241, 243, 253n289, 254n291, 274	2:1–10	83n25, 199, 206, 243, 246, 247, 249, 257n302, 272
1:14—3:21	245	2:1–8	203n46
1:14	254n292	2:1–3	212n81, 288
1:15—2:22	200n30	2:1f	243
1:15–23	206	2:1	243, 247
1:15–21	212n81	2:2–3	252n285
1:15–17	239, 244, 249	2:2f	252n284
1:15–17a	239	2:2	234, 252n283, 261
1:15ff	199	2:3–8	234
1:15–16	206	2:3	244, 261

Ephesians (continued)

2:4–7	212n81
2:4	235, 246, 247
2:5ff	261
2:5–8	256n300, 259
2:5–7	256, 260n313
2:5–6	243
2:5f	243
2:5	202, 202n43, 212n83, 229, 230, 247, 253n289, 254n291
2:5b	247
2:6	237, 252n285, 253n289, 254n291
2:7–9a	246
2:7	210, 229, 252, 253n289, 254n291
2:8–10	247, 272
2:8–9	212n79, 257
2:8	230, 240, 247n264
2:9	230, 247n264
2:10–22	213
2:10	230, 253n289, 254n291
2:11ff	229
2:11–22	142n19, 158n57, 199, 203n46, 205n56, 206, 246, 249, 257n302, 258, 278, 283, 283n409
2:11–16	243
2:11–15	243
2:11–13	278, 283n409
2:11–12	200n26
2:11f	260
2:11	206, 210, 247, 257, 283
2:12ff	212
2:12–22	246
2:12	251n282
2:13–17	243, 260n313
2:13	202, 207, 230, 253n289, 254n291, 283, 283n409
2:14ff	236, 249, 283
2:14–18	210, 240, 275, 278
2:14–16	257n302
2:14–15	247, 274
2:14	238n240, 251n282, 260n316, 272
2:15–18	212n81
2:15	202n43, 253n289, 254, 254n291, 257
2:16	253n289, 274
2:17–22	243
2:17	230
2:18–22	235
2:19–22	212n81, 278, 283
2:19	212, 230
2:20–22	202, 229, 240, 260n313
2:20	221, 237, 240, 240n250, 250, 258
2:21	248, 253n289
2:22	240, 253n289, 254n291
3:1—4:24	200n30
3:1ff	212n83
3:1–14	249
3:1–13	207, 243, 245
3:1–12	72n5
3:1	200, 200n28, 210, 255n292
3:2ff	259
3:2–13	200, 200n28, 203n46, 205n57
3:2–12	210, 234, 246, 257, 258, 274, 283
3:2–11	212n82
3:2–7	212n81
3:2	202, 202n43, 207, 210
3:3ff	241
3:3–6	235
3:3–5	288n428
3:3	221, 258
3:4–10	158n57, 249
3:4–6	257n302
3:5–7	258
3:5–6	210
3:5	237, 261

3:6	221, 250, 253n289, 254n291	4:6	252, 253n287
3:8–12	212n81	4:7ff	250
3:8	257	4:7–16	201, 204, 258, 278
3:9–11	257n302	4:7–14	243
3:9–10	202	4:7–12	240, 260n313
3:9	229, 252	4:7	235, 281n400
3:10	252n285	4:8	252n285, 253
3:11f	253	4:8–13	281
3:11	253, 254n291	4:8–12	260
3:12	253n289, 254n291	4:8–11	210, 246
3:13	202, 210, 254n292, 289	4:9f	236
		4:9	211, 253
3:14ff	259	4:10	252n285, 278
3:14–21	245	4:11–22	284
3:14–19	200, 207, 212n81, 243, 246, 274	4:11–16	212n81
		4:11	270n361, 277, 277n388, 281n400
3:14f	252	4:12–14	270, 283
3:14	212n83, 255n292	4:12f	274, 281n400
3:15	212n80, 238n240	4:12	270
3:16f	243	4:13–16	278
3:16	235, 243	4:13	210n71, 243, 251n282, 270, 270n361, 278
3:17	260n316		
3:18	252n285	4:14	210, 258, 269, 270, 270n361, 271, 273, 281, 283, 285n415
3:19	247		
3:20–21	142n18, 200, 207, 239, 243		
3:20	207, 252n286	4:15–16	243
3:21	253n287, 253n289, 254	4:15b–16	246, 248
		4:16–17	207
4–6	272	4:16	247, 278, 281, 281n400
4:1—6:20	200, 207		
4:1—6:9	200n30	4:17ff	241, 245
4:1ff	245	4:17–24	201, 207n63, 208, 213
4:1–16	200, 207, 207n63, 277, 281n400		
		4:17–21	243, 246
4:1–6	243, 270n362, 278	4:17–19	257n302
4:1	201, 202, 202n43, 207, 210, 213, 239, 281n400	4:17f	235
		4:17	201, 202n43, 207, 288
4:2–6	207	4:18	243
4:2–4	244	4:19	21n1
4:2	234, 238n241, 246	4:20	230, 270n362, 288
4:3	251n282	4:21	253, 254n291
4:4–16	202	4:22—5:6	245
4:4–6	182n14, 233n208	4:22ff	245
4:4	281n400		
4:5–7	246		

INDEX 331

Ephesians (*continued*)

4:22–24	202n43, 208, 229, 240, 244, 256n300
4:22	230
4:23	281n400
4:24–31	246
4:24	201, 230
4:25—6:20	200n30
4:25—6:9	277
4:25—5:14	201, 208
4:25—5:5	213
4:25-32	207n63
4:25-31	244
4:25-30	246, 260n313
4:25	233, 235, 240, 281n400
4:26–30	238
4:26	238n239
4:26a	230, 230n198
4:26b	230, 230n198
4:27	238n239, 252n283
4:28	22n3, 22n5, 238n239, 238n241, 254n292, 281n400
4:29	244
4:30	134n15, 209, 233, 238n239, 253n289, 256
4:31	235, 249
4:32—5:1	244
4:32	238n241, 254n291, 257n302
5	256, 271n366
5:1-2	207n63
5:1	260n316
5:2	240, 257n302, 260n313
5:3–14	207n63, 256
5:3–7	56
5:3–6	244
5:3–4	212n80
5:3	21n1
5:4ff	56
5:4	243, 254n292
5:5	21n1, 204, 257n302
5:5–14	288
5:6	210, 243, 255n292, 257n302
5:7ff	241
5:7–18	244
5:7–14	246
5:8	230, 234, 235, 235n216, 254n291, 257n302, 261
5:11	254n292, 281n400
5:12	237
5:13f	236, 282
5:14	253, 259, 260n313
5:15—6:9	208
5:15-21	201, 208
5:15-20	207n63
5:15f	244
5:15	202n43, 208
5:17-23	212n81
5:17	260n313, 281n400
5:18-19	230
5:18	212n80, 246
5:19-20	244, 245
5:19f	214
5:20	252n286
5:21—6:9	207n63, 245
5:21ff	235, 249
5:21-33	233n209, 275, 276n384
5:21-23	203n46
5:21-22	244
5:21	202n43, 208
5:22ff	229, 276n384
5:22-33	201, 202, 208, 233n209, 276n384, 282
5:22-32	233
5:23-24	244, 246, 247
5:23	204, 240
5:25ff	237, 257n302
5:25-33	203n46, 212n82, 260n313
5:25-32	204
5:25-28	212n81
5:25	232
5:25a	244
5:25b-33	244, 246, 247

5:26–32	246
5:27	243
5:28–33	240, 260
5:28	244
5:29	232
5:30	233
5:31f	210, 271n365, 283, 284
5:31	255n292, 271
5:32	153n44, 253, 282
5:32b	282n405
5:33	244
5:35	249
6:1–9	201, 208, 244
6:2–3	246, 260n313
6:2	212n80, 253, 254n292
6:5	235
6:8	212n80
6:9	247
6:10ff	289
6:10–20	201, 208, 245
6:10–17	244
6:10f	202n43
6:10	208
6:11ff	235
6:11–17	257n302
6:11–13	246
6:11f	252n284
6:11	252n283
6:12	251n282, 252n285
6:13–17	260n313
6:13	209
6:14–18	240
6:14–17	246
6:14	238n241
6:16	212n80
6:17	253
6:18–20	244, 249
6:18	238n241
6:19–20	202, 210
6:19f	72n5
6:21–24	201
6:21–22	199, 209, 210, 244, 245, 249, 266
6:21f	199n23, 267n346, 268, 281
6:21	202n43, 209, 210, 212n80
6:23–24	199, 201, 209, 245, 266
6:23	244
6:24	237, 244

Philippians

	33, 33n37, 211, 238, 241, 250
1:1	29n24, 33n37, 266
1:3–11	141n10
1:3	33n37
1:4	33n37
1:5	33n37
1:6	73n7, 113
1:7	33n37
1:8	141n9
1:9–11	86, 239
1:10–11	73n7
1:15	45n18
1:18	33n37, 211n74
1:25f	33n37
1:27	239
1:28	254n292
2	8
2:2	33n37
2:5—3:17	72n5
2:8	282n405
2:9–11	239
2:17f	33n37
3:1f	33n37
3:2–3	257
3:3–11	111
3:4–11	5, 72, 136
3:6	4n5
3:7ff	96
3:8–11	83n25
3:8	94
3:12	112
4:1	33n37
4:3	141n13
4:6–7	239
4:10ff	29n24, 33n36
4:10–20	33n37
4:10–18	48n21
4:10	141n10

Philippians (continued)

4:11–13	34
4:11	22n4
4:14	141n10
4:18	34
4:19	141n10

Colossians

	16, 17n13, 72n5, 113, 205, 205n58, 209, 210, 211n75, 213, 215, 216, 217, 218, 219, 220, 220n132, 221, 222, 223, 224, 225, 226, 227, 235, 236, 238, 239, 240n248, 241, 242, 245, 246, 247, 248, 249, 249n268, 250, 250n278, 251, 252n282, 253, 253n289, 254n292, 260, 260n313, 261, 262, 262n392, 263, 263n326, 263n329, 265, 267, 268, 268n351, 269, 272n369, 273, 274, 277n385, 277n388, 279, 279n392, 280, 281, 286
1–2	17n14
1	223
1:1–2	205n58, 242, 244
1:1	280
1:2—2:7	205n58
1:2	266, 266n342
1:3—2:5	205
1:3–29	245
1:3–11	244
1:3f	243
1:3	242
1:5–8	243
1:5	242
1:6–8	245
1:9ff	245
1:9–29	246
1:9f	243
1:9	242, 243
1:10	243
1:11–22	245
1:11–19	243, 245, 246
1:11	243, 244
1:12–14	235, 235n216
1:12	235n216, 242, 243
1:13	246
1:14	242, 248, 254n291, 276
1:15ff	149n34
1:15–20	248
1:15–17a	245
1:15b–16	221
1:16	243
1:18	243, 244
1:19	243, 254n291
1:20–22	243, 245, 246
1:20	242
1:21	243
1:22f	73n7
1:22	242, 244, 246, 266
1:23–29	72n5, 243, 245
1:23	243
1:24	243, 245
1:26–27	246
1:26	243
1:27	243
1:28	73n7, 243, 244
1:29	243
2	223, 277n385
2:1–5	245
2:1–3	243, 245, 246, 268
2:1–2	141n11
2:2	243, 268n352
2:3	245
2:4–8	245
2:4–5	243, 245
2:4	268
2:6—4:6	205
2:6ff	245
2:6–8	245
2:6–7	243, 246
2:7	242 ??????, 243
2:8–23	205n58
2:8	243, 245

INDEX 335

2:9–15	83n25, 245, 246, 247	3:15	244
2:9–10	243	3:16–17	244, 245
2:9f	243	3:18—4:1	245
2:9	243, 254n291	3:18	244
2:10	243, 248, 254n291	3:19	232n205, 244
2:11–15	243	3:20—4:1	244
2:11	243, 246, 254n291	3:20	244
2:12	243, 245, 254n291, 247	3:22–25	247, 250
		3:22–24	280n396
		4:2–6	245
		4:2–4	244
2:13	243, 246, 247	4:3	243
2:14	243, 246	4:5–6	244
2:15	254n291	4:6	244
2:16–18	243, 245	4:7ff	267n346
2:16	242, 274	4:7–18	205n58
2:18f	270n362	4:7–9	199, 199n23, 210, 244, 245, 268
2:18	254n292, 274		
2:19	243, 245, 246, 247, 248	4:9–17	250
		4:9	280n396
2:20–23	243, 245, 274	4:9a	245
2:20–22	211n74	4:10ff	262n394
2:20	245	4:10–17	244, 245
2:22	243	4:10–14	263, 280, 280n396
2:23	254n292	4:10–11	262, 264
3:1—4:6	205n58	4:10	263
3:1–4	243	4:11	262n393
3:1	243	4:12–13	268
3:5–15	245	4:13	141n12, 268
3:5–12	245	4:15	27n20
3:5–9a	244	4:16	265n336, 267, 267n346, 267n349, 268, 268n354
3:5–8	244		
3:5–6	56		
3:5	21n1, 243, 245		
3:6f	243	4:17	280n396
3:6	243	4:18	244
3:7	243	5:4	244
3:8–9	246		
3:8	244	**1 Thessalonians**	
3:9–11	256n300		7, 56n39, 138, 138n1, 204, 205, 209, 211, 238, 241, 242, 246, 250
3:9–10	240		
3:9b–11	244		
3:10f	243		
3:11	245, 272n369	1:1–10	205n56
3:12–15	243	1:1–2	205n56
3:12–13	244	1:1	205n56
3:12	244, 246	1:2—5:25	205n56
3:14–15	244		

INDEX

1 Thessalonians (continued)

1:2—3:13	205n56
1:2–10	205n56
1:3—2:11	72n5
1:3ff	204
1:6	31n31
1:9f	235n216
2:1—5:11	205n56
2:1–12	205n56
2:1–4	205n56
2:3–12	31n31
2:5	31
2:5–12	205n56
2:12	239
2:13—3:13	205n56
2:13	204
2:14–16	138, 138n1
2:16	138
2:17—3:10	205n56
2:19	211n74
3:5	252n283
3:9–13	141n10, 204
3:9	211n74
3:11–13	142n18
3:13	73n7
4–5	86
4:1—5:25	205n56
4:1—5:11	205n56
4:2ff	56
4:2–6	56n39
4:3–6	56
4:11	239
4:11–12	24n10
4:11f	22n3
4:12	22n4
4:13—5:11	156n51
4:13ff	24n10
4:13–17	204
4:13	142n16, 239
5:1–5	204
5:4	239
5:8	240, 257n302
5:9	239
5:12–22	205n56
5:12	29n23
5:14	24n10
5:23–28	205n56
5:23–24	205n56
5:23	73n7
5:25–28	205n56
5:26–28	205n56

2 Thessalonians

	220n132, 238, 239, 241, 246, 250, 252n282
2:1ff	24n10
2:1	52n29
3:1	252n283
3:6ff	24n10
3:6–15	48n21
3:10–12	22n3
3:11	45n18
3:13	22n5

1 Timothy

	22, 252n282
1:6	45n18
1:11ff	72n5
1:11–16	234
1:19	45n18
2:3–7	234
2:5–7	72n5
3:16	129n9
4:1–5	285n415, 286
4:1	45n18
6:6–9	22n2
6:6	22n4
6:10	22n2, 45n18
6:17–19	22n2
6:21	45n18

2 Timothy

	252n282
1:8–12	72n5, 234
2:18	59n43, 286
2:20	254n292, 287n426
4:12	267n346

Titus

	252n282
1:1–3	72n5
1:2–3	234
1:11	254n292

2:14	147n30		236n221, 237,
3:3–7	234		248, 263, 287n424
3:5–7	96, 103	1:3	235, 287n424
		1:3–5	235
Philemon		1:3–12	235
	204, 204n52, 205,	1:3	235, 287n424
	211, 216, 221,	1:10–12	235
	222, 239, 241,	1:12	287n424
	242n255, 247,	1:13	235
	250, 261, 262,	1:14f	235
	262n394, 263,	1:18	235
	263n329, 265,	1:23	287n424
	279, 280	2:1	235
1	280	2:2	287n424
2	27n20	2:4–10	235
4ff	280n395	2:4–8	240n250
4–7	27, 141n10	2:6–8	148n32
4–6	204n52, 239	2:9–10	147n30
7	204n52	2:9	235, 235n216
8ff	46n19	2:10	287n424
8	254n291	2:18	235
9–13	141n13	2:20	26n16
12	254n292	2:25	287n424
19	28, 239, 279	3:1	235
22–24	263	3:4	235
22	280	3:7	235
23–24	262n394, 280	3:9	26n16
23f	280n396	3:13f	26n16
		3:18	129n9
Hebrews		3:21	287n424
	64, 101, 215,	3:22	235
	215n100, 216, 233	4:10	235
1:2–3	149n34	5:8	235
1:5	131n12	5:10	254n291
3:1–6	131n12	5:13	263
3:7	253n288		
4:9	147n30	**2 Peter**	
8:10	147n30		246
James		**1 John**	
	215, 215n100		114, 115, 287n426
2:19	179	1:6f	115
4:6	253n288	1:8—2:2	114
		1:8	114
1 Peter		1:9	95
	64, 101, 214n93,	2:7–11	115
	215, 231, 235, 236,		

1 John (continued)

3:9	114
3:16–18	115
4:7–21	115
5:1–3	115

3 John

2	76n13

Jude

	246

Revelation

	156, 161n2, 237
2–3	237
3:21	237
10:7	237
10:11	237
10:18	237
18:4	147n30, 237
19:7	237
21:2	237
21:3	147n30
21:4	237
21:7	128n7
21:14	237, 258n307
22:21	237

www.ingramcontent.com/pod-product-compliance
Lightning Source LLC
Chambersburg PA
CBHW030431300426
44112CB00009B/956